Crisis,
Conflict and Instability

The International Crisis Behavior (ICB) Project

The International Crisis Behavior (ICB) Project was set up in 1975 as a large-scale investigation into international and foreign policy crises during the twentieth century. Through the compilation of quantitative data sets, two complementary paths with distinctive methodologies have been followed: in-depth case studies of states coping with external military-security crises, and an aggregate study of the international and foreign policy crises of more than 100 states in the global system from 1929 up to the end of 1985. The aim of the research has been to illuminate crisis behavior by identifying patterns of crisis onset, development and outcome.

Crises in the Twentieth Century
    Volume I: Handbook of International Crises
    Volume II: Handbook of Foreign Policy Crises

The results of the ICB Project's analysis of international and foreign policy crises for the years 1929–79 were published in two volumes by Pergamon Press in 1988. These *Handbooks* document the Project's methodological background, provide profiles of the most crisis-active states and summaries of 278 international crises, and outline the major findings from its descriptive survey. Further information about the scope and content of the *Handbooks* is available by returning the reply card provided in this volume.

Crisis, Conflict and Instability

As part of its research work, the ICB Project also prepared preliminary analyses of segments of the data set, focusing on specific issues, themes or controversies, and ranging across macro- and micro-level topics. At the macro-level these include: the relationship between polarity, stability, and crisis and between system and crisis; the differences between international crises which occur within and outside of protracted conflicts; the record of global organization involvement in international crises; and regional patterns of crisis management with an emphasis on the Middle East and Africa. At the micro-level, the topics include: superpower behavior in international crises and a comparative analysis of their involvement and effectiveness; the effect of structural factors on international crisis behavior; and an exploration of the "conflict-begets-conflict" tendency with reference to the relationship between perceived threat to values and violent response. These more analytical findings are reported in a systematic, integrated form in this volume. By doing so, *Crisis, Conflict and Instability* emphasizes the importance of the scope and content of the ICB Project in this crucial domain of world politics. It also includes details of the hitherto unreported crises for the years 1980–85 and concludes with a theoretically-focused agenda for future analysis in the areas of international conflict and crisis.

Crisis,
Conflict and Instability

by

MICHAEL BRECHER
McGill University

JONATHAN WILKENFELD
University of Maryland, College Park

with contributions by
Patrick James, Hemda Ben Yehuda,
Mark A. Boyer and Stephen R. Hill

PERGAMON PRESS
OXFORD · NEW YORK · BEIJING · FRANKFURT
SÃO PAULO · SYDNEY · TOKYO · TORONTO

Press plc, Headington Hill Hall,
3 0BW, England

Press Inc., Maxwell House, Fairview Park,
New York 10523, U.S.A.

Press, Room 4037, Qianmen Hotel, Beijing,
People's Republic of China

OF CHINA

FEDERAL REPUBLIC OF   Pergamon Press GmbH, Hammerweg 6,
GERMANY   D-6242 Kronberg, Federal Republic of Germany

BRAZIL   Pergamon Editora Ltda, Rua Eça de Queiros 346,
                      CEP 04011, Paraiso, São Paulo, Brazil

AUSTRALIA   Pergamon Press Australia Pty Ltd., P.O. Box 544,
                      Potts Point, N.S.W. 2011, Australia

JAPAN   Pergamon Press, 5th Floor, Matsuoka Central Building,
                      1-7-1 Nishishinjuku, Shinjuku-ku, Tokyo 160, Japan

CANADA   Pergamon Press Canada Ltd., Suite No. 271,
                      253 College Street, Toronto, Ontario, Canada M5T 1R5

First edition 1989

Library of Congress Cataloging-in-Publication Data
Brecher, Michael.
Crisis, conflict and instability / by Michael Brecher, Jonathan
Wilkenfeld; with contributions by Patrick James . . . [et al.] – 1st ed.
p.   cm. – (Crises in the twentieth century; v. 3)
Bibliography: p.
Includes indexes.
1. World politics – 20th century. 2. International relations.
I. Wilkenfeld, Jonathan. II. James, Patrick, 1957– . III. Title IV. Series:
Brecher, Michael, Crises in the twentieth century; v. 3.
D443.B713 vol. 3   [D445] 327′.09′04—dc19 89-3831

British Library Cataloguing in Publication Data
Brecher, Michael
Crisis, conflict and instability
1. International relations
I. Title II. Wilkenfeld, Jonathan III. James, Patrick
303.4′82
ISBN 0-08-036503-5 Hardcover
ISBN 0-08-036502-7 Flexicover

Printed in Great Britain by BPCC Wheatons Ltd, Exeter

Contents

List of Figures and Tables

FIGURES

TABLES

Preface

Since 1975, the International Crisis Behavior (ICB) Project has been engaged in a large-scale investigation of international and foreign policy crises during the twentieth century. Two complementary paths have been followed, with distinctive methodologies. One is in-depth case studies of states coping with external military–security crises, comprising, thus far: Israel in the 1967 and 1973–74 Middle East crises/wars; Syria in the Lebanon Civil War upheaval of 1975–76; the United States in the Berlin Blockade of 1948–49; the US in the Lebanon imbroglio of 1958, the Syria–Jordan confrontation of 1970, and the superpower near-collision in the October Yom Kippur War of 1973–74; the Soviet Union in the Prague Spring of 1968; Germany in the aftermath of the trauma of Stalingrad in 1942–43; India in the China Border conflict of 1962; Hungary during the 1956 Uprising; Zambia in the challenge of Rhodesia's UDI in 1965–66; and a preliminary report on crisis management by several states since World War II.*

The second path is an aggregate study of international and foreign policy crises of more than 100 states in the global system from 1929 to the end of 1985. Data were compiled for each of 323 international crises on variables grouped into seven clusters of crisis dimensions: breakpoint–exitpoint (or trigger–termination); crisis management techniques; great power/superpower activity; international organization involvement, outcome and severity. A similar quantitative exercise was undertaken for the 698 foreign policy crises for individual states. And the two data sets were analyzed in terms of several crucial system *demarcation points* or control variables: geography; polarity; system level; conflict setting; power discrepancy; major power involvement; and war. Several actor-level demarcation points were also used, notably regime type, age of a crisis actor, capability, power status, location of a crisis, and the gravity of value threat. The results, including the methodology, profiles of the most crisis-active states during the half-century, and the major findings from our descriptive survey were reported in two volumes in 1988 (Brecher and Wilkenfeld, *et al.*; Wilkenfeld and Brecher, *et al.*)†

As part of this ongoing research program we prepared preliminary analyses of segments of the data set, focusing on a specific issue, theme, puzzle or controversy in the endlessly fascinating and momentous world of crisis, conflict, and war. These islands of analysis ranged from such macro-level topics as polarity and stability, and third party intervention in crises by major powers and international organizations, to micro-level subjects such as threat and violence in foreign policy crises and crisis management by the two superpowers, along with a combined system/actor-level analysis of protracted conflicts and their impact on crises. Most of these were confined, in data terms, to the three decades after World War II.

With the completion of the two largely descriptive handbooks of crises, we turned to the task of presenting our findings in a systematic, integrated form. These draw upon the updated data set, from 1929 to 1985, including the hitherto unreported set of crises from the beginning of 1980 to the end of 1985 (see Appendix A and B to this volume). This is the *raison d'être* of *Crisis, Conflict and Instability*, the third volume of *Crises in the Twentieth Century*. It also serves to demonstrate the scope and substance of the ICB research program in a crucial domain of world politics.

Preliminary versions of some of these islands of analysis have been published in the last decade, and we are grateful to the publishers of the following journals for permission to use material from these articles:

Michael Brecher and Hemda Ben Yehuda, "System and Crisis in International Politics," *Review of International Studies* **11** (1985), 17–36. (Chapter 2)
Jonathan Wilkenfeld and Michael Brecher, "International Crises, 1945–1975: The UN Dimension," *International Studies Quarterly*, **28** (1984), 45–67. (Chapter 5)

---

* For the details of these publications, see Chap. 1, n. 12 below.
† The ICB datasets for the 1988 volumes comprised the years 1929–79; the current volume covers the period 1929–85.

Michael Brecher and Patrick James, "International Crises in the Middle East, 1929–1979: Immediate Severity and Long-Term Importance," *Jerusalem Journal of International Relations*, **9** (1987), 1–42; Patrick James, Michael Brecher, and Tod Hoffman, "International Crises in Africa, 1929–1979: Immediate Severity and Long-Term Importance," *International Interactions*, **14** (1988), 51–84. (Chapter 7)

Patrick James and Jonathan Wilkenfeld, "Structural Factors and International Crisis Behavior," *Conflict Management and Peace Science*, **7**, 2 (1984), pp. 33–53. (Chapter 8)

Michael Brecher, "International Crises and Protracted Conflicts," *International Interactions*, **11**, 3–4 (1984), pp. 237–297. (Chapters 9 and 10)

Michael Brecher and Patrick James, "Patterns of Crisis Management," *Journal of Conflict Resolution*, **32**, 3 (1988), pp. 426–456. (Chapter 11)

Michael Brecher, Jonathan Wilkenfeld and Stephen R. Hill, "Threat and Violence in International Crises," in K. Mushakoji and H. Usui (eds.), *Theoretical Frameworks of the Contemporary World in Transition, Vol. I.* Tokyo: Yushindo Kobunsha, 1987: 57–102. (Chapter 12)

Jonathan Wilkenfeld and Michael Brecher, "Superpower Crisis Management Behavior," in C.W. Kegley and P. McGowan (eds.), *Foreign Policy: USA/USSR.* Beverly Hills: Sage, 1982: pp. 185–212. (Chapter 13)

Among those who contributed to this volume, Patrick James deserves special mention. A doctoral student of Wilkenfeld at Maryland and, since 1984, a colleague of Brecher at McGill, he co-authored five chapters, as noted in the Contents. He also read the rest of the volume in a spirit of empathetic criticism. Hemda Ben Yehuda of the Hebrew University of Jerusalem, Mark Boyer of the University of Connecticut, and Stephen Hill of the University of Maryland each contributed as a co-author of a chapter of this book. We are grateful to Joel Schleicher of the Hebrew University of Jerusalem and Brigid Starkey and Alice Schott of the University of Maryland for invaluable and devoted research assistance in gathering data on 45 international crises from 1980 to 1985. Glenda Kershaw, Social Sciences Desk Editor at Pergamon Press, prepared the splendid index, as she did for the authors' *Crises in the Twentieth Century* (1988). We also thank Sandy Hin for using superior word processing skills in the preparation of the final typescript.

As in the earlier stages of this project, McGill University has been generous in extending annual research leaves to Brecher and research grants to sustain the enterprise. The Computer Science Center of the University of Maryland has continued to provide computer support to the project. The 1980–85 data were collected under a subcontract to the University of Maryland of a National Science Foundation grant to the University of Illinois-Champaign for "Data Development in International Relations." To all of these persons and institutions, and to the many readers of parts of this volume, we are grateful.

Michael Brecher
McGill University

Jonathan Wilkenfeld
University of Maryland, College Park
April 1989

Part I
Introduction

1 Framework

Michael Brecher and Jonathan Wilkenfeld

Michael Brecher and Jonathan Wilkenfeld

Introduction

Why study crises in the twentieth century? One reason is that "crisis" is among the most widely-used verbal symbols of turmoil in the politics among nations. Statesmen, in their memoirs and elsewhere, often portray themselves as being besieged by crises throughout their term of office; in fact, they mean any problem of decision-making and its attendant stress. Journalists and scholars, too, often write about incidents, disputes, riots, rebellions, etc., as crises. In short, "crisis" is a pervasive term to describe disruption and disorder in the global arena.

Another reason for studying "crisis" is that it is closely related to two other concepts which are central to an understanding of world politics, namely, conflict and war. Social conflict is as old as the human adventure. However, serious inquiry into conflict dates to the nineteenth century, notably to Marx and his followers, social Darwinists such as Spencer and Sumner, and classical theorists of power, influence and revolution – Mosca, Michels, Pareto and Sorel. The twentieth-century literature on conflict is vast, from Simmel (1908) and Weber (1917), to Rapoport (1974) and Gurr *et al.* (1980).[1] In the domain of international conflict and war, too, there has been a large and impressive body of knowledge, from Sorokin (1937) and Wright (1942), to Haas (1974) and Singer *et al.* (1972, 1979, 1980).[2]

"Conflict phenomena," according to Gurr (1980: pp. 1–2), "are the overt, coercive interactions of contending collectivities." These interactions have "four distinguishing properties . . .

1. two or more parties are involved;
2. they engage in mutually opposing actions;
3. they use coercive behaviors, 'designed to destroy, injure, thwart or otherwise control their opponent(s)' (Mack and Snyder, 1957: p. 218); [and]
4. these contentious interactions are overt . . ."

This definition is broad enough to encompass political riots, insurrection, revolution and war, all of which are examined in Gurr's review of the literature on political conflict. Conspicuously absent is higher-than-normal tension, often accompanied by violence. Periods of high tension often generate crises.

An international crisis, to be defined later in this chapter, is not synonymous with an international conflict. The former is issue-specific and narrower in focus than the latter. Moreover, crises may occur within or outside a protracted conflict[3] (e.g., respectively, Suez-Sinai Campaign of 1956–57, in the Arab-Israel Conflict, and Bizerta in 1958, between France and Tunisia). Even when a crisis is very long it can be distinguished from a conflict, for example, the 1947–48 and 1965–66 Kashmir Crises, as distinct from the India–Pakistan Conflict over Kashmir and related issues since both states became independent in 1947. An international conflict often encompasses many crises, either over the same issue, as with the East–West crises over Berlin (the Blockade in 1948–49, Deadline in 1957–59 and Wall in 1961), or over multiple issues, as in the Arab–Israel and India–Pakistan Conflicts since 1947.

Just as crisis is related to conflict, so too is it related to war. For Wright (1942: II, pp. 685, 700), "wars have been characterized by (1) military activity, (2) high tension level, (3) abnormal law, and (4) intense political integration. . . . War is thus at the same time an exceptional legal condition, a phenomenon of intergroup social psychology, a species of conflict, and a species of violence." Singer and Small (1972: p. 381) operationalized the concept of interstate war to mean "[C]onflict involving at least one member of [the] interstate system on each side of the war, resulting in a total of 1000 or more battle deaths."

The complex relationship between crisis and war, especially that between violence and crisis, will be a recurrent theme in the chapters to follow. Suffice it to note here that, with the exception of the Hungarian Uprising in 1956, all interstate wars listed

3

in the Correlates of War (COW) Project (Small and Singer, 1982: Appendix A) for the 1945–1980 period are coded as full-scale wars in the International Crisis Behavior (ICB) dataset, CRISBANK, as well.[4] The ICB list of 41 crises involving full-scale war for that period is considerably larger than the COW list of 16 wars because a number of those wars produced clusters of international crises, e.g., India–Pakistan – 3, Israel Independence – 2, Korean War – 2, Vietnam – 8, Chad–Libya – 3.[5]

The third and most important reason for studying "crisis" is the fact that many crises escalate to war, as evident in the crises of 1914 and 1939 and the cataclysms which followed. Some crises do not so escalate (e.g., Cuban Missiles in 1962). Further, crises take place during, as well as prior to, and after, a war (e.g., respectively, Stalingrad in 1942–43, Munich in 1938, and Turkish Straits in 1946).[6] More generally, the persistence of organized, large-scale, collective violence, especially in an era of advanced weapons technology, poses a challenge to the survival of all who inhabit the planet Earth.

Of the three concepts which attempt to illuminate turbulence, disruption and disorder in global politics, crisis was the last to emerge as the focus of systematic research. This can be traced to four contributions in the 1960s: the Stanford studies of the link between perceptions and decisions in the 1914 Crisis (e.g., Zinnes, North and Koch, 1961; and Holsti, 1965); McClelland's (1962, 1964) use of macro-level quantitative data to examine a sequence of crises in two "conflict arenas," Berlin and the Taiwan Straits; and conceptually, the micro-level definitions of crisis by Robinson (1962) and Hermann (1963, 1969).

Other notable studies are: Paige's (1968) "guided reconstruction" of United States decision-making at the outset of the Korean War; Allison's (1971) three models of the Cuban Missile Crisis; George and Smoke's (1974) "structured focused comparison" of deterrence in 11 United States crises, from the Berlin Blockade to the Missile Crisis; Snyder and Diesing's (1977) dissection of the bargaining process in 16 international crises from 1898 to 1973; the Stein and Tanter (1980) model of Israel's multiple paths to choice in the 1967 Middle East Crisis; Lebow's (1981) analysis of cognitive closure and crisis management in 26 cases from 1898 to 1967; Leng et al.'s (1979, 1982, 1983, 1988) quantitative studies of bargaining in twentieth-century crises; George's (1983, 1984, 1986) studies of crisis prevention; studies of a closely-related phenomenon, namely "militarized interstate disputes" (e.g., Gochman and Maoz, 1984; Leng and Singer, 1988); several analyses of deterrence and crisis management (Huth and Russett, 1984, 1988; Jervis, Lebow and Stein, 1985; Lebow and Stein, 1987; Winham et al., 1988); Bracken (1983), Betts (1987) and Lebow (1987) on nuclear crisis management; and James (1988) on crisis and war.

These impressive works notwithstanding, much remained obscure about crisis: crisis perceptions and the decision-making process of the Soviet Union;[7] most twentieth-century crises in regions other than Europe;[8] crises of weak international actors;[9] the role of alliance partners in crisis management; the precipitating causes of crises; crisis outcomes; and the consequences of crises for the power, status, behavior and subsequent perceptions of participant states. Nor is there an accepted theory of crisis.[10]

It was a growing awareness of these shortcomings and of the pervasiveness of this phenomenon that led to the initiation of the ICB Project in 1975.[11] Four objectives guided its research: the codification of knowledge about all international and foreign policy crises during the twentieth century; the framing and testing of hypotheses about the effects of crisis-induced stress on coping and choice by decision-makers; the discovery of patterns regarding core crisis dimensions – outbreak, actor behavior and crisis management, major power activity, involvement by international organizations, and outcome; and the application of the lessons of history to the advancement of international peace.

To achieve these goals we launched an inquiry into the military-security crises of all international (state) actors across all regions, cultures, and political and economic systems in the contemporary era. Its methods are qualitative and quantitative, that is, selected case studies in depth of perceptions and decisions by a single state[12] and studies in breadth of aggregate data on all crises during the twentieth century, initially, 1929–79.[13]

The ubiquity of crisis in world politics is evident in a few simple statistics. During the 57 years explored thus far, there were 323 international crises, that is, an average of 5.67 per year. These encompassed 698 states confronting foreign policy crises, that is, an average of 12.25 crisis actors per year over the half-century. And for the

51-year period, January 1929–August 1939 and September 1945–end of 1985, there were almost two crises in progress each day somewhere in the global system.

Before proceeding to an analysis of crucial dimensions of crises in the twentieth century, we present the definitions of crisis which guided the inclusion and exclusion of cases, the research design, and an overview of the ICB data set through various perspectives which were used to organize our findings and insights.

Definitions

The ICB definitions of crisis build upon those of McClelland (1968) and Young (1968), among others, at the macro-level, and Robinson (1962) and Hermann (1969) at the micro-level; but they also attempt to correct their deficiencies, as delineated in Chapter 2 below. Moreover, our definitions are designed to differentiate the two levels of analysis yet relate them to each other.

An *international* (macro-level) crisis is based upon *behavioral* data about conflictual interaction among states.

> An *international crisis* is a situational change characterized by an increase in the intensity of *disruptive interactions* between two or more adversaries, with a high probability of *military hostilities* in time of peace (and, during a war, an *adverse change* in the *military balance*). The higher-than-normal conflictual interactions destabilize the existing relationship of the adversaries and pose a *challenge* to the existing *structure* of an international system – global, dominant and/or sub-system.[14]

An illustration of such a situational change is the Soviet-supported attempt by Iran's *Tudeh* Party on 23 August 1945 to take over the Azerbaijan capital of Tabriz, the beginning of the Azerbaijan Crisis. International crises end with exitpoints, that is, events which denote a significant reduction in conflictual activity. In the Azerbaijan case this occurred as a result of the withdrawal of Soviet troops from Iran on 9 May 1946.

A *foreign policy* (micro-level) crisis, by contrast, is based upon *perceptual* data.

> A *foreign policy crisis*, that is, a crisis viewed from the perspective of an individual state, is a situation with three necessary and sufficient conditions deriving from a change in a state's external or internal environment. All three are perceptions held by the highest level decision-makers of the actor concerned: *a threat to basic values*, along with the awareness of *finite time for response* to the external value threat, and a *high probability of involvement in military hostilities*.[15]

A foreign policy crisis is triggered by an act, event or situational change which generates the necessary crisis conditions of perceived threat, time pressure and war likelihood (e.g., the shelling of the islands of Quemoy and Matsu by the People's Republic of China beginning on 3 September 1954, triggering crises for the Republic of China on Taiwan and the United States – and, with it, the first international crisis over the Taiwan Straits). The termination of a foreign policy crisis is evidenced by the reduction of these stress-creating perceptions to their pre-crisis level. In the case noted above, an offer to negotiate by China's Premier Chou En-Lai on 23 April 1955 reduced stress for the US and Taiwan.

In this illustration, as in all foreign policy crises, trigger and termination are perceptual in character; that is, a crisis for a state derives from the decision-maker(s)' image of pressures to cope with stress. So, too, termination is associated with awareness of declining stress. Both are subjective in focus.

Every international crisis contains one or more foreign policy crises for a state (e.g., crises for Iran, the UK, the US and the USSR, the four actors in the Azerbaijan Crisis, and, as noted, crises for the PRC, Nationalist China and the US in the Taiwan Straits Crisis). More generally, international crises which occur in a pre-war setting (Entry into World War II 1939, with 21 actors), during a war (Dien Bien Phu 1954, with three actors), or after a war (Turkish Straits 1946, with two actors) do not differ regarding the necessary conditions of a macro-level crisis, namely, more intense disruptive interactions and the military dimension (high likelihood of an outbreak of military hostilities or of a change in the military balance).

It is these interactions and the challenge to international system stability posed by the accompanying turmoil which constitute one major strand of ICB inquiry into crises. The other, closely-related focus is the effects of crisis-generated turmoil on foreign policy decisions. Thus intra-war crises (IWCs), like defeat in a major battle (e.g., Stalingrad in 1943) or technological escalation during a war (e.g.,the dropping of atomic bombs on Japan in 1945, leading to its surrender), profoundly affected the decisions of German and Japanese leaders during the Second World War. Indeed, the effects of these IWCs were more significant in terms of the sweep of world politics than the consequences of many non-intra-war crises for behavior and subsequent events. It is this relationship between crisis-induced stress and decisions, whether the stress is created in a non-war or war setting, that is the second strand of ICB research, as reflected in the in-depth case studies noted earlier.

Research Design

Data have been collected on four sets of variables, two at the micro/state level, two at the macro/international level. The first two sets – actor attributes and actor-case dimensions – relate to the year in which a foreign policy crisis begins. The other two data sets – crisis attributes and crisis dimensions – refer to the international crisis as a whole. Two separate codebooks were designed to tap these attributes and dimensions at both levels of analysis.

All variables are incorporated into a two-level conceptual scheme. For the international crisis (Figure I.1.1.), there are seven clusters of Crisis Dimensions – Setting, Breakpoint–Exitpoint, Crisis Management Technique, Major Power Activity, International Organization Involvement, Outcome and Severity. Each cluster contains one or more specific variables, as indicated in the Map. There are also six control variables, representing different perspectives for the classification of data and findings – Geography, Polarity, System Level, Conflict, Power Discrepancy, and Involvement by Powers.

At the actor level (Figure I.1.2.), there are five clusters of Crisis Dimensions – Trigger, Actor Behavior, Major Power Activity, International Organization Involvement and Outcome. There is also an array of controls: the same contextual variables as those noted above at the macro-level, along with war; and several Actor Attributes – Age, Territory, Regime, Capability, Values and Conditions. Their choice is based upon the assumption that these dimensions and attributes will affect both the propensity to become a direct crisis participant and behavior in a crisis.

A crisis can – and should – be addressed in both macro and micro terms. The focus of the macro-level is interactions among states in an international crisis. The focus of the micro-level is images held, and actions taken, by a state's decision-makers.[16]

Core Data on Crises: An Overview

Crises occur in many settings. One is geographic, both their regional location and their distance from the territory of the participating states. Another context is structural, that is, the type of power configuration in the system in which a crisis occurs. Crises may – or may not – erupt within an ongoing conflict or war. The adversaries may be equal or unequal with respect to capability. And the major powers may be aloof from – or actively involved in – an international crisis. Thus crises during the half-century were explored in terms of all these perspectives – geography, polarity, system level, conflict, war, power discrepancy, and involvement by the powers. They also serve as useful categories for the presentation of a summary of core data on crises at both levels of analysis.

Initially, each international crisis was located in one of 18 sub-regions. These were collapsed into five regions, with the following *geographic* distribution of the 323 cases: Africa (28%); Americas (12%); Asia (23%); Europe (18%); and Middle East (19%). At the micro-level, the location of a foreign policy crisis for a state was specified as: its home territory (58% of 698 actor-cases); its sub-region (17%); its continent (Africa, Americas, Asia, Europe or Middle East) (12%); or elsewhere, that is, beyond its continental domain (13%).

For the 57 years examined here, the 323 international crises were placed into one of four periods of system-*polarity* according to the first breakpoint of a crisis, i.e., the trigger date for its first crisis actor. The polarity distribution of international crises was as follows: multipolarity (1929–39 – [12%]); Second World War (1939–45 – [9%]); bipolarity (1945–62 – [29%]); and polycentrism (1963–85 – [50%]). The corresponding distribution among the 698 actor-cases is 14%, 11%, 30%, and 45%.

Every international crisis occurs, exclusively or primarily, within the dominant system or in one of several regional subsystems, which together constitute the global system.[17] Thus every case was classified according to the *system level* at which it took place. There were: subsystem (66%) (e.g., Chad/Libya VI 1983–84); mainly subsystem, i.e., predominantly subsystem in focus, but with a spillover to the dominant system, usually when one or more major powers was a crisis actor (14%) (e.g., Angola 1975–76); mainly dominant system, with a spillover to a subsystem (9%) (e.g., Suez-Sinai 1956–57); and dominant system (11%) (e.g., Berlin Deadline 1957–59). For foreign policy crises, the system-level categories were collapsed into two, with the following distribution among the 698 actor-cases: subsystem or mainly subsystem (70%); mainly dominant and dominant system (30%). Combined expert judgement by three independent coders was used to determine the system level assigned to each case.

Some international crises, as noted, take place in a setting free from long-term hostility. Others erupt in a context of prolonged dispute over several issues, with a legacy of periodic violence or an ongoing war, and spillover effects on other domains of their relationship. The 323 cases were therefore divided into three categories of *conflict* setting: non-protracted conflict (46%), protracted conflict (34%), and long-war protracted conflict (20%). After locating all international crises in one of the three conflict categories, each actor-case was recoded to determine whether or not the relevant crisis actor was a direct party to the conflict of which its international crisis was a part. The corresponding figures are 47%, 32% and 21%, respectively.

Foreign policy crises were also classified according to whether or not they occurred during a *war* and, if so, the type of catalyst. Of the 698 cases, 34% were intra-war crises (IWCs), 66% were non-IWCs. The distribution of triggering acts, events or environmental changes among the IWCs was as follows: exit of a major actor from an ongoing war (13%); entry of a new major actor (3%); technological escalation of a war (1%); major non-technological escalation (11%); defeat in a significant battle (2%); anticipated entry of a major actor into a war (1%); internal deterioration (1%); and other (2%).

Power discrepancy (PD) refers to the capability gap between adversaries, whether individual states or coalitions. The power score for each crisis actor is the sum of six separate scores on scales measuring size of population, GNP, territorial size, alliance capability, military expenditures, and nuclear capability. The scores were collapsed into three categories: high power discrepancy – 98 cases (34%); medium PD – 95 cases (32%); and low PD – 99 cases (34%) (World War II cases were excluded due to missing data). At the actor level, the numerical power discrepancy scores for each pair of adversaries were collapsed into five categories, with the following distribution: high negative PD (11% of all pairs); low negative PD (24%); no PD (24%); low positive PD (32%); and high positive PD (9%). These data made possible an exploration of the link between power/capability relationships among adversaries and their behavior in crises.

Major power involvement in international crises incorporates two elements – content and effectiveness. Two scales were devised to measure great power/superpower participation in a crisis. The first, for the 1945–85 period, extends from the role of both the US and the USSR as crisis actors to low or no involvement by both superpowers. Low involvement refers to political or economic activity, while high involvement refers to direct military, semi-military or covert activity. These same categories were applied to great power participation from 1929 to 1939. There were 191 international crises in which the involvement by both superpowers was low or none (1945–85) and 63 cases where they were highly involved. The comparable figures for the great powers in the decade before World War II were high involvement (21) and low/no involvement (17).

In addition to contextual variables, a group of actor attributes were used to classify micro-level data: age, regime, capability, values, and economic and socio-political conditions.

A crisis actor's *age* was determined from the date of its independence in the modern (post-1648) international system. All states fell into three categories: old – pre-1815 (35%); recent – 1815–1945 (31%); and new – post-1945 (34%).

Two *regime* variables were used. One measured the *duration* of the political authority within a state at the outbreak of its foreign policy crisis. Some indicators of regime change were the transfer of power from military to civilian rule, or the reverse, the institutionalization of a different governmental system, and a new constitution. The frequency distribution for the 698 crisis actors was: 0–2 years' duration (17%); 3–25 years (58%); and more than 25 years (25%). A second control measured regime *type*, with the following clusters: western democratic (42%); civil authoritarian (38%), and direct or indirect military rule (20%).

CRISIS DIMENSIONS

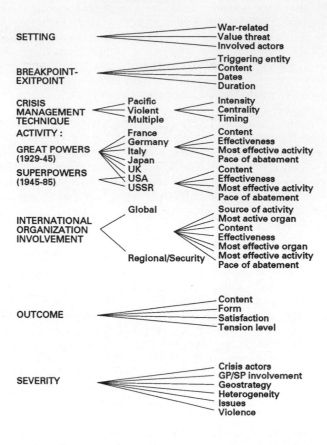

CONTROLS

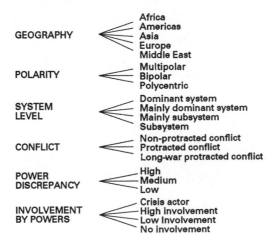

FIGURE I.1.1. Conceptual Map: Macro Level

CRISIS DIMENSIONS

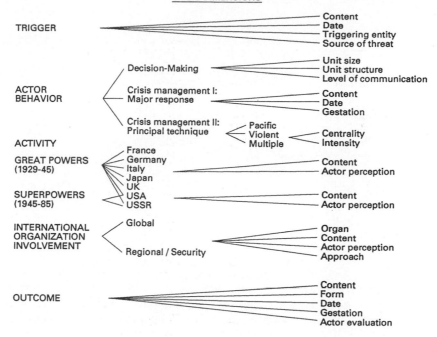

CONTROLS

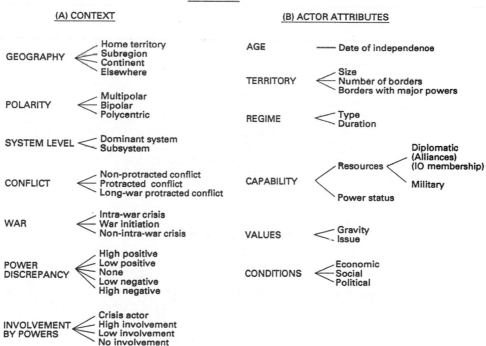

FIGURE I.1.2. Conceptual Map: Micro Level

Similarly, two strands of *capability* were introduced. One focused on a crisis actor's material power or *resources*, a composite of nuclear capability, military expenditure, alliance with a major power, population, territory and GNP at the onset of a foreign policy crisis. The frequency distribution among the 621 crisis actors, in global terms (World War II cases were excluded due to missing data problems), was: low capability (49%); medium (26%); high (13%); very high (12%). The corresponding figures, using a dominant system scale, were 32%, 14%, 26% and 28%, and in subsystem power terms, 54%, 30%, 9%, and 7%.

As for *power status*, all crisis actors were divided into four groups – superpowers, great powers, middle powers, small powers. Status refers to a state's place in the power hierarchy of the system in which its foreign policy crisis took place, at the time the crisis began. The distribution of cases at the subsystem level was: small powers (45%); middle powers (24%); great powers (23%); and superpowers (8%); and, for dominant system cases, 38%, 8%, 30%, and 24%, respectively.

The gravest *value* threatened at the onset of a foreign policy crisis was specified for each actor, with the following clusters: high value threats – to existence or of grave damage (24%); medium values – influence in the international system, territorial integrity, political or social system (63%), and low values – economic interests or a limited threat to population and property (13%).

The presence or absence of change in a group of six indicators (cost of living, unemployment, inflation, food prices, labor disruption and consumer goods shortages) and its direction, during the period four years prior to a crisis until its outbreak, were combined to indicate the *economic condition* of a crisis actor. Finally, in preparing the ground for a multi-pronged analysis of crises in the twentieth century, a combined category for a crisis actor's *socio-political conditions* was generated from four variables measuring societal unrest, mass violence, government instability and regime repression in a state at the outbreak of a crisis, compared to the situation six months earlier.

The underlying assumption in the selection of these perspectives, in the form of control variables, is that each will affect one or more crisis dimensions. Thus the spatial aspect of an international crisis, that is, the region in which it occurs, is likely to impinge on the primary crisis management technique, the extent of major power and international organization involvement, and its outcome. So too the conflict setting will affect many dimensions, from the type of breakpoint (trigger) to the substance and form of outcome. The same is anticipated from power discrepancy between adversaries. And, finally, it is assumed that the dynamics of an international crisis cannot be impervious to the extent of participation by the powers, ranging from a role as crisis actor to aloofness: what the powers do is likely to affect every facet of an international crisis. Similarly, foreign policy crises can be expected to be influenced by some of these contextual variables, as well as by one or more crisis actor attributes – its age, regime and capability, its perceived value threat, and its economic and socio-political conditions at the time of a crisis. The task is to discover the effects of these contextual and actor attributes on the unfolding of a crisis from onset to termination.

A Reader's Guide

In the two aggregate volumes of the ICB Project (Brecher and Wilkenfeld *et al.*, 1988; Wilkenfeld and Brecher *et al.*, 1988), an attempt was made to map the world of crisis in half of the twentieth century. The objectives of the Project, the definitions of crisis, the research design of the *Handbooks*, and an overview of the core data have been recapitulated in this introductory chapter – for those who are not familiar with the ICB dataset and its *raison d'être*. It remains to provide a guide to the main strands of this volume, with some illustrative findings.

In the largest sense, Volume III of *Crises in the Twentieth Century* is designed as interconnected "islands of analysis;" that is, one or more chapters will focus on an enduring issue, theme or question in the study of world politics and will present the salient findings, in order to shed light on unresolved controversies, to offer fresh insights, and to illuminate murky areas of the field, through both (macro-level) analyses of international crises and (micro-level) studies of foreign policy crises.

Definitions and concepts relating to system and crisis are elaborated in Chapter 2. More specifically, we present a fresh approach to the concepts of international system and crisis and unit-system linkages, or the "level-of-analysis" problem focused on crisis. This paves the way for several clusters of macro-level analysis:

system stability/instability (Chapters 3 and 4); third party intervention in crises (Chapters 5 and 6); the consequences of crises for regional subsystems and their actors (Chapter 7); and the impact of structural factors on crisis outcomes (Chapter 8).

Chapters 3 and 4 are devoted to the relationship of polarity to stability, that is, the role of different structures – bipolarity, multipolarity, etc. – in the generation of international conflict. One chapter presents a critique of the state of the art on that "great debate" and sets forth new directions for inquiry, focusing on a model of the comparative costs of security regimes in terms of (in)stability. The other chapter tests the model and its central hypothesis on the ranking of polarity structures *vis-à-vis* stability, using evidence on international crisis(macro)-generated turmoil.

Chapters 5 and 6 focus on the involvement and effectiveness of global IOs and superpowers in international crises. They are guided by two research questions: (1) what is the relationship between the attributes of international crises and the extent, substance and effectiveness of United Nations/League of Nations and US/USSR activity; and (2) under what conditions is UN and superpower intervention in crises likely to lead to favorable outcomes? In the first of these studies of third party intervention, we found that: UN involvement in serious crises was considerably higher than its overall involvement in crises; that it was most effective in abating crises which had escalated to full-scale war; and that crises in which the UN was involved were more likely than others to terminate in some form of agreement between the adversaries.

Chapter 7 analyzes international crises as political earthquakes. Indexes of Severity (intensity) and Importance (impact) are delineated and applied to half a century of crises in two regions of high turmoil, the Middle East and Africa, in an attempt to test the hypothesis that the severity of a crisis predicts its consequences three years thereafter, for the adversaries and for the system in which a crisis occurs.

Part II concludes with Chapter 8, an analysis of the impact of structural dimensions of the overall crisis and coping mechanisms. These structural dimensions include breakpoint-trigger (here conceived of as a defining characteristic of the interactions among the parties to the crisis), group size, and homogeneity of world view among the actors.

These analyses at the macro-level will be followed by three chapters which bridge the two levels of analysis by using both macro and micro findings (Part III). A protracted conflict-crisis model is specified in Chapter 9 and tested with the evidence of half a century on eight crisis dimensions: breakpoint/trigger; value threat; actor behavior; major power activity; international organization involvement; duration; and outcome, both form and substance. In Chapter 10, system level is added to the model as the intervening variable. And the expanded protracted conflict-crisis model is tested with ICB evidence on the dominant (East–West) system and two regional subsystems, the Middle East and South Asia.

Chapter 11 extends the analysis of the relationship between protracted conflict (PC) and crisis by presenting a five-stage comparison of patterns of crisis management: Arab–Israel (PC) versus other (non-PC) Middle East crises; Middle East crises compared to those in the rest of the world; Arab–Israel crises compared to all others in the global system; Arab–Israel crises compared to all others outside of protracted conflicts; and Arab–Israel cases compared to all other crises within PCs. Contrary to the conventional wisdom of area specialists, it was postulated that patterns of crisis management depend on whether or not a crisis occurs within a protracted conflict, not on its geographic location.

The combined macro-micro analyses of conflict and crisis lead to two studies of state behavior in crises (Part IV). Chapter 12 focuses on the venerable theory of human behavior based on the notion of stimulus-response. The dual hypothesis is: a) that the violence-begets-violence dynamic, which underlies the interactions of states in crises, will be strengthened under conditions of high stress for decision-makers; and b) that the impact of the stress level on crisis decision-making will be affected by three conditions – polarity of the international system, level of power of the crisis actor, and type of conflict setting.

Chapter 13 is devoted to US and USSR crisis behavior. Four dimensions of super-power crises are explored: their triggers; actor behavior, that is, their crisis management techniques, including the role of violence; the substance and form of their crisis outcomes; and their duration. The findings clearly point to: a US-dominated global system during the bipolar period (1945–62); a diminished US ability to manage crises in the polycentric era (1963–85); and, generally, reduced US influence in world politics over time. Moreover, it was discovered that, in direct confrontation between the superpowers, the Soviet Union almost always backed off. Finally, both used violence successfully in crises to achieve specific goals.

The concluding chapter to this volume presents a pre-theory of crisis. Operational definitions of concepts are offered at both system (macro) and actor (micro) levels of analysis. Variables are specified, as are models to explain: (1) an international crisis (system level), in terms of a logical sequence of four domains – onset, escalation, deescalation and impact, culminating in a dynamic, inter-phase model to explain the linkages among them; and (2) a foreign policy crisis (actor level), in terms of perceptions of value threat, time pressure and war likelihood, induced by change(s) in the environment, and the effects of these perceptions on coping and choice by decision-makers. These macro and micro models are then integrated into a holistic model of crisis.

Notes

1. Major figures in the analysis of social conflict, following Simmel and Weber, were the Chicago School of Sociology – Cooley (1918), Park and Burgess (1924), and Ross (1930); Sorokin (1928); and, since the Second World War, Lewin (1948), Bernard (1950, 1957), Coser (1956) and Dahrendorf (1959).

   Extensive surveys of the literature on social conflict are Lasswell (1931), Mack and Snyder (1957), McNeill (1965), Coser (1968), Fink (1968), North (1968), Nicholson (1970) and Gurr (1980).
2. Other notable contributions to the conflict/war literature are Aron (1957, 1959); Waltz (1959); Kahn (1960); Rapoport (1960); Richardson (1960a, 1960b); Schelling (1960, 1966); the Stanford School – North *et al.* (1960); Boulding (1962); K. J. Holsti (1966); Pruitt and Snyder (1969); Barringer (1972); O. R. Holsti (1972); Blainey (1973); Brodie (1973); Choucri and North (1975); Rummel (1975–1981); Nelson and Olin (1979); Organski and Kugler (1980); Beer (1981); Bueno de Mesquita (1981); Gilpin (1981); Mitchell (1981); Small and Singer (1982); Levy (1983); Howard (1984); Modelski and Morgan (1985); Stoessinger (1985); Luard (1986); Midlarsky (1986, 1988); Brown (1987); Modelski (1987); Goldstein (1988); Huth (1988); Nogee and Spanier (1988); Patchen (1988); Thompson (1988); and Mueller (1989).
3. The concept of protracted conflict and its impact on the major attributes and dimensions of crisis are discussed in Chapters 9–11 below.
4. The intensity of violence for the Hungarian Uprising is designated "serious clashes," not full-scale war.
5. A subsidiary COW-generated data set, known as Militarized Interstate Disputes, is much closer to the ICB data set in volume and to crisis as a concept. It reports an average number of 6.7 "disputes begun per year" for 1929–1945, and 12.7 for 1946–76 (Gochman and Maoz 1984).
6. For brief summaries of the crises cited here and elsewhere in this volume, see Brecher and Wilkenfeld *et al.* (1988, Part V).
7. For attempts to overcome this *lacuna*, see Adomeit (1982), K. Dawisha (1984), George (1983), Horelick (1964), S. S. Kaplan (1981), Triska and Finley (1968), Valenta (1979), Valenta and Potter (1984) and Wilkenfeld and Brecher (Chapter 6, this volume).
8. Noteworthy exceptions are Stremlau (1977) and Whiting (1960).
9. This is indirectly explored in M. Singer (1972).
10. For insightful surveys of the theoretically-oriented literature see M. Haas (1986), Holsti (1979), Hopple and Rossa (1981), and Tanter (1978).
11. Several of the volumes cited above in the text and most of those in the preceding notes had not yet appeared.
12. The ICB case studies published thus far are Brecher (1979); Brecher with Geist (1980); A. I. Dawisha (1980); Shlaim (1983); Dowty (1984); K. Dawisha (1984); and Jukes (1985). Three other studies are approaching completion: Hungarian Uprising 1956, for Hungary (Geist); India/China Border 1959–62, for India (Hoffmann); and Rhodesia's UDI 1965–66, for Zambia (Anglin).
13. Several considerations shaped our choice of this time frame. First, it maximizes the bases for comparison: crises in multipolar, bipolar and polycentric international systems with diverse global and regional organizations. Second, by incorporating the 100 new actors emerging at the end of the European imperial era, we achieve great variation in such characteristics of states as their age, size of territory, population, regime type, regime duration, belief system, economic development, and so forth. Third, we can thereby explore the crisis-laden years of Germany's reascent to major power status and the approach of World War II from 1933–39, as well as the profusion of crises in Africa during the 1970s. Finally, the set of cases to be generated would be large enough to permit statistical analysis of the aggregate data. While the two *Handbooks* (Brecher and

Wilkenfeld *et al.*, 1988; Wilkenfeld and Brecher *et al.*, 1988) present the data set for 1929–79, this volume incorporates the enlarged data set – forward to the end of 1985.

14. Theoretically, the probability of military hostilities (war likelihood) can range from an infinitesimal value above 0 to .99$\ddot{9}$. Operationally, "high probability" (or "*perceived* high probability of involvement in military hostilities," in the definition of foreign policy crisis above, p. 5) may be designated as .500 to .99$\ddot{9}$, that is, at least a 50/50 possibility. However, a marked change in the probability of military hostilities, for example, from .10... .30, may be just as salient as a move into a high probability range, especially in cases where protracted conflict predisposes states to expect crisis. What is crucial to the existence of an international (and foreign policy) crisis is a high – or substantial change in – (perceived) war likelihood.

    The notion of "adverse change in the military balance . . . during a war" clearly implies that an intra-war crisis (IWC) for one state, that is, the state which experiences the adverse change, is not a crisis for the state experiencing a favorable change in the military balance.

    The base for "higher-than-normal conflictual interactions" is a "normal relations range," as discussed in Chapter 2.

15. Our point of departure was Hermann's widely-held view of a crisis for a state as a situation involving a threat to high-priority goals, short time for response and surprise. The ICB definition incorporates five specific changes based upon empirical evidence and the logical imperative of the crisis-stress nexus: the deletion of surprise; the addition of perceived high probability of war or, more precisely, the perceived likelihood of military hostilities; the replacement of short time by finite time for the major response; the inclusion of internal environmental changes as potential triggers to crises; and a shift from high-priority goals to basic values. In a recent essay, Hermann (1988 p. 148, n. 3) noted "the movement toward consensus on a definition of crisis, at least from a decision-making perspective." He termed his revised definition "a variation on Brecher's modification of my own earlier efforts. I accept his introduction of the expectation of military hostilities as particularly appropriate for delimiting . . . [crises]."

    The ICB Project focuses on military-security crises. We recognize – but have not explored – other types of crises, such as political, economic and cultural.

16. The rationale for, and the links between, the two levels of crisis analysis are presented in "Unit-System Linkages" in Chapter 2 below.

17. The dominant system is identified by many international relations theorists with interaction among the major powers in world politics. For the more than half-century of our study, this meant the European great powers, the US and Japan in the 1930s, and the US–USSR inter-bloc system since 1945.

2 System and Crisis

Michael Brecher and Hemda Ben Yehuda

We begin this analytic study of crises in world politics by undertaking two fundamental and interrelated conceptual tasks. First, building upon earlier contributions, a new definition of international system is offered and its essential properties – structure, process, equilibrium, stability – are discussed. The second requirement is a fresh approach to crisis and the forging of links between its unit and system levels. This, in turn, will facilitate the analysis of crises as catalysts to system change (Chapter 7 below).

International System   In a trenchant essay on system transformation, Zinnes (1980) asserted that a satisfactory definition of international system must address two basic questions: (1) "how do we know one when we see one" and (2) what distinguishes one from another? The first can be met by a definition which builds upon earlier writings but restores the balance between structure and process within an integrated set of system components.

> An international system is a set of *actors* which are situated in a configuration of power *(structure)*, are involved in regular patterns of interaction *(process)*, are separated from other units by *boundaries* set by a given *issue*, and are constrained in their behavior from within *(context)* and from outside the system *(environment)*.[1]

Actors are the basic units that form a system. Systems vary according to the number of participants – at least two but often more, and their type – nation–state, international organization and transnational entity.

Structure refers to how the actors in a system stand in relation to each other. Its basic variables are the number of actors and the distribution of power among them, from unipolar through bipolar to multipolar or polycentric.

Process designates the interaction patterns among the actors of a system. The basic interaction variables are type, identified along a conflict/cooperation dimension, and intensity, indicated by the volume of interaction during a given period of time.[2] A link between structure and process is postulated: every structure has a corresponding interaction process; and a structure creates and maintains regular interaction.

International systems do not require the physical proximity of actors, though this trait is frequently present. Another distinctive property of a system, which serves to demarcate its boundaries, is *issue*. This concept may be defined as a specific shared focus of interest for two or more actors. There are war–peace issues; for example, K. J. Holsti (1972: pp. 452–455) noted several issues in his set of 77 international conflicts and crises from 1919 to 1965: territory; composition of a government; rights or privileges to bases; national honor; unlimited aggrandizement or imperialism; liberation; and unification. There are economic and developmental issues, such as fishing, commercial navigation, offshore drilling, and military uses in the issue-area of oceans, space and resources, as well as exchange rates, reserve assets, international capital movements, and adjustment, liquidity, and confidence in a regime within the international monetary issue-area (Keohane and Nye, 1977: Part II). There are also political, cultural, status and technological issues within broader categories of issue-area (Potter, 1980).

The inclusion of subsystems within our definition enables us to resolve a paradox in the globally-oriented concept of international system and thereby to address the other system properties, namely, boundaries, context and environment. The paradox is simple yet fundamental. Every system has boundaries, which demarcate members from other units. However, the concept of global international system excludes *a priori* the possibility of non-member units and, therefore, of boundaries. It has the additional shortcoming of negating the existence of an environment as a phenomenon distinct from the system itself. That in turn makes impossible a distinction between two kinds of effects on the behavior of actors – contextual, those arising from within a system, and environmental, those from outside. As Young (1968a: p. 23) observed, a global system can be characterized only by its context since "there is nothing outside the system which can be labeled environment." The concept of environment, he continued, is useful when dealing with subsystems, for these "may be affected by various factors (including other organized entities) located outside its boundaries in spatial terms."

There are several usages of the concept of *boundaries* in international politics. They may be conceived in vertical terms, that is, boundaries in time (Rosecrance, 1963, Chap. 11; M. Haas, 1974); as horizontal, that is, in spatial terms (Singer, 1971: pp. 12–13); or diagonal, that is, time and space boundaries together (Rosenau, 1972: p. 149). The notion of boundaries presented here is derived from the generic definition of international system above. As such, they make possible the spatial distinction between context and environment. *Context* and *environment* incorporate all geographic, political, military, technological, societal and cultural elements which affect the structure and process of a system, from within and from outside the system, respectively.

The definition of international system presented above enables us to identify a system. Other concepts are needed to distinguish among systems. These are stability and equilibrium, which have been dealt with extensively in the mainstream of international relations literature. In general, more emphasis has been given to stability. Moreover, its relationship to equilibrium has not been fully developed.[3] The restoration of equilibrium to a co-equal status with stability among the attributes of an international system is a precondition to developing the concept of international crisis.[4] Closely related conceptual tasks are definitions of stability and equilibrium and a specification of relationships between them so as to facilitate a differentiation among international systems.

The concept of change is the key to the distinction between stability and equilibrium, as well as to the link between them. Change may be defined as a shift from, or an alteration of, an existing pattern of interaction between two or more actors in the direction of greater conflict or cooperation. It is indicated by acts or events which exceed the bounds of normal fluctuations or a "normal relations range" (Azar, 1972; Azar *et al.*, 1977, 196–197, 207). Following Ashby (1952: p. 87) four types of change may be distinguished: full function – no finite interval of constancy; part function – finite intervals of change and of constancy; step function – finite intervals of constancy separated by instantaneous jumps; null function – no change over the whole period of observation. Change may also occur in the structure of a system, namely, an increase or decrease in the number of actors and/or a shift in the distribution of power among them.

Stability may be defined as change within explicit bounds. *Instability* designates change beyond a normal fluctuation range. These concepts may be operationalized in terms of the quantity (number) of change(s) in the structure of a system, its process or both, ranging from no changes to many changes. This continuum denotes degrees of stability. The absence of change indicates pure stability, its presence, some degree of instability. Any system can thus be designated as stable or unstable. Instability in the international system can be measured by change in the volume of conflictual interaction inherent in such phenomena as wars or crises. They may also induce structural change and thereby accentuate system instability.

Equilibrium may be defined as the steady state of a system, denoting change below the threshold of reversibility. *Disequilibrium* designates change beyond the threshold of reversibility. This meaning is broader than the notion of balance of power, a widely-used synonym for equilibrium in the world politics literature. These concepts may be operationalized in terms of the quality (significance) of change in structure, process or both, ranging from total reversibility to total irreversibility. This continuum denotes degrees of equilibrium. Incremental change indicates a state of equilibrium which has no effect on the system as a whole. Step-level or step function (irreversible) change indicates disequilibrium, which inevitably leads to system transformation, that is, a change in essential actors and/or the distribution of power among them. The new system, with properties which significantly differ from those of its predecessor, denotes a new equilibrium, that is, changes within it which are reversible. These system attributes are presented in Figure I.2.1.

Every system has explicit or implicit "rules of the game." Many international systems permit resort to violence as an instrument of crisis management, its legit-

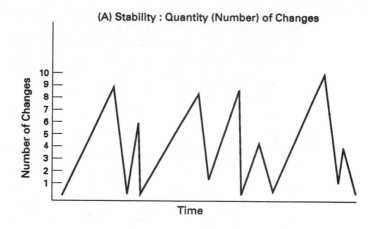

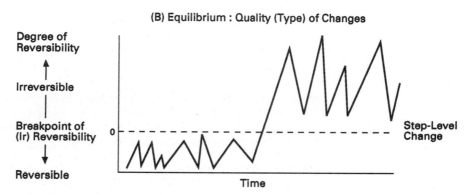

FIGURE **I.2.1.** Stability and Equilibrium

imacy deriving from the legal sovereignty of international actors. This is evident in the inherent right of individual and collective self-defense, enshrined in the international institutions of the twentieth-century multipolar system (League of Nations) and bipolar/polycentric systems (United Nations). Violence which exceeds the bounds of normal fluctuation, even when legitimized by the "rules of the game," constitutes, in our terms, instability, but not disequilibrium, unless this violence challenges the structure of the system.

Acute disruptions in an existing structure or process or both may, or may not, lead to disequilibrium:

> a "distortion" [i.e., instability] *per se* – an increase in temperature in an air-conditioned room, the rise of a single powerful state in a balance of power system, or a sharp increase in price because of a sudden upsurge in demand – does not suggest that a system is in disequilibrium: rather, it tests that hypothesis by allowing us to see whether adjustments take place. Does the air-conditioning bring the temperature back to the normal level, do coalitions form to counter the power of the rising state, do new sources of supply appear in response to price increases? . . . Disequilibrium of a system . . . appears only when the 'forces tending to restore the balance' (Arrow's phrase in a discussion of equilibrium) fail to operate. Air-conditioning that heats a room to 100 degrees F.; "bandwagoning" that leads to hegemony by a single power; prices that rise sharply and continuously without bringing forth new supply – these are indications of disequilibrium (Keohane, 1981).

There are additional linkages between stability and equilibrium. The logically-possible four states of a system are: stability–equilibrium; stability–disequilibrium;[5] instability–equilibrium, and instability–disequilibrium. These, along with illustrations and systemic outcomes, are presented in Table I.2.1.

In summary, approaches to international systems have been assessed. A revised definition has been proposed based upon six system components – actors, structure, process, boundaries, context and environment. Furthermore, the two basic system

TABLE I.2.1. System Attributes: Links

		Equilibrium	Disequilibrium
S T A B I L I T Y	A	No change or few *reversible* changes in structure or process or both and thus no effect on the system as a whole	Few, *irreversible* changes in structure or process which lead to system transformation
	B	Ideologically-based coalitions in bipolar system and flexible alignment patterns in multipolar system preserve existing structure	Exit of major actor from bloc leading to basic change in system polarity
	C	System unchanged: Equilibrium and Stability maintained	System transformed: new Equilibrium
I N S T A B I L I T Y	A	Many but *reversible* changes in structure and/or process which do not lead to system transformation	Many *irreversible* changes in structure, process or both which lead to system transformation
	B	Limited wars in scope, intensity, objectives	World war – likely to lead to destruction of existing structure
	C	System unchanged: Equilibrium maintained, Stability restored	System transformed: new Equilibrium, new Stability

Code: A = State of the System.
     B = Illustration.
     C = System Outcome.

attributes, stability and equilibrium, have been redefined and the links between them specified. Thus the dual task of identifying and differentiating systems has now been completed. The next section will focus on the concept of systemic crisis both within a given system and as a catalyst to system transformation.

International Crisis

Definitions of international crisis, based upon concepts related to international system, can be classified into two groups: process and combined structure-interaction.

Process definitions view international crisis as a turning point at which there occurs an unusually intense period of conflictual interaction. According to McClelland (1968: pp. 160–161), "a crisis is, in some way, a 'change of state' in the flow of international political actions . . ." Elsewhere McClelland (1972: pp. 6,7) noted that crisis "interaction is likely to affect the stability or equilibrium of the system . . ." Similarly, for Azar (1972: p. 184) "[I]nteraction above the . . . upper critical threshold . . . for more than a very short time implies that a crisis situation has set in." Snyder and Diesing (1977: p. 6), too, defined an international crisis as "a sequence of interactions between the governments of two or more sovereign states in severe conflict, short of actual war, but involving the perception of a dangerously high probability of war." These definitions emphasize stages of conflictual behavior among states, types of activity, the direction and speed of behavioral change, and shifts that indicate changes in the interaction process.

Well-operationalized concepts exist (Azar, Brody and McClelland, 1972). And scales facilitate the ranking of various behavioral groups (Azar *et al.*, 1977; Corson, 1970; McClelland, 1968; Tanter, 1966). The shortcomings of process definitions are analytical. The logic for designating the beginning and end of a crisis is not precisely indicated. Changes in process are not related to structure. There is no attempt to uncover causes and effects of international crisis. The result is a group of studies more valuable for their empirical findings than for their conceptual clarity (e.g., Burgess and Lawton, 1972; Eckhardt and Azar, 1978; McClelland, 1968, 1972; Peterson, 1975; Tanter, 1974; Wilkenfeld, 1972).

Combined *structure-interaction* definitions view an international crisis as a situation characterized by basic change in processes which might affect structural variables of a system. Thus Young (1968c: p. 15) identified "a crisis in international politics [as] a process of interaction occurring at higher levels of perceived intensity than the ordinary flow of events and characterized by . . . significant implications for the stability of some system or subsystem. . . ." Integrating structure into a process definition serves as a good analytical corrective by specifying the essential conditions and potential effects of crisis situations. There is, however, little operationalization of the crucial concept of structure or related empirical research.

There is another group, comprising Kaplan (1957), Pruitt (1969), Waltz (1979) and others, for whom systems are characterized by normal periods of equilibrium and stability with occasional shifts to disequilibrium and instability. Although such situations are not explicitly termed crises, these transitions are clearly related to the concept of crisis. Except for Kaplan, however, emphasis was placed on the traits of a specific system, not on changes from one system to another.

A problem common to crisis definitions is the mixture of unit- and system-level concepts. Snyder and Diesing (1977: pp. 6, 7), as noted above, specifically include a unit-level concept – "the perception of a dangerously high probability of war," which they term "[T]he centerpiece of our definition . . ." Moreover, "[T]he perceived probability must at least be high enough to evoke feelings of fear and tension to an uncomfortable degree." For Young (1968c: pp. 10, 14), "crisis concerns the probabilities that violence of major proportions will break out," a point which "explicitly refers to subjective perceptions about the prospects of violence rather than to a more objective measure of the probability of violence." Another illustration is Wiener and Kahn's (1962) twelve generic dimensions of crisis. Among them are system-level indicators such as a turning point in a sequence of events, a new configuration of international politics as a crisis outcome, and changes in relations among actors. There are also unit-level indicators: a perceived threat to actor goals; a sense of urgency, stress and anxiety among decision-makers; increased time pressure; and so forth.

In summary, there are several shortcomings in existing definitions of international crisis:

(1) they do not integrate the key concepts – change in interaction, type of structure, degree of disequilibrium, and instability;
(2) they focus clearly on interaction processes but do little to explain their sources and diverse effects on a system; and
(3) they mix system concepts with unit-level components such as perception, stress and values.

Moreover, there has been little attempt to link definitions at the two levels of crisis (McCormick, 1978; Tanter, 1978).

In an effort to overcome these weaknesses we present a definition of international crisis based upon the system properties discussed in the first section of this chapter. An international crisis, as noted in Chapter 1, may be defined as a situational change characterized by two necessary and sufficient conditions:

(1) an increase in the intensity of *disruptive interactions* among system actors, with the likelihood of *military hostilities* (or, during a war, an *adverse change* in the *military balance*), and
(2) a challenge posed by such higher-than-normal conflictual interactions to the existing *structure* of an international system, more precisely, to one or more structural attributes – power distribution, actors/regimes, rules and alliance configuration.

This definition refers to crises in the military–security (war–peace) issue-area only. International crisis encompasses change. System change, however, need not occur by leaps and jumps, that is, crises; it may result from cumulative events. Such change is the product of something other than a crisis.

The ICB definition specifies change in process and structure. It is also linked to stability *and* equilibrium, for the necessary conditions indicate a shift from stability-equilibrium to one of the three other logically-possible "states of a system" set out in Table I.2.1. In schematic terms: few distortions in process or few challenges to a structure denote low instability, whereas many changes indicate high instability; minor (reversible) distortions in process or minor challenges to a structure denote equilibrium, while major (irreversible) changes indicate disequilibrium; instability, defined as changes beyond a normal fluctuation range but within bounds, is present in all international crises; disequilibrium, that is, irreversible change, is not.

The two crisis conditions and the linkages among system properties can be illustrated by the Berlin Blockade Crisis of 1948–49 (dominant system level) and the Kashmir Crisis of 1965–66 (subsystem level).

Berlin 1948–49[6]   Tension between the Western Powers and the Soviet Union centered on the issue of occupied Germany. The 1945 Potsdam Agreement had divided Germany into four zones but had provided that they were to be treated as one economic unit under the Allied Control Council. On 7 June 1948 the three Western Powers published the recommendations of the March 1948 London Conference (to which the Soviet Union had not been invited) calling for a merger of their zones in Germany. This conflictual act broke an existing, though fragile, East/West consensus on Germany and set in motion several changes in rapid succession. The Soviet Union responded on 24 June by blocking all Western transportation into and out of Berlin. President Truman countered on 26 June with an order to step up the airlift into Berlin, which had begun two months earlier, and to expedite plans for the rehabilitation of Germany as part of Western Europe. Talks among the crisis actors began on 2 August 1948. An informal consensus on the future of Germany was reached by the Four Powers on 21 March 1949. An agreement was signed on 12 May formalizing the partition of Germany. These events indicated an accommodation by the system, the latter event marking the end of the Berlin Blockade Crisis.

In international crises changes vary in quality as well as in quantity: they are reversible in some cases, irreversible in others. Thus a sharp increase in conflictual interactions between the Western Powers and the USSR clearly indicated system instability between 7 June 1948 and 12 May 1949. The Berlin Crisis also affected the East/West equilibrium. Distortions were step-level in nature; that is, neither the interaction pattern nor the structure of the dominant system in world politics at the time was the same before and after the crisis. The agreement of 12 May 1949 illustrates this point. It left Germany divided, creating two new embryonic international actors, the FRG and the GDR, and tightened the polarization between the superpowers. Furthermore, the interaction pattern between the Western Powers and the Soviet Union after the agreement on Berlin came into effect differed substantially from that during the occupation of Germany by the Four Powers. The system during the Berlin Blockade Crisis was in a state of high instability leading to disequilibrium. As such, it helped to catalyze the transformation of the international system from embryonic bipolarity (1945–48) to tight bipolarity.

The threshold events between phases of the Berlin Blockade Crisis, as well as the overall links between crisis conditions and the system attributes of equilibrium and stability, are summarized in Table I.2.2.

TABLE I.2.2. International Crisis and System Properties: Berlin 1948–49

| Crisis Phase | Dominant System Components | | Dominant System Attributes | |
	Process	Structure	Stability	Equilibrium
Pre-Crisis: July 1945–7 June 1948	Interaction among the Four Powers ruling Germany within a normal relations range	Embryonic bipolarity	Stable	Equilibrium
Crisis: 7 June 1948–21 March 1949	Rapid increase in (irreversible) conflictual interaction between the USSR and the Western Powers	Grave challenge to the existing structure of the dominant system	Unstable	Disequilibrium
Post-Crisis: 21 March– 12 May 1949	Decline in conflictual interaction, system accommodation	Tight bipolarity	Stable	(New) Equilibrium

Kashmir 1965–66[7] A similar analysis will now be undertaken for an international crisis at the subsystem level, the India/Pakistan struggle over Kutch and Kashmir in 1965–66. A South Asian regional subsystem had emerged in 1947 with the transfer of power from the United Kingdom to India and Pakistan. For almost a quarter of a century, until the sundering of Pakistan in the crisis leading to the creation of Bangladesh in 1971, India and Pakistan were the relatively equal major powers in the South Asian system, with several minor powers on the geographic periphery of the subcontinent, Ceylon (Sri Lanka), Afghanistan and Nepal.

The normal pattern of interaction between India and Pakistan was characterized by mistrust and verbal hostility, with periodic disruptions of crisis intensity as those over the post-partition territorial issues of Junagadh, Kashmir and Hyderabad (1947–49) and the Punjab War Scare (1951). There were also long-standing disputes over diverse issues like refugee compensation and repatriation, and the division of river water in the Indus Valley. Among them was the princely state of Kutch. Its ruler had acceded to the Indian Union in 1947, but Pakistan claimed that the northern section of the Rann of Kutch was part of its Sind Province. Incidents occurred in 1956, but Indian control over the disputed territory was quickly restored.

The India/Pakistan crisis over Kutch and Kashmir began in April 1965 and ended in January 1966. The initial breakpoint (trigger) occurred on 8 April when India launched an attack on the Kutch border. Pakistan responded with a counter-attack the same day. Much higher than normal hostile interaction continued until the end of June 1965. Pakistani forces initially repelled local Indian troops. In response, on 26 April, India placed its armed forces on alert, thereby escalating the crisis. A British call for a cease-fire and negotiations was accepted in principle on 11 May, but hostilities continued until 30 June when both parties agreed to the terms of a UK-mediated package – mutual withdrawal of forces, direct negotiations, and arbitration if these failed to settle the dispute. High instability characterized the South Asian subsystem during those months, but its basic equilibrium remained unchanged. Third party intervention led to partial system accommodation.

A second phase of this international crisis began in August 1965 and lasted until January 1966. The breakpoint occurred on 5 August when Pakistan-supported guerrillas infiltrated into the Indian-held part of Kashmir in an attempt to spark a large-scale uprising. The overall distribution of power between India and Pakistan in South Asia was at stake, making the challenge to the structure of the regional system much greater than in the April–June phase over the Rann of Kutch. India responded on 25 August by sending several thousand troops across the 1949 Kashmir Cease-Fire Line, capturing most areas through which the infiltrators came. The crisis escalated further on 1 September when Pakistan sent an armored column across the Cease-Fire Line in southern Kashmir threatening the vital road linking the Kashmir capital, Srinagar, with the plains of India. This led to a further escalation, namely, India's invasion of West Pakistan on 5 September.

The sharp increase in the volume of disruptive interaction indicated greater system instability. This was accentuated by China's denunciation of India's "aggression" against Pakistan and its "provocation" on the Sikkim–Tibet border. Moreover, Beijing issued an ultimatum to Delhi to dismantle all border military fortifications and to stop all alleged intrusions into Tibet. While rejecting China's demands on the 17th, India hinted at a willingness to make minor concessions. The next day Chinese troop movements were reported to be within 500 meters of Indian border positions. But on 21 September China withdrew its ultimatum announcing that India had complied with its demands. This moderate decrease in conflictual interaction denoted partial accommodation at the systemic level; change had not risen above the threshold of irreversibility.

The threat of direct Chinese military involvement in a South Asian crisis generated mediation efforts by the superpowers through the Security Council. A cease-fire resolution in mid-September, which also provided for a UN observer group in Kashmir, was accepted by India and Pakistan. This did not, however, indicate an end to the crisis, for both armies continued to occupy each other's territory, a situation which was soon followed by violations of the Cease-Fire Agreement. Another pacific strand of third party intervention began on 17 September when Soviet Prime Minister Kosygin offered to convene a conference in Tashkent between President Ayub Khan of Pakistan and Indian Prime Minister Shastri. The conference was held between 4 and 10 January 1966. It ended with a declaration affirming the intentions of both parties to restore diplomatic and economic relations following the withdrawal of their troops from all occupied territory, as well as the repatriation of prisoners-of-war. Thus 10 January 1966 marked the end of the crisis and successful accommodation by the South Asian system. The challenge to its structure had been overcome, the pre-crisis equilibrium had been restored, and instability had reverted to its long-term norm of protracted conflict (see Chapter 9).

As with the Berlin Crisis of 1948–49, the links between crisis conditions and the system attributes of equilibrium and stability in the 1965–66 India/Pakistan Crisis are summarized in Table I.2.3.

Thus far our analysis focused exclusively on the systems level. In the next section we address the level-of-analysis problem with respect to crisis. In so doing we prepare the ground for a confrontation with the dimension of system change.

TABLE I.2.3. International Crisis and System Properties: India/Pakistan 1965–66

Crisis Phase	Subsystem Components		Subsystem Attributes	
	Process	Structure	Stability	Equilibrium
Pre-Crisis: 1. 8 April–30 June 1965	Increase in (reversible) conflictual interaction over Kutch	Bipolarity	Unstable	Equilibrium
2. 1 July–4 August 1965	Decline in conflictual interaction	Bipolarity	Stable	Equilibrium
Crisis: 5 August–16 September 1965	Rapid increase in (irreversible) conflictual interaction over Kashmir	Grave challenge to the existing structure of the South Asian subsystem	Unstable	Disequilibrium
Post-Crisis: 17 September 1965–10 January 1966	Marked decline in conflictual interaction, system accommodation	Bipolarity	Stable	(Restored) Equilibrium

Unit-System Linkages

In all fields there are several levels of analysis, each with distinct concepts, research questions and methodologies. Every level is capable of illuminating a segment of knowledge within a discipline. To provide insights into a part of any whole is admirable. However, the ultimate challenge is to link the findings at all levels into an aggregate of the whole and its parts in order to comprehend as much as possible of the total universe of knowledge in any field.[8]

This perspective reflects a conviction that a focus on a single level of analysis is inadequate. To examine the two levels – unit and system – would enable us to move beyond the position of blind men attempting to grasp the elephant. In the words of North (1967: p. 394):

> As research scholars and would-be theorists in international relations we might all derive at least three useful lessons from the old fable about the blind men and the elephant. The first is that the elephant [crisis] presumably existed; the second is that each of the groping investigators [at the unit and system levels], despite sensory and conceptual limitations, had his fingers on a part of reality; and the third is that if they had quieted the uproar and begun making comparisons, the blind men might – all of them – have moved considerably closer to the truth.

It is in this spirit that we now approach the task of linking the unit (micro) and system (macro) levels of crisis analysis.

Since the early 1960s there has been a large body of research on state behavior in external crises, the counterpart to studies of conflictual interactions among states (M. Haas, 1986; Hopple and Rossa, 1981; O. R. Holsti, 1980; Tanter, 1978). They differ in definitions, conceptual frameworks and techniques of analysis. The approach to follow emphasizes points of convergence while maintaining a clearcut distinction between the two levels and their diverse effects.

As noted in Chapter 1, a unit-level (or foreign policy) crisis derives from perceptions, whereas a system-level (or international) crisis is objective. Stated differently, the focus of the former is image and action, while that of the latter is reality and interaction. There is no one-to-one relationship between unit- and system-level crises: the former occurs for a single state; the latter is predicated upon the existence of distortion in the pattern of interaction between two or more adversaries in a system.

Definitions of crisis at both levels have already been presented. At the unit level there are crisis actors, that is, states whose decision-makers perceive a threat to basic values and a high probability of involvement in military hostilities (along with the awareness of finite time for response to the external value threat). There are parallel concepts at the system level, as presented in Table I.2.4.

For the threat component the counterparts are values of decision-makers and structure of the system. Basic values, such as existence, influence in the global and/or regional systems, territorial integrity, economic welfare, and others are the elements which guide goals, decisions and actions of states. Similarly, at the system level, structure provides the setting for continuity in interaction processes. Threat at the unit level indicates (subjective) perceptions by decision-makers. Challenge at the

TABLE I.2.4. Unit- and System-Level Crisis Components

Component	Crisis Level	
	Unit	System
Threat	Threat to Basic Values	Challenge to System Structure
Violence	Increase in War Likelihood	Increase in Disruptive Interaction

system level means an (objective) possibility of change in the structure. A challenge to the structure may or may not materialize just as a threat to basic values may or may not be realized.

In the 1948–49 Berlin Crisis the mutual threats to Soviet and US influence in Germany and, more generally, in the international system generated a sharp increase in conflictual interaction. This distortion, the counterpart of an increase in perceived likelihood of military hostilities, posed a challenge to the existing structure of the dominant system, namely, to the number of actors (two or more Germanys) and the tighter polarization of Europe around the superpowers as a result of the crisis.

A crisis may thus be addressed in macro and micro terms. While the former deals with systemic interactions and the power configuration among actors, the latter focuses on a crisis actor. In that context, there are situational changes in which only one state perceives a crisis for itself, that is, actions by one (or more) state(s) or non-state actor(s), or internal development(s) which trigger images of threat, time pressure and war likelihood for a single actor (e.g., the massing of Indian demonstrators on the border with Goa in 1955, creating a crisis for Portugal – but not for India). In other instances, two or more states experience a crisis over the same issue, as with the Western Powers and the USSR and some Soviet bloc members over Berlin in 1948–49, 1957–59 and 1961.

The link between unit- and system-level concepts of crisis may be illustrated by two different cases: when a crisis for all actors is identical in time; and when their crises overlap but are not identical in time. Establishing this link requires the clarification of static and dynamic concepts at both levels. The former are trigger/termination at the unit level and breakpoint/exitpoint at the system level. The latter are escalation/deescalation and distortion/accommodation, respectively. These concepts are presented in Table I.2.5 below.

TABLE I.2.5. Static and Dynamic Concepts of Crisis

Nature of Concept	Crisis Level	
	Unit	System
Static	Trigger/Termination	Breakpoint/Exitpoint
Dynamic	Escalation/Deescalation	Distortion/Accommodation

At the unit level, a trigger, a static act, is defined as the catalyst to a foreign policy crisis. In the 1948–49 Berlin Crisis the trigger to the Soviet Union's crisis was, as noted, the publication by the Western Powers on 7 June 1948 of the recommendations of the March London Conference. The trigger for the United States, Britain and France was the Soviet decision on 24 June to block all Western transportation to and from Berlin. In terms of a dynamic process, a trigger denotes an escalation, for an actor, of perceived threat, time pressure and the likelihood of military hostilities.

The termination of a crisis at the unit level is the point in time when decision-makers' perceptions of threat, time pressure and war likelihood decline to the level existing prior to the crisis trigger. In the Berlin case the termination date for each of the Four Powers was 12 May 1949, when an agreement regarding West and East Germany as separate entities was signed. Thus the triggers did not coincide, but the termination dates did. In dynamic process terms, termination for crisis actors marks the final deescalation in perceived threat, time pressure and war likelihood during a foreign policy crisis.

At the system level parallel notions exist – breakpoint and exitpoint as counterparts of trigger and termination. A breakpoint is a disturbance to a system created by the entry of an actor into a crisis.[9] An international crisis erupts with an initial breakpoint event, such as the Western Powers' challenge to Moscow on 7 June 1948 regarding the integration of their zones of occupation in Germany. In dynamic terms, this change denoted distortion in the pattern of East/West interaction. Similarly, an exitpoint refers to a significant reduction in conflictual activity, such as the formal agreement among the Four Powers on 12 May 1949 about the future of Germany and the lifting of the blockade. This change indicates accommodation, that is, a shift to a less intense level of hostile interaction than that during the crisis.

The duration of an international crisis is measured from the first breakpoint to the last exitpoint which, in unit-level terms, means from the crisis trigger for the first actor to crisis termination for the last actor. For the initial breakpoint to occur there must be two or more adversarial actors in higher-than-normal conflictual interaction. They may both or all be crisis actors simultaneously, a rare occurrence, for this requires triggers the same day, as in the 1965–66 India/Pakistan crisis over Kutch--Kashmir. More often, they comprise one crisis actor and one adversary who triggers its crisis; the latter may later become a crisis actor, as with Belgium and the Congo in the 1960 Congo Crisis,[10] or it may not. A variant is one initial crisis actor and one adversary, with the latter joined by another in the process of becoming crisis actors, as with the US and, later, the USSR and Cuba in the 1962 Missile Crisis.[11] Another variation is one crisis actor at the outset with several adversaries who later become crisis actors simultaneously, as with the USSR and the US–UK–France in the 1948–49 Berlin Crisis. As for the winding down of an international crisis, the majority of cases reveal a simultaneous termination for all crisis actors and, therefore, simultaneous accommodation by the system, as in the Berlin and India/Pakistan cases noted above.

Distortion may be gradual or rapid; so too with accommodation. In general, international crises are characterized by multiple breakpoints, that is, gradual distortion and, by contrast, few exitpoints, that is, rapid accommodation. The reason is that the onset of an international crisis is usually a process in which crisis actors cumulatively challenge one another. The result is that breakpoints tend to differ in time and, therefore, distortion is gradual. Accommodation, however, usually requires agreement, either formal or tacit. Thus exitpoints tend to coincide in time. However, as long as any crisis actor has not terminated its crisis, accommodation has not yet been completed: termination of the unit-level crisis for the last participant and the end of the system-level crisis are identical in time.

Breakpoints and exitpoints also indicate the entry or departure of actors in an international crisis. Each breakpoint denotes an increase in conflictual interaction relative to the pre-crisis phase, whereas exitpoints signal accommodation at the system level. Linking unit-level upward to system-level, the effects of trigger/termination on breakpoints/exitpoints are immediate and direct; that is, a trigger at the unit level always denotes a breakpoint at the system level and thus a further distortion in systemic interaction. In the Berlin case, the acts of both 7 June and 24 June 1948, which were triggers at the unit level for the Soviet Union and the Western Powers, respectively, were also immediate breakpoints in the system-level crisis. However, when international crisis is linked downward to actors the effects of exitpoints on deescalation are immediate and direct for some but may be delayed and indirect for others. Stated differently, not all system-level (interaction) changes affect all actors at once and equally in a readily identifiable way. The Berlin Crisis provides an example of direct and immediate effects: the last exitpoint, on 12 May 1949, denotes final deescalation for the Four Powers. In general, international crises have more significant effects than foreign policy (unit-level) crises because they pose a dual danger, namely, to the structure of the system and to its actors, whereas unit-level crises affect actors only.

In summary, an international crisis requires behavioral change on the part of at least two adversarial actors. That disruption and the ensuing conflictual interaction contribute to one of four combinations of stability, instability, equilibrium, disequilibrium, that is, four states of an international system. Although an international crisis is catalyzed by actions, these actions, the triggers to foreign policy crises for a state, can always be traced to their perceptual origin. Here lies the link between the two levels of crisis. Finally, the evidence from both levels, that is, international and foreign policy crises in the twentieth century, will provide the empirical basis for the "islands of analysis" to follow, as outlined in the Reader's Guide in Chapter 1.

Notes

1. Conceptually, an *international system* ranges across a broad spectrum, from the global system through the dominant system to subsystems. The major attempts to integrate system concepts into international relations theory focused on the great powers in world politics, a synonym for Singer and Small's (1972: p. 381) "Central Sub System," that is, "the most powerful, industrialized, and diplomatically active members of the interstate system, generally coinciding with the 'European state system'." M. A. Kaplan (1957: pp. 4, 9) referred to a "system of action" as a set of five interrelated variables whose relationship is characterized by behavioral regularities – essential rules, transformation rules, actor, capability and information variables; but he did not explicitly define an international system. For Hoffmann (1961: p. 207), the concept of international system is blurred by its all-inclusive nature; it incorporates the structure of the world, the nature of the forces which operate across or within the major units, capabilities, pattern of power, and political culture of the units. Rosecrance (1963: pp. 5, 6) emphasized the historical dimension of international systems and treated them at length; but he distinguished among his nine systems from 1740 to 1960 mainly by "significant changes in diplomatic style." Aron (1966: pp. 94, 95) appears to restrict the term to an "ensemble" of political units "capable of being implicated in a generalized war." E. Haas (1964: pp. 62–63) noted the need for "definitional clarity, verbal and operational" among key system properties – inputs, outputs, units, environment, attributes, structures and functions – but the links were not developed. McClelland (1966: p. 20) distinguished between boundaries and environment but confined the meaning of system to interaction, i.e., process. Young (1968a: p. 6) specified four essential components: actors, structure, process and contextual limitations, but his distinction between structure and process is blurred. Keohane and Nye (1977: pp. 20–21) clarified this distinction by identifying the former with "the distribution of capabilities among similar units" and the latter with "bargaining behavior within a power structure." Waltz (1979: p. 40), too, asserted the need for a clear-cut demarcation of structure and interaction but, like McClelland with process, he overemphasized structure.

   There are two strands in the *subsystems* literature: *geography* and *issue*. On the first, see Binder (1958), Modelski (1961), Brecher (1963), Hoffmann (1963), Russett (1967), Zartman (1967), Bowman (1968), Kaiser (1968), Cantori and Spiegel (1970), M. Haas (1970), Dominguez (1971). Among the most careful in using a geographic criterion is M. Haas (1974: pp. 336–56), whose empirical analysis of 21 subsystems combined geographic and issue criteria, providing a rare link to the second strand in the subsystems literature. For an overview of the geographic subsystems literature see Thompson (1973).

   On issue subsystems, see Hanrieder (1965), Russett (1967), Zimmerman (1972), K. J. Holsti (1972), M. Haas (1974), Dean and Vasquez (1976), Keohane and Nye (1977, 1987), Mansbach and Vasquez (1981), Vasquez and Mansbach (1983), and indirectly, Rosenau (1988). Lampert (1980) was the most direct in asserting the primacy of issue over geography as the basic component of subsystem.

   Thoughtful critiques of systems theory applied to international relations are Young (1968a), Stephens (1972), E. Haas (1975) and Morgan (1987).

   E. Haas was also among the earliest proponents of the most recent variation on the systems theme, namely, the concept of international regime. The literature on regimes is vast, including all issues of *IO* from the summer of 1975 onwards. See, especially, Krasner (1983), Keohane (1984), Young (1986) and, for a comprehensive survey of the regime literature, Haggard and Simmons (1987). A regime, in the largest sense, may be termed an issue subsystem and, in narrower terms, the rules of the game within such a system. For a historically-based view that functional regimes have replaced territorial boundaries in the international system of states, see Kratochwil (1986).

   Another current strand of systems theory, with two distinct paths, is "world systems" theory, primarily associated with Modelski and Wallerstein, respectively. See, for example, Hollist and Rosenau (1981) and Bergesen (1983).

2. In the literature on systems, though not on *international* systems, process is also used to denote growth and decay, concepts which are closely linked to system transformation. The latter is discussed below in relation to stability and equilibrium. Growth and decay with respect to political actors is discussed in Mansbach and Vasquez (1981: pp. 143–185). For a review of recent literature on long cycle theory relating to international relations, see Rosecrance (1987).

3. Kaplan (1957: pp. 21, 35–36) designated his "six distinct international systems" as "six states of equilibrium of an ultrastable international system;" that is, equilibrium is synonymous with system. Equilibrium is the normal state of a system; and his concern was with "the expectations for stability of each of the systems." The concept of "ultrastable system" was developed by Ashby (1952: pp. 100–122). The first wave of analysts in the ongoing debate over the relationship between polarity and stability (see Chapter 3 below) (Waltz, 1964; Deutsch and Singer, 1964; Rosecrance, 1966; Young, 1968a) virtually omitted discussion of the concept of equilibrium, Aron (1966) had an extensive discussion on equilibrium, but it was treated as a policy, not a concept. And Waltz (1967: p. 229, fn. 18) related structure to stability: "By 'structure' I mean the pattern according to which power is distributed; by 'stability,' the perpetuation of that structure without the occurrence of grossly

destructive violence." Thus a change in structure means system transformation and a new stability. Just as Kaplan equated system with equilibrium, so Waltz equated system with stability.

Several international relations scholars did focus on equilibrium. In this they share the emphasis of general systems theorists and economists who identify stability and instability as "states of equilibrium" (Arrow, 1968: pp. 384, 387). Richardson's conception of stability "referred simply to any set of conditions under which the system would return to its equilibrium state . . ." (Deutsch and Singer, 1964: p. 391). Liska (1957: p. 13) relied "mainly on the ideas of progressive, stable, and unstable equilibrium." And for Pruitt (1969: pp. 20, 36–37) "Instability is defined as the *likelihood of sudden (basic) change* . . ." Moreover, "Stable relations are usually characterized by oscillations around an equilibrium point . . ."

4. Michael Haas' treatise on international conflict (1974), for example, has a 23-page appendix on "Definitions of Concepts," in which equilibrium is conspicuously absent. By contrast, Boulding (1978) and Gilpin (1981: pp. 156–185) devote considerable attention to this core concept.

5. The concept of stability-disequilibrium seems to contradict common usage which assumes that a state of disequilibrium is necessarily unstable. However, a stable disequilibrium is well-illustrated by medical science's characterization of a gravely-ill patient as being in a "critical but stable state," namely, an uncertain period between recovery and death. By this is meant a crisis which is generated by a fundamental change in a patient's health, e.g., a massive heart attack, where the routine performance charts of the vital organs following the attack are within normal ranges and are said to be under control. The former – fundamental change – represents disequilibrium; the latter – normal performance – represents stability. The two are linked in the descriptive analysis of the patient's condition.

Boulding (1978: p. 330), too, drew attention to the coexistence of stability and disequilibrium in socio-political life by an imaginative metaphor, the "iceberg effect," which he applied to political change ranging from *coups d'état* to revolutions.

6. Evidence pertaining to this crisis was derived from Acheson (1969), Shlaim (1983), Truman (1956), Ulam (1971), and Windsor (1963). See also Brecher and Wilkenfeld *et al.* (1988: p. 213).

7. Sources for the following discussion are Barnds (1972), Brines (1968), Choudhury (1968) and Lamb (1966). See also Brecher and Wilkenfeld *et al.* (1988: pp. 274, 275–276).

8. Among the pioneers of systems theory in the social sciences, Boulding (1956: pp. 201, 202) introduced the idea of system rungs or levels. Deutsch (1974: pp. 152–156) set out a ten-level political system, including four levels in international politics. McClelland (1955: p. 34; 1958) was perhaps the first to specify levels in the study of world politics. The "level-of-analysis problem" was first given explicit formulation by Singer (1961; also 1971). See also Andriole (1978).

9. The ICB definition of a crisis, as noted earlier, refers to the war–peace issue-area. However, breakpoints may occur in any foreign policy issue, and the study of international political, economic, and status crises might yield no less valuable findings. For these types an appropriate change is necessary in the second condition of an internationsl crisis specified above.

10. The crisis trigger for Belgium, on 5 July 1960, was a mutiny among soldiers of the Congolese *Force Publique*, which rapidly turned into a general movement against Belgian and other European residents. Belgium responded on the 8th by announcing its intention to send military reinforcements to the Congo. A crisis was triggered for the Congo two days later when Belgian troops went into action.

11. The Missile Crisis for the United States was triggered on 16 October 1962 when photographic evidence of the presence of Soviet offensive missiles in Cuba was presented to President Kennedy. The US major response, on 22 October, was a decision to blockade all offensive military equipment *en route* to Cuba. This, in turn, triggered crises for the Soviet Union and Cuba.

Part II
International Crises

3 Polarity, Stability, Crisis: The Debate over Structure and Conflict Twenty-Five Years Later. I. State of the Art and New Directions

Michael Brecher and Patrick James

Prologue There have been several "great debates" in the study of world politics, some of them unresolved. Idealism, as expressed in the legal-institutional school which held sway before the Second World War, faced the challenge of power politics.[1] During the resultant hegemony of realism an unresolved debate over method erupted in the sixties and has long divided the discipline.[2] Macro-theorists asserted the primacy of the international system over its actors, while decision-making theorists emphasized autonomous choice in state behavior.[3] Eventually, systems theory yielded to the claims of regime analysis, demonstrating the controversy that can emerge even from within a given school of thought.[4] The focus on "high politics" (conflict and war) ultimately was challenged by the "low politics" (economic issues) of the interdependence school.[5] Neo-realism has faced severe criticism from proponents of a system paradigm and neo-Marxists calling for a return to a normative approach.[6] And throughout, the universal contention between deductive theorizing and inductively-generated knowledge has accentuated the multiple divisions in a discipline in ferment.[7]

State of the Art

The Debate

One of the most prominent "great debates" concerns the link between structure and conflict. It transcends the controversies just described, encompassing issues related to theory, method and the philosophy of inquiry. More specifically, this debate focuses on the presumed impact of different polarity configurations on the level of instability in the international system. It first crystallized in the aftermath of the Cuban Missile Crisis, when Waltz (1964) made a cogent case for *bipolarity* as an inherently more stable system. He argued that two integrated blocs with acknowledged patron–leaders would have a shared interest in maintaining the global balance and the power to do so. This arrangement would produce more predictable behavior by all actors, including the bloc leaders; a lower likelihood of miscalculation – of capability, coalitions and intent, so often the generator of war; the "recurrence of crises" but their more effective control in the mutual interest of preserving the *status quo*; and the lesser danger of destabilization by weak third states.[8]

Deutsch and Singer (1964), supporting M. A. Kaplan's (1957: pp. 34–36) view that *multipolarity* is more stable, emphasized the greater uncertainty about likely outcomes of conflict in a multipolar system and, therefore, the greater caution in initiating potentially disruptive behavior. They also looked favorably on: the wider range of options, leading to cross-cutting cleavages, which could reduce the rigidity of alignments and conflicts among states; the dispersion of attention among members of a multipolar system; and slower-to-mature arms races in an environment of changing alliances.[9] Aron (1966: p. 139, but not unequivocally), and Hoffmann (1968: pp. 14–15), too, were advocates of multipolarity as a more stable system, in the early stages of the debate.

Rosecrance (1966) criticized the two competing hypotheses and advocated an intermediate international system, *bi-multipolarity*, as likely to be the most stable. His reasoning, too, was plausible. Each bipolar bloc leader would engage in both cooperative and competitive relations, restraining conflict but preventing hegemony by its adversary. So too would the lesser states. Zero-sum games would be avoided; conflicts would be limited in stakes; the possibility of war would be less, and the consequences of war would be more tolerable.

Young (1968a), too, criticized the bipolar/multipolar dichotomy as too narrow and proposed a *discontinuities* model as an alternative conceptual approach to a changing international system. Whereas bipolarity focuses on a single dominant axis, to which all lesser actors are related and subordinate, the discontinuities model acknowledges both dominant system and subsystem factors and their interrelationships. Similarly, Young dealt with subsystems, not individual states, as did the protagonists of multipolarity.

Other mixed models include Hanrieder's (1965) *heterosymmetrical bipolarity*, essentially a synthesis of Kaplan's loose bipolar and Master's multi-bloc structures; Hoffmann's (1968: pp. 21–46, 356–364) *multi-hierarchical* system, a very similar construct to Rosecrance's bi-multipolarity, combining bipolarity, multipolarity and a polycentric level, a rare use in the literature of the last type; and Spiegel's (1970, and 1972: pp. 127–128) *bimodal* structure which, like Hoffmann's, acknowledges the primacy of bipolarity but recognizes the role of small and middle powers in the international hierarchy.

Disagreement persists over the relative merits of bipolarity and multipolarity. Is it desirable to have two preeminent powers regulating a system of lesser (weaker) states? Or is a dispersion of influence among several great powers more likely to be stable? Or, again, would a hybrid system be preferred, with bipolarity along some dimensions and multipolarity on others? The initial task of this chapter is to reformulate the debate in order to facilitate a more compelling empirical judgment of the competing claims. To this end, a review of basic concepts is necessary.

Concepts: Polarity and Stability   The concept of polarity is riddled with ambiguity (Nogee, 1975; Jackson, 1977). Among the earliest attempts at clarification were M. Haas' (1970: pp. 99, 100) definitions of a *pole* as "a militarily significant cluster of units within an international arena," and of *stratification* (polarity) as "the distribution of resources within a subsystem, including . . . the number of members, their relative power, alliance ties . . . and . . . the number of power centers . . ." Several other scholars have also noted the multi-dimensional character of polarity. Bueno de Mesquita (1975, 1978) referred to three attributes: the number of poles or clusters of states; their tightness and discreteness, and the degree of inequality in the distribution of power. Rapkin and Thompson with Christopherson (1979) distinguished between polarity (the distribution of power) and polarization (the tendency for actors to cluster around the system's most powerful states). Wayman (1984) differentiated power polarity (power distribution) from cluster polarity (alliance clustering). Hart (1985: p. 31), too, distinguished between polarity – "the number of autonomous centers of power in the international system" – and polarization – "the process by which a power distribution is altered through alignment and coalition formation." And Wallace (1985: p. 97) defined polarization in terms of two key structural attributes of a system: the distribution of military capability and the configuration of military alliances within it. In sum, most studies have defined polarity in terms of the number of autonomous power centers or the distribution of power or resources.

Practical applications of this concept highlight its ambiguity. For example, a myriad of terms was used to designate the structure of international politics after 1945: "bimodal, bipolar, loose bipolar, very loose bipolar, tight bipolar, bimultipolar, bipolycentric, complex conglomerate, détente system, diffuse bloc, discontinuity model, heterosymmetrical bipolarity, multipolar, multihierarchical, multibloc, pentapolar, polycentric, oligopolistic, tripolar, and three-tiered multidimensional system within a bipolar setting" (Nogee, 1975: p. 1197). However, as Nogee correctly added, three broad categories existed in the literature: bipolarity; multipolarity; and a combination of the two. This is evident in Table II.3.1., which summarizes the conventional wisdom on the phases of post-World War I polarity: multipolarity (1919–39); bipolarity (1945–62); and a hybrid system (1963–   ). All the scholars who addressed the first phase identified multipolarity with multiple power and decision centers, flexible alignments, and balance of power politics. Similarly, bipolarity was, by consensus, shaped by the existence of two superpowers and US- and Soviet-led blocs; some noted the emergence of supranational actors, including global and regional international organizations. By contrast, polycentrism remains blurred in the literature, a structure different from bipolarity; many noted reduced bloc cohesion and less superpower confrontation; but its unique, hybrid character remained ill-defined.

Interpretations of (in)stability have been diverse, as in the case of polarity. For

TABLE II.3.1. Conventional Wisdom on Phases of Polarity[1]

Author(s)	Multipolarity 1919–39	Bipolarity 1945–62[2]	Polycentrism 1963–[3]
Morgenthau (1948, 1973)	Multipolarity, seven great powers at the outbreak of WWII	Bipolar world-two bloc system	Polycentrism not acknowledged[4]
Kaplan (1957)	Balance of power system	Tight and loose bipolar systems, with bloc leaders and bloc actors such as NATO and WTO	No discussion of polycentrism[5]
Aron (1966)	Multipolarity more evident in pre-1914 system[6]	Bipolar system, with two coalitions preserving the equilibrium	Challenge to bipolarity from emergence of China as a major power in the 1960s
Rosenau (1966)	Multipolarity	Loose bipolar system Supranational actors, such as the UN and NATO, are involved	Trend away from bipolarity in the 1960s New independent states, more superpower cooperation, gradual diffusion of power
Waltz (1979)	Multipolar system	Bipolar world	No acknowledgement of polycentrism
Craig and George (1983)	Multipolar	Cold War system	Shift away from acute bipolarity to more viable system after Cuban crisis Superpower accommodation
Holsti (1983)	Not discussed	Bipolarity	No longer a strictly bipolar system. Small group of important industrialized states
Keylor (1984)	Implied multipolarity	Tight bipolarity (1945–53); loose bipolarity (1953–62)	Détente and multipolarity. New nuclear powers, declining bloc cohesion, new states emerge in Third World
Ziegler (1984)	Multipolar system, balance of power, prevention of hegemony	Bipolarity (from 1949)	Declining dominance of superpowers Emergence of China, Japan, and Western Europe as major powers
Pearson and Rochester (1984)	Multipolar period. Flexible alignment	Bipolarity.[7] Highly polarized system	Polycentrism. Declining bloc cohesion
Kegley and Wittkopf (1985)	Not discussed	Unipolar (1945-49). Bipolar period (from 1949). Bloc actors arise, WTO and NATO	Bipolycentric period[8]
Russett and Starr (1985)	Multipolar system	Loose bipolar system[9]	Multipolar characteristics embedded in a bipolar system. Unusable nuclear weapons, other centers of conventional power and economic influence

Notes for Table II.3.1

1. Seven of these books are listed by Alker and Biersteker (1984: p. 140) as the most "widely used" texts by instructors of international relations theory. The other studies also have obtained some degree of prominence among scholars of world politics.
2. There is a universal consensus about the prevalence of bipolarity after World War II. In addition to those cited above see, for example, Lasswell and Kaplan (1950: p. 256); Herz (1959: pp. 111–166); Wolfers (1959, 1962: pp. 127–128); Kaplan and Katzenbach (1961: pp. 50–55); Russett (1965: Ch. 1). At the same time, there is a considerable diversity in the demarcation of subperiods. For example, E. Haas (1967–68: pp. 19–29) identified four categories: unipolar (1945–46); tight bipolar (1948–51); loose bipolar (1952–55), and tripolar (1956–60). Hopkins and Mansbach (1973: p.125) specified tight bipolarity (1947–56) and loose bipolarity (1957–62). Rosecrance (1963: pp. 256–266) used the term "tripolarity" to describe the last of his nine international systems, 1945–60. On tripolarity, see also Maillard (1970) and Yalem (1972).
3. As with the time frame of bipolarity and its subperiods, there are diverse views about the date of its replacement by some other structure. E. Haas (1967–68), as noted above, places it after 1960; Holsti, in an earlier version of his textbook (1972: pp. 93–94) cited 1955–56. Herz (1959: p. 34) suggested that bipolarity might be passing into history. Rosecrance (1963: pp. 212–213), Bull (1977) and Spanier (1972: p. 82) cited 1962 – the year indicated in this chapter as the date of structural change. And Shulman (1970: p. 2) perceived a trend towards "diminishing bipolarity" except for nuclear war capability, along with an emerging "multiple balance of power system."
4. The emergence of other power centers was viewed by Morgenthau (1973: pp. 345–346) as a return to multipolarity, not the creation of a third type of system.
5. Kaplan's analysis appeared prior to the 1960s.
6. Aron (1966: p. 134) saw multipolarity as a compromise between anarchy and the rule of law. The balance between the two clearly shifted away from a legal disposition of issues during the inter-war period.
7. Pearson and Rochester (1984: p. 60) refer to "tripolarity" as emerging in the late 1950s. However, that term pertains to the nonaligned movement and not a third superpower.
8. The US and the USSR continue to be more powerful than all other states but the blocs had loosened by the 1960s (Kegley and Wittkopf, 1985: p. 465).
9. Russett and Starr (1985: p. 103) see bipolarity emerging at the outbreak of World War II.

Richardson, "instability means . . . any state of affairs that would . . . continue to change until reaching some limit or breakdown point of the system" (Deutsch and Singer, 1964: p. 391). For M. A. Kaplan (1957: pp. 21, 35–36), instability will "shift it [a system] from its existing equilibrium . . . [and] transform it into a different system." Hoffmann (1961: p. 208) distinguished between a stable system, ". . . one in which the stakes of conflict are limited . . . and the main actors agree on the rules according to which the competition will take place," and a revolutionary [unstable] system, ". . . one in which the incompatibility of purposes rules out such an agreement."

For Rosecrance (1963: pp. 220–221, 296), "a system aiming at stability" comprises four elements: "a source of disturbance or disruption (an input);" a regulator; a list of environmental constraints; and outcomes. And he identified the sources of international instability: "virulent ideological conflict; chronic internal instability . . .; regulative activity inadequate to cope with the planned disturbance; and environmental capacity insufficient to neutralize the clash of major inputs." Deutsch and Singer (1964: pp. 390–392) defined stability as "the probability that the system retains all of its essential characteristics; that no single nation becomes dominant; that most of its members continue to survive; and that large-scale war does not occur." Taken together, these early assessments of stability incorporate a wide range of theoretical elements, such as continuity, anti-hegemonic forces and limitations on conflict.

Other treatments of stability emphasized patterns of behavior, statics and dynamics and probability. Thus, for Young (1968a: p. 42), stability in static terms is the persistence of a system's essential variables (i.e., actors, structures, processes, and context), within the bounds of recognizability over time . . . In dynamic terms, on the other hand, "stability can be thought of as the tendency of a system to move in the direction of equilibrium following disturbances." For Waltz (1979: pp. 161–162), stability means the maintenance of a system's structure, that is, its distribution of power, without excessive violence. M. Haas (1970: pp. 99, 100), too, viewed stability as behavioral change over time, with instability defined as "the number of wars of various types."

Efforts toward clarification have persisted into the 1980s, yet a consensus on the meaning of stability still has not emerged. Gilpin (1981: p. 91) suggested "another meaning of stability/instability, namely, the propensity in a system under particular sets of conditions for relatively small causes to lead to disproportionately large effects." Levy (1985: p. 44) observed, as did Zinnes (1967: p. 271) indirectly, that stability has two distinct and not entirely compatible meanings in the world politics literature – maintenance of the *status quo* and the relative absence of war. And Midlarsky (1986: p. 86) identified its obverse in very narrow terms: "The concept of instability is here limited to the propensity toward systemic breakdown as measured by departures from the equilibrium condition, and validated by the onset of systemic war."

Linking Polarity to Stability: A Critique of the Findings

The debate on polarity and stability has consisted mainly of theorizing about logically-expected relationships. Waltz, Deutsch and Singer, Rosecrance and other contributors delineated the rationale for their competing propositions about the impact of structure on conflict; but none of them tested their views against empirical evidence. Deutsch and Singer (1964: p. 390) asserted that the greater stability of multipolar systems "has seemed so intuitively reasonable that a few historical illustrations have been accepted as sufficient." At the same time, they acknowledged: "This is, on balance, not enough to support a lawful generalization; it must eventually be put to the historical test."

The first foray into the evidence was Rosecrance's (1963) historical analysis of nine international systems from 1740 to 1960. Focusing on a system regulator's ability to cope with disturbances to an existing distribution of power, he concluded that multipolarity was more stable than bipolarity because, *inter alia*, it reduces the effects of conflict among the powers by spreading their rivalry and competition evenly throughout the system. Haas (1970) went beyond the Eurocentric Great Power system and analyzed in depth the stability/polarity link in 21 international subsystems from 1649 to 1965, including eight within Europe. He concluded (p. 121): "multipolarity entails more violence, more countries at war, and more casualties; bipolarity brings fewer but longer wars."

From the late 1960s onward, studies using Correlates of War (COW) Project data from 1816 to 1965 constituted the main effort toward systematic testing. The initial COW study on this issue (Singer and Small, 1968) yielded a mixed finding about the relationship between the tightness of alliance commitments and the magnitude and severity of war, namely, mostly negative correlations for the nineteenth century (1815–99), mainly positive for the twentieth (1900–45). In a similar longitudinal study, Singer, Bremer and Stuckey (1972) discovered that power parity and a fluid power hierarchy among states were associated with less war in the nineteenth century while, in the twentieth, a lower incidence of war was associated with the preponderance of power in the hands of a few states and relative stability in the rank order among major powers. Another COW study (Wallace, 1973), traversing the same time frame, found a strong curvilinear relationship between alliance polarization and war, that is, a much greater likelihood of increased war when polarization was extremely low or extremely high.

Bueno de Mesquita, using different indicators but essentially the same COW data (1975: p. 207, 1978), found the opposite of Wallace's study, namely, that "the bipolarization of the international system and the reduction of the system's tightness are likely to reduce the amount of war involving major powers." Wayman (1984: p. 76) suggested that polarity's two components – power distribution and alliance clustering – have opposite effects on the incidence of war among the major powers. On the basis of COW data he found that the correlational evidence supported Waltz regarding power bipolarity for the entire 150-year period and Deutsch and Singer regarding cluster multipolarity for the twentieth century. Thus, he concluded, ". . . a combination of power bipolarity and alignment multipolarity is the formula for stability in the modern era."

In a group enterprise by Correlates of War researchers, Garnham (1985: p. 20) cited four generalizations supported by systemic studies:

1. There is a curvilinear relationship between the number of poles in the inter-state system and the probability of major power war . . . .
2. . . . the magnitude and severity of war . . . are maximized at very low and very high levels of polarization.
3. Systemic tightness is positively correlated with the onset of war during the twentieth century.
4. The magnitude of war in the major power subsystem is related to the distribution of power within the system.

For Midlarsky (1986: pp. 98, 100; see also 1988), as a result of tests of his hierarchical equilibrium theory of systemic war:

> The first and most striking [empirical finding] is that in all of the time periods studied [1816–99, 1893–1914, 1919–39, 1946–64], the great power conflicts alone demonstrated stability and it was only in conjunction with other conflict sets that instability was discovered. . . . The results . . . suggest the essential role of the smaller powers in relation to the onset of systemic war. . . .
>
> Polarity, as a variable in and of itself, has been found to bear no relationship to the onset of systemic war.

Rather than putting the research to rest, these findings indicate the need for further investigation. Why should the linkage be curvilinear? How can the extremes of polarization produce similar, devastating results? Why is the intensity of alliance commitment linked to disruption? These and other questions suggest that other approaches to polarity and stability might be able to enhance understanding of structure and conflict.

Casting his empirical net far beyond the Correlates of War data or even that of Rosecrance and Haas, Levy (1985: pp. 54, 66) concluded the following about polarity and stability in the "Eurocentric Great Power system" from 1495 to 1975:

> . . . bipolar systems have been historically more stable than multipolar systems. They have been characterized by significantly lower levels of war for many of the indicators, including the critical severity and magnitude dimensions [as defined by the Correlates of War Project]. The intensity and concentration of war have generally been lower in bipolar periods, and general wars have never occurred during bipolarity. . . . [However, i]f the system were conceived in global terms, the definition and measurement of polarity would be different, and so might the results.

Other recent studies have tended to favor bipolarity. Focusing on the four decades since the end of World War II, Gaddis (1986, 1987) provided an explanation of the "long peace" in terms of structural and behavioral elements of stability in the bipolar system, strongly supporting the Waltz thesis. First, that system accurately reflected the distribution of military power, then and now. Moreover, bipolarity is a simple structure, easier to sustain than the multipolar system prior to 1939 and, consequently, alliances have been more stable. Defections – from both blocs – also were more tolerable. These structural factors were supplemented by stabilizing traits of the US-Soviet relationship: their mutual *in*dependence, made possible by geographic remoteness and economic self-sufficiency; and the absence of domestic pressures to risk war. At the behavioral level, Gaddis credited the leaders of both superpowers with caution due to several factors: the development of nuclear weapons and an effective nuclear deterrent; the "reconnaissance revolution," which greatly reduced the danger of surprise attack; ideological moderation by both parties; and a mutually-recognized set of rules of the superpower game, including respect for spheres of influence, the avoidance of direct military confrontation, and eschewing the use of nuclear weapons. The upshot has been the longest era of stability in the twentieth century and a period of peace comparable to only a few in modern world history.

Thompson (1986) compared two approaches to the relationship between polarity and war (Waltz vs. Modelski's long cycle of global politics), adding unipolarity and near-unipolarity to the conventional dichotomy – bipolarity and multipolarity. His empirical domain was almost identical to that of Levy, 1494–1983; his findings "strongly support the long-cycle prediction" while also not contradicting Waltz's argument. More specifically, considerably less warfare is associated with unipolar, near-unipolar and bipolar periods than with multipolarity, and the last class reveals a much higher proportion of "weighted warfare" (44.2%) than its proportion of time as the global structure (23.3%). However, when the 490 years are disaggregated into six long-cycle periods, "bipolarity can, at times, be just as destabilizing as multipolarity," for example, UK/Netherlands and France/UK rivalries in the seventeenth and eighteenth centuries and Anglo-German rivalry in the early twentieth century. These findings, in short, are inconclusive.

Finally, Most and Starr (1987) called for improved logic, theory and empirical analysis. They also offer several clues to the puzzle about the generation of international conflict: system size is no less important than system polarity regarding the conflict potential of different structures; neither parity nor preponderance alone explains dyadic conflict initiation; and while system-level phenomena set limits to the amount of possible conflict, states are free to act within these constraints. Their overall conclusion reaffirmed the conventional view: "Factors at both levels are important. Structural factors appear to define opportunities and set the 'menu' of available options . . . . the choices which [actors] do or do not make can be significant" (pp. 256–257).

All of these findings relate to *war proneness* and *intensity of war*, not to the broader concept of system *instability*. Valuable as the studies are, they are inadequate on several grounds to the task of evaluating competing hypotheses about polarity and stability. First, they equate stability with the absence of war, and instability with the presence of war, more narrowly, low- and high-proneness to war. All other sources of system instability are excluded. Secondly, the preoccupation with the "central subsystem" and Great Power wars in the works reviewed above, except for Haas and Young, leaves out large geographic segments of the global system encompassing the vast majority of autonomous political actors in twentieth-century world politics.[10] Finally, the most important shortcoming, as suggested earlier, lies in the conceptually-limited and operationally-narrow view of stability/instability.

Stated differently, war has been the conventional indicator of disruption and nascent structural change. However, it is misleading to assess instability strictly in terms of the frequency and intensity of war. Many international conflicts do not involve violence yet still manage to pose grave threats to system stability; for example, the three superpower confrontations over Berlin (the Blockade, 1948–49, the Deadline, 1957–59 and the Wall, 1961) did not escalate to war but they severely challenged the dominant central subsystem of world politics. Especially in the modern era, with its ever-present potential for a nuclear exchange, the presence or absence of war, or any level of violence, is not the optimal indicator of the intensity of an international conflict and its disruptive effects.

New Directions

This investigation is motivated by dissatisfaction with the state of the art on the relationship between system structure and international conflict. Fresh approaches to the debate, concepts and indicators are proposed. This will culminate in a model of security regimes, designed to break new ground on the unresolved "great debate." The theory will be tested in the following chapter, using a new set of indicators within a large new body of data on disruptive international interactions.

The Debate   None of the approaches or definitions cited earlier is capable of resolving the polarity/stability conundrum. In essence, the dichotomy of bipolarity and multipolarity is flawed: these alternatives are too narrow. Other structures are neglected, such as unipolarity (incorporated only in Thompson's work) and polycentrism, to be discussed below. Similarly, the concept of stability/instability encompasses a wider range of disruptive interactions among states in the system than the most extreme type of destabilization, namely, war.

As will become apparent, these difficulties with concept formation and measurement reflect the lack of a fully developed explanation for the presumed linkage of structure to conflict. This will entail more accurate specifications of the central concepts, polarity and stability. Specifically, the concept of polarity, the independent variable, must be extended to include polycentrism. And a broader indicator than war must be used to operationalize stability/instability, the dependent variable. As noted, a model of security regimes also will be presented, incorporating the revised concepts in a more comprehensive approach to the nexus of structure and conflict.

Revising the Concepts: In order to make progress towards resolving the debate over structure and conflict,
Polarity and Stability   the first task is to define polarity, and to delineate the various types of system structure. *Polarity*, in its revised form, refers to the number of power and decision centers in a relevant international system, global, dominant or subordinate. Theoretically, a system may be unipolar, bipolar or multipolar, the approximate counterparts to monopolistic, duopolistic, and oligopolistic market systems (Keohane and Nye, 1977: p. 20). These are structures with one, two, and more than two centers of power and decision, respectively. Hybrid systems, with unequal numbers of power and decision centers, also are possible.

The theoretically-possible combinations of power polarity and decision polarity, with illustrations, are presented in Figure II.3.1. Each of the six pairs generates disruptive interactions among the participating units. Which structure is the most stable and which the most unstable is a matter of *a priori* reasoning, to be set out later in this chapter, and of empirical investigation, to be reported in its sequel.

A *unipolar* structure would require an overwhelming concentration of military capability and political decisions in one entity, a "world state" which would thereby shape the rules of the system, dominate relations among lesser actors, and assert its

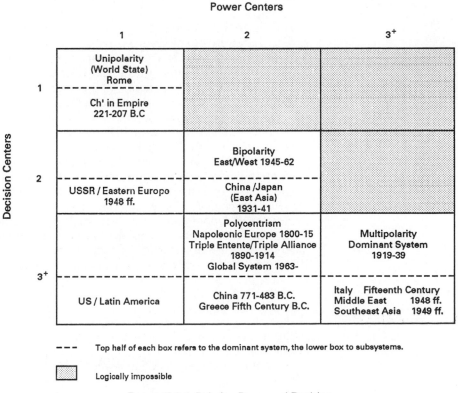

Power Centers

	1	2	3+
1	Unipolarity (World State) Rome - - - - Ch' in Empire 221-207 B.C		
2	USSR / Eastern Europo 1948 ff.	Bipolarity East/West 1945-62 - - - - China /Japan (East Asia) 1931-41	
3+	US / Latin America	Polycentrism Napoleonic Europe 1800-15 Triple Entente/Triple Alliance 1890-1914 Global System 1963- - - - - China 771-483 B.C. Greece Fifth Century B.C.	Multipolarity Dominant System 1919-39 - - - - Italy Fifteenth Century Middle East 1948 ff. Southeast Asia 1949 ff.

(Decision Centers on vertical axis)

- - -   Top half of each box refers to the dominant system, the lower box to subsystems.

[░░]   Logically impossible

FIGURE **II.3.1.** Polarity: Power and Decision

hegemony at will. There is no historical case of pure unipolarity at the dominant (or global) system level. Rome at the height of its power and authority constituted quasi-unipolarity. At the regional subsystem level, the Ch'in Empire was the unipolar center of China for a very brief period (221–207 B.C.). In the contemporary era, both the USSR (in Eastern Europe) and the US (in Latin America) have exhibited subsystemic power unipolarity, but with at least one other autonomous decisional center – Tito's Yugoslavia in the former and several in the latter, meaning Argentina, Brazil, Mexico and, most visibly since 1961, Castro's Cuba.

Bipolarity indicates a concentration of power and decision in two relatively equal actors, whether individual units or tight coalitions. Bipolarity in an international political system is not the exact counterpart of duopoly in an economic system, just as unipolarity denotes less than a monopoly of power. Nevertheless, the two polar centers are preeminent in determining the conditions of stability, the limits of independent behavior by bloc members or unaffiliated actors, and the outcomes of major wars in the system.

Power bipolarity has characterized the global system since the end of World War II. However, in the wider meaning of hostile centers of power *and* decision, the term applies to the years from mid-1945 to late 1962. Within that time frame there have been distinct phases. *Embryonic bipolarity and bipolarization* lasted from the end of World War II to the spring of 1948, when the power preeminence of the US and the USSR, and the emerging bloc structure, had not yet fully crystallized. *Power bipolarity and tight bipolarization*, referring to two centers of decision, as well as power, emerged with "turning points" closely related in time: the assertion of Communist hegemony in Czechoslovakia (February 1948) and the eruption of the Berlin Blockade Crisis (June 1948), culminating in the formal creation of NATO in 1949 and the Warsaw Pact in 1955. The entry of the Soviet Union into the nuclear club in 1949, superimposed upon its conventional military power, marked the advent of bipolarity in the power sense. Finally, *power bipolarity and loose bipolarization* was ushered in by the passive cooperation of the superpowers in the Suez Crisis (October–November 1956), continuing until late 1962. At the subsystem level, China and Japan in East Asia from 1931 to 1941 illustrate power and decision bipolarity.

Multipolarity signifies diffusion of military power and political decision among three or more relatively equal units (e.g., Italy in the fifteenth century, the principal units being Venice, Milan, Genoa, Florence and Naples (Mattingly, 1955); and most of the Western state system, 1648–1919 (Schuman, 1933)). The diffusion of military power traditionally has led to a flexible alliance configuration in "international" relations.

The entire inter-World War period was a *multipolar* system *par excellence*, with several relatively equal great powers recognized by each other and by all other members of the system as sharing the apex of the power pyramid: France, Germany, Great Britain, Italy, Japan, the Soviet Union and the United States. Unlike unipolarity and bipolarity, the structure of the inter-World War system was characterized by multiple centers of power and decision, and uncertainty about behavior by the other great powers in the system.[11] At the subsystem level, the Middle East since 1948, and Southeast Asia after 1949 qualify as multipolar systems.

Polycentrism identifies a hybrid structure, with two preeminent centers of *military power* and multiple centers of *political decision*. As such, it resembles both bipolarity and multipolarity. The empirical referent for polycentrism at the global level in the twentieth century is from late 1962 onward. However, this type of structure was also present in premodern "international" systems: the Greek city-state system on the eve of the Peloponnesian War, with Athens- and Sparta-led military coalitions, along with a diffusion of decisional authority among the lesser members (Thucydides, 1930); the Indian state system of antiquity (Ghoshal, 1947 and Modelski, 1964); and the Ch'i- and Ch'u-led alliances of northern and southern states during the later phase of the "Spring and Autumn" period of the Chinese state system, 771–483 B.C. (Walker, 1953). This duality also existed in early nineteenth-century Europe, with Napoleonic France and the coalition of traditional European powers – England, Austria, Prussia and Russia – exhibiting power bipolarity but with each state an independent decisional unit. A similar pattern of power bipolarity and multiple decisional centers characterized the period before World War I, with the loose coalitions of Triple Alliance and Triple Entente (Rosecrance, 1963).

Polycentrism began to reemerge in the late 1950s. The international system remained essentially bipolar in terms of military capability. At the same time, intra-bloc cohesion was seriously undermined by the assertion of independence within the US- and USSR-led coalitions, notably China's withdrawal from the Soviet bloc and France's military disassociation from NATO, a process dating from soon after De Gaulle's return to power in 1958. More broadly, the global system experienced a profound structural change created by the vast and sweeping process of decolonization. The retreat from empire spilled over from the Middle East and South Asia in the late 1940s to North Africa in the fifties and thereafter to sub-Saharan Africa: in 1956 there were only four independent states throughout that continent; by 1962 there were more than 30. The global system had moved in the direction of universality and a notable diffusion of decisional authority from the bipolar concentration of decisions organized around the US- and Soviet-led bloc organizations – NATO and WTO, EEC and COMECON, etc. In short, by 1963 polycentrism had arrived.

While a precise date marking the onset of contemporary polycentrism is uncertain, the change can be identified with the immediate aftermath of the Cuban Missile Crisis and the Sino-Indian Border war, both in October-November 1962. In the former, the superpowers withdrew from the brink of nuclear war, dramatizing the constraints on overwhelming military capability; and, in the latter, the deepening Sino-Soviet split became irrevocable. Together they indicated that power bipolarity and decision bipolarity in world politics are not synonymous and that other centers of decision in the global system could no longer be controlled by the US and the USSR.

To recapitulate the conceptual distinctions and similarities: multipolarity is characterized by wide dispersion among many centers of military power, while polycentrism retains the bipolar concentration of power; they are similar in that both have many centers of political decision. Thus, the difference between the conception of polarity specified here and definitions cited earlier is the addition of polycentrism as a distinctive structural type, a hybrid between bipolarity (dual power concentration) and multipolarity (diffusion of decisional centers). In both conceptual and operational terms, this means a trichotomous independent variable at the global level.[12]

One further point about Figure II.3.1. should be made regarding the cells in the matrix, which reveal a disjuncture between the number of centers of decision and power. In all cases the number of decision centers is greater; other combinations are excluded. It would be inconceivable that a state with a noteworthy level of power would fail to function independently in terms of decision; even the choice of isolationism would constitute an individual selection of policy. In sum, every center of power is, *ipso facto*, a center of decision, but the reverse does not obtain.

Regarding stability, the dependent variable of the debate on structure and conflict, our differences with prior definitions are no less fundamental. The key to stability, as noted in Chapter 2, is the concept of change, but not necessarily drastic change, such as system transformation, large-scale war, or system breakdown. These lie at the extreme of the stability/instability continuum, while change itself may be defined as any alteration of an existing pattern of interaction between two or more actors in the direction of greater conflict or cooperation. Thus *stability* was defined as change within explicit bounds, and *instability* as change beyond a normal fluctuation range. Conflict – violent or otherwise – which exceeds the bounds of normal fluctuation constitutes instability; but even violent disruptions do not always challenge the structure of a system. In short, as elaborated in Chapter 2, stability and instability refer to few, and many, reversible changes. They are not synonymous with system *status quo* or system transformation, that is, equilibrium or disequilibrium.

In the light of the preceding critique, another "new direction" is necessary, namely, the use of a broader indicator than war in order to tap a wider range of disruptive interactions among states. That indicator is *international crisis*, a much more comprehensive indicator of conflict, as demonstrated in Chapter 2. Some crises are accompanied by violence – minor or serious clashes, or full-scale war – while others are not. Yet all crises cause disruption within an international system; that is, they are sources – and thus an excellent indicator – of instability.

An international crisis, as noted earlier, erupts with a breakpoint event, act or change, that is, a disturbance which creates a foreign policy crisis for one or more actors. Other illustrations of crisis initiation are: the crossing of the Thag La Ridge in the North East Frontier Agency by Chinese forces on 8 September 1962, setting in motion the Sino-Indian Border Crisis; and the dispatch of Egypt's 4th Armored Division into Sinai on 17 May 1967, along with its overflight of Israel's nuclear research center at Dimona the same day, leading to the Six Day War Crisis. These events created the subjective conditions of a foreign policy crisis. The exitpoints – crisis termination – for these cases were, respectively, the unilateral declaration of a cease-fire by Beijing on 1 December 1962 and the end of the Six Day War on 11 June 1967.

Polarity, Stability and Security Regimes: A Model

In a preliminary theoretical treatment of structure and conflict, James and Brecher (1988) concluded that the post-1962 system – referred to as polycentrism – should be the most unstable, followed by multipolarity and bipolarity. They reasoned that each system would result in different, security-related costs to its members. These costs could be divided into two initial categories: decision-making and implementation.

Costs of decision-making include the time spent reaching agreement on the components of a security regime and the externalities created for those left out of the process. The former increases with the number of decision centers while the latter decreases. This tradeoff function is illustrated in Figure II.3.2. Costs of decision time (C), combined with externalities (D), reach a minimum at an unspecified point "K," somewhere between monopoly over decisions and full participation along the continuum of decision centers. It was also argued that, given the likely pattern of the tradeoff, two decision centers would be preferred, i.e., K = 2. Externalities would be relatively high with either two or a few more participants, while three (or more) decision centers would introduce the possibility of time-consuming coalitional dynamics and confounding issues. Thus, in terms of decision-making as related to security regimes, polycentrism and multipolarity would be more costly than bipolarity.

Implementation encompasses fixed and variable costs. The fixed costs pertain to the creation of the working components of a security regime, while variable costs refer to ongoing system management. Problems arising from collective action suggest that two power centers would experience lower fixed costs than three (or more), hence favoring bipolarity and polycentrism. Variable costs are expected to be greater when a system is troubled by status inconsistency, in other words, an unequal number of power and decisional centers. This would argue in favor of the greater instability of polycentrism.

Combining the two sets of costs, bipolarity clearly ranks first with regard to stability. When comparing the other two international systems, fixed costs of implementation are higher for multipolarity, while polycentrism has higher variable costs. In this tradeoff multipolarity is deemed better off, hence polycentrism is hypothesized to be the most unstable structure.

The expectation that polycentrism will be the most unstable type of international system is reinforced by several interrelated processes and a structural trait which, together, produce exceptionally high variable costs. First, the larger number of

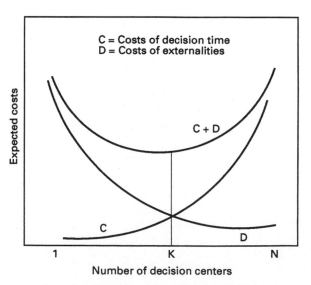

FIGURE **II.3.2.** Costs of Decision-Making

autonomous decision centers in polycentrism increases the theoretically-possible number of adversarial pairs and coalitions which tend, *per se*, to generate more disruption (see Chapter 8 below). This tendency is accentuated by the status/capability gap – legal sovereignty with little military power – which afflicts most of these entities.

Four specific sources of instability are involved:

(a) uncertainty about likely behavior in future interstate relations;
(b) miscalculation about probable alignment and coalitional configurations, especially on the periphery of the international system;
(c) attempts at manipulation of the weak by the strong, notably the bloc leaders; and
(d) continuous striving by weak actors for alliance or protector relationships with more powerful states.

All this compounds the tendency to periodic disruptive interaction which is inherent in a system with many politically autonomous members.

Another ongoing source of instability in polycentrism is the independence process itself. Most autonomous entities, regardless of the historical and ideological settings in which they emerge, become members of the international system through violence or tense confrontation. Their leaders are inclined to view coercion and violence as the norm for behavior and necessary to the achievement of goals, domestic and external. A closely-related factor is that many new states remain uncrystallized, disunited and vulnerable to a myriad of internal sources of dissension, all of which imposes upon their élites a need to find compensating objects of attention to ensure their tenure.

The concentration of military power in two states or blocs (power bipolarity) induces a stable equilibrium in their direct relationship, as noted; that is, no change or few reversible changes in structure or process and thus no fundamental effect on the dominant system. However, this does not extend to the plethora of lesser autonomous decision centers on the periphery of the system, which are frequently engaged in disruptive conflicts, crises and wars, leading to (often intense) destabilization. Furthermore, the bloc leaders, seeking hegemony, tend to a policy of permissiveness about disruptive interactions among less powerful members of the system, including war, as long as destabilization on the periphery does not spill back to the central core of the international system. This is especially evident in most of Africa's interstate crises and conflicts since 1960. The major powers are, however, often drawn into non-bloc disputes, and their activity generates more disruption. In sum, the structure and process of polycentrism constitutes the least effective security regime.

The central thesis is that the regime costs of formulating, implementing and maintaining security arrangements are lowest with two preeminent powers (bipolarity), higher with a greater dispersion of power (multipolarity), and highest when there is an unequal number of power and decisional centers (polycentrism).

This hierarchy has been derived in a purely theoretical manner. In order to operationalize this theoretical ranking, a more concrete assessment of instability will now be presented for one polarity configuration – bipolarity in the post-World War II era. This analysis will focus on specific international crises as manifestations of the various types of cost for a security regime.

Costs of decision time are reflected in immediate post-World War II crises such as Kars-Ardahan, Azerbaijan, Communism in Poland, the Turkish Straits, the Greek Civil War II, Communism in Hungary, and the Truman Doctrine.[13] These interactions were bargaining episodes in a two-year process of decision-making (1945–47) culminating in a new global security regime; that is, bipolar competition emerged as the norm, replacing wartime coalitional negotiations.

Kars-Ardahan and the Turkish Straits Crisis solidified the Western position in West Asia, with decisive naval responses from the US and the UK to a renewed, but relatively minor, Soviet probe.[14] The Azerbaijan Crisis served a similar purpose:[15] the successful response by the US to a Soviet threat to Iran created another geographic boundary as part of the costs of decision time in the formulation of a bipolar security regime.

The crisis over communism in Poland provided initial Western recognition of a vital Soviet interest: control over the traditional invasion routes from the West.[16] Conversely, the Greek Civil War II established Greece as part of the US sphere of influence.[17] Finally, an early international crisis over Communism in Hungary reaffirmed Soviet control over that country. Crises involving the alignment of states such as Turkey, Iran, Poland, Greece and Hungary served, *inter alia*, as decision-making forums for the US and the USSR. Bipolarity emerged gradually as bloc identification solidified in part of Europe and the Middle East. This process of decision-making culminated in the Truman Doctrine (12 March 1947) which symbolized the emergent bipolar system of crisis management that had first revealed itself in conferences at London and Potsdam. So, too, did the Soviet veto of any UN activity to police Greek border violations, a warning that the USSR would not be discouraged from supporting what it considered to be wars of liberation. In short, a two-year period of international crises had set the boundaries and rules of the game for the bipolar regime.

Externalities, the other type of decision costs, appear to be significantly higher than those of decision time in the case of bipolarity. Several areas of the world experienced instability because some governments had autonomous (albeit implicit) status outside the US and Soviet spheres of influence. In other words, the new inter-bloc security regime had not provided for their control by either coalition, leaving open the possibility of intense competition by the "two camps" for their allegiance.

Numerous international crises in Asia and the Middle East in the late 1940s and 1950s reflected this contest of wills. An obvious instance is Korea in 1950. Although the US ultimately played a central role in that conflict, initially it had treated the Korean peninsula as an area open to competition – Acheson's reassertion in January 1950 that Korea was not part of the US' defense perimeter. This appeared to encourage the attack from the North a few months later (Dougherty and Pfaltzgraff, 1986: p. 80). Another example of destabilization in Asia was the crisis over Dien Bien Phu in 1954.

The decision-making costs for a bipolar security regime, when viewed in terms of international crises, suggest a somewhat higher proportion of externalities compared to decision time. Of course, the sheer number of international crises is not a completely valid indicator of cost; relative intensity also must be considered. All other things being equal, however, the far greater number of crises apparently resulting from externalities is consistent with theoretical expectations.

Implementation costs for bipolarity are expected to be minimal compared to those of other security regimes. Fixed costs of implementation refer to the establishment of an administrative apparatus for the regime. An obvious turning point was the crisis over the Marshall Plan, a crucial mechanism for European economic recovery which led to an East-West confrontation.[18]

Most components of the bipolar security regime did not, however, develop directly within international crises. The Council for Mutual Economic Assistance (COMECON), a Soviet version of the Marshall Plan; the Communist Information Bureau (COMINFORM); the North Atlantic Treaty Organization (NATO); the Warsaw Treaty Organization (WTO); and the Central Treaty Organization (CENTO) were all instituted with minimal international disruption. Given the relative simplicity of bipolarity – two central powers and well-understood coalitions – it is not surprising that the fixed costs of implementation are relatively low for this structure.

Variable costs also appear to be limited. These costs of regulating the system are reflected in crises such as Guatemala and the Hungarian Uprising. The first case concerned the US' sphere of influence in the Americas. It began on 12 December 1953 when the left-leaning Guatemala regime learned about US sponsorship of an anti-government "liberation" movement. Guatemala responded by requesting arms from the Soviet bloc. This signalled an incipient breakdown within the US sphere of influence; Washington imposed an embargo on arms shipments to Guatemala and backed an invasion by pro-US rebels. The invasion succeeded and Guatemala resumed its position in the US camp.

The Hungarian Uprising created similar difficulties for the USSR within its bloc. On 23 October 1956 about 200,000 Hungarian demonstrators, in Budapest and elsewhere, demanded the withdrawal of Soviet troops and other measures that would lead to Hungarian autonomy. The Soviets responded decisively by removing the Nagy government by force and replacing it with a compliant regime. As in the case of Guatemala, bloc cohesion was restored through swift action by the preeminent state.

On balance, however, there are few intra-bloc crises to report. Until the waning days of bipolarity in late 1962, the variable costs of implementation remained low. This completes the operational discussion of costs and crisis-generated instability.

Conclusion

Twenty-five years later, the debate over systemic structure and international conflict remains unresolved. Its central concepts, polarity and stability, continue to generate controversy. Problems of concept formation and measurement account, at least in part, for the failure to obtain a verdict in this lengthy trial. So, too, does the lack of a comprehensive approach toward ranking the various structures with regard to propensity toward conflict.

Some new directions have been advocated in the preceding review. Polarity requires revision; decisional autonomy should receive recognition alongside the hierarchy of power. The concept of stability also has been found wanting. Instability should be assessed more thoroughly than in the past, with international crisis being a logical replacement for war as the key indicator. Finally, a comprehensive model of security regimes has been used to derive a ranking of polarity configurations vis-à-vis stability.

Testing of this model, the logical next step, will proceed using macro-level data on international instability. This process of theorizing and testing will culminate in an overall assessment of the role of structure in the generation of international conflict.

Notes

1. Examples of the legal-institutional approach are Oppenheim (1905–6), Brierly (1928), Eagleton (1932) and Zimmern (1936). The classic expositions of power politics are Schuman (1933), Carr (1939) and Morgenthau (1946, 1948).
2. This debate was forcefully expressed in the exchange between Bull (1966) and Kaplan (1966). More recent expositions include Bueno de Mesquita (1985), Krasner (1985) and Jervis (1985). For a discussion of the long-term supremacy of Realism, see Vasquez (1983).
3. Examples of the former are Kaplan (1957) and Waltz (1975), with the latter represented by Snyder, Bruck and Sapin (1962), Rosenau (1966) and Brecher *et al.* (1969).
4. Regime studies include Krasner (1983) and Young (1986).
5. Some of the most prominent examples are Keohane and Nye (1972, 1977, 1987) and Keohane (1984).
6. Prominent exponents of these three viewpoints are: (1) Waltz (1979) and Gilpin (1981); (2) Modelski (1978), Wallerstein (1974, 1980) and Hollist and Rosenau (1981); and (3) Ashley (1984) and Alker and Biersteker (1984).
7. The two sides of this debate are well-represented by Young (1969, 1973) versus Russett (1969) and Singer (1972). For an insightful discussion of the many points of division among students of world politics, see K. Holsti (1985).
8. The greater stability of a bipolar structure was also argued by Riker (1962: pp. 182–187) and Zoppo (1966: p. 601).
9. Prior to the explicit phase of the debate, Morgenthau (1948: pp. 271–272) had noted that the possibility of more – and changing – coalitions contributed to stability through uncertainty, just as a balancer in a multipolar system could maintain or restore a viable balance of power by appropriate behavior, in its own interests, as well as those of adversarial states or coalitions. Wright (1942: p. 755) and Gulick (1955: pp. 94–95), arguing in a similar vein, and Masters (1961: p. 789) also supported multipolarity.
10. Several research projects in progress are moving beyond the dominant system and great power foci. Among these are Gochman and Leng on militarized interstate disputes, deriving from the Behavioral Correlates of War Project, Midlarsky on major-minor power wars, and Pearson on international military interventions (DDIR, 1987).
11. The period 1939–45 was essentially a self-contained transition from the multipolar system of the 1930s to the bipolar system after 1945; that is, it exhibits many centers of decision, resembling the former, along with intense inter-coalitional conflict and intra-coalitional cohesion, like the latter. There were, too, some changes in the power hierarchy: France ceased to be a great power from June 1940 until the end of World War II; so too did Italy from 1943 onwards; and Germany replaced Great Britain as the preeminent member of the group, from the fall of Western Europe in the spring of 1940 until the defeat at Stalingrad in early 1943.
12. The other two hybrid systems (second and third cells, first column of Figure II.3.1.) have empirical referents at the subsystemic level only.
13. The following capsule summaries of international crises are based upon Brecher and Wilkenfeld *et al.* (1988: I. Part V).
14. The Soviet Union had long aspired to control the Turkish Straits. Soviet proposals on 7 June 1945 to revise the *status quo*, established by the Montreux Convention of 1923, triggered a crisis for Turkey and constituted a test of US and UK patron commitments.

In April 1946 the US reaffirmed its support for Turkey as an independent state through a diplomatic response. This action helped to establish one of the earliest boundaries of the post-war geostrategic world.

15. Decisive diplomatic action by the United States through the UN played a major role in convincing the Soviet Union to withdraw its troops in May 1946.

16. The US and the UK conceded *de facto* recognition of Soviet control over Poland through very mild responses to elaborately-staged elections in January 1947, which ensured the USSR's hegemony.

17. Greek Civil War II started on 13 November 1946 when Greek guerrillas launched a major attack, threatening a Communist takeover. The UN became involved through a fact-finding mission of the Security Council. The crisis ended in February 1947 when the US invited Greek officials to make a formal request for aid, and President Truman asked Congress to provide military and economic assistance to Greece, thereby signalling Yugoslavia and the USSR of the US position on Greece – the Truman Doctrine.

18. Severe winters in 1945 and 1946 and a drought in 1947 had caused great economic hardship in Czechoslovakia. The announcement of the Marshall Plan in June 1947 resulted in favorable responses from the Eastern and Central European states. Specifically, the Czech Cabinet's acceptance of a Western invitation to participate in the Plan triggered a crisis for the USSR, which feared for its control over Eastern Europe. Pressure on Czechoslovakia resulted in withdrawal from the Marshall Plan and set a precedent for other Soviet bloc states with similar inclinations.

4 Polarity, Stability, Crisis: The Debate over Structure and Conflict Twenty-Five Years Later. II. Weighing the Evidence

Michael Brecher, Jonathan Wilkenfeld and Patrick James

Introduction

In a symposium on paths to knowledge in world politics, Bueno de Mesquita (1985: p. 135) observed:

> Knowledge will best be gained when those with the "traditionalist" skills for evaluating the patterns within individual events, those with the "behavioralist" training in the analysis of general patterns, and those with the skills of the axiomatic theorist communicate and cooperate with each other in an effort to move the discipline forward.

This persuasive call for multiple methods of analysis is especially appropriate to the unresolved debate over systemic structure and international conflict, for that dialogue reveals a record of isolated inquiry. Historians have speculated about polarity and stability across the centuries. Social scientists with quantitative expertise have collected and analyzed data about polarity and the frequency and intensity of warfare. Theorists have engaged in rigorous, deductive assessments of the logic underlying the presumed linkage. Yet, despite the abundance of scholarly efforts, an integrated assault on the complex problem of polarity and stability is still not apparent.

Cumulation of knowledge has been limited because of the compartmentalized nature of research thus far. This is evident from the preceding chapter, which surveyed the theoretical literature, discussed historical cases of international conflict in the context of theory and summarized quantitative findings. The continuing puzzle over the link between structure and conflict, which emerged from that review, stimulated a new approach including a model which ranks several types of polarity configuration in terms of (in)stability. The essence of that model, it will be recalled, is the comparative costs of security regimes, referring to decision-making (time and externalities) and implementation (both fixed and variable). The general hypothesis ranks bipolarity the most stable, followed by multipolarity, with polycentrism the most unstable.

The purpose of this chapter is to test the model and the hypothesized ranking of international systems. Bivariate and multivariate findings on more than half a century of crises, 1929–85, will be employed. The testing will focus on the macro-level (Brecher and Wilkenfeld et al., 1988) in an attempt to measure the volume of instability generated by interaction among states in international crises.

The key to (in)stability, as noted in Chapter 2, is the notion of change, that is, more cooperative or more conflictual interaction. The latter type of change frequently escalates to crisis and, less often, to war. Whatever the issue(s) in dispute, whether tangible or intangible, of high or low value, crisis generates disruption and turmoil at the system level. That, in turn, may affect one or more core components of an international system: its power hierarchy, alliance pattern, rules of the game, and the most basic interests of system members, including survival. In short, acute conflictual interaction may, but need not, lead to system breakdown or transformation, that is, disequilibrium or a new equilibrium, respectively. Both would maximize system instability.

The rationale for macro-level testing of the polarity-stability hypothesis is twofold. One reason flows from the crucial fact that turmoil, or crisis-generated change, is capable of more precise measurement than that achieved in the past. The other reason is that polarity and stability are systemic concepts; that is, the debate has focused on an international, not actor-level, phenomenon. As such, turmoil is the preeminent – but not exclusive – indicator of the extent of instability in an international system for any time frame – a day, month, year, or a block of time with which a specific type of international structure is associated (e.g., bipolarity, 1945–62). Thus macro-level findings on turmoil constitute a body of evidence which can shed new light on the "great debate" over structure and conflict 25 years after its inception (Waltz, 1964, Deutsch and Singer, 1964). Both individual variables and a multivariate index will be used to measure instability.

Bivariate Testing

Indicators

The most appropriate strategy in the selection of indicators is comprehensive coverage of an international crisis, from onset to outcome and legacy. A set of 11 variables will be used to provide a thorough mapping of crisis turmoil. These comprise, apart from the average annual number of crises in a polarity configuration: the gravity of threatened values; breakpoint (trigger); crisis management technique; intensity of violence; number of involved actors; extent/type of major power activity, and its effectiveness in crisis abatement; form of outcome; extent of satisfaction with crisis outcome; and crisis legacy in terms of subsequent tension level.

The breakpoint or trigger to a crisis gauges the extent of turmoil in the initial setting. Gravity of threat to values measures the intensity of the issues at stake. Crisis management techniques and intensity of violence offer an appraisal of turmoil once a crisis is in motion. Further indicators, namely, the number of involved actors and, especially, the extent and type of major power activity, indicate the salience of a crisis to the existing international order. Finally, the form of outcome, the degree of satisfaction among participants, and the subsequent level of tension among crisis actors provide instructive measurements of potential impact on the relationship among the adversaries and the legacy to the system in which the crisis occurs. It is appropriate to probe all of these crucial variables in the phenomenon of crisis as a whole.

The gravity of *threatened values* identifies the object of gravest threat as perceived by the decision-maker(s) of any of the crisis actors during the course of an international crisis, as follows: *low/political* threat – e.g., limited threat to population and property, intervention in domestic politics; threat to *territorial* integrity – e.g., annexation of a part of a state's territory; threat to *influence* in the global system or a regional subsystem; threat of *grave damage* or to *existence* – e.g., large casualties in war, survival of population.

The *breakpoint* or *trigger* to an international crisis is the specific act, event or situational change that catalyzes a crisis for the earliest crisis actor, that is, perceptions of value threat, time pressure, and likely military hostilities. The many types of triggers, for purposes of this analysis, are grouped into four categories: *non-violent*, including verbal act – e.g., protests; political act – e.g., severance of diplomatic relations; economic act – e.g., nationalization of foreign property; and external change – e.g., change in weapon system; *internal*, that is, a verbal or physical challenge to a regime or élite – e.g., *coup d'état*; *non-violent military* – e.g., mobilization of forces; *violent*, including indirect and direct violent acts – e.g., attack on an ally, invasion of an adversary's territory.

Crisis actors employ various methods to cope with a crisis. This variable indentifies, for the international crisis as a whole, the highest *crisis management technique* (CMT) used by any actor along a scale from non-violence to violence: *pacific*, including negotiation – e.g., formal bilateral exchanges; mediation – e.g., by global or regional organization; multiple techniques not including violence; and non-military pressure – e.g., withholding promised economic aid; *non-violent military* – both physical acts – e.g., maneuvers, and verbal acts – e.g., threat to use violence; *violence*.

The *intensity of violence* refers to the intensity of hostile physical interaction as a crisis management technique in the crisis as a whole: it may be *no violence*, *minor clashes* involving few or no deaths or injuries; *serious clashes* short of full-scale war; or *full-scale war*.

Involved actors are those states which are perceived by the crisis actors to be involved in an international crisis (including the crisis actors themselves).[1] Involvement refers to any of the following types of activity, as elaborated below: political; economic; covert; semi-military, and direct military activity. Involved actors range from two crisis adversaries, the minimal number of participants in a crisis, to more than 11 actors.

Major power activity is any substantive verbal or physical involvement in an international crisis, by the superpowers (from 1945 to 1985) and by one or more of the seven great powers (from 1929 to 1939). Such involvement is grouped into three categories: *no/low* activity, including political – e.g., statements of (dis)approval by authorized government officials, and economic – e.g., financial aid to a crisis actor; *semi-military*, including covert aid – e.g., military advisors, without participation in combat; *direct military* – e.g., dispatch of troops in support of an ally during a war.

The *effectiveness* of *major power activity* in crisis abatement refers to its role in preventing the outbreak of hostilities or in contributing to the termination of an international crisis. The scale for this variable is as follows: *no* activity; *no or negative* contribution to crisis abatement; *marginal* effect; *important* or *single most important* contribution.

The *form of outcome* indentifies the form in which an international crisis terminates: *agreement*, formal or semi-formal – e.g., cease-fire, oral declaration; *tacit* – mutual understanding by adversaries, unstated, unwritten; *unilateral act*; no agreement – e.g., crisis fades with no known termination date.

The *extent of satisfaction* refers to the evaluation of the outcome by the crisis actors: *all satisfied*, *mostly satisfied* – more actors satisfied than dissatisfied; *equally mixed* – an identical number of satisfied and dissatisfied actors; *dissatisfied* – mostly dissatisfied and all dissatisfied.

Crisis *legacy* assesses the effect of a crisis outcome on the bilateral tension level between the adversaries; tension *escalation* – a crisis between the principal adversaries recurred during the subsequent five-year period; tension *reduction* – a crisis did not recur during that period.

The variables having been specified, we turn now to the bivariate analysis of half a century of international crises.

Analysis The bivariate findings on the individual indicators of turmoil will be presented in a series of tables. Each table has the same structure. Polarity appears as a trichotomous independent variable, the categories being multipolarity (1929-39), bipolarity (1945–62) and polycentrism (1963-85).[2] The dependent variables correspond to the components of an international crisis described in the preceding section. The evidence is based upon 292 cases from the International Crisis Behavior (ICB) Project's data set.

An *a priori* indicator of crisis-generated turmoil is the *number of crises* associated with each type of system structure.[3] The average number of international crises per year increased 51.4% from the multipolar to the bipolar system (3.56 to 5.39 crises), and 29.9% (5.39 to 7.00) from bipolarity to polycentrism (see Table II.4.1.). In 1958, for example, a year of high crisis turmoil, there were nine international crises: Berlin Deadline, Formation of the UAR, Tunisia/France II (over Bizerta), Sudan/Egypt Border, Indonesia–Aborted Coup, Lebanon/Iraq Upheaval, Taiwan Straits II, Cambodia/Thailand, and Mexico/Guatemala Fishing Rights. Their combined duration was 921 crisis-days in that year (some began in 1957, others continued into 1959; those days were excluded). Thus, in terms of crisis-generated turmoil, this general indicator points to multipolarity as the most stable structure, with polycentrism as the most unstable.

TABLE II.4.1.   Number of International Crises

System (a)	Time Span (b)	Number of Years (c)	Number of Crises (d)	Average No. of Crises per Year (e) = (d)/(c)
Multipolar	1929–39	10.67	38	3.56
Bipolar	1945–62	17.25	93	5.39
Polycentric	1963–85	23.00	161	7.00

The first within-crisis indicator of turmoil is gravity of threatened *values*.[4] Table II.4.2. presents overall findings for the three system-periods, followed by statistical tests for each pair. These findings indicate substantial differences among the types of structure. Threats to existence, the most fundamental value for state actors, and threats of grave damage were much more frequent, relatively, in multipolarity crises

TABLE II.4.2. Polarity and Threat to Values

	Low/Political		Territorial		Influence		Grave Damage/ Existence			
Multipolarity 1929–39	4	10%	11	29%	6	16%	17	45%	38	13%
Bipolarity 1945–62	23	25%	20	21.5%	30	32%	20	21.5%	93	32%
Polycentrism 1963–85	45	28%	45	28%	42	26%	29	18%	161	55%
	72	25%	76	26%	78	27%	66	22%	292	100%

$$X^2 = 17.45, p = .008*$$

Multipolarity – Bipolarity: $N = 131$, $X^2 = 11.09$, $p = .011*$
Multipolarity – Polycentrism: $N = 199$, $X^2 = 14.65$, $p = .002*$
Bipolarity – Polycentrism: $N = 254$, $X^2 = 2.35$, $p = .503$
* $p \leqslant .05$

than in either the bipolar or polycentric systems – 45%, 21.5% and 18%, respectively. Conversely, the proportion for low and political threats combined was much lower in multipolarity than in either bipolarity or polycentrism – 10%, 25% and 28%, respectively. This suggests that an international system with extensive diffusion of power and decision is least able to protect its members from high value threats. In short, the evidence on values indicates that multipolarity is much more conducive to instability than are bipolarity or polycentrism.

Among the behavioral measures of turmoil, a logical starting point is the type of *breakpoint* (*trigger*) to an international crisis. Table II.4.3. and the accompanying statistics indicate that, in terms of crisis onset, polycentrism is the most unstable: 60% of its crises were triggered by violence, in sharp contrast to both multipolarity and bipolarity cases (39% and 31%); in the latter, non-violent, non-military triggers occurred more than twice as often, proportionately, as in polycentrism crises (45%–21%). These figures reinforce other findings on the conspicuous increase in violence in twentieth-century world politics generally, as well as indicating the greatest turmoil in polycentrism.

A plausible explanation is the explosive increase in the number of states in the global system in the 1960s and 1970s, many of which were born in violence and carried that violence into their post-independence external (and internal) behavior. Moreover, many of these new states were internally disunited, with unstable regimes and leaders who sought to divert domestic opposition and dissatisfaction by resort to external adventures (Wilkenfeld, 1968). The very similar distribution of trigger

TABLE II.4.3. Polarity and Crisis Breakpoint (Trigger)

	Non-Violent		Internal		Non-Violent Military		Violent			
Multipolarity 1929–39	14	37%	3	8%	6	16%	15	39%	38	13%
Bipolarity 1945–62	42	45%	10	11%	12	13%	29	31%	93	32%
Polycentrism 1963–85	33	21%	12	7%	20	12%	96	60%	161	55%
	89	30%	25	9%	38	13%	140	48%	292	100%

$$X^2 = 23.99, p = .000*$$

Multipolarity – Bipolarity: $N = 131$, $X^2 = 1.37$, $p = .712$
Multipolarity – Polycentrism: $N = 199$, $X^2 = 5.99$, $p = .112$
Bipolarity – Polycentrism: $N = 254$, $X^2 = 22.59$, $p = .000*$
* $p \leqslant .05$

types for multipolarity and bipolarity crises strengthens this explanation: although these structures differed sharply in power configuration – diffusion versus concentration – their basic units, states, remained relatively stable. It was only with the advent of polycentrism, a hybrid structure of power and decision, as a consequence of the rapid expansion of new states and non-state actors, that a fundamental shift occurred in the pattern of triggers.

Another behavioral indicator of turmoil is the relative frequency of violence as the primary *crisis management technique* in different international structures. For this variable, the results, as shown in Table II.4.4., are somewhat inconclusive statistically: while violence was more prevalent as the primary CMT in polycentrism crises (59%), compared to bipolarity (48%) or multipolarity (45%), these differences are not statistically significant at the .05 level. Based upon the earlier findings on breakpoint, namely, that violent triggers were far more frequent during polycentrism, one would have expected a similar finding on the use of violence in crisis management (the notion that violence-begets-violence). However, a comparison of Tables II.4.3. and II.4.4. indicates that, while the proportion of polycentrism cases with violent triggers and violent CMTs was stable (60% and 59%), violence in crisis management unexpectedly increased for the other two structures, particularly bipolarity (31% to 48%).

TABLE II.4.4. Polarity and Crisis Management Technique

	Pacific		Non-Violent Military		Multiple Including Violence		Violence			
Multipolarity 1929–39	15	39%	6	16%	13	34%	4	11%	38	13%
Bipolarity 1945–62	31	33%	18	19%	21	23%	23	25%	93	32%
Polycentrism 1963–85	41	25%	26	16%	51	32%	43	27%	161	55%
	87	30%	50	17%	85	29%	70	24%	292	100%

$$X^2 = 8.45, p = .207$$

Multipolarity – Bipolarity: N = 131, X^2 = 4.52, p = .210
Multipolarity – Polycentrism: N = 199, X^2 = 5.62, p = .132
Bipolarity – Polycentrism: N = 254, X^2 = 3.45, p = .328

Since the multipolarity-polycentrism paired comparison approaches significance at the .05 level, and is in the predicted direction, it is worth noting that violence as the primary crisis management technique was less visible in the multipolar system of the thirties than in polycentrism of the sixties, seventies and eighties, 11% and 27%, respectively. This is also true of extended violence, as noted.

A plausible explanation for these findings lies in the comparative effectiveness of security regimes, as delineated in the preceding chapter. The "rules of the game" are much less ambiguous in multipolarity than in polycentrism. This, in turn, is due to the sharper awareness, in the former, of the power discrepancy between the strong and the weak. Thus a security regime, as an informal consensus about "rules of the game," is more effective in limiting disruption, that is, containing instability, in a multipolar system (Jervis 1983: pp. 185-189). Moreover, self-imposed restraint on the use of violence by crisis actors is more likely to occur and to be effective in a balance-of-power type of international structure of relatively equal powers, that is, multipolarity, than among weak states dominated by two military power blocs which are unwilling or unable to constrain violent behavior by the unaligned, that is, polycentrism.

An indicator closely related to crisis management technique is the *intensity of violence* used by states to manage their crises. Table II.4.5. and the summary statistics reveal some interesting paired comparisons. The basic differences between multipolarity and polycentrism are clear: 50% of all crises in the former (19 of 38) exhibited no violence as a CMT, compared to 34% for the latter; and secondly, while the two structures showed a similar pattern for full-scale war as their primary CMT, serious clashes were far more prevalent in polycentrism cases (32%–13%).

TABLE II.4.5. Polarity and Intensity of Violence

	No Violence		Minor Clashes		Serious Clashes		Full-Scale War			
Multipolarity 1929–39	19	50%	5	13%	5	13%	9	24%	38	13%
Bipolarity 1945–62	37	40%	21	22%	22	24%	13	14%	93	32%
Polycentrism 1963–85	55	34%	21	13%	52	32%	33	21%	161	55%
	111	38%	47	16%	79	27%	55	19%	292	100%

$X^2 = 12.33$, p = .055*

Multipolarity – Bipolarity: N = 131, X^2 = 4.82, p = .185
Multipolarity – Polycentrism: N = 199, X^2 = 4.96, p = .104*
Bipolarity – Polycentrism: N = 254, X^2 = 6.65, p = .084
* p ≤ .05

The differences between bipolarity and polycentrism crises were not as sharp. Nevertheless, the latter exhibited more violence in crisis management generally, and more intense violence. Using the combined data for full-scale war and serious clashes as an additional indicator of violence-generated turmoil during international crises, the ranking changes somewhat; polycentrism is the most disruptive, with 53% of its cases showing high intensity of violence, while bipolarity and multipolarity were almost equal, 38% and 37%, respectively.

Another measure of turmoil is the number of *involved actors* in international crises; this indicates, *inter alia*, their scope and complexity. As evident in Table II.4.6., polycentrism accounted for more than twice as many 11+ actor-cases, proportionately, as multipolarity or bipolarity crises (15%, 8%, 6%). Moreover, crises with 11 or more involved actors in polycentrism comprised 24 of 33 such cases, many of them in Africa where the OAU and its members displayed a strong tendency toward activism in crisis resolution. More significantly, both the multipolar and polycentric systems were characterized by great breadth in terms of crisis interaction, with a high frequency of crises in the 6–11+ actor range – 61% and 47%, compared to only 33% for bipolarity. By contrast, bipolarity crises were prone to minimal involvement – 42% of all 2–3 involved actor-cases (33 of 79), constituting 36% of all bipolarity cases. The finding of high numerical involvement in multipolarity crises is even more impressive in the light of the small size of the pre-World War II global system, compared with those after 1945. One explanation is that the presence of seven great powers in multipolarity and the consequent uncertainty of alliance configuration made them more prone to involvement in crises so as to reduce the danger from potential adversaries.

TABLE II.4.6. Polarity and Number of Involved Actors

	2–3 Actors		4–5 Actors		6–10 Actors		11+ Actors			
Multipolarity 1929–39	7	18%	8	21%	20	53%	3	8%	38	13%
Bipolarity 1945–62	33	36%	29	31%	25	27%	6	6%	93	32%
Polycentrism 1963–85	39	24%	46	29%	52	32%	24	15%	161	55%
	79	27%	83	29%	97	33%	33	11%	292	100%

$X^2 = 14.60$, p = .024*

Multipolarity – Bipolarity: N = 131, X^2 = 8.84, p = .032*
Multipolarity – Polycentrism: N = 199, X^2 = 5.72, p = .126
Bipolarity – Polycentrism: N = 254, X^2 = 6.91, p = .075*
* p ≤ .05

Crises also vary in the *extent/type of major power activity*, that is, the most intense verbal or physical act, regardless of whether the major power is itself a crisis actor. The small number of military-security crises during multipolarity (1929–39) does not justify a separate breakdown for each of the great powers – France, Germany, Italy, Japan, the UK, the US, and the USSR. Thus the highest type of activity by any great power in a crisis – scaled from low to direct military – was taken as the involvement for an entire crisis. Similarly, superpower involvement refers to the highest type of activity by the US, the USSR, or both.

Two important findings from the overall and paired data for the three system-periods are evident in Table II.4.7. First, there is a remarkable similarity between the patterns exhibited by bipolarity and polycentrism: low-level or no activity by the superpowers in 60% of the crises in both systems, and military involvement in only 12–13% of their cases. The explanation would seem to be the wish to minimize the risk of superpower confrontation in crises. Second, multipolarity was noteworthy for the relatively high proportion of crises with low or no great power activity (39.5%), and for the relatively high proportion of crises in which at least one great power was involved militarily (39.5%). Thus, for this indicator of turmoil, bipolarity and polycentrism can be viewed as more stable than multipolarity.

Table II.4.8. reports findings on the relative *effectiveness in crisis abatement* of the great powers in the multipolar system and the superpowers in the bipolar and polycentric systems. Multipolarity and bipolarity exhibited similar patterns of effective crisis activity by the great powers or superpowers – 52% and 44% effectiveness,

---

TABLE II.4.7. Polarity and Activity by Major Powers

	No/Low		Semi-Military		Military			
Multipolarity 1929–39	15	39.5%	8	21%	15	39.5%	38	13%
Bipolarity 1945–62	56	60%	25	27%	12	13%	93	32%
Polycentrism 1963–85	96	60%	45	28%	20	12%	161	55%
	167	57%	78	27%	47	16%	292	100%

$$X^2 = 17.79, p = .001*$$

Multipolarity – Bipolarity: N = 131, X^2 = 11.74, p = .003*
Multipolarity – Polycentrism: N = 199, X^2 = 15.58, p = .000*
Bipolarity – Polycentrism: N = 254, X^2 = .04, p = .981
* p ≤ .05

TABLE II.4.8. Polarity and Effectiveness of Activity by Major Powers

	No Activity		Ineffective		Marginal		Important or Most Important			
Multipolarity 1929–39	3	8%	9	24%	6	16%	20	52%	38	13%
Bipolarity 1945–62	15	16%	31	33%	6	7%	41	44%	93	32%
Polycentrism 1963–85	50	31%	54	34%	16	10%	41	25%	161	55%
	68	23%	94	32%	28	10%	102	35%	292	100%

$$X^2 = 23.34, p = .001*$$

Multipolarity – Bipolarity: N = 131, X^2 = 5.14, p = .162
Multipolarity – Polycentrism: N = 199, X^2 = 15.49 p = .001*
Bipolarity – Polycentrism: N = 254, X^2 = 12.29, p = .006*
* p ≤ .05

respectively. Polycentrism, on the other hand, exhibited only a 25% effectiveness rate, while its rate of non-involvement by superpowers in crises was 31%, sharply higher than was the case for the other two systems.

The *form of outcome* is another indicator of crisis-generated turmoil. Overall, more than half (53%) of all international crises during the three system-periods terminated in some form of agreement or understanding – formal, informal, or tacit (Table II.4.9.). An additional third ended through a unilateral act, the most disruptive form of outcome. Multipolarity showed the highest propensity to agreement, 60%, compared to 42% for bipolarity and 39% for polycentrism. Thus, multipolarity is the most stable system on this indicator, with bipolarity and polycentrism as relatively equal in the extent of instability.

Still another measure of turmoil relates to the degree of *satisfaction* among the parties about the outcome of their crisis. Table II.4.10. reveals that, while the pattern for multipolarity does not differ significantly from that of the other two structures, there is a statistically significant difference between bipolarity and polycentrism. Interestingly, the rate for all parties satisfied was 41% for polycentrism, compared to only 21% for bipolarity; that is, crises among members of the two blocs tended much more than crises among non-bloc, mostly Third World, actors, to zero-sum disharmony in their perception of outcomes. For satisfaction with outcome, then, bipolarity is clearly the most unstable structure, with polycentrism and multipolarity equally stable on this dimension.

Our final bivariate measure of turmoil is the legacy of a crisis outcome in terms of the *subsequent tension level* between the adversaries. As evident in Table II.4.11., bipolarity stands out as the most stable structure for this indicator: 67% of its crises

---

TABLE II.4.9. Polarity and Form of Outcome

	Agreement		Tacit		Unilateral		No Agreement			
Multipolarity 1929–39	23	60%	4	11%	7	18%	4	11%	38	13%
Bipolarity 1945–62	39	42%	14	15%	26	28%	14	15%	93	32%
Polycentrism 1963–85	63	39%	12	8%	62	38%	24	15%	161	55%
	125	43%	30	10%	95	33%	42	14%	292	100%

$$X^2 = 11.77, p = .067$$

Multipolarity – Bipolarity: $N = 131$, $X^2 = 3.75$, $p = .290$
Multipolarity – Polycentrism: $N = 199$, $X^2 = 7.62$, $p = .055$
Bipolarity – Polycentrism: $N = 254$, $X^2 = 5.34$, $p = .149$

TABLE II.4.10. Polarity and Satisfaction with Outcome

	All Satisfied		Mostly Satisfied		Equally Mixed		Dissatisfied			
Multipolarity 1929–39	7	37%	3	16%	8	42%	1	5%	19	12%
Bipolarity 1945–62	10	21%	7	14%	23	47%	9	18%	49	32%
Polycentrism 1963–85	35	41%	14	16%	23	27%	14	16%	86	56%
	52	34%	24	15.5%	54	35%	24	15.5%	154*	100%

$$X^2 = 9.45, p = .150$$

Multipolarity — Bipolarity: $N = 68$, $X^2 = 3.17$, $p = .366$
Multipolarity – Polycentrism: $N = 105$, $X^2 = 2.63$, $p = .453$
Bipolarity – Polycentrism: $N = 135$, $X^2 = 7.75$, $p = .050$**
*There were 138 cases in which the adversary was not a crisis actor or there was missing data.
**$p \leqslant .05$

TABLE II.4.11. Polarity and Escalation/Reduction of Tension

	Escalation	Reduction		
Multipolarity 1929–39	25 66%	13 34%	38	13%
Bipolarity 1945–62	31 33%	62 67%	93	32%
Polycentrism 1963–85	87 55%	70 45%	157†	55%
	143 50%	145 50%	288	100%

$$X^2 = 15.95, p = .000*$$

Multipolarity – Bipolarity: $N = 131$, $X^2 = 10.32$, $p = .001*$
Multipolarity – Polycentrism: $N = 195$, $X^2 = .95$, $p = .328$
Bipolarity – Polycentrism: $N = 250$, $X^2 = 10.56$, $p = .001$
* $p \leqslant .05$
† Four cases in the 1963–85 period could not be coded on the tension variable.

resulted in tension reduction, compared to 45% for polycentrism and 34% for multipolarity. This finding is especially interesting, since bipolarity did not show any unique characteristics in terms of definitiveness of outcome – a tendency to terminate in agreement. Crises within the multipolar and polycentric systems, both characterized by diffuse state decision-making centers, exhibited a similar distribution of tension escalation and reduction.

The essence of the bivariate findings on crisis-generated turmoil is summarized below.

★ *Multipolarity* exhibited relatively high turmoil and, therefore, instability on five of 11 indicators: it was the most unstable structure on value threat and major power activity; and, along with polycentrism, it was most unstable on resort to full-scale war in crisis management, number of involved actors and subsequent tension level.
★ *Bipolarity* exhibited relatively high turmoil on two indicators – extent of satisfaction with crisis outcome and, along with polycentrism, form of outcome. For the potentially preeminent indicator – subsequent tension level – it is far and away the most stable system.
★ *Polycentrism* exhibited relatively high turmoil on nine indicators. It was the most unstable system for: crises per year, violent trigger, violent crisis management technique, high intensity of violence, and effectiveness of major power activity. It shared with multipolarity higher turmoil on full-scale war in crisis management, number of involved actors, and subsequent tension level. And it was, with bipolarity, most unstable on form of outcome.

In short, assuming relatively equal weight for all measures of instability, the bivariate findings on crisis-generated turmoil reveal polycentrism as the most unstable structure by far, followed by multipolarity, with bipolarity the most stable type of international system, the ranking postulated in our costs of security regimes model.

Multivariate Operationalization of Instability

Thus far turmoil has been operationalized in terms of ten separate indicators – threat to values, breakpoint (trigger), crisis management technique, intensity of violence, number of involved actors, extent and effectiveness of major power activity, form of and satisfaction with outcome, and crisis legacy. The results of these bivariate analyses have shown conclusively that polycentrism was the most unstable structure, while bipolarity was the most stable.

In the sections below, the bivariate approach to the investigation of polarity and stability will be extended in two ways. First, factor analysis will be employed in order to generate a smaller set of indicators of turmoil for further analysis. Second, an overall Index of Instability will be proposed, based on the indicators of turmoil and other relevant crisis attributes. The combination of these two extensions is referred to below as multivariate analysis.

Dimensions of Turmoil   Factor analysis was applied as a statistical technique suited for uncovering the underlying dimensions of turmoil among the ten indicators examined above. The factors identified, and the factor scores assigned to each of the 292 cases on these factors, are then used as overall measures of turmoil in the Index of Instability to be outlined below. Table II.4.12. presents the results of a three-factor solution.

Factor 1, labeled "behavior," accounts for 41.2% of the common variance, and is clearly the dominant factor in this solution. This factor groups three behavioral variables: intensity of violence, crisis management technique, and, to a lesser extent, breakpoint. Factor 2, labeled "third party activity," accounts for 32.8% of the common variance, and groups the variables representing the extent and effectiveness of great power/superpower activity. Finally, Factor 3, labeled "threat," accounts for 26% of the common variance; and loads a single variable, threat to values.

In light of these findings and, in particular, the dominant position of the behavior dimension (Factor 1), this single measure was used as the sole indicator of turmoil in the subsequent analysis. Accordingly, factor scores were generated for the 292 cases on the behavior dimension of turmoil.

TABLE II.4.12. Factor Analysis of Indicators of Turmoil*

Variables	Factor 1	Factor 2	Factor 3	H^2 Communality
Threat to Values	−.08	.32	(.82)	.79
Breakpoint	(.43)	.00	−.04	.18
Crisis Management Technique	(.76)	.10	.32	.69
Intensity of Violence	(.86)	.20	.25	.84
Number of Actors	.28	.29	.15	.18
Extent of GP/SP Activity	.19	(.44)	.17	.26
Effectiveness of GP/SP Activity	−.11	(.95)	−.16	.93
Form of Outcome	−.02	−.10	−.04	.01
Satisfaction with Outcome	.24	.14	.31	.17
Escalation/Reduction of Tension	−.11	−.03	−.26	.08
% of Total Variance	17.1%	13.6%	10.8%	41.5%
% of Common Variance	41.2%	32.8%	26.0%	100%

* Verimax rotation with 1.0 inserted as the diagonal element.
Parentheses indicate high loadings on a particular factor.

Index of Instability   Construction of a multivariate Index of Instability involves both the simultaneous use of several scaled indicators of turmoil, and the incorporation of two additional crisis attributes: power status of the actors, and duration of the crisis. The inclusion of power status recognizes that the degree of systemic disruption resulting from an international crisis is a function not only of the type of behavior exhibited by the parties to the crisis (pacific versus violent behavior, minor clashes versus full-scale war), but also reflects the power status of these actors; that is, crises with more powerful actors, *ipso facto*, generate more turmoil than crises with less powerful participants. Furthermore, the inclusion of duration for each actor recognizes that systemic disruption will be more extensive the longer the crisis from trigger to termination.

The overall Index of Instability is represented by the following equation:

$$[1] \qquad I_j = (T_j) \left(\log_{10} \left[\sum_{i=1}^{N} (P_i(D_i)) + 1 \right] \right)$$

where

I_j = instability generated by crisis "j" (j = 1,..., 292).
T_j = turmoil associated with crisis "j".
P_i = power status of actor "i" in international crisis "j".
D_i = duration in days as a crisis actor for actor "i" in crisis "j".

The instability generated by an international crisis is a function of its turmoil, the relative power status of its participants and its duration. The role of each component of Equation 1 in the overall assessment of instability will be explained in turn.

Turmoil (T_j) in Equation [1] will be represented by the major factor to emerge from the factor analysis of the ten bivariate turmoil indicators – behavior.

The power status (P_1) of an actor in a crisis is measured on a four-point scale, ranging from superpower (4), through great power (3), middle power (2), to small power (1).

The duration of an international crisis is measured from the first breakpoint to the last exitpoint which, in unit-level terms, means from the crisis trigger for the first actor to crisis termination for the last actor to exit from an international crisis. These events signal systemic distortion and accommodation, respectively.[5] In Equation 1, duration (D_1) refers initially to the elapsed time between trigger and termination for an individual actor in a crisis.

It will be noted that the Index of Instability measures the weighted duration for each actor. Thus, duration is weighted by the power status of the actor in question. Furthermore, a log transformation is introduced, in order to reduce the potentially overwhelming impact of very lengthy crises.[6] The combined weighted duration for each actor in an international crisis thus derived is then multiplied by turmoil to achieve an Instability score for that crisis.

The October–Yom Kippur (Middle East) Crisis of 1973–74 will be used to illustrate the operationalization of the Index of Instability and its three components – turmoil, power status and duration. As noted earlier, *turmoil* is operationalized as Factor 1, with strong loadings from two behavioral variables – crisis management technique and intensity of violence. The data for this case reveal that the predominant crisis management technique was multiple techniques including violence, while the intensity of violence employed in crisis management was full-scale war. The overall score for turmoil in the October-Yom Kippur Crisis was +.786.

Power status is complex for the October–Yom Kippur War participants. The US and the USSR were superpowers; thus $P_1 = 4$, and $P_2 = 4$. Egypt and Israel were great powers in the Middle East subsystem; thus P_3 and P_4 each $= 3$. And Syria was then a middle power; that is, $P_5 = 2$.

With respect to the *duration* of the October-Yom Kippur Crisis, the first breakpoint was the evidence of an impending Egypt-Syria attack, on 5 October 1973, triggering a crisis for Israel. The other four states became crisis actors at different points in time – Syria on 10 October, the US on the 12th, Egypt on 18th October, and the USSR on the 22nd. Similarly, the actors exited at different points in time, e.g., Egypt on 18 January 1974, when the Disengagement Agreement with Israel was signed. The last exits were on 31 May 1974, when Israel and Syria signed a Disengagement Agreement. This was the termination date for Israel, Syria, the US, and the USSR. The duration for actors in that crisis was as follows: US, 232 days; USSR, 222 days: Egypt, 93 days; Israel, 239 days; and Syria, 234 days. Thus, $D_1 = 232$; $D_2 = 222$; $D_3 = 93$; $D_4 = 239$; and $D_5 = 234$.

Having derived values for turmoil, power status and duration, the Index of Instability for the October–Yom Kippur Crisis can be calculated according to Equation 1:

$$I = (.786) \log_{10} (4(232) + 4(222) + 3(93) + 3(239) + 2(234) + 1)$$
$$= 2.764$$

Analysis of Polarity and Instability

Table II.4.13. reports the findings for each of the three polarity structures, utilizing the Index of Instability as described above. For each structure, it reports the mean Index of Instability score, standard deviation, number of cases, and minimum and maximum values. Difference of mean tests are also computed for each pair of polarity structures, and t-tests and significance levels are reported. It should be noted that a positive mean score on the Index of Instability indicates greater instability in the system, as measured primarily by violent crisis management techniques and the use of more intense forms of violence (serious clashes and full-scale war). Negative mean scores on the Index indicate greater stability in the system, i.e., pacific crisis management techniques and no violence or only minor clashes.

The findings clearly show that the polycentric system, 1963–85, was the least stable in terms of the multivariate Index of Instability. Its mean score of .568 is statistically different from those reported for both multipolarity and bipolarity, as measured by the t-tests performed. The lowest Instability scores are exhibited by the bipolar system, although the difference between its scores and those reported by multipolarity are not statistically significant. Nonetheless, the results of this multivariate test of our central proposition confirm the findings obtained in the bivariate analysis earlier in this chapter; i.e., polycentrism is the most unstable system, followed by multipolarity, with bipolarity exhibiting the greatest stability.

TABLE II.4.13. Polarity and Index of Instability

Multipolarity		
	$\bar{X} = -.214$	Minimum = -4.325
	$s = 2.481$	Maximum = 3.738
	$N = 38$	
Bipolarity		
	$\bar{X} = -.358$	Minimum = -6.430
	$s = 2.169$	Maximum = 4.908
	$N = 93$	
Polycentrism		
	$\bar{X} = .568$	Minimum = -4.239
	$s = 2.063$	Maximum = 4.434
	$N = 159\ddagger$	

Difference of Means Test:
Multipolarity – Bipolarity: $t = .329$ (not significant)
Multipolarity – Polycentrism: $t = 1.990$*
Bipolarity – Polycentrism: $t = 3.380$†
* $p \leq .05$
† $p \leq .001$
‡Two cases with missing data.

Conclusion

Twenty-five years from its inception, the debate over structure and conflict continues to hold a fascination for students of world politics. Yet, as noted at the outset, an integrated intellectual assault on this topic had not emerged. Consequently, the approach taken in this inquiry consciously blends together theory, history and data. The first (conceptual) part (Chapter 3 above) culminated in a deductively-derived model of security regimes, which ranked bipolarity, multipolarity and polycentrism in descending order of stability. Historical examples were cited in the description of the model and, in the second (empirical) part, assisted in clarifying the measurement of variables.

As for the quantitative analysis, the findings from bivariate and multivariate testing confirmed the most salient expectations from the model. Polycentrism, a hybrid structure of power and decisional centers, showed much more instability than the other two polarity configurations. Statistical testing strongly supported bipolarity over multipolarity as the more stable system. And the very important indicator focusing on subsequent tension level favored bipolarity. In sum, the comparative costs of security regimes model and the evidence from more than half a century of crisis-generated instability provide a strong theoretical and empirical basis for resolving the debate over structure and conflict in world politics.

Notes

1. Involved actors, unlike crisis actors, do not perceive a situational change as posing a crisis – threat-time-war likelihood – for themselves; they are lesser participants.
2. The starting point for post-World War I multipolarity is generally regarded as 1919, with polycentrism continuing through the 1980s. However, since the ICB Project data set currently extends from 1929 through 1985, this defines the time boundaries of our quantitative analysis.
3. Like other bivariate indicators of turmoil, this has a high degree of "face" validity. More specifically, the sheer number of crises in a given system has a plausible linkage to instability.

   It will be noted that the findings on the average number of crises per year are not weighted by the number of states in the global system at any point in time. The rationale derives from the competing hypotheses proposed by the protagonists of bipolarity and multipolarity; that is, that a large number of states is likely to induce more/less conflict.
4. The collection and coding of data for threat to values and each of the other variables is explained in Brecher and Wilkenfeld *et al.* (1988: I. Parts II and III).
5. These concepts – breakpoint, exitpoint, distortion and accommodation – were discussed in Chapter 2 above.
6. The following chart demonstrates the effects of the logarithmic transformation on any variable X:

X	Log X
1	0
10	1
100	2
1000	3

Thus, increments of X produce diminishing increments under the transformation. It should also be noted that the logarithm of 1 is 0, and a score of 0 for the duration component would be unacceptable because it would result in a 0 value for the entire Index of Instability. Hence, 1 is added to the expression prior to the transformation.

5 Third Party Intervention I: The Global Organization Dimension

Jonathan Wilkenfeld and Michael Brecher

Introduction

The involvement of third parties in the search for pacific settlement of disputes has been an enduring—some would add, necessary—part of world politics in the twenti- eth century. It received initial quasi-institutional expression at The Hague Peace Conferences of 1899 and 1907. It was enshrined in the Covenant of the League of Nations (Articles 11-13, 15, 17) and, after World War II, in the United Nations Charter (Chapter VI). A legitimate role in international disputes was also assumed by regional organizations such as the Organization of American States, the League of Arab States, the Organization of African Unity, and also security organizations like NATO and the Warsaw Pact and, to a lesser extent, political bodies like the Council of Europe. Individual states, notably the great powers of the inter-war period and the superpowers since 1945, have also been involved in the resolution of con- flicts, crises, and disputes among other states.

Third party intervention has been defined as "any action taken by an actor that is not a direct party to the crisis, that is designed to reduce or remove one or more of the problems of the bargaining relationship and, therefore, to facilitate the termination of the crisis itself" (Young, 1967: p. 34). The rationale for such intervention derives from the essentially anarchic character of the international sys- tem and, more generally, from conflict resolution relating to all human relations. Parties to a dispute can often achieve accommodation only by the involvement of a "disinterested" person or institution—or by arbitration or adjudication on the part of quasilegal or legal bodies with the full authority of a universally accepted regime. Such authority, present in most domestic political institutions, is conspicuously absent in the global international system. Moreover, given the unequal distribution of capabilities and resources, and the autonomy of political decision-making, dis- putes among states carry the potential of more dangerous spillover, affecting the fragile stability of the global system or one of its subsystems. In the absence of authoritative institutions and binding rules for the resolution of disputes, state actors have granted international organizations the authority to seek pacific settlement and, where violence occurs, to restore international peace and security (Article 16 of the League Covenant, and Chapter VII of the UN Charter). This involvement is usually initiated by member-states in quest of legitimation and support for their claims.

The institutional *sources* of third party intervention in international disputes are thus very broad: global, regional and security organizations, superpowers and great powers, and on occasion, lesser actors as well. So too is the *scope* of third party activity. This may be viewed along a scale of involvement, beginning with no dis- cussion of an approach, complaint or request by one or more members, followed by discussion without decision, and decision without provision for action. These activit- ies are verbal and passive in form, with no commitments. Greater involvement is evident in an array of field operations, "the 'acid test' of the concern of the world's governments for world peace. Field operations imply the expenditure of time, money, reputations, and even lives away from organization (or third state) head- quarters" (Haas, Butterworth and Nye, 1972: p. 36). This too may be modest, such as fact-finding in a dispute, an offer of good offices, even a willingness to mediate or suggest a formula for conciliation. Mediation may, however, extend to proposing the specific terms of a compromise solution. Still higher on the scale of involvement is a call for economic and/or military sanctions. Highest is a direct military presence to maintain a fragile cease-fire, armistice or peace agreement, such as truce super- vision through the placing of observers in the contested territory, the stationing of a peacekeeping force in a neutral zone between the parties, and, at the apex of involvement, the use of emergency military forces to interpose and/or monitor com- pliance.

Research on third party involvement in interstate disputes has generated a large body of literature, mostly from the perspective of traditional international law and organization (for example, Claude, 1964; David Davies Institute, 1972; Eagleton, 1957: Chaps. 17, 18; Falk and Mendlovitz, 1966: Parts 8, 9; Goodspeed, 1967: Chaps. 7, 8; Henkin, 1968: Chaps. X, XI; James, 1969; Nicholas, 1971; and Stone, 1954: Chaps III–VII, X). Social science contributions have been fewer. Notable examples are: Haas, Butterworth and Nye, 1972; Butterworth, 1978; Haas, 1983, 1986; Young, 1967: Pelcovits and Kramer, 1976; Zacher, 1979; Finlayson and Zacher, 1980.

In a study of international conflict and collective security, Zacher examines the activity of the UN and regional organizations in 93 international wars and crises between 1946 and 1977. A *war* was considered to have taken place "where at least 500 armed individuals entered a state with the approval of their state of origin for the purpose of altering the government's policies and/or its character, or for the purpose of defending the government against attacks by internal opponents" (Zacher, 1979: p. 21). A *crisis*, according to this treatment, existed when

> both of the immediate conflicting parties, or one of the conflicting parties and a permanent member of the UN Security Council, did one of the following things: (1) stated that a war was a significant possibility in the near future; (2) stated that if one party did not change a particular policy, it would use military force; or (3) mobilized some or all of their armed forces for either offensive or defensive purposes in such an anticipated war (Zacher, 1979: p.21); see also Finalyson and Zacher, 1980).

For Haas, Butterworth and Nye, the unit of analysis is a dispute defined as meeting the following conditions:

> there must be a definable issue at stake . . .; there must be clearly visible parties with specific claims on one another, particularly an identified government as defendant; the dispute must be of an interstate character . . . (Haas, Butterworth and Nye, 1972: p. 4; see also Butterworth, 1976, and E. Haas, 1983, 1986).

For Small and Singer, a conflict qualified as an *interstate war* when it led to a minimum of 1000 battle fatalities among all the system members involved (Small and Singer, 1982: p. 55).

Third parties can take on a variety of functions in international crisis situations. In a very useful summary of these functions, based primarily on the work of Young (1967) and Touval (1975), Bobrow (1981) makes the following points:

> In principle, third parties can contribute to crisis regulation and settlement in two ways. First, they can make a direct positive contribution. Familiar examples include focusing the parties on a particular termination agreement, devising a formula to avoid hard issues, providing an agenda, and manipulating timing. Second, third parties can work to weaken constraints on the primary parties; that is, they can make it easier for the primary parties to do what they would in some sense like to do anyway. Third parties do this by lowering the net costs associated with a more flexible bargaining position, including the internal political penalties. In effect, third parties provide face-saving assistance for the primary conflict participants. They may do so by providing rationalizations for the disavowal of previous stands, by certifying the benefits of an agreement, and by providing insurance against the risks should an agreement fail.

In this chapter, our attention shifts from disputes and wars in general to a more narrow focus on *international crises* as defined in Chapter 1. The majority of international crises comprise at least two crisis actors, that is, states whose decision-makers manifest the perceptions of threat, time pressure and war likelihood, the necessary and sufficient conditions of a foreign policy crisis, as noted earlier. However, there are also single-state international crises, comprising one crisis actor, with the presence of one or more involved actors, whose decision-makers may have initiated the crisis and, in any event, are involved but do not perceive all three conditions as applying to themselves (e.g., the Dominican Republic in a 1947 crisis with Guatemala, with the latter as an involved actor; Egypt, in its 1955 Baghdad Pact Crisis, with the UK, the US, Iraq and Turkey as involved actors; Portugal in its Goa Crisis the same year, with India as an involved actor). Since global organization involvement in an international crisis presupposes a disagreement between two or more states, a single-state international crisis, with the involved adversarial actor specified, fits the category of third party cases.

Third party intervention in this analysis will focus on the involvement of global organizations—the League of Nations and the United Nations—in crisis management. This chapter spans the period 1929–39 for the League and 1945–85 for the UN. A total of 292 crises have been identified for these 51 years, and they form the data base for the analysis to follow.

The Role of Global Organizations in International Crises

Our attention will focus on three aspects of global organization intervention in crises. First, we will be concerned with the *level* of such involvement in terms of specific organs which play an active role in crisis management (the Council, the Assembly, the Secretary-General for the League of Nations; and the Security Council, the General Assembly, and the Secretary-General for the United Nations). Second, we will examine the *extent* of such involvement, i.e., low-level (fact-finding, discussion without resolution, good offices, general), medium-level (mediation, condemnation, call for action), and high-level (arbitration, sanctions, observers, emergency military forces). Third, we will assess the *effectiveness* of global organization involvement in abating a crisis, that is, in preventing hostilities or contributing to crisis termination. League or UN involvement was considered to have been effective when it was the single most important contributor to crisis abatement, or when it had an important impact, along with action by other international actors.

Before proceeding to a discussion of hypotheses relevant to the role of the League and the UN in international crises, it would be useful to examine briefly the empirical record of global organizations in terms of crisis intervention. The League became involved in 14 of 38 or 37% of international crises during the 1929–39 period, while the UN became involved in 150 of 254 or 59% of international crises in the 1945–1985 period. The League was effective in three of the 14 cases or 21%, compared to 34 of 150 or 23% for the UN.

Table II.5.1. presents a yearly breakdown in terms of the number of crises per year, the number of crises in which the League or the UN became involved, and the number of cases in which their actions were judged to have been effective in terms of crisis abatement. At first glance, the record speaks for itself. It is possible, however, to note some trends in the data, and it is the explanations of these trends which we will try to identify as the analysis proceeds.

Table II.5.2. highlights the peak periods of crisis for the international system (bearing in mind that the number of actors has grown dramatically, particularly during the last two decades under analysis). It also notes the peak year/periods of global organization involvement and effectiveness in crisis abatement. Finally, it indicates the years which delineate the transition points in the evolution of the international system: 1939—transition from multipolar to World War II; 1948—from embryonic bipolar with the US, the USSR, and the UK/Commonwealth as power centers, to tight bipolarity; 1956—from tight bipolarity to loose bipolarity; and 1962—transition to polycentrism, with the two superpowers maintaining their duopoly in military capability but with a great diffusion of influence among other decision-making centers (France, China, Japan, EEC).

Table II.5.2. indicates that the peak periods of crisis for the international system are generally matched by peaks in global organization involvement in crises. Heightened involvement, however, does not necessarily lead to greater effectiveness: only three periods in the span of 51 years under investigation show all three factors of higher frequency of crisis, peak global organization involvement, and peak global organization effectiveness: 1947–48, 1960–63, and 1976–78. Two of these periods include transition years in the international system: 1948 and 1962.

Before turning to the central questions of this chapter—the link between crisis attributes and global organization involvement, and between global organization involvement and crisis outcome—it will be useful to explore such involvement from the perspective of polarity in the international system. As noted in Chapters 3 and 4 above, the polarity structure of the international system—multipolarity, bipolarity, and polycentrism—has a profound impact on crisis characteristics and state behavior. It is our expectation that global organization involvement in crises will also reflect the critical differences among the three types of systems.

Table II.5.3. summarizes the distribution of cases for the three international sys-

TABLE II.5.1. Yearly Totals for Crises, Global Organization Involvement and Effectiveness

Year	Total Number of Crises	Number of Crises in which Global Organization Involved	Number of Crises in which Global Organization was Effective
1929	3	1	0
1930	0	0	0
1931	1	1	0
1932	3	3	1
1933	2	1	0
1934	3	2	1
1935	5	1	0
1936	3	3	1
1937	5	1	0
1938	6	1	0
1939 (to 1 Sept)	7	0	0
1945 (from 2 Sept)	3	2	1
1946	3	1	0
1947	8	4	2
1948	9	7	2
1949	3	1	0
1950	2	2	0
1951	3	3	0
1952	1	0	0
1953	7	5	1
1954	2	1	0
1955	6	2	1
1956	4	3	1
1957	7	3	0
1958	8	5	1
1959	3	1	0
1960	7	4	1
1961	11	5	1
1962	6	2	1
1963	10	5	1
1964	7	6	0
1965	6	6	1
1966	2	2	0
1967	3	2	1
1968	7	6	0
1969	7	3	0
1970	5	3	1
1971	5	3	1
1972	4	1	0
1973	7	2	0
1974	2	2	1
1975	7	7	1
1976	11	5	2
1977	11	4	1
1978	12	8	2
1979	12	9	1
1980	9	4	1
1981	12	5	3
1982	5	4	1
1983	7	4	1
1984	7	6	2
1985	3	2	1
Total	292	164	37

tems in terms of global organization involvement. Involvement increased from 37% for the League in the pre-World War II multipolar system, to 55% for bipolarity and 61% for polycentrism. While the small increase in the rate of UN involvement in crises from bipolarity to polycentrism does not warrant elaborate conclusions, it is interesting to note that this finding is considerably higher than that of E. Haas (1986; p. 9), who focuses on a set of 319 disputes between July 1945 and September 1984, of which 137 or 43% were referred to the United Nations. This discrepancy—59% for UN involvement in *crises*, 43% in *disputes*—may point to an important distinction between international organization intervention in these two types of conflict.

TABLE II.5.2. Peak Years of International Crises, 1929–85

Peak Periods of Crises in the International System	Peak Periods of GO Involvement in Crises	Peak Periods of GO Effectiveness	Transition Points of System Polarity
1937–39	1936		1939
1947–48	1947–48	1947–48	1948
	1953		
1957–58	1956–58		1956
1960–65	1960–65	1960–63	1962
1968–69	1968		
	1975		
1976–79	1978–79	1976–78	

TABLE II.5.3. Polarity and Global Organization Involvement

	No Involvement	Involvement		
Multipolarity 1929–39	24 — 63%	14 — 37%	38	13%
Bipolarity 1945–62	42 — 45%	51 — 55%	93	32%
Polycentrism 1963–85	62 — 39%	99 — 61%	161	55%
	128 — 44%	164 — 56%	292	100%

$X^2 = 7.68$, $p = .021$

Table II.5.4. provides a finer breakdown on global organization involvement in crises for the three system-periods. The patterns are quite different, and point to some important structural changes in the international system. Constant across all three systems is the role of the Security Council (Council, for the League), handling 57% to 63% of all crises. The relative prominence of the Secretary-General and the General Assembly (Assembly, for the League) changed markedly across the three system-periods. Crisis management in the League relied considerably on the Assembly (36%), but the role of the UN General Assembly diminished to only 7% of crises in the polycentric system. Polycentrism, on the other hand, showed a considerable role for the Secretary-General in crisis management (21%), compared to only 10% for bipolarity. The Secretary-General was never a factor in League crisis management during the decade of multipolarity. This latter finding is a reflection of the large increase in UN membership (from 55 in 1959 to 159 in 1985), making centralized organizational activity more unwieldy.

Clearly, we must look more closely at a number of factors which have a bearing on the gross trends observed here. While the initial results are somewhat discourag-

TABLE II.5.4. Polarity and Locus of Global Organization Involvement

	General	Secretary-General	(General) Assembly	(Security) Council		
Multipolarity 1929–39	1 — 7%	0 — 0%	5 — 36%	8 — 57%	14	9%
Bipolarity 1945–62	6 — 12%	5 — 10%	11 — 21%	29 — 57%	51	31%
Polycentrism 1963–85	11 — 11%	21 — 21%	5 — 7%	62 — 63%	99	60%
	18 — 11%	26 — 16%	21 — 13%	99 — 60%	164	100%

$X^2 = 19.07$, $p = .004$

ing, in terms of an effective role for the global organization in the maintenance of international peace and security, we must now turn to an evaluation of sets of hypotheses in order to fill out the picture. In this regard, two general research questions guide the current analysis:

1. What is the relationship between the attributes of international crisis and the extent of global organization involvement?
2. Under what conditions is global organization intervention in international crises likely to lead to favorable outcomes?

We will now examine these questions in some detail and then propose and test several hypotheses.

Crisis Attributes and Global Organization Intervention

The data presented thus far reveal that global organizations became involved in barely half of the 292 international crises during the 1929–39 and 1945–85 periods. Given their mandate in the area of international conflict and crisis, what explains this relatively low involvement? On the surface, it could be plausibly argued that global organizations, with primary interest in the maintenance of international peace and security, will become involved in those situations which pose the most serious threat to peace and security. Traditionally, this threat has been judged in terms of such indicators as extent of violence, number of participants, and involvement of major powers. In this regard, the first research hypothesis may be formally stated as follows:

Hypothesis 1: The more serious an international crisis, the more likely it is that the global organization will intervene.[1]
The concept of seriousness of crisis may be operationalized in several ways. Five indicators will be used here.

Violent Crisis Triggers (Breakpoints): The trigger to an international crisis, as noted in Chapter 2, is the act, event or situational change which induces more intense disruptive interaction than normal between two or more adversaries, by catalyzing a crisis for the initial crisis actor. Triggers set the tone for an international crisis in that they inhibit or enhance the probabilities of certain types of behavior on the part of participants. For example, the behavior-begets-behavior literature argues that violent crisis triggers increase the probability of violent responsive crisis management techniques on the part of the actors (Phillips, 1973, 1978; Wilkenfeld, 1975; Hopple *et al.*, 1977 and Ward, 1982). Thus our first subhypothesis may be stated as follows:

Hypothesis 1a: The more violent a crisis trigger, the more likely it is that the global organization will become involved.

Gravity of Threat to Values: The level of threat in an international crisis is represented by the gravest threat experienced by any of the actors. In this formulation, the most serious situations are considered to be those associated with a threat to the existence of one of the actors and a threat of grave damage to an actor. The second subhypothesis is as follows:

Hypothesis 1b: The graver the threat to actor values in an international crisis, the more likely it is that the global organization will become involved.

Number of Crisis Actors: Generally, one might expect that the larger the number of states in a crisis situation, the more serious that situation is in terms of the peace and security of the international system. In fact, such seriousness may increase geometrically rather than linearly as the number of crisis actors increases, posing problems for the bargaining and negotiation process (Coase, 1960, 1981; Avaizian and Callen, 1981 and Chapter 8 below). Thus, the third subhypothesis may be stated as follows:

Hypothesis 1c: The larger the number of crisis actors, the more likely it is that the global organization will become involved.

Intensity of Violence: While the trigger variable captures the violence which sets a crisis in motion, intensity refers to the subsequent employment of violence by the actors as a crisis management technique. While a variety of crisis management techniques may be used, ranging from negotiation and other pacific methods to violence, those crises characterized as serious usually exhibit a degree of violence in crisis management. Hence, the fourth subhypothesis is as follows:

Hypothesis 1d: The more intense the violence employed as a crisis management technique, the more likely it is that the global organization will become involved.

Great Power or Superpower Involvement: While involvement by superpowers in crises will almost automatically imply seriousness, there are clearly gradations in such an assessment. The most serious of such situations are those in which the US and the USSR are both directly involved as crisis actors in the post-World War II era. Less serious are cases in which only one major power is a crisis actor, or where involvement is limited to the political, economic or propaganda spheres; (for an analysis of superpower crisis management behavior, see the following chapter). The final subhypothesis of this section is as follows:

Hypothesis 1e: The higher the level of major power involvement in a crisis, the more likely it is that the global organization will become involved.

Global Organization Intervention and Crisis Outcomes

The second major question examined in this chapter focuses on the extent to which global organization intervention affects crisis outcomes. In particular, we are concerned with identifying the conditions under which global organization involvement in a crisis is likely to lead to favorable outcomes, both from the point of view of the individual actors (in terms of their own goals and satisfaction) and of the peace and security of the international system in general (diffusion of tensions). In this regard, we are guided by the following general hypothesis.

Hypothesis 2: The more active and effective the global organization is in an international crisis, the more likely it is that outcomes will be favorable to the participants and the international system in general.
The concept of favorable outcome will be operationalized through three indicators.

Termination in Agreement: It is our contention that one way to evaluate the outcome of an international crisis is the extent to which the parties achieve some form of agreement. Crisis resolution can be achieved formally through treaties, armistices, or cease-fires, as well as semi-formally, as in letters and oral declarations. The thrust of global organization activity in a crisis is usually to incorporate the terms of a solution into a formal document, such as a Security Council resolution or a General Assembly report of the results of good offices, fact-finding missions, or mediation efforts. A more specific subhypothesis will guide our analysis:

Hypothesis 2a: The more active the global organization is in an international crisis, the more likely is the achievement of formal or semi-formal agreement.

Satisfaction with Outcome: The second indicator of favorableness of outcome pertains to the relative satisfaction of the parties with the conditions under which a crisis terminates. Here the assumption is that global organization intervention will have the effect of promoting compromise among the parties, and therefore a more satisfying outcome than would have been the case had they been left to their own devices.[2] The relevant subhypothesis follows.

Hypothesis 2b: The more active the global organization is in an international crisis, the more likely it is that all parties will be satisfied with the outcome.

International Tension: Crisis resolution should be assessed not only in terms of the immediate outcome for the parties, but also in terms of the long-run consequences for the system as a whole. Clearly, global organization intervention seeks to achieve resolution at both levels. Such activity, which is designed to reduce hostility among adversaries, is likely (through third party intervention) to enhance stability and peaceful relations among them with the result that further crises are less likely to occur in the foreseeable aftermath.[3] The appropriate subhypothesis follows:

> **Hypothesis 2c: The more active the global organization is in an international crisis, the more likely it is that long-term tensions among the parties will be reduced.**

Analysis

Crisis Characteristics
and UN Intervention

The initial set of analyses explores the relationship between the seriousness of international crises and the level of UN intervention. That is, we will assess the extent to which the indicators of seriousness – trigger to crisis, value threat, crisis management technique, intensity of violence, number of actors, and major power activity – explain whether or not the UN was likely to have become involved in an international crisis during the period 1945–85. The results of our earlier examination of the role of polarity in the explanation of crisis phenomena (see Chapters 3 and 4 above) warrant the imposition of a polarity control as part of the analysis of global organization intervention in crisis. This will be done for the bipolar and polycentric systems only, since the paucity of crises in multipolarity (38) and the small number of cases in which the League of Nations became involved (14) does not justify extended analysis. We will conclude this section with profiles of cases which meet the criteria of seriousness of crisis and UN involvement.

The indicators of seriousness have already been discussed in some detail. The central dependent variable in this section is UN involvement, which will be dichotomized: low-level includes general activity, activity of sub-organs and specialized committees, and Secretary-General activity; high-level includes the activity of the General Assembly and the Security Council.

Table II.5.5. presents the findings on the relationship between type of trigger and extent of UN involvement.[4] Crisis triggers are grouped into the following categories: non-violent (verbal, political, economic, external change, non-violent internal challenge); non-violent military; and violence (including violent internal challenge). The original hypothesis assumed that the more violent a trigger to an international crisis, the more likely it is that the UN would become involved. The two systems exhibit quite different patterns for trigger: violence triggered only 38% of bipolarity crises, compared to 64% for polycentrism. For bipolarity, differences in triggers produced quite sharp variation in the extent of UN involvement: crises triggered by violence were characterized by UN involvement of the highest organs – General Assembly and Security Council – (57%), whereas crises with non-violent or non-violent military triggers showed lower levels of involvement by these organs – 41% and 8%, respectively. These distinctions were more blurred for the polycentric system. For both systems, non-violent military triggers exhibited the lowest rates of UN involvement in crises: 42% for bipolarity, 50% for polycentrism.

Table II.5.6. deals with the level of threat to actor values and the level of UN involvement. As noted previously, the level of threat in an international crisis is represented by the gravest threat experienced by any of the crisis actors. Low-level threat, as noted earlier in this volume, refers to limited threats to population and property, as well as threats to the social system and economic interests. The scale then moves up to threat to the political system, territorial integrity, influence in the international system, threat of grave damage and threat to existence.

TABLE II.5.5. Type of Crisis Trigger and Level of UN Involvement

	Bipolarity						*Polycentrism*				
	No UN Involvement	Low-Level Organs	High-Level Organs				No UN Involvement	Low-Level Organs	High-Level Organs		
Non-Violence	22 48%	5 11%	19 41%	46	49%		14 37%	10 26%	14 37%	38	24%
Non-Violent Military	7 58.3%	4 33.3%	1 8.3%	12	13%		10 50%	2 10%	8 40%	20	12%
Violence	13 37%	2 6%	20 57%	35	38%		38 37%	20 19%	45 44%	103	64%
	42 45%	11 12%	40 43%	93	100%		62 38%	32 20%	67 42%	161	100%
	$X^2 = 11.88$, p = .018						$X^2 = 2.89$, p = .576				

TABLE II.5.6. Threat to Values and Level of UN Involvement

	Bipolarity					Polycentrism				
	No UN Involvement	Low-Level Organs	High-Level Organs			No UN Involvement	Low-Level Organs	High-Level Organs		
Low Threat	3 — 75%	1 — 25%	0 — 0%	4	4%	7 — 31%	4 — 17%	12 — 52%	23	14%
Political	9 — 47%	3 — 16%	7 — 37%	19	20%	13 — 59%	2 — 9%	7 — 32%	22	14%
Territorial	11 — 55%	1 — 5%	8 — 40%	20	22%	20 — 44%	9 — 20%	16 — 36%	45	28%
Influence	15 — 50%	3 — 10%	12 — 40%	30	30%	16 — 38%	9 — 21%	17 — 41%	42	26%
Grave Damage	3 — 30%	3 — 30%	4 — 40%	10	11%	3 — 15%	7 — 35%	10 — 50%	20	12%
Existence	1 — 10%	0 — 0%	9 — 90%	10	11%	3 — 33%	1 — 11%	5 — 56%	9	6%
	42 — 45%	11 — 12%	40 — 43%	93	100%	62 — 38%	32 — 20%	67 — 42%	161	100%

$X^2 = 17.48$, $p = .064$ (Bipolarity) $X^2 = 12.51$, $p = .252$ (Polycentrism)

Unlike the data on trigger, the bipolar and polycentric systems do not differ markedly in the distribution of cases across the six categories of threat. However, the data reveal considerable differences between the two systems as regards UN involvement. For bipolarity, we find a clear indication that, as the level of threat to values increases, so too does the propensity for the UN to become involved: the sharpest contrast is 25% involvement for low threat and 53% for political threat, compared to 70% for threat of grave damage and 90% of UN involvement for crises involving threats to existence. Nine of the ten crises with threat to existence involved activity of the highest UN organs, with seven of these nine cases exhibiting Security Council activity – Indonesia Independence 1945, 1947, 1948–49; Israel Independence 1948–49; Korea I 1950; Taiwan Straits I 1954–55; and Kuwait Independence 1961 – and two involving General Assembly activity – Korea II 1950 and Korea III 1953. For polycentrism, there appears to be no relationship between level of threat and UN involvement. We do note, however, a modest increase in the involvement of low-level organs in UN crisis management during polycentrism, particularly in crises concerning territorial threat, threat to influence, and threat of grave damage. This latter finding reflects the increased activity of the Secretary-General in crisis management during the polycentric system. In sum, while the data on value threat in the bipolar system provide strong support for the seriousness/UN involvement hypothesis, this relationship does not persist during polycentrism.

Table II.5.7. presents findings on the relationship between techniques of crisis management (CMT) and extent of UN involvement in crises. Three general types of management techniques are available to individual crisis actors, as noted earlier: pacific techniques; non-violent military; and violence. As with the other indicators of seriousness, the highest level of crisis management (from pacific to non-violent military to violence) exhibited by any actor in a crisis was taken as the highest level for the international crisis as a whole.

It is interesting to note that violence in crisis management accounts for 58% of all polycentrism crises, compared to 47% for bipolarity. Despite this difference, neither system exhibited a relationship between crisis management technique and extent of UN involvement. Although the findings are not statistically significant, it does appear that, for polycentrism, the data run counter to the hypothesized relationship between seriousness and UN involvement: crises involving pacific crisis management techniques show a greater propensity for involvement by high-level UN organs than do crises characterized by violence in crisis management.

Table II.5.8. examines the relationship between intensity of violence employed as a crisis management technique and extent of UN involvement. Here our reasoning

TABLE II.5.7. Crisis Management Technique and Level of UN Involvement

Bipolarity

	No UN Involvement	Low-Level Organs	High-Level Organs		
Pacific	15 48%	4 13%	12 39%	31	33%
Non-Violent Military	10 56%	2 11%	6 33%	18	20%
Violence	17 39%	5 11%	22 50%	44	47%
	42 45%	11 12%	40 43%	93	100%

X² = 1.99, p = .738

Polycentrism

	No UN Involvement	Low-Level Organs	High-Level Organs		
Pacific	13 32%	7 17%	21 51%	41	26%
Non-Violent Military	15 58%	6 23%	5 19%	26	16%
Violence	34 36%	19 20%	41 44%	94	58%
	62 38%	32 20%	67 42%	161	100%

X² = 7.54, p = .110

TABLE II.5.8. Intensity of Violence and Level of UN Involvement

Bipolarity

	No UN Involvement	Low-Level Organs	High-Level Organs		
No Violence	20 54%	4 11%	13 35%	37	40%
Minor Clashes	13 62%	3 14%	5 24%	21	22%
Serious Clashes	8 36%	3 14%	11 50%	22	24%
Full-Scale War	1 8%	1 8%	11 84%	13	14%
	42 45%	11 12%	40 43%	93	100%

X² = 14.57, p = .024

Polycentrism

	No UN Involvement	Low-Level Organs	High-Level Organs		
No Violence	24 44%	10 18%	21 38%	55	34%
Minor Clashes	8 38%	2 10%	11 52%	21	13%
Serious Clashes	22 42%	10 19%	20 39%	52	32%
Full-Scale War	8 24%	10 30%	15 46%	33	21%
	62 38%	32 20%	67 42%	161	100%

X² = 6.32, p = .388

is that it is not merely the occurrence of violence which compels UN activity, but also its extent or intensity. Values range from no violence, minor clashes, serious clashes, to full-scale war. The data reveal a notable increase in the intensity of violence in crisis management as we move from the bipolar to the polycentric system: serious clashes and full-scale war as crisis management techinques account for 38% of bipolar crises, increasing to 53% for the polycentric system. For bipolarity, as hypothesized, crises which exhibited the most intense forms of violence in crisis management – serious clashes and full-scale war – exhibited the highest rate of UN involvement – 92% involvement for full-scale war, 64% involvement for serious clashes. Among these most serious crises, UN involvement was confined almost exclusively to the highest organs of that organization (General Assembly and Security Council – 11 of 12 crises involving full-scale war, 11 of 14 crises involving serious clashes.

Once again, the hypothesized relationship between seriousness and UN involvement is not evident during the polycentric system-period. Whereas 92% of the bipolarity cases of full-scale war exhibited UN involvement (with this activity occurring almost exclusively in the highest level organs), only 76% of the polycentrism cases of full-scale war exhibited UN involvement, with high-level UN organs involved in three-fifths of these cases. In fact, for the polycentric system, minor clashes were much more likely than serious clashes or full-scale war to produce high-level UN involvement. It should be noted, however, that many of the full-scale war cases with no UN involvement in the polycentric period occurred in the periphery of the global system, e.g., Black September 1970, North/South Yemen I 1972,

Ogaden II 1977, Chad/Libya II 1978, Chad/Libya III 1978, and North/South Yemen II 1979.

Table II.5.9. explores the relationship between the number of actors in a crisis and the extent of UN involvement. (Single-actor cases are those in which the adversarial state (or states) is not itself experiencing a crisis.) The largest international crises for the 1945–85 period are War in Angola 1975–76, with seven actors, and the Middle East crises of 1948–49, 1956–57, and 1967, Berlin Wall 1961, and Prague Spring 1968, each with six actors.

We have hypothesized that the larger the number of actors in a crisis, the more serious the crisis in terms of its implications for peace and security in the international system, and hence the greater the likelihood of UN involvement. Although there is some variation across systems, the data for both system-periods clearly show that as the number of actors in crises increases, the likelihood of UN involvement also increases.

The final portion of this analysis deals with the relationship between the extent of superpower activity and the likelihood of UN involvement. In Table II.5.10., we rank-order the crises in terms of the degree of superpower activity, ranging from cases of no activity by either power, cases of involvement by one or both powers, to cases in which one or both superpowers were crisis actors.

The data reveal a strong trend in the direction of the hypothesized link between seriousness of crisis and extent of UN involvement. For both bipolarity and polycentrism, as the extent of superpower activity increased, the level of UN involvement increased as well. (In this regard, see Pelcovits and Kramer, 1976). If we disaggregate our highest indicator of superpower activity so as to isolate those crises in which

TABLE II.5.9. Number of Actors and Level of UN Involvement

	Bipolarity					Polycentrism				
	No UN Involvement	Low-Level Organs	High-Level Organs			No UN Involvement	Low-Level Organs	High-Level Organs		
Single Actor Case	19 66%	1 3%	9 31%	29	31%	36 49%	11 15%	26 36%	73	45%
2–3 Actors	22 43%	7 14%	22 43%	51	55%	24 32%	19 25%	32 43%	75	47%
4+ Actors	1 8%	3 23%	9 69%	13	14%	2 15.5%	2 15.5%	9 69%	13	8%
	42 45%	11 12%	40 43%	93	100%	62 38%	32 20%	67 42%	161	100%
	$X^2 = 13.06$, $p = .011$					$X^2 = 9.98$, $p = .041$				

TABLE II.5.10. Superpower Activity and Level of UN Involvement

	Bipolarity					Polycentrism				
	No UN Involvement	Low-Level Organs	High-Level Organs			No UN Involvement	Low-Level Organs	High-Level Organs		
Superpowers not Involved	11 73%	0 0%	4 27%	15	16%	29 62%	7 15%	11 23%	47	29%
US or USSR Involved	18 37%	9 18%	22 45%	49	53%	26 29%	21 24%	41 47%	88	55%
US and/or USSR Actors	12 43%	2 7%	14 50%	28	31%	7 27%	4 15%	15 58%	26	16%
	41 45%	11 12%	40 43%	92*	100%	62 38%	32 20%	67 42%	161	100%
	$X^2 = 8.77$, $p = .067$					$X^2 = 16.75$, $p = .002$				

*1 case with missing data.

both superpowers were actors, we find 12 cases at this most serious level. Nine of these 12 cases showed involvement of the highest UN organs – Security Council in Azerbaijan 1945–46, Berlin Blockade 1948–49, Congo II 1964, Six Day War 1967, October–Yom Kippur War 1973–74, Angola 1975–76, Afghanistan 1979–80; General Assembly in Korea War II 1950 and Suez–Sinai Campaign 1956–57.

To summarize, we have noted considerable contrast between the bipolar and polycentric systems regarding the hypothesized relationship between seriousness of crisis and UN intervention. For bipolarity, five of the six indicators of seriousness – trigger, threat to values, intensity of violence, number of crisis actors, and super-power activity – are strongly related to UN involvement; that is, as seriousness increased, the likelihood of UN intervention increased, and the most potent UN organs – the General Assembly and the Security Council – were likely to become involved. A seriousness profile for the bipolar system would indicate violent trigger, threat of grave damage or threat to existence, serious clashes or full-scale war, four or more crisis actors, and one or both superpowers as crisis actors. Four international crises fit this profile, and all four exhibited UN involvement at the highest level: Korea I 1950 (Security Council), Korea II 1950 (General Assembly), Korea III 1953 (General Assembly), and Suez–Sinai Campaign 1956 (General Assembly).

The polycentric system did not exhibit the same strong relationship between seriousness and UN involvement in crises. In fact, only two of the seriousness indi-cators – number of actors and superpower activity – were related to UN involvement. In the case of the other indicators, not only were the findings not statistically signifi-cant, but they were also in the opposite direction to that hypothesized. We will return to this contrast between bipolarity and polycentrism once we have concluded the second part of the analysis, pertaining to UN involvement and outcome of crisis.

UN Intervention and Crisis Outcomes

Thus far we have been concerned with the relationship between the seriousness of an international crisis and the propensity of the UN to become involved. In this section our focus shifts to an assessment of the impact of UN involvement and its effectiveness on the outcomes of crises. The working hypothesis is that, the more active the UN is in a crisis, and the more effective that activity, the more likely it is that favorable outcomes will emerge, both from the point of view of individual actors and from the perspective of the international system as a whole. Favorableness of outcome is assessed on the basis of three indicators: form of outcome, actor evalu-ation of outcome, and escalation or reduction of tension. Once again, this section will focus on the contrasting patterns of bipolarity and polycentrism.

In Tables II.5.11. a. and b. we examine the relationship between UN involvement and effectiveness, and form of outcome. *Agreement* denotes formal agreements, such as treaties, armistices, and cease-fires, as well as semi-formal agreements, such as letters and oral declarations. *Tacit agreements* are mutual understandings by adversaries, neither written nor stated. *Unilateral acts* are actions undertaken by a single actor, without the voluntary agreement of the adversary, which terminate a crisis. *No agreement* includes crises which fade, which have no known termination date and no known agreement among the adversaries.

TABLE II.5.11.a. UN Involvement and Form of Outcome

	Bipolarity					Polycentrism				
	Agreement	Tacit	Unilateral Act	No Agreement/ Other		Agreement	Tacit	Unilateral Act	No Agreement/ Other	
No UN Activity	13 31%	7 17%	17 40%	5 12%	42 45%	29 47%	4 6%	22 36%	7 11%	62 38%
Low-Level Organs	6 55%	3 27%	0 0%	2 18%	11 12%	10 31%	2 6%	14 44%	6 19%	32 20%
High-Level Organs	20 50%	4 10%	9 22.5%	7 17.5%	40 43%	24 36%	6 9%	26 39%	11 16%	67 42%
	39 42%	14 15%	26 28%	14 15%	93 100%	63 39%	12 7%	62 39%	24 15%	161 100%
	$X^2 = 10.45$, p $= .107$					$X^2 = 3.31$, p $= .770$				

TABLE II.5.11.b. UN Effectiveness and Form of Outcome

	Bipolarity					
	Agreement	Tacit	Unilateral Act	No Agreement/ Other		
No Contribution/ Escalation	13 38%	5 15%	8 23.5%	8 23.5%	34	67%
Marginal	2 40%	2 40%	0 0%	1 20%	5	10%
Important/ Most Important	11 92%	0 0%	1 8%	0 0%	12	23%
	26 51%	7 14%	9 17.5%	9 17.5%	51	100%

$X^2 = 14.22$, p $= .027$

	Polycentrism					
	Agreement	Tacit	Unilateral Act	No Agreement/ Other		
No Contribution/ Escalation	24 37%	4 6%	26 41%	10 16%	64	65%
Marginal	3 20%	3 20%	7 47%	2 13%	15	15%
Important/ Most Important	7 35%	1 5%	7 35%	5 25%	20	20%
	34 34%	8 8%	40 41%	17 17%	99	100%

$X^2 = 5.45$, p $= .488$

In Table II.5.11.a. we note that, for bipolarity, agreement as the form of outcome was least common among crises with no UN involvement: only 31% of these cases ended in agreement, compared with 55% for low-level UN involvement and 50% for cases with high-level UN involvement. Although the chi-square is only approaching significance, the trend in the data is in the hypothesized direction. Among the cases with no UN involvement, a large proportion (40%) terminated through a unilateral act by one of the actors. For polycentrism, although the findings are not statistically significant, the trend is in the opposite direction to that hypothesized: agreement was the most likely outcome among crises with no UN activity. Among polycentric crises with low-level UN involvement, 44% terminated in unilateral acts, contrasting sharply with no cases for bipolarity.

Table II.5.11.b. focuses on UN effectiveness in crisis abatement and the form of outcome, and examines only those cases in which there was some UN involvement. For bipolarity, we find a strong relationship in the predicted direction: as UN effectiveness increased, the proportion of cases which ended in agreement also increased. In fact, 11 of the 12 bipolarity crises in which the UN was an important or the most important factor in crisis abatement ended in agreement: Azerbaijan 1945–46, Kashmir I 1947–48, Indonesia Independence II 1947, Israel Independence 1948–49, Indonesia Independence III 1948–49, Suez Nationalization 1956, Suez–Sinai Campaign 1956–57, Cambodia/Thailand 1958, Congo I: Katanga 1960, West Iran II 1961, and Cuban Missiles 1962. As we shall see later (see Table II.5.13. below), five of these crises in which agreement was reached reemerged as crises in a subsequent period.

Once again, the data for polycentrism do not exhibit a clear trend, and are not statistically significant: the probability of a crisis terminating in agreement was virtually the same for crises in which UN involvement did not contribute to resolution or actually led to escalation, and crises in which UN involvement was judged to have been important or most important in crisis abatement. Among the 20 cases in which UN involvement was an important or the most important factor in crisis abatement, seven ended in agreement: Cyprus I 1963–64, Kashmir II 1965–66, Cyprus II 1967, Moroccan March–Sahara 1975, US Hostages–Iran 1979–81, Operation Askari 1983–84, Basra/Kharg Island 1984. Seven others terminated with a unilateral act by one of the crisis actors: Cyprus III 1974–75, Operation Thrasher 1976, Aegean Sea 1976, Litani Operation 1978, Nicaraguan Civil War 1978, Operation Smokeshell 1980, and Iraq Nuclear Reactor 1981.

In Tables II.5.12.a. and b. we examine the relationship between UN involvement and effectiveness, and the participants' evaluation of the outcome.[5] The first category of evaluation of outcome includes crises in which either all or most of the actors were satisfied with the outcome. The second category groups crises in which the actors were equally divided, or where most or all were dissatisfied.

While overall satisfaction with outcomes was generally lower in bipolarity than in polycentrism (35% versus 57%), the data for UN involvement in bipolarity cases do show a trend toward higher rates of satisfaction as the level of UN involvement

TABLE II.5.12.a. UN Involvement and Evaluation of Outcome

	Bipolarity				Polycentrism			
	All/Mostly Satisfied	Dissatisfied			All/Mostly Satisfied	Dissatisfied		
No UN Activity	2 12%	15 88%	17	35%	14 52%	13 48%	27	31%
Low-Level Organs	3 37.5%	5 62.5%	8	16%	10 53%	9 47%	19	22%
High-Level Organs	12 50%	12 50%	24	49%	25 62.5%	15 37.5%	40	47%
	17 35%	32 65%	49*	100%	49 57%	37 43%	86*	100%
	$X^2 = 6.45$, $p = .040$				$X^2 = .93$, $p = .627$			

TABLE II.5.12.b. UN Effectiveness and Evaluation of Outcome

	Bipolarity				Polycentrism			
	All/Mostly Satisfied	Dissatisfied			All/Mostly Satisfied	Dissatisfied		
No Contribution/ Escalation	12 57%	9 43%	21	66%	22 52%	20 48%	42	71%
Marginal	0 0%	1 100%	1	3%	6 75%	2 25%	8	14%
Important/ Most Important	3 30%	7 70%	10	31%	7 78%	2 22%	9	15%
	15 47%	17 53%	32*	100%	35 59%	24 41%	59*	100%
	$X^2 = 2.92$, $p = .233$				$X^2 = 2.92$, $p = .232$			

*Single actor-cases excluded from this analysis.

increased (Table II.5.12.a.). Thus, while only 12% of cases with no UN involvement exhibited satisfaction with the outcome, the rate rose to 50% for crises in which the highest level UN organs were involved. For polycentrism, we observe little fluctuation in the rate of satisfaction with outcome, although satisfaction rates are higher than those for bipolarity at all levels of UN involvement.

In Table II.5.12.b., which deals with UN effectiveness, relatively few crises remain for analysis once single-actor cases and cases with no UN involvement are removed. And the results are not significant for bipolarity or polycentrism. In fact, the direction of the data is contrary to our expectations in bipolarity and conforms to it in polycentrism; that is, in bipolarity, UN effectiveness is inversely related to satisfaction with outcome, whereas in polycentrism the relationship is direct. For example, only 30% of the bipolarity cases where the UN was important or most important in crisis abatement resulted in satisfaction with outcome, compared to a 78% rate of satisfaction for polycentrism.

Tables II.5.13.a. and b. deal with the relationship between UN involvement and effectiveness, and the extent to which tension among the parties was reduced, as measured by the absence of crisis among the principal adversaries in the subsequent five-year period. Overall, the data reveal a trend toward greater tension in the international system: while 67% of bipolarity crises terminated with a reduction in tension, only 45% of the polycentrism crises did so. As noted from Table II.5.13.a., the extent of UN involvement has little impact on escalation or reduction of tension.

In Table II.5.13.b., we examine the impact of effectiveness of UN activity on escalation or reduction of tension. While the data for bipolarity do not support our

TABLE II.5.13.a. UN Involvement and Escalation or Reduction of Tension

	Bipolarity				Polycentrism			
	Escalation	Reduction			Escalation	Reduction		
No UN Activity	13 31%	29 69%	42	45%	32 52%	29 48%	61	39%
Low-level Organs	3 27%	8 73%	11	12%	19 61%	12 39%	31	20%
High-Level Organs	15 37.5%	25 62.5%	40	43%	36 55%	29 45%	65	41%
	31 33%	62 67%	93	100%	87 55%	70 45%	157	100%

$X^2 = .60$, $p = .740$ $X^2 = .65$, $p = .723$

TABLE II.5.13.b. UN Effectiveness and Escalation or Reduction of Tension

	Bipolarity				Polycentrism			
	Escalation	Reduction			Escalation	Reduction		
No Contribution/ Escalation	12 35%	22 65%	34	67%	37 60%	25 40%	62	64.5%
Marginal	1 20%	4 80%	5	10%	11 79%	3 21%	14	14.5%
Important/ Most Important	5 42%	7 58%	12	23%	7 35%	13 65%	20	21%
	18 35%	33 65%	51	100%	55 57%	41 43%	96	100%

$X^2 = .72$, $p = .700$ $X^2 = 6.80$, $p = .033$

original hypothesis, a statistically significant relationship is evident for polycentrism: whereas crises in which the UN was an important or the most important contributor to crisis abatement resulted in a 65% rate of tension reduction, the rate for lower levels of UN effectiveness was considerably lower. Thus, while the polycentric system overall yielded considerably lower rates of tension reduction than bipolarity, the one circumstance in which the trend was reversed was in those cases in which the UN was effective in crisis abatement. Examples of such polycentrism crises are: Kashmir II 1965–66, Cyprus II 1967, Portuguese Invasion of Guinea 1970, Caprivi Strip 1971, Cyprus III 1974–75, Moroccan March–Sahara 1975, Aegean Sea 1976, Nicaraguan Civil War 1978, US Hostages–Iran 1979–81, Essequibo II 1981–83, Iraq Nuclear Reactor 1981, Lesotho Raid 1982, and Operation Askari 1983–84.

Summary and Conclusion

By way of conclusion, let us return to the original hypotheses upon which these analyses were based and evaluate their overall ability to explain aspects of global organization intervention in international crises. In the first hypothesis, we proposed that the global organization was more likely to intervene in crises when a serious threat to the peace and security of the international system and its member-units existed. The indicators of seriousness were evaluated separately for the bipolar system (1945–62) and the polycentric system (1963–85). The data for bipolarity strongly supported the hypothesized relationship between seriousness and UN intervention, as summarized below:

(1) Violent triggers occurred in 38% of all bipolarity international crises. Crises triggered by violence were more likely than others to generate UN intervention; and such intervention was likely to involve the highest-level UN organs – Security Council and General Assembly.

(2) The probability of UN intervention increased as the threat to values became more serious. The UN intervened in 90% of the crises involving a threat to existence, with the Security Council and General Assembly accounting for all such serious cases.

(3) Crises which exhibited the most intense forms of violence in crisis management had the highest rate of UN involvement – 92% for full-scale war and 64% for serious clashes. All but four of these 26 most serious crises were handled by the Security Council and the General Assembly.

(4) The larger the international crisis in terms of number of crisis actors, the more likely it was that the UN would intervene. The larger the crisis, the more likely it was that such intervention was expressed through the highest-level UN organs.

(5) The rate of UN intervention was highest in crises in which the superpowers were active, either as crisis or involved actors.

As noted previously, the data for the polycentric system generally do not support the seriousness/UN intervention hypothesis. There were exceptions among cases in which a large number of actors was involved, and those in which the superpowers were very active. For both these indicators, the data for polycentrism support the seriousness/UN intervention hypothesis.

In general, then, these findings demonstrate that while the UN intervened in only 59% of international crises from 1945 to 1985, its rate of intervention in "serious" crises was actually considerably higher, particularly for the bipolar system-period. Furthermore, those crises with the highest seriousness scores were most likely to generate UN activity by its highest organs – Security Council and General Assembly. E. Haas (1986: pp. 20, 96), in his study of conflict management by international organizations, also found that 60% of the serious disputes involving military operations were referred to the UN. Furthermore, he found that 44% of the 34 cases involving active warfare showed a limited or great success by the UN in dispute management. Thus, these findings on UN intervention in international crises are more encouraging than those with which we began this analysis.

Our second hypothesis concerned the impact of UN intervention on crisis outcomes. More specifically, we proposed that the more active the UN was in a crisis, and the more effective that activity, the more likely it was that favorable outcomes would emerge. The findings are summarized below:

(1) For bipolarity, termination in agreement among the parties was most likely among crises in which the UN became involved. Furthermore, effective UN involvement was associated with a very high rate of achievement of agreement. Neither of these trends was in evidence during polycentrism.

(2) Although bipolarity exhibited a lower rate of satisfaction with outcome than polycentrism (35% versus 57%), level of UN involvement and satisfaction with outcome were related as hypothesized for bipolarity (and not for polycentrism).

(3) Irrespective of UN effectiveness, the data reveal a trend toward greater tension in the international system as we move from bipolarity to polycentrism. However, effective UN activity was likely to lead to tension reduction in polycentrism, though not in bipolarity.

In conclusion, our analysis has revealed that the bipolar system-period showed a substantial relationship between seriousness of crisis and the tendency for the UN to become involved as a crisis manager; but this relationship did not carry over into the polycentric system. Further, UN intervention in bipolarity crises was associated with agreement and satisfaction with outcome. However, it was the polycentric system which exhibited the greatest degree of tension reduction as a consequence of UN intervention.

Notes

1. Finlayson and Zacher (1980) suggest that alignment configuration is an important factor in determining whether or not the UN will become involved in a particular crisis. In essence, they suggest that the one type of conflict which is most likely to evoke UN attention is that involving threats or acts of force by aligned against non-aligned states. While we find this notion intriguing, its implications are beyond the scope of the present analysis.

2. Satisfaction is a relational indicator, having to do with the actor's own perception of satisfaction relative to the perceived satisfaction of the other crisis actors. An international crisis is classified as exhibiting a satisfactory outcome where all parties are satisfied with the outcome, even when some perceived others to be dissatisfied.
3. Operationally, tensions were considered to have been reduced when no crisis involving the principal adversaries occurred during the subsequent five-year period.
4. In these and subsequent tables, chi square and significance levels are reported, and will be used to assess the strength of a relationship between two variables.
5. For purposes of the analysis of the impact of UN intervention on the degree of satisfaction among the parties to a crisis, we have had to exclude all single-actor cases, as well as cases in which all crisis actors (as opposed to all involved actors) were on the same side of an issue. Examples of this latter type of crisis are Turkey, Greece and the US in the Truman Doctrine Crisis of 1947, Syria, Egypt, Lebanon and Iraq in the Palestine Partition Crisis of 1947, and Bahrain and Saudi Arabia in the Coup Attempt in Bahrain 1981–82.

6 Third Party Intervention II: The Superpowers as Crisis Managers

Mark A. Boyer and Jonathan Wilkenfeld

Introduction

Implicit throughout the earlier chapters on polarity and stability was the idea that the structure of the international system has an effect on the behavior of states in crisis. In multipolarity, a number of great powers exhibit somewhat different characteristics from the less powerful states in the system. In bipolarity, there are two superpowers that are distinct from the rest of the states in the system. In polycentrism, there are numerous centers of international decision, although dominant powers, such as the superpowers in the contemporary international system, still exist. Accordingly, one can hypothesize that a state's foreign policy behavior will be affected by its role within a particular type of international system. In other words, state behavior is influenced by structural constraints.

In line with these ideas, one study of superpower foreign policy behavior concluded that "[t]here are conspicuous similarities in American and Soviet external conduct which derive in large measure from similar conceptions of the 'superpower role' " (Jonsson, 1984: p. 222). Building on a number of earlier studies of the effects of international role on foreign policy behavior (see for instance, Brecher, Steinberg and Stein, 1969; Holsti, 1970; Wish, 1977, 1980; Backman, 1970; Walker, 1979, 1981),[1] Jonsson sought to determine whether superpower foreign policy behavior is influenced more by the characteristics and requirements of the superpower role than by particular national characteristics such as ideology, culture or historical tendencies (1984: pp. 6–7). Examining three post-World War II issue-areas – foreign aid, crisis management in the Middle East, and nonproliferation – Jonsson (p. 222) found that the Soviet Union tended to emulate American behavior in an effort to acquire equal status with the United States and legitimize its role as a superpower. He also concluded that cooperation, tacit or otherwise, emerged between the superpowers in each of these issue-areas.

Holsti (1970) suggested that a nation's international role emanates from two sources: a state's own role conception and the role prescriptions held by other actors with regard to that state's expected behavior. Both sources will likely be conditioned by the structure of the international system at any point in time and will influence a nation's status in the system. That status, in turn, has an impact upon a nation's foreign policy role performance. In other words, a nation's foreign policy behavior is constrained (or, at least, conditioned) by a state's own and other states' perceptions of what its behavior should be. Jonsson (1984: p. 28) puts it more precisely by stating that national role conceptions should be viewed "as intervening variables, mediating the impact of traditional background factors or 'sources' of foreign policy behavior." As a result, one can hypothesize that the differences in international behavior commonly ascribed to the United States and the Soviet Union would likely be more prominent if not for the constraints of the superpower role. One can further hypothesize that during the bipolar period (1945–62), when the Soviet Union was still attempting to catch up to the United States in a variety of ways, the foreign policy behavior of the two superpowers would be less similar than during the polycentric period (since 1963), during which the superpowers have operated at a level of approximate parity and have had some incentive to maintain the international *status quo*.

In this vein, Jonsson, drawing on Holsti (1970) and Wish (1977), identified 15 superpower role conceptions (Table II.6.1.). As evident from the list, these conceptions suggest often contradictory roles for the superpowers in the global system. For instance, the superpowers are considered violators *and* promoters of universal values, interveners *and* mediators, and liberators *and* exploiters. But these apparent contradictions can be understood by examining the particular role conceptions held by a superpower's own policy-makers and those ascribed to each superpower by other states' policy-makers. Table II.6.2. displays the six most frequently cited role conceptions by a superpower's policy-makers, while Table II.6.3. shows those ascribed to the superpowers by other policy-makers.

Table II.6.2. shows that US and Soviet policy-makers cite five of the same six role conceptions as indicative of their international role, indicating a large degree

---

TABLE II.6.1. Superpower Role Conceptions

Promoter of universal values
Violator of universal values
Promoter of own value system
Preventer of other superpower's values
Model
Developer
Liberator
Liberation supporter
Regional protector
Bloc leader
Exploiter
Intervener
War instigator
Mediator
Protector of own state

Source: Jonsson, 1984: p. 19.

TABLE II.6.2. Six Role Conceptions Most Frequently Cited by Superpower Policy-Makers

	Rank		Number of Respondents	
1. United States	1.	Promoter of Universal Values	54	(42%)
	2.	Regional Protector	22	(17%)
	3.	Liberation Supporter	18	(14%)
	4.	Developer	18	(14%)
	5.	Promoter of Own Values	11	(8%)
	6.	Mediator	6	(5%)
Total			129	(100%)
2. Soviet Union	1.	Promoter of Universal Values	74	(52%)
	2.	Liberation Supporter	22	(15%)
	3.	Regional Protector	18	(12%)
	4.	Promoter of Own Values	14	(10%)
	5.	Protector of Own State	8	(6%)
	6.	Developer	7	(5%)
Total			143	(100%)

Source: Jonsson, 1984: p. 20.

TABLE II.6.3. Six Role Conceptions Most Frequently Cited by Other States' Policy-Makers

	Rank		Number of Respondents	
1. United States	1.	Violator of Universal Values	144	(37%)
	2.	Intervener	96	(25%)
	3.	Exploiter	69	(18%)
	4.	War Instigator	56	(14%)
	5.	Developer	12	(3%)
	6.	Promoter of Universal Values	11	(3%)
Total			388	(100%)
2. Soviet Union	1.	Violator of Universal Values	91	(44%)
	2.	Intervener	45	(22%)
	3.	Exploiter	23	(11%)
	4.	Promoter of Universal Values	23	(11%)
	5.	War Instigator	19	(9%)
	6.	Developer	7	(3%)
Total			208	(100%)

Source: Jonsson, 1984: p. 21.

of consensus among superpower policy-makers in this regard. Many of the seemingly contradictory role conceptions listed in Table II.6.1. can be explained by noticing in Table II.6.3. that the role conceptions ascribed to the superpowers by others are often mirror images of those in Table II.6.2. Even more interesting, the same six role conceptions were ascribed to both the United States and the Soviet Union by other policy-makers, even though they are given a somewhat different ranking for each superpower. Moreover, along the lines of Holsti's analysis, these two types of role conceptions ultimately work to produce foreign policy behavior. As a result, Tables II.6.2. and II.6.3. suggest that, if role conceptions influence foreign policy behavior, the United States and the Soviet Union should exhibit similarities in their international activities as discussed above. Empirical analyses performed by CACI (1980), Wish (1980), Wilkenfeld and Brecher (Chapter 13 below) and Jonsson (1984) have provided at least some support for that proposition.

Notwithstanding the findings from these studies, there is a widespread view in both policy-making and academic communities that emphasizes divergence in US and Soviet foreign policy behavior. For instance, many politicians in the United States owe their electoral success to their ability to capitalize on anti-Soviet sentiments in the American public. Rightly or wrongly, these electoral efforts usually require that the politician delineate the behavioral *differences* that exist between the United States and the Soviet Union. The Soviet Union is often painted as an aggressively expansionist power, while the United States is seen as working toward the maintenance of order and stability in the international system. The success of Reagan's 1980 campaign was at least in part the result of his aggressive anti-Soviet rhetoric.

The academic community, too, has spawned a large body of literature emphasizing the singularity of the foreign policy behavior of the superpowers. In Soviet foreign policy studies, at least three schools of thought can be identified, each providing an alternative set of dominant motivating factors in Soviet foreign policy. Griffiths (1984: pp. 3–4) discusses three schools of thought: the first focuses on the nature of a totalitarian political order committed to world domination; the second emphasizes the external or international constraints on Soviet international activities;[2] and the third concentrates on the quasi-pluralistic nature of Soviet foreign policy-making and the internal political tradeoffs it entails.[3] Welch (1970) derives a classification scheme for analyses of Soviet foreign policy that focuses on the degree to which the analyst believes Soviet leadership is committed to its rhetorical statements. His three schools of thought are: (1) the ultra-hard image of the great beast, (2) the hard image of the mellowing tiger, and (3) the mixed image of the neurotic bear. Additionally, Nacht (1985) identifies two schools of thought, aggressive versus defensive, and places such analysts as Richard Pipes in the former and George Kennan in the latter.[4]

One can construct similar classification systems for studies of United States foreign policy. Over the last two decades, a host of process-oriented studies, similar to those of Griffiths' third school on Soviet policy, have emerged in American foreign policy studies. Bureaucratic politics explanations of US foreign policy behavior achieved renown with Allison's (1969, 1971) study of the Cuban Missile Crisis and have been expanded by many other authors.[5] Nacht (1985) also focuses attention on internal factors in the American system by pointing to the problems caused for US international activities by the persistence of contradictory foreign policy goals. Other scholars have attributed US foreign policy behavior to its desire to contain the Soviet Union and maintain its primacy in the international system, and therefore the *status quo*, with evaluations of American behavior taking similar form to those based in role theory (Hoffmann, 1979–80; Gaddis, 1982). Still others view American foreign policy problems as the result of a misalignment of foreign policy goals and the means available to achieve those goals (Calleo, 1987).

As the preceding discussion suggests, there is a lack of consensus within the academic community over the motivations of and similarities between superpower foreign policies. The purpose of this chapter is to investigate the extent to which the superpower role suppresses the impact of other "traditional" sources of foreign policy behavior for the US and the USSR. In particular, this chapter will provide some insight into the influence of international role on superpower *crisis* behavior. In this respect, it will complement the work of Jonsson and others on international role and superpower foreign policy behavior by providing a test of the tenets of role theory as they apply to the crisis environment.

International crisis is used as the focal point for analysis for a number of other reasons. First, we assume that crises provide a microcosm of the foreign policy process overall in that they force a state to act efficiently in a constrained and pressure-filled environment. Second, few attempts[6] have been made to analyze systematically superpower foreign policy behavior at an aggregate level for the entire post-World War II period. Only the CACI studies (1976, 1978, 1980) have focused aggregate analysis on crisis behavior. Other empirical analyses, e.g., George and Smoke (1974), Brecher (1980), Adomeit (1982), Shlaim (1983), Dowty (1984) and Dawisha (1984), have employed case studies and have not examined the patterns of superpower behavior beyond that level. As a result, more evidence is required to evaluate the aggregate patterns of the impact of international role on crisis behavior.

The empirical evidence in this chapter should fill a gap in the literature on role theory left by earlier studies that have focused on non-crisis foreign policy behavior and by those not specifically focusing on the superpowers. If a large degree of similarity exists in the crisis behavior manifested by the superpowers, some credence will thus be given to the propositions put forth by role theory. The extent to which behavioral differences exist between the superpowers will help gauge the influence causal factors other than international role play in superpower behavior. If little difference exists at this aggregate level, then the arguments regarding differences in foreign policy behavior between the superpowers can be seen primarily as discussions of the margin of superpower behavior and not as differences in general behavior. If large differences exist, then deeper investigation of other causal factors will be required.

Variables

A number of ICB variables will allow us to gain insight into the impact of superpower role on crisis behavior. The analysis is broken into two main parts. The first section examines the ways the superpowers became involved in international crises during the 1945–1985 period. Activity is coded as follows: (1) inactive; (2) low-level activity, including political or economic assistance or propaganda efforts; (3) semi-military or covert activity, including military aid or the employment of military advisors without actual fighting; and (4) direct military activity, including the dispatching of troops, aerial bombing, and naval assistance.

The second section examines the effectiveness of superpower activity in crises. Effectiveness is understood in terms of preventing the outbreak of hostilities or otherwise contributing to the termination of an international crisis. Effectiveness is coded as follows: superpower activity (1) did not contribute to crisis abatement; (2) escalated the crisis; and (3) contributed to crisis abatement.[7]

In both sections cross-tabulations will be performed with a number of other variables to help discern the similarities and differences that exist between the activities of the two superpowers. In particular, geographic region and system structure will be used. Geographic region is coded as: (1) Asia, (2) Middle East, (3) Africa, (4) Europe and (5) the Americas. This variable should yield some insight into superpower crisis behavior within and outside their own spheres. In regions where one of the superpowers is the dominant actor, one would expect to find greater divergence in the behavior of the superpowers. But in regions where influence is low or in an area of historical confrontation (e.g., Europe), greater similarities in behavior should exist.

System structure is coded as: (1) bipolarity (1945–62) and (2) polycentrism (1963–85). If the tenets of role theory hold, one would expect to find greater similarity in the crisis behavior of the superpowers under polycentrism than under bipolarity. In the polycentric system, the United States and the Soviet Union both have a stake in preservation of the international *status quo* because of their roles as dominant actors and the rise of other power and decision centers in world politics. In the bipolar system, differences in behavior should exist because Soviet international status and role were somewhat different from that of the United States.

Analysis of Superpower Crisis Activity

Turning first to superpower activity generally, we note from Table II.6.4. that, of the 254 post-World War II international crises until the end of 1985, the US was involved at some level in 69% and the USSR in 55%, indicating frequent involvement in international crises by both states. The higher overall level of US involvement might be explained by a number of factors.

First, the US was more globally oriented than the USSR during the immediate post-war period, when the latter was preoccupied with managing and consolidating

TABLE II.6.4. Superpower Activity in International Crises, 1945–85

		USSR Activity								
		None		Low		Semi-Military or Covert		Direct Military			
US Activity	None	64*	82%† 56%	10	13% 13%	4	5% 8%	0	0% 0%	78	31%
	Low	38	36% 33%	40	37% 50%	21	20% 45%	8	7% 62%	107	42%
	Semi-Military or Covert	11	24% 9%	18	38% 23%	16	34% 34%	2	4% 15%	47	18%
	Direct Military	2	9% 2%	11	50% 14%	6	27% 13%	3	14% 23%	22	9%
		115	45%	79	31%	47	19%	13	5%	254	100%

$$X^2 = 72.93, p = .000$$

* The 64 international crises in which neither superpower was active are distributed as follows:

Region	Frequency	%
Asia	7	11%
Middle East	11	17%
Africa	39	61%
Europe	2	3%
Americas	5	8%
Total	64	100%

† The upper figure is the row percentage, the lower figure the column percentage.

communist regimes (Ulam, 1974: p. 408), particularly in Eastern Europe, but also at other points around its periphery such as North Korea and its aborted attempts in Iran. Moreover, not until Khrushchev's rhetoric for wars of "national liberation" in the Third World in the mid- to late-1950s did the USSR develop a more globalist foreign policy (Nacht, 1985: p. 11). Paralleling the USSR's rise to globalism was a military buildup that provided it with a global naval presence and nuclear parity with the US. The US, on the other hand, was at the center of the international system from the end of World War II. International efforts to stabilize, and institutionalize to a certain extent, the post-war international system demanded an active and global US presence. US efforts to fill the vacuum left by the retreat of Great Britain around the world caused the US to become active internationally at an unprecedented level. US willingness and capability to rebuild the international economy through the implementation of the Bretton Woods System (1944) and the Marshall Plan (1947) are indications of US globalism at that time.

A second factor which may have contributed to less USSR activity in other states' crises is caution in Soviet foreign policy generally: this tended to inhibit the use of military force in situations where the US was integrally involved and in situations where long-term commitments were seen by the USSR as likely (Adomeit, 1982: p. 322).[8] Studies of political uses of military force in the post-war era by the US (Blechman and Kaplan, 1978) and the Soviet Union (S. S. Kaplan, 1981) also indicate greater Soviet caution and lower activity: there were more incidents cited for the US (215 from January 1946 to May 1975) than for the USSR (190 from June 1944 to February 1979). Particularly in crises, which often require quick action and also present riskier foreign policy situations, Soviet caution could preclude participation, especially if the USSR tends to be rather risk averse, as Triska and Finley (1968: p. 347) concluded. In this regard, Soviet intervention and lengthy involvement in Afghanistan, from 1979 to 1989, can be viewed as an unusual case for the USSR.

Table II.6.4. also presents the 254 post-1945 crises as a cross-tabulation of US and Soviet levels of activity. Sixty-two of the 64 cases (24% of the total) without any superpower involvement occurred in the Third World (the two exceptions were the Malta/Libya Dispute of 1980 and the Aegean Naval Crisis of 1984). This is not surprising because the Third World was secondary to the interests of the super-powers and the competition between them. Furthermore, of those 64 cases, 61% occurred in Africa. This finding conforms to many of the ideas in the literature about regional aspects of superpower competition. Africa has essentially been peripheral to US and Soviet foreign policy efforts. For the US, many of the conflicts in Africa were looked upon as problems of colonialism and decolonization. Hence, because of extensive commitments elsewhere, American decision-makers seem to have decided to remain aloof from Africa or to leave its post-colonial crises to the former European rulers. Until the mid-1970s American foreign policy toward Africa was "low-profile and cautious" (Oye *et al.*: p. 337). The only major exceptions were the Congo in 1964 and Angola in 1975–76, where the USSR was active as well.

For the USSR, too, Africa was an area of secondary concern. The first real venture into African politics did not occur until 1959, after Guinea declared its independence from France (Calvocoressi, 1982: p. 421). And, while the Soviets did become involved in Africa thereafter, for example in the Congo, Africa remained outside its sphere of high interest until recently. The Angolan and SWAPO commitments have tended to raise superpower competition in Southern Africa to a higher level.

More striking than the data on non-involvement cases is the fact that 49% of the total (125 cases: the addition of the southeast nine cells in Table II.6.4.) saw some activity by both superpowers in the same crisis. Further, in those crises in which one superpower was highly involved (direct military semi-military, or covert activity), the level of involvement for the other superpower tended to be lower. Of the crises with direct military activity – 22 for the US and 13 for the USSR – there were only three crises in which both were active militarily: the Berlin Blockade 1948–49, the second Korean War Crisis 1950–51, and the Berlin Wall Crisis 1961.[9] Yet the events of all three crises basically support the overall findings in relation to US/USSR confrontation: caution on the part of the superpowers with little likelihood of high-risk direct military confrontation.

During the Berlin Blockade, the USSR had ample opportunity to escalate the crisis, due to the continued US airlift, but it refrained from doing so. Instead, Soviet forces were used for the ground blockade, while US forces were engaged in the airlift. In the second Korean War Crisis, Soviet forces in the Far East were merely put on alert due to the potential of US troops advancing to the Korea-Soviet border; the crisis ended for the USSR when the tide of battle shifted in favor of the PRC and North Korea. The Berlin Wall Crisis also showed superpower caution and restraint: although various instances of "saber-rattling" did occur, neither superpower did more than reinforce its troops in Berlin, possibly to signal commitment rather than intent to fight. Ultimately, although the possibility of direct military conflict was slightly higher in the Berlin Wall Crisis, both superpowers were able to avoid a direct confrontation, just as in the other two instances of minimal military activity. This suggests that the behavior of both the US and the USSR was constrained by their roles in the global system.

Returning to superpower crisis activity in general: although the overall US level is somewhat higher than that of the USSR, the basic patterns of involvement show little difference in the distribution of cases across the three types of activity for both superpowers. This similarity in overall behavior may mask the effects on superpower crisis activity of two variables discussed briefly and indirectly earlier: geography and system structure. As noted with reference to Africa, the impact of region upon superpower crisis activity is rather conspicuous. One might expect that the pattern of activity would accord with historical spheres of influence and with changes in the international system after World War II.

In this context George (1983: p. 381) discusses superpower rivalry in terms of several types of interest symmetry and how these affect the level of superpower confrontation in various regions:

1. high interest symmetry – areas where both sides have very strong, if not vital interests.
2. low interest symmetry – areas where both sides have modest interests.
3. interest asymmetry favoring the USSR.
4. interest asymmetry favoring the US.
5. disputed interest symmetry – areas where the superpowers do not agree on the relative balance of interests.
6. uncertain interest symmetry – areas where ambiguity and fluidity of situation dominate.

George goes on to state that situations 1 through 4 generally lead to the development of rules for superpower behavior (pp. 383–384), along the lines of role constraints, suggesting that certain regions, such as the Americas and Europe, would have defined rules for superpower behavior. The African region would fit into type 2, making it unnecessary for any rules at all. The Middle East and, possibly, Asia, would fit into types 5 or 6 and therefore would see a high incidence of superpower activity due to uncertain rules. While not directly specifying the level of regional involvement, the George typology implies the presence of spheres of influence and of regions where differences in superpower behavior will occur.

Tables II.6.5.a. and b. and Tables II.6.6.a. and b. present data on superpower activity and region. Looking first at Tables II.6.5.a. and b., we note that the implications of the George typology are manifested in the crisis data for the superpowers. It is not surprising that the Asian region has the highest proportion of involvement cases for both superpowers (26% for the US, 30% for the USSR), followed by the Middle East and Africa. US activity in the Korean and Vietnam Wars, its backing of Nationalist China on Taiwan, and its commitments to Japan indicate a high involvement in the region in general. Soviet commitments and involvement in both

TABLE II.6.5.a. Superpower Crisis Activity by Region, 1945–85: US

	Asia		Middle East		Africa		Europe		Americas			
Not Active	11	14%	14	18%	44	56.5%	4	5%	5	6.5%	78	31%
Active	45	26%	43	24%	40	23%	22	12%	26	15%	176	69%
	56	22%	57	23%	84	33%	26	10%	31	12%	254	100%

$X^2 = 28.74, p = .000$

TABLE II.6.5.b. Superpower Crisis Activity by Region, 1945–85: USSR

	Asia		Middle East		Africa		Europe		Americas			
Not Active	15	13%	19	17%	55	48%	5	4%	21	18%	115	45%
Active	41	30%	38	27%	29	21%	21	15%	10	7%	139	55%
	56	22%	57	23%	84	33%	26	10%	31	12%	254	100%

$X^2 = 38.28, p = .000$

TABLE II.6.6.a. Level of Superpower Crisis Activity by Region, 1945–85: US

	Low		Semi-Military/Covert		Direct Military			
Asia	20	44%	12	27%	13	29%	45	26%
Middle East	29	67%	12	28%	2	5%	43	24%
Africa	25	62.5%	13	32.5%	2	5%	40	23%
Europe	19	86%	1	5%	2	9%	22	12%
Americas	14	54%	9	35%	3	11%	26	15%
	107	61%	47	27%	22	12%	176	100%

$X^2 = 23.88, p = .002$

TABLE II.6.6.b. Level of Superpower Crisis Activity by Region, 1945–85: USSR

	Low	Semi-Military/Covert	Direct Military		
Asia	29 / 71%	9 / 22%	3 / 7%	41	30%
Middle East	19 / 50%	17 / 45%	2 / 5%	38	27%
Africa	14 / 48%	14 / 48%	1 / 4%	29	21%
Europe	11 / 53%	3 / 14%	7 / 33%	21	15%
Americas	6 / 60%	4 / 40%	0 / 0%	10	7%
	79 / 57%	47 / 34%	13 / 9%	139	100%

$X^2 = 25.28, p = .001$

Asian wars and periodic Soviet support for, and conflict with, the PRC help explain the similar finding for the USSR in Asia.

As expected from the George typology, too, the US was much more frequently involved in crises in the Americas than was the USSR. The five cases of US inactivity in this region were: the Dominican Republic/Cuba Crisis of 1947; the Luperon Crisis for the Dominican Republic in 1949; the Mexican/Guatemala Fishing Rights Crisis of 1958–59; the Belize Crisis for the United Kingdom in 1975; and the Essequibo II Crisis for Guyana in 1981. All five crises were characterized by low/no violence, and no Soviet activity; and they were relatively minor crises. The ten cases in the Americas where the USSR was involved were: Guatemala 1953–54; the Assassination Attempt on the Venezuelan President in 1960; Bay of Pigs in 1961; Cuban Missile Crisis of 1962; Dominican Republic/Haiti Crisis of 1963; the Dominican Republic Crisis of 1965; the Cienfuegos Base Crisis of 1970; the Falklands/Malvinas War of 1982; the Invasion of Grenada in 1983; and the Nicaragua MIG-21 Crisis of 1984. In seven of those 10 cases the US was a crisis actor, the only exceptions being the Assassination Attempt/Venezuela 1960, the Dominican/Haiti 1963 Crisis and the Falklands/Malvinas War of 1982. In none of these cases did the USSR use direct military force, although Soviet semi-military activity was present in four cases.

In European crises, as expected, both superpowers were almost always involved. However, the extent of their activity differed. In 86% of the cases the US was active at a low level (see Table II.6.6.a.). The two Berlin crises mentioned earlier account for the incidents of US military activity. The USSR (Table II.6.6.b.), by contrast, was active at low levels only 53% of the time, and engaged in direct military activity in a third of the crises. All of the cases of Soviet direct military activity were in Eastern Europe. These findings, too, tend to support the George typology in that the USSR perceives itself as freer to do as it pleases in a region of interest asymmetry, while in the rest of Europe, both superpowers tend to get involved at a low level. These findings also suggest the existence of tacit rules for US/Soviet crisis behavior in Europe.

It is also noteworthy that in both the Middle East and Africa, George's type 5 or 6 regions, the extent of superpower activity differed considerably. The USSR exhibited a much higher proportion of semi-military/covert activity in these regions than it did in Europe or Asia and a higher proportion than did the US in Africa and the Middle East. One possible explanation is that in type 5 or 6 situations, the USSR perceives opportunities for gains in overall superpower competition. In these "grey areas," although Soviet interests may be low (possibly even type 2), uncertain or disputed, the USSR may be induced to pursue its foreign policy goals at a higher level of activity. If crises are interpreted as threats or opportunities (Bobrow et al., 1977: p. 204), the USSR viewed crises in the Middle East or Africa as opportunities to achieve benefits in the global competition with the other superpower. In type 5 or 6 situations, then, superpower role has less influence on behavior than in other George-type situations.

A second relevant variable is the structure of the international system, defined in terms of the interaction and relationship between the superpowers. The bipolar system spanned the period 1945–62 and was characterized primarily by the dynamics of US/Soviet conflicts. The polycentric system from 1963 onward exhibits some distinct differences in the overall thrust of international relations. The influx of new actors and issues into the international system during the 1960s, 1970s and 1980s led to a relative decline of East/West issues in the system. While the superpowers have not explicitly acknowledged this shift within their own foreign policies, more varied international interaction is conspicuous. Tables II.6.7.a. and II.6.7.b. basically support the conclusion about the relative decline of superpower participation in international crises: although no drastic shift is evident, these tables show a slight decline in the percentage of superpower involvement from bipolarity to polycentrism.

As for types and levels of crisis activity across system-periods, Tables II.6.8.a. and II.6.8.b. reveal several significant findings. For the US, the distribution among the three categories of activity was almost identical for bipolarity and polycentrism. Of the 15 cases of direct US military activity in the polycentric period, nine occurred in Southeast Asia, mostly during the Vietnam War. The six other cases were scattered: Congo 1964; Dominican Republic 1965; EC-21 Spy Plane 1969; Iranian Hostages 1979–81; Gulf of Syrte 1981; and Invasion of Grenada 1983. In sum, these findings for the two systems tend to support the hypotheses generated by role theory.

For the USSR the distribution was rather different across system-periods. Low-

TABLE II.6.7.a. Superpower Crisis Activity by System Structure, 1945–85: US

	Bipolarity		Poly-centrism			
Not Active	23	29%	55	71%	78	31%
Active	70	40%	106	60%	176	69%
	93	37%	161	63%	254	100%

$X^2 = 2.04$, p = .153

TABLE.II.6.7.b. Superpower Crisis Activity by System Structure, 1945–85: USSR

	Bipolarity		Poly-centrism			
Not Active	34	30%	81	70%	115	45%
Active	59	42%	80	58%	139	55%
	93	37%	161	63%	254	100%

$X^2 = 3.96$, p = .047

TABLE II.6.8.a. Level of Superpower Crisis Activity by System Structure, 1945–85: US

	Low		Semi-Military /Covert		Direct Military			
Bipolarity	45	64%	18	26%	7	10%	70	40%
Polycentrism	62	59%	29	27%	15	14%	106	60%
	107	61%	47	27%	22	12%	176	100%

$X^2 = .857$, p = .652

TABLE II.6.8.b. Level of Superpower Crisis Activity by System Structure, 1945–85: USSR

	Low		Semi-Military /Covert		Direct Military			
Bipolarity	36	61%	15	25%	8	14%	59	42%
Polycentrism	43	54%	32	40%	5	6%	80	58%
	79	57%	47	34%	13	9%	139	100%

$$X^2 = 4.39, p = .111$$

level and direct military activity decreased from bipolarity to polycentrism, while semi-military or covert activity increased. The decline in Soviet direct military activity reflects more secure Soviet hegemony in Eastern Europe. The rise in semi-military and covert activity corresponds to the regional findings for Soviet behavior; that is, as the USSR became a global power, it became more actively involved in crises in regions that were once peripheral to Soviet interests.

Effectiveness of Superpower Crisis Activity

In analyzing superpower effectiveness in international crises we will proceed as in the earlier part of this chapter, that is, by examining levels/types of activity, region, and the post-World War II system-periods as potential discriminating factors in the effectiveness of superpower crisis activity. In Tables II.6.9.a. and II.6.9.b., types of activity and US/USSR effectiveness in crisis abatement are shown. Overall, the US contributed to crisis abatement in 53% of the cases in which it was involved and escalated crises 11% of the time. Eight of the 19 crises where US activity escalated a crisis were part of one of the two Asian conflicts, Korea and Vietnam. The USSR,

TABLE II.6.9.a. Superpower Effectiveness in Crises by Level of Activity, 1945–85: US

	Did not Contribute		Escalated		Effective			
Low	53	49%	6	6%	48	45%	107	61%
Semi-Military/ Covert	11	24%	3	6%	33	70%	47	27%
Direct Military	0	0%	10	45.5%	12	55.5%	22	12%
	64	36%	19	11%	93	53%	176	100%

$$X^2 = 47.25, p = .000$$

TABLE II.6.9.b. Superpower Effectiveness in Crises by Level of Activity, 1945–85: USSR

	Did not Contribute		Escalated		Effective			
Low	49	62%	11	14%	19	24%	79	57%
Semi-Military/ Covert	21	45%	14	30%	12	25%	47	34%
Direct Military	0	0%	9	69%	4	31%	13	9%
	70	50%	34	25%	35	25%	139	100%

$$X^2 = 23.97, p = .000$$

by contrast, exhibited a much lower proportion of positive contribution to crisis abatement – 25% – with the largest number of its cases falling in the "not contributed" category. The implications of these differences will be discussed later.

There were also differences in superpowers' effectiveness with respect to cases of direct military activity. Among 22 US cases, it contributed to crisis abatement in 12 (55.5%), while in ten cases it escalated the crisis (but six of those cases were among the Asian cases mentioned above). The other four cases of US escalation were the Berlin Blockade, the Dominican Republic 1965, Mayaguez 1975, and the Gulf of Syrte 1981, all incidents where the US stood to benefit from escalation. Soviet direct military activity, on the other hand, contributed to crisis abatement in four cases (31%) and escalated nine crises (69%). Three of the escalated crises were in Eastern Europe. The others were: Azerbaijan 1945-46; the second Korean War Crisis 1950-51; the Catalina Affair 1952; the second War of Attrition 1970; the second Ogaden Crisis 1977-78; and the Afghanistan Invasion 1979. It is also worth noting that, while semi-military or covert involvement was the most effective activity for the US, this type of activity, when employed by the USSR, either had no effect or escalated a crisis. This finding may be attributable to a Soviet preference for proxies in an effort to avoid direct military participation in crises, as suggested by Adomeit (1982: p. 322).

In Tables II.6.10.a. and II.6.10.b., we examine the effect of level of superpower activity on the effectiveness of the other superpower in crises. We observe that, as the level of USSR involvement in crises increased, US effectiveness declined (from 59% when the USSR was not involved to 31% when the USSR was involved in direct military action). By contrast, USSR effectiveness, while considerably less

TABLE II.6.10.a. Superpower Effectiveness in Crises by Level of Other Superpower's Activity, 1945–85: US Effectiveness

		US Effectiveness				
		Did not Contribute	Escalated	Effective		
	Not active	17 33%	4 8%	30 59%	51	29%
	Low	23 33%	6 9%	40 88%	69	39%
USSR Activity	Semi-Military/Covert	17 40%	7 16%	19 44%	43	25%
	Direct Military	7 54%	2 15%	4 31%	13	7%
		64 36%	19 11%	93 53%	176	100%

$X^2 = 6.16, p = .406$

TABLE II.6.10.b. Superpower Effectiveness in Crises by Level of Other Superpower's Activity, 1945–85: USSR Effectiveness

		USSR Effectiveness				
		Did not Contribute	Escalated	Effective		
	Not Active	10 72%	3 21%	1 7%	14	10%
	Low	33 48%	17 25%	19 27%	69	50%
US Activity	Semi-Military/Covert	16 44%	10 28%	10 28%	36	26%
	Direct Military	11 55%	4 20%	5 25%	20	14%
		70 50%	34 25%	35 25%	139	100%

$X^2 = 4.09, p = .664$

frequent than that of the US, appears to have been unaffected by the type of US activity, other than no involvement. Stated differently, the US has been more constrained by higher levels of Soviet crisis activity than the USSR by US activity.

It is also interesting to note that, while the US effectiveness rate was relatively high among crises in which the USSR was not involved (59%), the USSR was effective in only one crisis in which the US was uninvolved (Mozambique Raid 1981). This finding is probably an artifact of the types of crises which one or the other superpower chooses to ignore. For example, two of the three crises in which USSR involvement escalated a US non-involved crisis were crises for Finland in 1948 and 1961 caused by Soviet pressure. The other was a relatively minor crisis, the 1960 Rottem Crisis between Egypt and Israel, which involved no violence and only Soviet political activity. Furthermore, among the 10 crises where there was no US involvement and the USSR did not contribute to crisis abatement, only three showed significant levels of violence and in only one case – the Vietnamese Invasion of Cambodia in 1977–78 – did Soviet activity go beyond political or economic involvement. The minor character of these crises or their location in the Soviet sphere of influence (Finland) was the likely cause of US non-involvement.

Following the earlier line of analysis, region, too, is assumed to have an impact upon superpower effectiveness. In Tables II.6.11.a. and II.6.11.b., we note that the US was more effective than the USSR in crisis abatement in all five regions. The highest success rate for the US (81%) is in the Americas, which is also the region of highest USSR contribution to abatement (40%), even though it was not often active

TABLE II.6.11.a. Superpower Effectiveness in Crises by Region, 1945–85: US

	Did not Contribute		Escalated		Effective			
Asia	11	24%	9	20%	25	56%	45	26%
Middle East	19	44%	1	2%	23	54%	43	24%
Africa	22	55%	2	5%	16	40%	40	23%
Europe	10	46%	4	18%	8	36%	22	12%
Americas	2	8%	3	11%	21	81%	26	15%
	64	36%	19	11%	93	53%	176	100%

$$X^2 = 27.72, p = .000$$

TABLE II.6.11.b. Superpower Effectiveness in Crises by Region, 1945–85: USSR

	Did not Contribute		Escalated		Effective			
Asia	22	54%	6	14%	13	32%	41	30%
Middle East	22	58%	6	16%	10	26%	38	27%
Africa	17	59%	9	31%	3	10%	29	21%
Europe	4	19%	12	57%	5	24%	21	15%
Americas	5	50%	1	10%	4	40%	10	7%
	70	50%	34	25%	35	25%	139	100%

$$X^2 = 22.46, p = .004$$

in that region's crises. This result supports the notion that the United States plays a dominant role in the Americas and that it tends to work toward preservation of the *status quo* through crisis abatement.

Both the US and the USSR were least effective as crisis managers in Africa and Europe. One explanation for ineffectiveness in Africa relates to the pervasiveness of change and conflict during the decolonization era. Much of Africa was experiencing recurring social and political upheaval, and Western nations in particular were looked upon with wary eyes. Some of the US effectiveness problems may have been due to its close ties with the former colonial powers. As for the USSR, its late start at foreign policy involvement in Africa may have impeded its efforts at crisis abatement in that region. Moreover, the USSR may also have perceived escalation of crises in Africa as a means to increase its influence at the expense of the West.

In Europe, the USSR was most inclined to escalate crises (57%), while the US most often did not contribute to crisis abatement. This finding is due to Europe's role as the the primary theater of superpower rivalry, at least during the bipolar period. Both superpowers at times drove up the ante of crises as displays of resolve and commitment. Furthermore, eight of the 10 cases where US activity did not contribute to crisis abatement occurred in Eastern Europe; that is, US effectiveness was severely constrained in the Soviet sphere of influence. Ten of the 12 European crises involving Soviet escalation were also located in Eastern Europe, such as the Hungary Uprising in 1956.

Tables II.6.12.a. and II.6.12.b., reveal some shifts in superpower effectiveness in relation to changes in the international system in the post-World War II era. Both superpowers show a modest decline in effectiveness from bipolarity to polycentrism. This parallels the decline in superpower activity across the two system-periods and, more generally, the decline in superpower dominance of international relations. No longer were the superpowers omnipotent international actors and no longer did states acquiesce in superpower pressure as readily as in the bipolar system. For the USSR, there was, too, a decline in the frequency of crisis escalation from bipolarity to polycentrism. This finding tends to support the view that the USSR developed a greater interest in stability than it had in the bipolar system, and that it did not as often perceive a need to escalate crises to achieve its foreign policy goals. In other words, the USSR, like the US, acquired a stake in preservation of the *status quo* in

TABLE II.6.12.a. Superpower Effectiveness in Crises by System Structure, 1945–85: US

	Did not Contribute		Escalated		Effective			
Bipolarity	21	30%	7	10%	42	60%	70	40%
Polycentrism	43	41%	12	11%	51	48%	106	60%
	64	36%	19	11%	93	53%	176	100%

$X^2 = 2.49, p = .288$

TABLE II.6.12.b. Superpower Effectiveness in Crises by System Structure, 1945–85: USSR

	Did not contribute		Escalated		Effective			
Bipolarity	21	36%	20	34%	18	30%	59	42%
Polycentrism	49	61%	14	18%	17	21%	80	58%
	70	50%	34	25%	35	25%	139	100%

$X^2 = 9.33, p = .009$

the international system. Thus the expectations of role theory appear to gain some support from this finding as well.

Conclusion

From the findings presented above we are able to draw a number of preliminary conclusions about the effectiveness of superpower activity in crises. First, the characterization of US foreign policy in general as ineffective is not substantiated by our data. The rate at which US involvement in crises contributed to crisis abatement indicates a rather high level of success for the US in this regard. Regardless of the type of involvement, US activities have had a beneficial influence and have been effective tools for crisis abatement. Even when it engaged in direct military activity, it aided in crisis abatement more often than not. Therefore, regardless of the institutional, bureaucratic, and reactive aspects of the American foreign policy process, it responded effectively overall to the demands of crisis situations. It should be remembered, however, that while US effectiveness was generally manifested in the data, there were significant differences between levels of effectiveness when controlling for region and the structure of the international system. Systemic constraints and the extent of regional interest and influence had a definite impact upon US crisis effectiveness and involvement more generally.

As for the USSR, conclusions on effectiveness in terms of crisis abatement are more difficult to draw. If analyzed in an approach similar to the analysis of US effectiveness, one must conclude that the USSR was somewhat less effective than the U.S. This can only be a tentative conclusion, however, at this point. In terms of effectiveness at crisis abatement, the USSR was not as omnipotent as portrayed by some international relations scholars.

As for the role theory hypothesis regarding superpower foreign policy behavior, we do find some support in the crisis data presented above. Although there are distinct differences between the superpowers, such as when controlling for geographic region, some degree of similarity exists in the general patterns of crisis activity by the US and the USSR. In particular, when examining superpower crisis activity in Table II.6.4. we found that the two superpowers became involved in crises in similar ways. As a result, we take this as some preliminary evidence of role constraints on superpower activity in crises. But as we move beyond the aggregate level other intervening factors, such as geography and system structure, had an influence on the exact nature of the activity in particular situations. Thus, determination of the influence of role constraints demands more indepth case analysis.

Notes

1. The following discussion will primarily focus on Jonsson's work in the area of role theory, because of its exclusive attention to superpower roles in the international system. Some important work in role theory and international relations, such as Brecher, Steinberg and Stein (1969), Holsti (1970), and Wish (1977, 1980), has discussed the superpower role, but was broader in scope and did not delve into specifics. Role theory studies by Walker (1979, 1981, 1987) were primarily concerned with the empirical congruence between national role conceptions and role enactments (or actual behavior). In this regard, Walker's work lends insight into the empirical validity of role theory hypotheses, but does not directly pertain to the discussion of superpower role conceptions that will follow. Hermann's (1987) perceptive work on superpower involvement with other states focuses on the regime orientation of the US and the USSR toward Third World countries.

2. In some respects the interpretations put forth by this school of thought fit with the general tenets of role theory explanations of superpower behavior.

3. The third school basically emerges as a bureaucratic politics model, along the lines developed in the American foreign policy literature (see Allison, 1971). For a critique of the bureaucratic politics model as applied to Soviet foreign policy decision-making, see K. Dawisha (1980).

4. Pipes (1981) provides a good overview of his interpretation of Soviet foreign policy motivations. Kennan's views are best described in his famous "X" article in *Foreign Affairs* (1947) or alternatively in Kennan (1983).

5. See, for example, the collection of studies proceeding from a bureaucratic perspective contained in Halperin and Kanter (1973).

6. The major exceptions to this are CACI (1976, 1978, 1980), Blechman and Kaplan (1978), S. S. Kaplan (1981), and the collection of studies of superpower foreign policy contained in Kegley and McGowan (1982).

7. Depending upon the foreign policy goals of a superpower during a particular crisis, the term "effectiveness" may be a bit misleading, since escalation of a crisis may well be the goal. However, if we assume that stable, peaceful international relationships are sought by both superpowers, as can be presumed from role theory, then effectiveness should in general be interpreted as success toward achieving crisis abatement.

8. Dawisha (1984) also supports at least some of these assertions in her study of Soviet intervention in Czechoslovakia in 1968. She states that Romania and Yugoslavia both felt that one of the main reasons the USSR intervened during the Prague Spring Crisis was because it perceived the risk of Western military counter-action to be negligible.

9. All descriptions of crises are drawn from Brecher and Wilkenfeld *et al.* (1988: I. Part V).

7 Severity and Importance of Third World Crises: Middle East and Africa

Michael Brecher and Patrick James

Introduction

International crises occur frequently in the Third World, especially in the Middle East and Africa. In some cases, these interstate conflicts are produced by political, economic and social upheavals at the domestic level. The ongoing turbulence in Lebanon is a notable illustration; the instability of that quasi-regime has transcended its borders, resulting in numerous international crises and significant changes. In other instances, external crises have fueled the fires of internal disruption. A dramatic example is the exacerbation of the struggle for power in Chad from 1978 onwards by the frequent military interventions of Qaddhafi's Libya. It would not be difficult to cite other important changes in foreign and domestic political systems that have resulted from crises in the Middle East and Africa.

Despite the high probability that international crises bring about systemic changes, it is difficult to predict their long-term effects. The crisis that accompanied the October-Yom Kippur War of 1973, for example, obviously had significant implications for the future of the Middle East state system. However, it would not have been easy at that time to anticipate the impact of the Yom Kippur War in specific terms. Would it change the existing power structure in the region? How likely was the 1973–74 Middle East Crisis to produce new alliances or overturn old ones? Could rules of the game be expected to change as a result of that crisis?

The search for a predictive device entails certain conceptual questions:

1. What is an international system?
2. What is an international crisis?
3. How are the immediate severity and long-term importance of a crisis related to one another?

The first two questions were carefully explored in Chapter 2 above. Suffice it, therefore to recall the definitions of these concepts.

An *international system* was defined in general terms as a set of actors who are situated in a configuration of power (structure), are involved in regular patterns of interaction (process), are separated from other units by boundaries set by a given topic (issue), and are constrained in their behavior from within (context) and from outside the system (environment). It is apparent that several systems exist simultaneously in the Middle East and in Africa.

In the former, the members of the Arab League may be regarded as actors in a system that encompasses most of the region. (The exceptions are Israel, Iran and Turkey. The first is excluded as a common enemy, while the other two are non-Arab Muslim states.) This system exists within boundaries set by several issues, among which Palestinian Arab self-determination has been a major concern of the organization almost since its inception. Members of the Arab League interact in the context of a common language and heritage and similar cultural traits.

In Africa, the member-states of the Organization for African Unity (OAU) are actors in an international system that is virtually coterminous with the continent itself; the Union of South Africa is the notable, long-term exception. That system exists within boundaries set by the issue of pan-Africanism, the central ideological goal of the OAU since its inception. African states interact in the context of a common colonial and racial heritage. As with the Middle East, the remainder of the international polity constitutes the environment of this subsystem, constraining action through its preponderant capabilities.

An *international crisis* was defined as a situational change in an international system characterized by two individually necessary and collectively sufficient conditions: (1) distortion in the type and an increase in the intensity of *disruptive interactions*, with an accompanying high probability of military hostilities; and (2) a *challenge* to the existing structure of the system. Conditions 1 and 2 denote a significant increase in the intensity of interactions and in the strain that structure undergoes. International crises encompass change. While it is recognized that developments in a system need not occur by leaps and bounds, and can result from cumulative events, such change is the product of something other than a crisis.

For purposes of analysis and prediction, the immediate intensity and long-term impact of an international crisis must be distinguished from each other. The intensity, i.e., the *severity* of a crisis, is assessed in terms of its destabilizing effects on an international system. Stability, it will be recalled (Chapter 2), was defined as change within explicit limits, while instability designates change beyond a normal range of fluctuating interaction. These concepts were operationalized in terms of the number of changes in the structure of a system, its process, or both. The absence of change indicates pure stability; its presence, some degree of instability.

The long-term impact of a crisis, its *importance*, is measured by the extent of disequilibrium it has produced in an international system. Equilibrium and disequilibrium were operationalized in terms of the quality (significance) of change in structure, process, or both, ranging from total reversibility to absolute irreversibility.

Acute distortions in an existing structure or process may – or may not – lead to disequilibrium. Thus disequilibrium, *ipso facto*, denotes a high level of instability, but the reverse does not necessarily obtain. Every international crisis entails instability. But not all crises will result in irreversible changes in structure or process. Such changes, that is, disequilibrium of a system, occur only when the forces that tend to restore a balance fail to operate.

Indicators of Severity and Importance

We turn now to the examination of the severity and importance of international crises in two Third World regions. Tables II.7.16. and II.7.17. at the end of this chapter present the 63 international crises in the Middle East and the 89 in Africa from 1929 to 1985 that have been identified by the ICB Project. The crisis actors in each case and its duration are also listed.[1] (The scores that appear for overall severity and importance will be explained at a later point.)

The Severity of an international crisis will be measured by six indicators: number of actors, great power or superpower involvement, geostrategic salience, heterogeneity, issues, and extent of violence. These variables cover a wide range of system characteristics. The number of crisis actors demarcates a set of participants and an attendant power structure. The extent of violence measures the intensity of the process of hostile interaction. Boundaries are set by the issues in dispute. The geostrategic salience of the location of a crisis provides a context for interaction, while involvement by major powers represents an environmental constraint. Heterogeneity bridges the gap between actor–level and international crisis, since it gauges diversity among participants. Each of these six severity indicators will now be defined in operational terms. Scales will be provided for the indicators, along with illustrations corresponding to the scale points.

One indicator of severity is the number of direct participants in an international crisis: the presence of more crisis actors signifies wider embryonic change during a crisis. As Tables II.7.1.a. and II.7.1.b. indicate, the *number of actors* ranges from one to six or more. It is noteworthy that most of the cases had one or two actors, for the Middle East and Africa are regions in which the spillover of conflict is assumed to be widespread.[2]

TABLE II.7.1.a. Scale for Actors: Middle East Crises

Scale Points	No. of Cases*	% of Cases*	Criterion	Example
6	3	5	6 (or more) crisis actors	Israel Independence 1948–49
5	2	3	5	October-Yom Kippur War 1973–74
4	7	11	4	Basra/Kharg Island 1984
3	7	11	3	Lebanon War 1982
2	19	30	2	Saudi/Yemen War 1933–34
1	25	40	1	Breakup of UAR 1961

* N = 63.

TABLE II.7.1.b. Scale for Actors: Africa Crises

Scale Points	No. of Cases*	% of Cases*	Criterion	Example
6	1	1	6 (or more) crisis actors	War in Angola 1975–76
5	1	1	5	Shaba II 1978
4	2	2	4	Congo II 1964
3	9	10	3	Chad/Libya VI 1983–84
2	31	35	2	Congo I: Katanga 1960–62
1	45	51	1	Expulsion of Tunisians 1985

* N = 89.

Other states and, frequently, transnational (non-state) actors were *involved actors*; that is, they provided verbal, political, economic, semi-military or direct military support to a crisis actor or its adversary. The analytical distinction between *crisis actor* and *involved/adversarial actor* – the latter does not perceive the situational change as a crisis for itself – partly explains the ubiquity of single actor-cases in Africa, even in many of the frequent bilateral border crises. For example, State A, perceiving a threat, but not the likelihood of war or time constraints – or both – mobilizes forces or moves troops to a frontier, triggering a crisis for State B. The former, while deeply involved as the triggering entity and adversary, is not a crisis actor if either of the other two necessary conditions of a unit-level, foreign policy crisis is absent.

This configuration occurs frequently in African cases, as illustrated by Raids on SWAPO, March 1979. The South African Defense Forces attacked soldiers and bases of the SWAPO liberation movement in neighboring Angola, triggering a crisis for Angola. South Africa was an involved actor as the triggering entity and Angola's adversary. SWAPO, too, was heavily involved as a non-state actor, like the United Nations. The latter, through a Security Council resolution on 28 March, condemned South Africa and demanded an immediate end to its provocative acts. While South Africa catalyzed that international crisis, Angola was the only state which perceived the situation as a crisis for itself.

Involvement refers to the extent of great power/superpower adversarial behavior in international crisis.[3] As illustrated by Tables II.7.2.a. and II.7.2.b., involvement

TABLE II.7.2.a. Scale for Involvement: Middle East Crises

Scale Points	No. of Cases	% of Cases	Criterion*	Example*
6	4	7	Both superpowers (SPs) crisis actors	Suez-Sinai Campaign 1956–57
5	2	4	One SP a crisis actor, the other high involvement	Lebanon/Iraq Upheaval 1958
4	3	5	Both SPs high involvement	North/South Yemen II 1979
3	4	7	One SP a crisis actor, the other low or no involvement	War of Attrition 1970
2	12	21	One SP high involvement, the other low or no involvement	Jordan/Syria Confrontation 1980
1	32	56	Both SPs low or no involvement	Iraqi Threat 1976

TABLE II.7.2.b. Scale for Involvement: Africa Crises

Scale Points	No. of Cases	% of Cases	Criterion*	Example*
6	2	3	Both superpowers (SPs) crisis actors	Congo II 1964
5	1	1	One SP a crisis actor, the other high involvement	Shaba II 1978
4	4	5	Both SPs high involvement	Ogaden I 1964
3	1	1	One SP a crisis actor, the other low or no involvement	Raid on Gafsa 1980
2	12	14	One SP high involvement, the other low or no involvement	Mozambique Raid 1981
1	64	76	Both SPs low or no involvement	Burkina Faso/Mali 1985–86

* Applies to cases 1945–85; excludes first five cases in Table II.7.17.

by the powers has ranged from low or no participation to both superpowers as crisis actors. The majority of crises in the Middle East have not involved the major powers directly, although several have included the United States and the Soviet Union as crisis actors: Azerbaijan 1945–46; Suez-Sinai Campaign 1956–57; Six Day War 1967; and October-Yom Kippur War 1973–74.

It is also clear that African crises have not stimulated a great deal of activity by the major powers. While that may change in the future, the past record is one of low or no involvement by the powers in most of the crises in Africa. Of course, there are exceptions. An example of the penultimate scale point is the Shaba II Crisis 1978. The United States and France were crisis actors, the former providing aid and logistical support to the latter which sent troops to help the Zairean government suppress the rebels. The Soviet Union supplied arms and trained the rebel forces.

Geostrategic salience refers to the location of an international crisis in terms of its natural resources, distance from major power centers, and so forth. Geostrategic assets vary over time: oil- and uranium-producing regions acquired greater salience since the 1950s; coal-producing regions became less significant. Key waterways and choke points such as the Suez Canal have retained their relevance over the decades. Tables II.7.3.a. and II.7.3.b. display the scale points for geostrategic salience with illustrations. They range from relevance to one subsystem up to the global system itself.

TABLE II.7.3.a. Scale for Geostrategic Salience: Middle East Crises

Scale Points	No. of Cases	% of Cases	Criterion	Example
5	3	5	Global system	Six Day War 1967
4	3	5	Dominant system and more than one subsystem	Middle East Campaign 1941
3	7	11	Dominant system and one subsystem	War of Attrition II 1970
2	8	13	More than one subsystem	Kuwait Independence 1961
1	42	66	One subsystem	Iraq Nuclear Reactor 1981

TABLE II.7.3.b. Scale for Geostrategic Salience: Africa Crises

Scale Points	No. of Cases	% of Cases	Criterion	Example
5	0	0	Global system	none
4	1	1	Dominant system and more than one subsystem	Ethiopian War 1935–36
3	6	7	Dominant system and one subsystem	Congo II 1964
2	10	11	More than one subsystem	Portuguese Invasion of Guinea 1970
1	72	81	One subsystem	Botswana Raid 1985

No less than 13 of the 63 Middle East crises were salient to the global or dominant system, for example, Occupation of Iran by British and Soviet forces in 1941–42, ostensibly to frustrate an Iranian shift to alignment with Germany during World War II. This pattern reaffirms the significance of events in the Middle East, although two-thirds of the crises within the region have been salient to only one subsystem, for example, Karameh 1968, a brief but sharp military encounter between the Israel Defense Forces and Jordan-backed PLO guerrillas.

As for African crises, none was relevant beyond the dominant system and more than one subsystem (e.g., the Congo II Crisis 1964 was salient to the Southern African subsystem, as well as the dominant East/West system because of direct superpower activity). If the World War II and colonial power crises in Africa are excluded, the scale points beyond the first would have significantly lower percentage frequencies: 81% of the crises have a minimal score. This, along with the distribution of data for involvement noted earlier, clearly illustrates the limited geostrategic significance of that continent and its peripheral nature *vis-à-vis* issues that are salient to the global system.

With respect to the extent of *heterogeneity*, severity is measured by the number, not the intensity, of attribute differences among adversaries.[5] The attributes are military capability, political regime, economic development, and culture. Tables II.7.4.a. and II.7.4.b. show the range of scale points, with no attribute differences at one extreme and four at the other. In 62% of the Middle East cases, there were three or more attribute differences (e.g., Gaza Raid, February 1955, with Egypt and Israel the adversaries, differing on political regime, i.e., military authoritarianism vs. Western democracy; economic development, i.e., developing vs. developed; and culture, i.e., Arab Islam vs. Judaism).

TABLE II.7.4.a. Scale for Heterogeneity: Middle East Crises

Scale Points	No. of Cases	% of Cases	Criterion	Example
5	19	30	Military, economic, political and cultural differences among adversaries	Syria Mobilization 1976
4	20	32	Three attribute differences	Basra/Kharg Island 1984
3	14	22	Two differences	Yemen War IV 1966–67
2	6	10	One difference	Lebanon Civil War II 1978
1	4	6	None	Formation of UAR 1958

TABLE II.7.4.b. Scale for Heterogeneity: Africa Crises

Scale Points	No. of Cases	% of Cases	Criterion	Example
5	31	35	Military, economic, political and cultural differences among adversaries	Ifni 1957
4	16	18	Three attribute differences	Libyan Intervention–Gambia 1980
3	26	29	Two differences	Omdurman Bombing Raid 1984
2	5	6	One difference	Algeria/Morocco Border 1963
1	11	12	None	Guinea Regime 1965

In over 80% of the African cases there were two or more attribute differences. Given that most African states exhibit limited divergence in economic development and military capability, it is unlikely that these attributes account for the high level of heterogeneity in African crises. The heterogeneity variable undoubtedly reflects the pervasiveness of cultural diversity. Designed by colonial powers, Africa's borders are inconsistent with tribal realities. In crises involving bordering states it is not uncommon for several cultures to be adversaries (e.g., the principal difference between Ethiopia and Somalia (Ethiopia/Somalia, Ogaden I and II Crises) is that Ethiopia is a primarily Christian, Amharic-speaking state, while the Somali nation is composed of Muslim clans speaking Arabic dialects).

Issue-areas denote generic substance, that is, groups or clusters of issues with a shared focus. These clusters can be grouped into four issue-areas: (1) military–security, incorporating territories, borders, free navigation, change in military balance, military incidents, and war; (2) political–diplomatic, including sovereignty, hegemony, and international influence; (3) economic–developmental, including the nationalization of property, raw materials, economic pressure such as boycotts and sanctions, and foreign exchange problems; and (4) cultural–status, comprising issues of ideology, and challenges to nonmaterial values and symbols. Tables II.7.5.a. and II.7.5.b. display the scale points for issues, which range from one nonmilitary issue to three issues. As evident, the overwhelming majority of Middle East crises focused on two issues, including military-security, or the latter by itself (e.g., Qalqilya 1956, affecting the military domain).

The majority of African crises focused on military–security issues alone. An example of broader issues at stake was the Rhodesian Settlement Crisis 1979–80, which incorporated three issues: the ongoing violence of the guerrilla war gave it a distinct military–security component; political–diplomatic issues arose as Rhodesia abandoned the illegal status conferred upon it as a result of its 1965 UDI and was succeeded by the newly-independent state of Zimbabwe; and the new state was

TABLE II.7.5.a. Scale for Issues: Middle East Crises

Scale Points	No. of Cases	% of Cases	Criterion	Example
5	1	2	Three issues	Israel Independence 1948–49
4	23	36	Two issues, including military–security	Azerbaijan 1945–46
3	29	46	Military–security alone	Onset Iran/Iraq War 1980
2	4	6	Two issues other than military–security	Palestine Partition 1947
1	6	10	One non-military–security issue	Jordan Waters 1963–64

TABLE II.7.5.b. Scale for Issues: Africa Crises

Scale Points	No. of Cases	% of Cases	Criterion	Example
5	2	2	Three issues	Rhodesian Settlement 1979–80
4	21	24	Two issues, including military–security	Rwanda/Burundi 1963–64
3	52	58	Military–security alone	Operation Askari 1983–84
2	2	2	Two issues other than military–security	Congo I: Katanga 1960–62
1	12	14	One non-military–security issue	Chad/Libya II 1978

culturally different from its predecessor: it was ruled by the black majority and adopted a socialist ideology). The narrow issue focus in understandable, given the instability of African boundaries and the ethnic conflicts that extend beyond the confines of a single state. By contrast, crises over three issues are scarce in Africa.

Last among the indicators of severity is the intensity of *violence* in an international crisis. Displayed by Tables II.7.6.a. and II.7.6.b., the scale points for violence range from none to full-scale war. Full-scale wars were the most common in the Middle East, followed closely by serious clashes: together they account for 35 of its 63 crises. This is in accordance with the universal image of the Middle East as a region in which escalating violence is almost the rule rather than the exception.

Minor and serious clashes are the most common levels of violence in African crises. This is plausible, for full-scale war means far greater cost for those who wage it. Since most African states are not in a position to engage in such a sustained high-level expenditure of resources, violence is less intense – but more frequent – than in the Middle East.

The extent of disequilibrium resulting from an international crisis, that is, its long-

TABLE II.7.6.a. Scale for Violence: Middle East Crises

Scale Points	No. of Cases	% of Cases	Criterion	Example
4	19	30	Full-scale war	Yemen War I 1962–63
3	16	25	Serious clashes	Litani Operation 1978
2	11	18	Minor clashes	Jordan Regime 1957
1	17	27	No violence	Bahrain Coup Attempt 1981–82

TABLE II.7.6.b. Scale for Violence: Africa Crises

Scale Points	No. of Cases	% of Cases	Criterion	Example
4	10	11	Full-scale war	Chad/Libya IV 1979
3	35	39	Serious clashes	Burkina Faso/Mali 1985–86
2	28	32	Minor clashes	Mauritania/Mali 1962–63
1	16	18	No violence	Nigeria/Cameroon Border 1981

term Importance, will be measured by four indicators of system change: change in power distribution; actors; rules of the game; and alliance configuration. The first two represent structural changes, while the latter two influence the process of interaction. Each of these effects is assessed three years after the end of a crisis. Although this time period is set arbitrarily, certain considerations favor it. Given the nature of macro-level changes, a shorter time would not permit them to unfold. This is true especially of rules of the game, for which change may be imperceptible unless measured in years. By contrast, if a longer period is selected, the competing effects of diverse crises and other international events could not be readily disentangled. As in the case of severity, the exposition of the indicators of importance will be accompanied by a descriptive analysis.

Effects on the *distribution of power* within an international system refer to change in both the number of power centers and the hierarchy of power. The scale points listed in Tables II.7.7.a. and II.7.7.b. range from no change in relative power among adversaries to change in the composition of states at the apex of a power pyramid. As evident, a change in the relative power of adversarial crisis actors is the modal outcome in the Middle East. Among the six cases of more extensive change, the most far-reaching is the Six Day War of 1967, which catapulted Israel to the top of the power pyramid at the expense of Egypt.

TABLE II.7.7.a. Scale for Change in Power: Middle East Crises

Scale Points	No. of Cases	% of Cases	Criterion	Example
4	1	2	Change in composition of states at the apex of the power pyramid	Israel Independence 1948–49
3	5	11	Change in the ranking of states among the five most powerful within the dominant system/subsystem	Formation of UAR 1958
2	26	57	Change in the relative power of adversarial crisis actors	Lebanon War 1982
1	14	30	No change in the relative power among adversaries	North/South Yemen II 1979

TABLE II.7.7.b. Scale for Change in Power: Africa Crises

Scale Points	No. of Cases	% of Cases	Criterion	Example
4	0	0	Change in composition of states at the apex of the power pyramid	None
3	1	2	Change in the ranking of states among the five most powerful within the dominant system/subsystem	East Africa Campaign 1940–41
2	25	45	Change in the relative power of adversarial crisis actors	Kenya/Somalia 1963–64
1	30	53	No change in relative power among adversaries	Lesotho Raid 1982

Given the lack of major power involvement, and generally limited geostrategic salience, Africa crises have less of an opportunity to affect the states at the top of the ladder. Consequently, there are no crises at the highest scale point. Change in the relative power of adversarial actors accounts for 45% of the Africa cases (e.g., Kenya emerged from a 1963–64 crisis with Somalia as the more powerful of the two as it demonstrated the ability to repulse Somalia's efforts to acquire its Northern Frontier District).

Change in *actors* comprises regime change, whether in orientation or type, and more basic structural shifts for one or more independent states as a result of an international crisis.[7] Tables II.7.8.a. and II.7.8.b. display the scale points which range from no change in actors to the creation/preservation/elimination of one or more state actors. Of the Middle East crises, 30% resulted in a change of some kind;

TABLE II.7.8.a. Scale for Change in Actors: Middle East Crises

Scale Points	No. of Cases	% of Cases	Criterion	Example
4	2	4	Creation/preservation/elimination of one or more state actors	Israel Independence 1948–49
3	1	2	Change in regime type	Lebanon/Iraq Upheaval 1958
2	11	24	Change in regime orientation	Lebanon War 1982
1	32	70	No change in actors or regimes	Lebanon Civil War II 1978

TABLE II.7.8.b. Scale for Change in Actors: Africa Crises

Scale Points	No. of Cases	% of Cases	Criterion	Example
4	7	13	Creation/preservation/elimination of one or more state actors	Gambia Coup Attempt 1981–82
3	3	5	Change in regime type	Nouakchott II 1977
2	1	2	Change in regime orientation	Chad/Libya IV 1979
1	45	80	No change in actors or regimes	Ogaden I 1964

for Africa, the figure is 20%. The relatively high frequency of the maximal scale point among African cases is interesting (e.g., as a result of the Rhodesian Settlement 1979–80, the state of Rhodesia was replaced by Zimbabwe). This result underscores the unsettled character of that Third World region.

Rules of the game refer to those norms derived from law, custom, morality or self-interest that serve as guidelines for legitimate behavior by the actors of a system. These rules may be informal or formally codified. As illustrated by Tables II.7.9.a. and II.7.9.b., the scale points range from no change to the creation or elimination of codified or tacit rules. Slightly more than one-half of the Middle East crises have been played out within the confines of accepted rules of the game. The most common change in rules is a decline in consensus, although there were 10 crises that generated more extreme changes, such as the Litani Operation in 1978, when large-scale Israeli forces penetrated deep into Lebanon, as they had not done before – a precedent for the Israeli invasion of Lebanon in 1982. In Africa, the overwhelming number of crises have been played out within the confines of the accepted rules of the game. The relative frequencies decline precipitously after that category.

Change in *alliance configuration* means a shift in the structure of international coalitions. Tables II.7.10.a. and II.7.10.b. list four scale-points, ranging from no

TABLE II.7.9.a. Scale for Change in Rules: Middle East Crises

Scale Points	No. of Cases	% of Cases	Criterion	Example
4	3	7	Creation or elimination of codified or tacit rules of the game	Biqa Valley Missiles 1981 1981
3	7	15	Breakdown in consensus	Shatt-al-Arab I 1959–60
2	11	24	Decline in consensus	Black September 1970
1	25	54	No change	North/South Yemen I 1972

TABLE II.7.9.b. Scale for Change in Rules: Africa Crises

Scale Points	No. of Cases	% of Cases	Criterion	Example
4	3	5.5	Creation or elimination of codified or tacit rules of the game	Entebbe Raid 1967
3	4	7	Breakdown in consensus	Raid on Angola 1979
2	4	7	Decline in consensus	Sahara 1975–76
1	45	80.5	No change	Sudan/Ethiopia Border 1983–84

TABLE II.7.10.a. Scale for Change in Alliances: Middle East Crises

Scale Points	No. of Cases	% of Cases	Criterion	Example
4	1	2	Formation/elimination of an alliance	October–Yom Kippur War 1973–74
3	4	9	Entry/exit of actor(s) into/from a formal or informal alliance	Azerbaijan 1945–46
2	8	17	Increase/decrease of cohesiveness within an existing alliance	Qalqilya 1956
1	33	72	No change	Cairo Agreement 1969

TABLE II.7.10.b. Scale for Change in Alliances: Africa Crises

Scale Points	No. of Cases	% of Cases	Criterion	Example
4	5	9	Formation/elimination of an alliance	Ethiopian War 1935–36
3	2	3	Entry/exit of actor(s) into/from a formal or informal alliance	Rhodesian Settlement 1979–80
2	10	18	Increase/decrease of cohesiveness within an existing alliance	Ogaden II 1977–78
1	39	70	No change	Chad/Nigeria Clashes 1983

change to the formation or elimination of an alliance. Among the Middle East crises, 28% resulted in a change in alliance. Only in one case, however, did an alliance form or break apart as the result of a crisis: the October–Yom Kippur War in 1973–74, when Egypt began to shift from a long-standing alignment with the Soviet Union to a pro-US posture, a consequence of superpower behavior during that crisis and its immediate aftermath.

Most Africa crises do not affect alliances. But there are numerous examples of change in alliance cohesion, possibly due to frequent regime changes and the highly personal nature of relationships among African Heads of State (e.g., upon its creation in 1980, Zimbabwe promptly joined a number of regional organizations: the OAU, the Southern African Development Coordinating Council, and the Front Line States.)

Six indicators of severity and four indicators of importance have been descriptively analyzed. The October–Yom Kippur Crisis will now be used as an in-depth illustration of the coding of these indicators for a specific international crisis.

Middle East Crisis 1973–74

The October–Yom Kippur Crisis is one of the most severe and important cases in the ICB Middle East data set.[8] The international crisis of 1973–74 began on 5 October with evidence of an impending massive disruption in the high level of conflictual interaction between Israel and its Arab adversaries. A concerted military

TABLE II.7.11.a. Index of Severity: 1973–74 Middle East Crisis

Severity Indicators		Weight	Assigned Score
S_1	Actors	4	5
S_2	Involvement	4	6
S_3	Geostrategy	2	5
S_4	Heterogeneity	2	5
S_5	Issues	2	4
S_6	Violence	1	4

$$\text{Severity Index}^* = S^1 = 0.134 \left(\sum_{k=1}^{6} W_k S_k \right) - 1$$
$$= 0.134(4(5) + 4(6) + 2(5) + 2(5) + 2(4) + 1(4)) - 1$$
$$= 9.18$$

*The coefficients used in the conversions to 10-point scales are derived as follows: the lower and upper boundaries (minimal and maximal weighted scores) for Severity are 15 and 82. In order to convert these scores to a 10-point scale, it is necessary to multiply by 0.134 and subtract 1 from each value. Similarly, the lower and upper boundaries for Importance are 8 and 32, making 0.375 and 2 the appropriate parameters.

TABLE II.7.11.b. Index of Importance: 1973–74 Middle East Crisis

Importance Indicators		Weight	Assigned Score
i_1	Power change	3	3
i_2	Actor change	2	2
i_3	Rules change	2	3
i_4	Alliance change	1	4

$$\text{Importance Index}^* = I^1 = 0.375 \left(\sum_{k=1}^{4} u_j l_j \right) - 2$$

$$= 0.375(3(3) + 2(2) + 2(3) + 1(4)) - 2$$

$$= 6.63$$

attack by Egypt and Syria the next day and other events that followed posed a serious challenge to the structure of the Middle East subsystem and, toward the end of the crisis, a challenge to the dominant system as well. The result, as evident in the aggregated scores for the ten indicators listed in Tables II.7.11.a. and II.7.11.b., is a very high Overall Severity (9.18) and Overall Importance (6.63). The structure of each index will be explained at a later point.

Background

The West Bank of the Jordan River, the Gaza Strip, the Sinai Peninsula, and the Golan Heights had been occupied by Israel since the Six Day War of June 1967. In March 1969, Egypt launched a War of Attrition against Israeli forces in the Sinai. A US-sponsored cease-fire was accepted by both sides in August 1970 – but not a US plan for peace in the region, the Rogers Plan. In April 1973, Israel's forces were mobilized when its leaders perceived Egyptian exercises to be a prelude to an invasion of Israel; the invasion was to occur six months later.

On 13 September 1973, 13 Syrian MIGs and one Israeli Mirage were shot down in an air battle over the Golan Heights. When Syria did not react immediately to this dramatic defeat, some Israeli leaders became suspicious that Damascus was planning a major retaliation. The Israel Defense Forces (IDF) in the north were strengthened, and precautionary measures were taken in the south. Syria's massing of three infantry divisions, tanks and artillery, and a mobilization of Syrian reserves, along with the evacuation of Soviet military advisors and their families from Damascus and Cairo, were all noted by Israeli intelligence. The IDF was put on the highest state of alert. Nevertheless, as late as 5 October 1973, the Director of Israel's military intelligence perceived an outbreak of war in the immediate future to be very unlikely. This erroneous judgment was based on two Israeli misperceptions: that Egypt's inferior air power would not permit it to launch a war against Israel, and that Syria would not go it alone, without Egypt's active participation.

Severity Indicators

Actors

Five states became crisis actors at different points in time during the Middle East upheaval of 1973–74 – Israel (5 October), Syria (10 October), the United States (12 October), Egypt (18 October) and the Soviet Union (22 October). There were also many involved actors, notably Arab states from the Near East Core such as Iraq and Saudi Arabia, and from North Africa such as Algeria, Libya and Morocco. These states supported the Arab crisis actors by several means, including the dispatch of token military contingents to the battlefield and a draconian oil price increase, along with an oil embargo against the Netherlands and the United States.

A deployment of Egyptian forces toward the Suez Canal on 5 October 1973 and a change from a defensive to an offensive posture triggered a crisis for Israel. That night, Israel's military intelligence reported an impending Egyptian attack across the Canal scheduled for the following day. Israel immediately raised the IDF's alert level and strengthened its forces along the northern and southern borders. The war began on 6 October with a simultaneous attack by Egyptian and Syrian forces. By the 10th, after heavy losses, Israeli forces succeeded in reversing the tide of battle in the north, triggering a crisis for Syria. Syria responded not only on the battlefield but also with an urgent call for an increase of Egyptian military pressure on Israel in the south and an appeal to the Soviet Union for aid. During the next three days, Israeli forces advanced ten kilometers beyond the 1967 cease-fire lines into Syrian territory.

Israeli Prime Minister Meir agreed to a cease-fire in place on 12 October. Its rejection by Egypt and Syria triggered a crisis for the United States, which feared a possible confrontation with the USSR: seven Soviet airborne divisions had been placed on an increased state of readiness. The Soviet commitment to the Arabs, in the form of a massive resupply of arms by air and sea, indicated to Washington that Moscow would not tolerate an unambiguous Arab defeat comparable to that of 1967.

The successful Egyptian crossing of the Suez Canal was followed on 14 October by the largest tank battle in military history, with Egypt suffering a major defeat. On the 16th, the Israelis crossed the Canal and threatened to surround the Egyptian Third Army. A crisis for Egypt was triggered when President Sadat became aware of its worsening military position. Egypt's response was to press the Soviet Union to obtain a cease-fire agreement. This was hastily arranged by Brezhnev and Kissinger in Moscow on 19–20 October; and the first cease-fire of the 1973 war, formally imposed by the United Nations, took effect on the 22nd. When the Egyptians continued their attempt to open up an escape route for their Third Army, fighting broke out once more.

Israeli violations of the 22 October cease-fire agreement triggered a crisis for the Soviet Union. Moscow responded on the 24th with a dispatch of naval vessels and a Note from Brezhnev to Nixon containing a clear warning that, unless the Israeli onslaught on the west bank of the Suez Canal was stopped at once, the USSR might intervene unilaterally on the battlefield. The United States responded with mounting pressure on Israel to stop fighting and to allow nonmilitary supplies to reach the Third Army. At the same time, President Nixon issued a sharp reply to Moscow: most of the US armed forces, including the Strategic Air Command with its nuclear capability, were put on a high state of alert, namely, Defensive Condition 3. The crisis escalated further when, on 25 October, a Soviet freighter arrived in Alexandria reportedly carrying nuclear weapons. Finally, on 26 October 1973, a US/Soviet-sponsored Security Council resolution calling for a second cease-fire was accepted by all the parties. Thus, in terms of the actor component, the October–Yom Kippur Crisis was one of the most severe international crises since the end of the Second World War, scoring 5 on a six-point scale of actor participation.

Involvement The crisis of 1973–1974 was even more severe in terms of involvement by the superpowers, point 6 on a six-point scale. The United States and the USSR were crisis actors in confrontation with each other, as demonstrated by the Soviet threat of direct military intervention in Sinai and the American counter-threat expressed in the nuclear alert. Only the Cuban Missile Crisis of 1962 was more acute in the nuclear dimension of superpower behavior.

More tangibly, both superpowers were lavish in the supply of arms and equipment to their client states – during and after the October–Yom Kippur War. The Soviets began a combined airlift/sealift on 8 October, the United States on the 14th. Apart from urgently-needed replacements for Israeli planes and tanks lost on both fronts, the latter extended $2.2 billion in emergency military assistance at the end of the war. Moreover, the cease-fire agreements were worked out between the superpowers. Premier Kosygin arrived in Cairo on 16 October to persuade Egypt to accept a cease-fire. At first unsuccessful, Soviet aerial reconnaissance persuaded Sadat within two days to accept this advice. Secretary of State Kissinger visited Moscow on 19–20 October; and he and Brezhnev hammered out a draft resolution for the Security Council calling for an immediate cease-fire. The Council adopted this resolution within hours.

The two superpowers remained dangerously involved during the peak stress phase of the 1973–74 crisis, from 22 to 26 October. The Soviets, as noted, threatened to land paratroops to save the encircled Egyptian Third Army from destruction. The United States signaled its determination to prevent direct Soviet military intervention. Ultimately, Israel yielded to US pressure on the Third Army issue, just as all the principal regional protagonists were to yield to American mediation.

Talks between Egypt and Israel, with the active participation of Kissinger, continued for two months and concentrated on withdrawal to the post-Six Day War lines, the problem of the encircled Third Army, and an exchange of prisoners. A Disengagement Agreement was signed on 18 January 1974, with Israel agreeing to withdraw twenty kilometers from the Canal and the size of both forces being reduced. The negotiations between Israel and Syria took much longer, with US involvement no less intense – or crucial – for the outcome. Israel's demand for a complete list of all Israeli prisoners-of-war was negotiated by Kissinger in February

1974. In March, Syria announced that it had decided to resume the war immediately. Shelling of Israeli-held positions in the north and firing back and forth continued through the spring of 1974 in a mini-war of attrition. On 2 May, Kissinger began a month of shuttle diplomacy, traveling between Damascus and Jerusalem with side trips to Riyadh, Amman and Cairo. In the final US-induced agreement, Israel returned parts of the Syrian town of Quneitra but kept control over two of the three strategic hills in the area where heavy weapons were forbidden. A UN buffer zone was established. As in the case of the Israel–Egypt agreement, a US Memorandum of Understanding, with pledges of large-scale military and economic aid, was given to Israel. The Israel–Syria Disengagement Agreement was signed on 31 May 1974, terminating the October–Yom Kippur Crisis–War for Israel, Syria, the Soviet Union and the United States.

Geostrategic Salience The geostrategic salience of the October–Yom Kippur Crisis, too, was the maximum, that is, point 5 on a five-point scale. The Suez Canal is a key choke point in the transportation nexus between Europe on the one hand and East Africa, South and Southeast Asia on the other. Furthermore, the vast oil resources of the Gulf region and the rapid increase in petroleum prices, along with the embargo, made this crisis salient to the global system as a whole, that is, to the dominant (super-power) system and almost all subsystems, which are dependent on a regular supply of imported oil.

The strategic significance of the Middle East is accentuated by two additional factors. Unlike Europe, this region remains a "grey zone" of competition in which the United States and the USSR assume the right – and perceive the obligation – to be actively involved lest their adversary enhance its influence with one or more formally uncommitted states. Moreover, the location of the Middle East in close proximity to Soviet Central Asia, with its large Muslim population and centers of industrial/military development, gives to this region very high power salience: to the United States, as a region of opportunity, along with economic and strategic resources; and to the Soviet Union, as a region of opportunity and high potential threat to the stability of heartland centers of population and industry. An international crisis in the Middle East, and especially within the Arab-Israel protracted conflict, is of higher salience to the superpowers than crises in any other Third World regional subsystem.

Heterogeneity The October–Yom Kippur Crisis was among a substantial group of cases in the entire ICB data set (110 of 323 of 34%) with the highest possible heterogeneity; that is, there were differences among pairs of adversaries on all four attributes – military capability, economic development, political regime and cultural traits. Thus, while the principal regional protagonists – Egypt, Israel, Syria – were middle powers in global terms, each was confronted with a superpower allied to an adversary. Similarly, an economically underdeveloped Egypt faced the most advanced industrial state in the international system, the United States. There were several types of regimes, from Western democracy in one coalition (US, Israel) to various kinds of authoritarianism in the other – Communist (USSR), combined military-party (Syria), a charismatic leader (Egypt). And in the cultural domain, Judaism confronted Islam in the Israeli–Arab confrontation. Heterogeneity in this crisis, notably cultural, was accentuated by acute "dissensus" on rules of the game among the Middle East crisis actors, for example, Arab nonrecognition of Israel's legitimacy and the corresponding Arab assumption of a right to expunge Israel as a sovereign state.

Issues There were military and political issues in the 1973–74 Middle East Crisis. Territory was a major focus of dispute, with Egypt and Syria trying to regain their lost territories of the 1967 War, Sinai and the Golan Heights, respectively, and Israel striving to retain those territories as bargaining chips in future negotiations for a peace settlement. Borders, too, remained in dispute, within the larger territorial issue. For the superpowers, the principal issue was relative influence in a resource-rich, strategically located region of predominantly nonaligned states. And for the less powerful crisis actors, there were the additional issues of the regional military balance and the survival of Israel as a viable state. Thus, this indicator of the 1973–74 crisis scored high but less than the maximum, 4 on a five-point scale.

Violence   The October–Yom Kippur Crisis ranks among the most severe of all post-World War II international crises in terms of violence. A full-scale war raged for twenty days. Casualties were in the tens of thousands. The tank battle of 14 October 1973 involved more than two thousand tanks. Losses of equipment on both sides were staggering. This very costly conventional war was aggravated by threats to use nuclear weapons, reportedly by Israel during the early days of setback on the battle-field, potentially, by Egypt in late October with the reported arrival of Soviet nuclear weapons in Alexandria, and implicitly by the United States through its nuclear alert. In short, the indicator of violence manifested the highest severity, 4 on a four-point scale, a full-scale war of exceptional intensity.

Taken together, the six indicators of severity in the October–Yom Kippur Crisis generate an overall score of 9.18 on a 10-point scale, as noted, making it one of the five most severe cases in the ICB data set of 323 international crises from 1929 to 1985.

Importance Indicators   The 1973–74 Middle East Crisis posed several challenges to the structure of the international system. At the global level, the oil embargo undermined the stability of the economies of Western Europe and Japan. In addition, many regions with underdeveloped economies came under grave pressure as a result of the unleashing of a powerful economic weapon by the Arab states. Alliances were tested. The pre-1973 hierarchy of power in the Middle East was assailed. And rule "dissensus" widened. What then were the consequences of this crisis for international systems in the years that followed?

Power Change   There were substantial changes in the distribution of power within the Arab–Israeli subsystem. Israel had been the preeminent state in terms of regional capability following its overwhelming victory in the Six Day War. The 1973 war, however, marked the resurgence of Egypt's and Syria's military capability, along with a shift in the Middle East power hierarchy. Israel's brief tenure as the regional superpower reverted to relative equality between Israel and Egypt at the apex of the Arab-Israeli power pyramid, with Syria a serious contender for equal status. It was, at a higher level of capability, similar to the hierarchy of power within the Arab–Israeli system after the 1956–57 Sinai–Suez Campaign.

As for the balance of influence between the superpowers in the Arab–Israeli conflict zone, the United States seems to have been the principal beneficiary. Almost from the outset (8 October), it befriended Israel – but later Egypt as well. Through the cease-fire negotiations and beyond, the United States attained credibility as a Middle East mediator, in the world generally and among the crisis actors in particular. It seemed able to persuade them of empathy for Egyptian and Syrian goals, as well as for vital Israeli security interests. The US role was enhanced by a change in its policy, namely, the supply of arms to Saudi Arabia and other lesser Arab states, at the same time that the historic commitment to Israel remained unchanged. The Soviets, by contrast, lost their effective bridgehead in Egypt; their support became confined to Syria. Thus the extent of power change registered 3 on a four-point scale, that is, a shift in relative power among adversaries.

Actor Change   No actor was eliminated; nor were new ones created. However, regime orientations changed markedly. At the outset of the October–Yom Kippur Crisis, Egypt was a Soviet client, though less so than in the Nasser era. It remained almost entirely dependent on the USSR for a wide range of advanced weapons, including bombers, fighter planes and tanks, without which the military option to regain control of Sinai was not feasible. That dependence was even more glaring during the October–Yom Kippur War, when the Soviet combined sealift/airlift operation enabled Egypt to sustain the heavy losses in equipment from 6 October onward. Syria's dependence on the Soviets was more striking at the outset and continued throughout the war, as replacements for lost equipment enabled the Syrian army to prevent an Israeli breakthrough to Damascus.

During the war, however, Egypt began the process of changing its alignment. Notwithstanding the Soviet threat to intervene on the battlefield in Egypt's favor, it was American diplomatic pressure on Israel that rescued the Egyptian Third Army from annihilation. Moreover, it was Kissinger's mediation that led to the Egypt–Israel Disengagement Agreement of January 1974 and a partial Israeli withdrawal from the Suez Canal. A US pledge to replace the Soviet Union as Egypt's principal arms supplier completed the process of a basic change in Egypt's orientation toward the superpowers at the conclusion of the crisis.

The shift in Egypt's alignment made the Soviets more interested in strengthening their Syrian connection – and made Syria more prepared to strengthen its alignment with Moscow. This had the major benefits for Syria of a steady and increasing flow of Soviet weapons, including advanced SAM batteries, planes and tanks, along with Soviet diplomatic and political support. For Israel, the experience of 1973–74 strengthened its dependence on the United States – for arms, economic aid, and political and diplomatic support in international organizations, where a pro-Arab phalanx in the Third World, supported by the Soviet bloc, threatened Israel's legitimacy as an international actor (e.g., the UN General Assembly's "Zionism as Racism" resolution of 1975). In short, actor change for this crisis registered 2 on a four-point scale.

Rules Change Informal rules were maintained during the 1973 war, apart from a brief resort to surface-to-surface missiles by Syria that caused heavy damage and casualties to an Israeli *kibbutz*, and a responsive bombing of Syrian urban centers by Israel. Much more significant was the setting in motion of a change in the basic rules of the Arab–Israeli game, dramatized by Sadat's journey to Jerusalem in November 1977. The deeply-rooted Arab consensus on Israel – politicide – was shattered by the ensuing Camp David Accords (1978) and the Egypt–Israel Peace Treaty (1979). Viewed in the perspective of this change in Arab–Israel rules of the game, the *de facto* King Hussein–Foreign Minister Peres agreement on the terms of an international peace conference, the 1987 "London Document," is a continuation of the process initiated by Egypt–Israel peaceful coexistence a decade earlier.

Alliance Change Alliances were severely shaken by the 1973–74 October–Yom Kippur Crisis. Fissures within NATO widened as the United States mounted an airlift to Israel while most of its European allies refused to cooperate. The cleavage widened further when, on 6 November 1973, the EEC issued a pro-Arab declaration of attitudes to the conflict, calling for Israeli withdrawal to pre-5 June 1967 borders and affirming the Palestinian Arab unfettered right to self-determination. Within the Middle East, the alliance between Egypt and Syria crumbled under the weight of divergence of policy toward the superpowers, especially during the negotiations leading to the disengagement of forces. And the Sadat peace initiative in 1977, gestating during the aftermath of the 1973-74 crisis, was to shatter the pattern of alliances among Middle East Arab states based on, *inter alia*, the illegitimacy of Israel as a state. Taken together, this registered point 4 on the four-point scale for alliance change. In short, the aftermath of the October–Yom Kippur Crisis was a transformation of the Middle East subsystem and basic change in the structure of both global and regional systems, which explains the very high score (6.63), as noted, for this crisis in terms of overall importance.

Having explained the coding of a major Third World international crisis, the next task is to create indices of severity and importance based on the two sets of indicators. This will facilitate the prediction of overall importance on the basis of overall severity.

Indices of Severity and Importance

Severity and importance are hypothesized to have a relation of cause and effect. The rationale is that destabilizing effects during a crisis (severity) can be expected to penetrate the structure of an international system and, over time, to generate change (importance), large or small.

All other things being equal, an index based on the presumed causal linkages among its constituents has more theoretical value than one that has been derived inductively. This is true for both severity and importance, because the structure of each index can then be understood in terms that are logical, as opposed to statistical. Accordingly, the initial development of indices is deductive. (Subsequent predictive performance can be used to argue for [or against] a role for an inductive generation of indices.)

The weight assigned to each indicator is based on its ostensible causal linkages with the others. Figures II.7.1. and II.7.2. display the networks of effects among the indicators of severity and importance, respectively.[9] Using the example of the October–Yom Kippur Crisis, Table II.7.11. shows how the scores for the 10 indicators have been weighted (based on the networks from Figures II.7.1. and II.7.2.) and aggregated to generate overall scores, that is, an *Index of Severity* and an *Index of Importance*. In the case of the 1973–74 Middle East Crisis, the final values of 9.18 and 6.63 for the respective indices result from the linear transformations demonstrated in the table. All of the scores in Tables II.7.16. and II.7.17. (at the end of this chapter) for Overall Severity and Overall Importance of Middle East and Africa crises, respectively, have resulted from the same conversions, and range somewhere from 1 to 10. This has been done in order to facilitate presentation and comparison.

Although the Severity and Importance scores in Tables II.7.16. and II.7.17. are based on indices that have been derived deductively, there are two reasons why the linkages among their components should be checked before proceeding with a quantitative/aggregate analysis of Severity and Importance. One is that each set of indicators is supposed to represent the same underlying concept. The components, therefore, should show a positive association with each other. The second reason is to make sure that the indicators are not too closely connected. Otherwise, one (or more) might be regarded as superfluous.

On the basis of these considerations, a moderate level of association among the indicators would be desirable. Tables II.7.12.a. and II.7.12.b. and II.7.13.a. and II.7.13.b. demonstrate that the components of the Severity and Importance indices have that property. Scanning the tables corresponding to the Middle East, 10 of the 15 bivariate correlations for Severity indicators are positive and statistically significant at the 5% level and, at the same time, none is overwhelming. The weakest linkage is heterogeneity with violence. All but one of the bivariate linkages for the importance indicators are statistically significant at the 5% level. As for the tables dealing with Africa, all of the bivariate measures of association are positive and, at the same time, none is overwhelming.

TABLE II.7.12.a.　Severity Indicators: Rank-Order Correlation Coefficients*: Middle East Crises

	S_2	S_3	S_4	S_5	S_6
S_1	0.41	0.47	0.36	0.16†	0.31
S_2		0.39	0.17†	0.20†	0.25
S_3			0.44	0.42	0.26
S_4				0.12†	0.07†
S_5					0.45

TABLE II.7.12.b.　Severity Indicators: Rank-Order Correlation Coefficients*: Africa Crises

	S^2	S^3	S^4	S^5	S^6
S^1	0.40	0.26	0.13†	0.51	0.42
S^2		0.42	0.18†	0.22	0.31
S^3			0.30	0.04†	0.43
S^4				0.10†	0.20
S^5					0.11†

* These coefficients and those in Tables II.7.13.a. and II.7.13.b. are generated by Kendall's tau, an appropriate measure of association between variables at the ordinal level. See Table II.7.11.a. for a listing of the indicators corresponding to $S_1, \ldots S_6$.
† $p > .05$

TABLE II.7.13.a.　Importance Indicators: Rank-Order Correlation Coefficients*: Middle East Crises

	i_2	i_3	i_4
i_1	0.38	0.25	0.48
i_2		0.12†	0.43
i_3			0.27

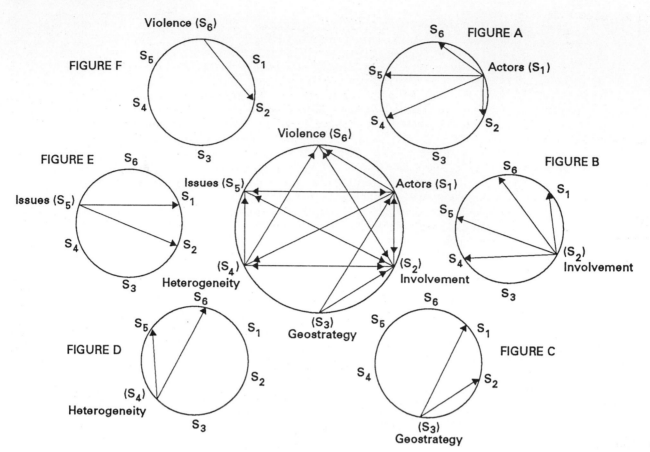

FIGURE II.7.1. Indicators of Severity: Network of Effects

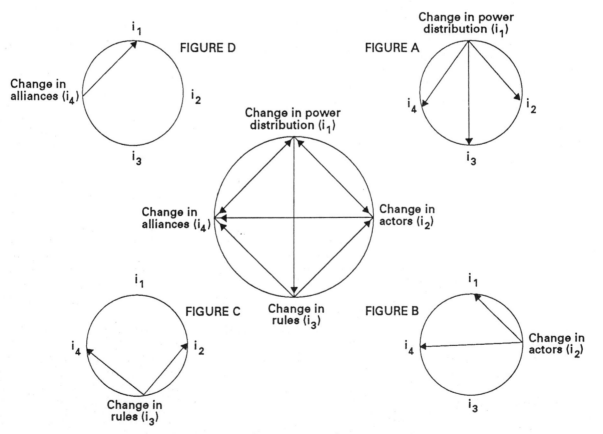

FIGURE II.7.2. Indicators of Importance: Network of Effects

TABLE II.7.13.b. Importance Indicators: Rank-Order Correlation Coefficients*: Africa Crises

	i^2	i^3	i^4
i^1	0.21†	0.17†	0.19†
i^2		0.23	0.41
i_3			0.39

* See Table II.7.11.b for a listing of the indicators corresponding to $i_1, \ldots i_4$.
† $p > .05$

Aggregate Analysis

There are two stages to the aggregate analysis of Severity and Importance. First, a contingency table will be used to probe for a general connection between the indices. Second, an ordinary least squares regression will be used to link Severity and Importance in a more precise manner. Since the emphasis of this inquiry is on patterns within the Third World, findings will be reported for the combined set of crises in Africa and the Middle East.

Severity and Importance scores will be converted to high and low categories for the tabular analysis. (An exact division at the median case is not feasible due to tied scores.) The breakpoints for Severity and Importance are 2.80 and 2.14, respectively.

Table II.7.14. reveals a connection between the indices. Of low-Severity crises, 61% scored low on Importance, while 55% of the high-Severity crises scored high on Importance. The tau b statistic for this table is 0.16, with a significance level of 5%. While hardly overwhelming, the linkage should be viewed in the context of the data, which are gathered from regions that are stereotyped as unpredictable.

TABLE II.7.14. Contingency Table for Severity and Importance

		Importance			
		High	Low		
Severity	High	29 / 55%	24 / 45%	53	52%
	Low	19 / 39%	30 / 61%	49	48%
		48 / 47%	54 / 53%	102	100%

TABLE II.7.15. Outliers from Regression Analysis

International Crisis	Severity	Importance	Standardized Residual
Israel Independence	6.24	9.25	3.72
Rhodesian Settlement	5.30	7.75	2.93
Ethiopian War	5.43	7.38	2.66
Breakup of UAR	1.95	5.88	2.50
Formation of UAR	1.55	5.50	2.35
Tan Tan	1.85	4.75	1.79
East Africa Campaign	4.63	5.50	1.61
Suez Canal	3.96	5.13	1.52
Mali Federation	2.08	4.38	1.48
Nouakchott II	1.28	4.00	1.43

In its general form the regression model linking Severity and Importance has achieved a modest level of success ($R^2 = .17$, N = 102). A closer look at the most poorly predicted cases may prove instructive. Table II.7.15. lists the 10 crises with the highest standardized residuals, along with their Severity and Importance scores. There is one obvious pattern in the table: all of the residuals are positive. In each instance, the Severity score produces an estimate of Importance that is too low. Perhaps some additional indicators of Severity would be useful in the quest to anticipate Importance, especially for those cases with the greatest impact on the international system.

Although several options could be pursued, limitations of space permit only one possibility to be suggested. As noted, for sequences of crises (such as Yemen War I–IV), only the final case can be assessed along the dimension of Importance. A modification of that practice might lead to an improvement in prediction. Perhaps the extent of protracted conflict should be included as a component of Severity for the last case in a sequence of crises. In other words, the longer the sequence, the greater the increment in Severity, subject to some upper limit.[10]

Conclusion

This chapter has focused on prediction of the long-term significance of crises on the basis of their immediate characteristics. Partial success has been achieved with respect to anticipating the importance of crises in the Middle East and Africa. Indices of Severity and Importance have been developed and used toward that end. These indices, however, may be applied to crises in any region of the world.

A final point – one of caution – is that the disequilibrium of Third World regions, such as the Middle East and Africa, will complicate prediction, regardless of how it is to be conducted.[11] For now, however, the development of a systematic approach toward the anticipation of crisis consequences should be regarded as satisfactory progress.

TABLE II.7.16. Middle East International Crises, 1929–85: Severity and Importance*

Case	Crisis Actors (in order of entry)†	Duration	Overall Severity	Overall Importance
Saudi/Yemen War	Saudi Arabia, Yemen	18/12/33–20/05/34	2.75	2.13
Alexandretta	Turkey, France	09/09/36–23/06/39	4.09	2.88
Middle East Campaign	Iraq, UK, Germany, Vichy France	29/04/41–14/07/41	6.64	–
Occupation of Iran	Iran	25/08/41–29/01/42	4.23	–
Iran	Iran	26/09/44–09/12/44	3.42	–
Syria/Free French Forces	Syria, France	17/05/45–03/06/45	4.76	2.13
Kars-Ardahan	Turkey	07/06/45–05/04/46	4.49	–
Azerbaijan	Iran, UK, USA, USSR	23/08/45–09/05/46	7.71	4.38
Turkish Straits	Turkey, USA	07/08/46–26/10/46	4.76	–
Palestine Partition	Egypt, Iraq, Lebanon, Syria	29/11/47–17/12/47	4.09	–
Israel Independence	Egypt, Iraq, Israel, Jordan, Lebanon, Syria	15/05/48–20/07/49	6.24	9.25
Sinai Incursion	Egypt, UK, Israel	25/12/48–10/01/49	4.36	–
Tel Mutillah	Syria, Israel	15/03/51–14/05/51	3.15	2.13
Qibya	Jordan	14/10/53–a	2.89	2.88
Baghdad Pact	Egypt	24/02/55–**/10/55	2.35	3.63
Gaza Raid	Egypt, Israel	28/02/55–23/06/56	4.23	1.75
Qalqilya	Jordan, Israel	13/09/56–**/10/56	3.15	2.50
Suez-Sinai Campaign	Egypt, USSR, France, Israel, UK, USA	29/10/56–12/03/57	9.27	5.88
Jordan Regime	Jordan	04/04/57–03/05/57	1.95	3.63
Syria/Turkey Border	Turkey, USA, Syria	18/08/57–29/10/57	4.76	2.50
Formation of UAR	Iraq, Jordan	01/02/58–14/02/58	1.55	5.50
Lebanon/Iraq Upheaval	Lebanon, Jordan, UK, USA,	03/05/58–**/10/58	6.91	3.63
Shatt-al-Arab I	Iraq, Iran	28/11/59–04/01/60	2.75	2.50
Rottem	Egypt, Israel	15/02/60–08/03/60	2.89	2.13
Kuwait Independence	Kuwait, UK	25/06/61–13/07/61	3.69	1.00
Breakup of UAR	Egypt	28/09/61–05/10/61	1.95	5.88
Yemen War I	Jordan, Saudi Arabia, Egypt, Yemen	26/09/62–15/04/63	4.90	–
Jordan Internal Challenge	Israel	21/04/63–04/05/63	2.62	1.00
Jordan Waters	Egypt, Jordan, Lebanon, Syria, Israel	11/12/63–05/05/64	4.23	2.13
Yemen War II	Egypt, Yemen, Saudi Arabia	00/05/64–08/11/64	3.82	–
Yemen War III	Egypt, Yemen, Saudi Arabia	03/12/64–25/08/65	4.36	–
Yemen War IV	Saudi Arabia, Egypt, Yemen	14/10/66–26/09/67	4.36	3.63
El Samu	Israel, Jordan	12/11/66–15/11/66	3.29	2.13

TABLE II.7.16. *Continued*

Case	Crisis Actors (in order of entry)†	Duration	Overall Severity	Overall Importance
Six Day War	Israel, Egypt, Jordan, USA, Syria, USSR	17/05/67–11/06/67	9.72	7.38
Karameh	Israel, Jordan	18/03/68–22/03/68	3.42	3.62
Pre-War of Attrition	Israel	07/09/68–07/11/68	3.96	–
Beirut Airport	Lebanon	28/12/68–**/01/69	2.48	3.63
War of Attrition I	Israel	08/03/69–28/07/69	2.75	–
Shatt-al-Arab II	Iran, Iraq	15/04/69–30/10/69	2.62	2.13
Cairo Agreement	Lebanon	22/10/69–03/11/69	2.62	3.63
War of Attrition II	Egypt, USSR, Israel	07/01/70–07/08/70	5.70	3.63
Black September	Syria, USA, Israel, Jordan	15/09/70–29/09/70	5.97	3.25
North/South Yemen I	North Yemen, South Yemen	26/09/72–28/11/72	2.75	1.00
Libyan Plane	Israel	21/02/73–21/02/73	3.15	2.88
Iraq Invasion – Kuwait	Kuwait	20/03/73–08/06/73	2.22	2.13
Israel Mobilization	Israel	10/04/73–**/06/73	2.35	–
October–Yom Kippur War	Israel, Syria, USA, Egypt, USSR	05/10/73–31/05/74	9.18	6.63
South Yemen/Oman	Oman	18/11/73–11/03/76	2.08	2.13
Lebanon Civil War I	Syria	18/01/76–30/09/76	2.08	–
Iraqi Threat	Syria	09/06/76–17/06/76	1.55	1.00
Syria Mobilization	Israel	21/11/76–13/12/76	2.62	2.88
Lebanon Civil War II	Syria	07/02/78–20/02/78	2.35	–
Litani Operation	Lebanon	14/03/78–13/06/78	2.62	3.25
North/South Yemen II	North Yemen, South Yemen	24/02/79–30/03/79	4.36	1.00
US Hostages in Iran	USA, Iran	04/11/79–20/01/81	5.16	4.00
Onset Iran/Iraq War	Iran	17/09/80–19/11/80	3.29	–
Jordan/Syria Confrontation	Jordan	25/11/80–14/12/80	2.62	1.00
Biqa Valley Missiles	Syria, Israel	28/04/81–24/07/81	3.02	3.25
Iraq Nuclear Reactor	Iraq	08/06/81–19/06/81	2.75	2.88
Bahrain Coup Attempt	Bahrain, Saudi Arabia	13/12/81–08/01/82	2.35	1.00
Khoramshar	Iraq	22/03/82–30/07/82	3.29	–
Lebanon War	Lebanon, Syria, Israel	05/06/82–01/09/82	4.36	2.88
Basra/Kharg Island	Iraq, Iran, Kuwait, Saudi Arabia	21/02/84–11/07/84	5.97	–

a The absence of a termination date indicates a faded crisis.

* Of the 63 Middle East international crises in the data set, all are scored for overall severity but only 46 receive an overall importance score. The reason for the discrepancy is to be found in the existence of clusters that together act as a catalyst to change in the system. Long-war crises are striking illustrations, notably those that occurred within World War II (1939–45) and Yemen (1962–67). Unlike severity, which measures the intensity of a crisis *during* the period of its existence – hence a severity score for every crisis – importance gauges the impact of a crisis several years *after* its termination. Therefore, the consequences of each crisis within a long war are accurately assessed as the impact of the entire cluster, not of any component part. For example, the importance score for the prolonged Yemen War is attached to the last of the crises within that cluster, namely, Yemen War IV, *not* Yemen War I, II or III. In other words, the importance of the cluster and of each crisis within it is gauged from the end of the Yemen War as a whole.

There are also clusters of crises that occur in close proximity in space and time and focus on a common issue – for example, the three Arab/Israel crises in 1947–49, namely, Palestine Partition, Israel Independence and Sinai Incursion. All derived from the struggle for Palestine on the eve of, and just after, the end of the British Mandate. Thus only Israel Independence, the last to terminate, was given an importance score.

Some international crises are parts of "unfinished" clusters the importance of which cannot yet be measured, such as the Lebanon Civil War cases of 1976 and 1978. The crises of these clusters were therefore given an empty cell for overall importance.

** A double asterisk means that an exact date could not be specified.

† The time of entry of crisis actors into an international crisis is subject to great variation. In some cases, all direct participants become crisis actors the same day (e.g., the six states in the Israel Independence Crisis, on 15 May 1948). At the other extreme, the five direct participants in the October–Yom Kippur Crisis of 1973–74 became crisis actors at different times, beginning with Israel on 5 October and ending with the Soviet Union on 22 October. Another variant is the Six Day War of 1967, with Israel becoming a crisis actor on 17 May, Egypt and Jordan on 5 June, the United States on 6 June, and Syria and the Soviet Union on 9 June. For the entry dates of all crisis actors in the 63 Middle East international crises, see Brecher and Wilkenfeld *et al.* 1988: Table II.7.

TABLE II.7.17 International Crises in Africa, 1929–85*: Severity and Importance†

Case	Crisis Actors	Duration	Overall Severity	Overall Importance
Wal-Wal	Ethiopia, UK	06/12/34–22/10/35	4.90	–
Ethiopian War	Ethiopia, France, Italy	02/10/35–05/05/36	5.43	7.38
Italian Colonial Demands	France	30/11/38–31/03/39	3.15	1.38
East Africa Campaign	UK, Italy	19/08/40–17/05/41	4.63	5.50
El Alamein	Germany, Italy	23/10/42–13/05/43	5.16	–
Suez Canal	Egypt, UK	30/07/51–30/01/52	3.96	5.13
Suez Nationalization	France, UK	26/07/56–06/11/56	4.36	–
Tunisia/France I	Tunisia	31/05/57–27/06/57	1.95	–
Ifni	Spain	23/11/57–* /11/57	2.62	2.13
Tunisia/France II	Tunisia	08/02/58–17/06/58	2.75	2.50
Sudan/Egypt Border	Sudan	09/02/58–25/02/58	2.08	1.00
Ghana/Togo Border	Ghana	* /03/60–01/04/60	1.81	2.13
Congo I: Katanga	Belgium, Congo	05/07/60–15/02/62	3.96	3.63
Mali Federation	Mali, Senegal	20/08/60–22/09/60	2.08	4.38
Ethiopia/Somalia	Ethiopia	26/12/60–* /12/61	2.35	1.00
Bizerta	France, Tunisia	17/07/61–29/09/61	3.69	1.00
Mauritania/Mali	Mauritania	29/03/62–18/02/63	2.22	1.38
Algeria/Morocco	Algeria, Morocco	01/10/63–04/11/63	2.62	1.00
Kenya/Somalia	Kenya	13/11/63–04/03/64	2.48	2.13
Dahomey/Niger	Niger, Dahomey	21/12/63–04/01/64	2.89	1.00
Rwanda/Burundi	Rwanda, Burundi	21/12/63–* /04/64	3.15	1.00
East Africa Rebellion	UK	19/01/64–30/01/64	2.22	2.50
Ogaden I	Ethiopia, Somalia	07/02/64–30/03/64	4.49	2.13
Congo II	Congo, Belgium, USA, USSR	04/08/64–30/12/64	7.98	3.63
Guinea Regime	Guinea	09/10/65–* /12/65	1.01	2.50
Rhodesia UDI	Zambia	05/11/65–27/04/66	2.62	2.13
Portuguese Invasion of Guinea	Guinea	22/11/70–11/12/70	2.62	2.13
Chad/Libya I	Chad, Libya	24/05/71–17/04/72	2.62	2.13
Caprivi Strip	Zambia	05/10/71–12/10/71	2.75	1.00
Uganda/Tanzania I	Uganda, Tanzania	20/10/71–25/11/71	2.75	–
Uganda/Tanzania II	Uganda, Tanzania	17/09/72–05/10/72	2.75	2.13
Zambia	Zambia	19/01/73–03/02/73	2.48	1.00
War in Angola	Zaire, Zambia, South Africa, Angola, USA, Cuba, USSR	12/07/75–27/03/76	9.18	3.63
Moroccan March-Sahara	Spain, Morocco	16/10/75–14/11/75	3.42	–
Sahara	Algeria, Morocco, Mauritania	14/11/75–* /04/76	5.57	3.25
Uganda Claims	Kenya	15/02/76–24/02/76	1.81	2.13
Operation Thrasher	Rhodesia, Mozambique	22/02/76–* /04/76	3.96	–
Nouakchott I	Mauritania	08/06/76–08/06/76	1.28	–
Entebbe Raid	Israel	30/06/76–04/07/76	3.02	4.38
Sudan Coup Attempt	Sudan	02/07/76–15/07/76	1.14	3.25
Nagomia Raid	Mozambique	09/08/76–* /11/76	2.48	–
Operation Tangent	Botswana	20/12/76–31/03/77	2.75	–
Shaba I	Angola, Zaire	08/03/77–26/05/77	3.96	–
Mapai Seizure	Mozambique	29/05/77–30/06/77	2.62	–
Nouakchott II	Mauritania	03/07/77–* /07/77	1.28	4.00
Libya/Egypt Border	Libya, Egypt	14/07/77–10/09/77	2.89	1.00
Ogaden II	Ethiopia, Somalia	22/07/77–14/03/78	4.63	–
Rhodesia Raids	Zambia	31/08/77–14/08/78	2.62	–
French Hostages	France, Algeria	25/10/77–23/12/77	3.56	4.38
Chimoio Tembue Raid	Mozambique	23/11/77–22/03/78	2.62	–
Chad/Libya II	Chad, Libya	22/01/78–27/03/78	2.48	–
Chad/Libya III	Chad, Libya, France	15/04/78–29/08/78	4.36	–
Cassinga Incident	South Africa, Angola	03/05/78–17/05/78	3.96	–
Shaba II	Angola, Zaire, Belgium, France, USA	11/05/78–30/07/78	7.44	2.13
Air Rhodesia	Rhodesia, Zambia	03/09/78–31/10/78	2.89	–
Fall of Amin	Tanzania, Libya, Uganda	30/10/78–10/04/79	4.09	4.00

TABLE II.7.17 *Continued*

Case	Crisis Actors	Duration	Overall Severity	Overall Importance
Angola Invasion Scare	Angola	07/11/78–14/11/78	2.62	–
Tan Tan	Morocco	28/01/79–* /03/79	1.81	4.75
Raids on ZIPRA	Rhodesia, Angola, Zambia	12/02/79–31/05/79	3.69	–
Raids on SWAPO	Angola	06/03/79–28/03/79	2.75	–
Goulimime–Tarfaya Road	Morocco, Algeria	01/06/79–25/06/79	2.22	1.00
Chad/Libya IV	Chad, France, Libya	12/04/79–10/11/79	4.36	2.88
Rhodesian Settlement	Rhodesia, Botswana, Mozambique, Zambia	15/07/79–04/03/80	5.30	7.75
Raid on Angola	Angola	28/10/79–02/11/79	2.75	3.63
Raid on Gafsa	Tunisia, Libya	27/01/80–* /04/80	4.76	1.00
Operation Iman	Morocco	01/03/80–09/05/80	2.35	1.00
Operation Smokeshell	Angola	07/06/80–02/07/80	2.89	–
Libya Threat–Sadat	Egypt, Libya	11/06/80–*	2.89	1.00
Libyan Intervention–Gambia	Gambia	27/10/80–07/11/80	1.81	1.00
East Africa Confrontation	Somalia	05/12/80–29/06/81	2.22	–
Chad/Libya V	France	06/01/81–16/11/81	2.08	–
Mozambique Raid	Mozambique	30/01/81–* /03/81	3.29	1.00
Nigeria/Cameroon Border	Nigeria, Cameroon	16/05/81–24/07/81	3.02	1.00
Gambia Coup Attempt	Senegal	30/07/81–31/01/82	1.81	3.25
Gulf of Syrte	Libya	12/08/81–01/09/81	3.56	1.75
Operation Protea	Angola	23/08/81–30/09/81	3.42	–
Polisario Attack	Morocco	13/10/81–09/11/81	1.81	–
Ogaden III	Somalia	30/06/82–* /08/82	2.89	–
Lesotho Raid	Lesotho	09/12/82–15/12/82	2.75	1.00
Libya Threat–Sudan	Sudan, Egypt, Libya	11/02/83–22/02/83	3.96	–
Chad/Nigeria Clashes	Chad, Nigeria	18/04/83–02/07/83	2.89	1.00
Chad/Libya VI	Chad, France, Libya	24/06/83–11/12/84	4.63	–
Botswana/Zimbabwe Border	Botswana	08/11/83–21/12/83	1.68	1.00
Sudan/Ethiopia Border	Sudan	20/11/83–20/02/84	2.75	1.00
Operation Askari	Angola	06/12/83–16/02/84	2.89	–
Omdurman Bombing Raid	Sudan, Egypt, Libya	16/03/84–* /* /84	4.09	1.00
Botswana Raid	Botswana	14/06/85–21/06/85	2.75	1.00
Expulsion of Tunisians	Tunisia	21/08/85–26/09/85	2.08	***
Burkina Faso/Mali	Mali, Burkina Faso	20/12/85–18/01/86	2.89	***

* An asterisk means that an exact date could not be specified.

† Of the 89 Africa international crises in the data set, all are scored for overall severity but only 56 receive an overall importance score. This discrepancy is explained at length in note * to Table II.7.16. Examples from the respective categories detailed in that note are the long-war cluster over Rhodesia (1973–80), the closely-connected Tunisia/France crises (1957–58) and the unfinished Chad/Libya cluster.

*** Data on the importance indicators are incomplete for these recent cases.

Notes

1. The ICB Project, as noted, concentrates on interstate crises and on the behavior of states under externally generated stress. At the same time, it analyzes in detail the multiple roles of suprastate actors (League of Nations, United Nations, regional organizations) in crisis management, as well as the (often significant) roles of substate actors (e.g., nationalist movements, tribal groups in Africa) as triggering entities, stimuli to state behavior, etc. Moreover, the activity of nonstate actors is discussed in the descriptive summaries of international crises contained in the Project's *Handbook of International Crises* (Brecher and Wilkenfeld *et al.*, 1988:I), from which the data for these indicators and the other variables to follow are taken.

2. In some international crises, only one actor perceived a crisis. However, other states and, frequently, transnational (non-state) actors were involved in these cases. Thus every crisis actor has a perceived adversary, usually the state that triggers its crisis and, therefore, the international crisis as a whole.

3. During the decade before World War II, Britain, France, Germany, Italy, Japan, the Soviet Union and the United States constituted the subset of great powers in the global system. From 1920 to 1956, Britain and France were the preeminent external powers in the Middle East. However, as with all post-World War II international crises in the ICB data set, only the involvement of the global superpowers, the United States and the Soviet Union, was monitored from 1945 to 1985.

4. In this case the superpowers were (passive) partners, not adversaries.
5. For cases with only one crisis actor, the comparisons are made with the adversarial actor(s).
6. The average length of time per Africa crisis supports this line of reasoning, since it increases substantially across the four categories of conflict.
7. Although the primary focus of the concept of importance is on change, it is recognized in the coding of indicators that reinforcement of the *status quo* may constitute a significant development. For example, Tables II.7.8.a. and II.7.8.b. include *preservation* of an actor within the highest scale point for change in actors. Other scale points across the four indicators of importance also allow for reinforcement of the *status quo* as a noteworthy occurrence. A further instance would be change in alliances (Tables II.7.10.a. and II.7.10.b.), with increasing cohesiveness of an existing alliance included as part of scale point 2.
8. The following exposition is based upon a number of sources: Aruri (1975); Bandmann and Cordova (1980); Bartov (1978); Brecher with Geist (1980); Dayan (1976); Dowty (1984); Eban (1977); Freedman (1975); G. Golan (1974, 1977); M. Golan (1976); Heikal (1975); Herzog (1975); Kalb and Kalb (1974); Kissinger (1982); Meir (1975); Monroe and Farrar-Hockley (1975); Nixon (1978); Quandt (1977); Sadat (1978); Schiff (1975); and Shimoni (1977).
9. These diagrams follow the exposition in Brecher and James (1986), where the linkages between the indicators are explained in detail. As an illustration of the deductively derived weights in Figure II.7.1., the issues indicator is given a weight of 2. First, as the range of issues increases, so will the number of actors, drawn into a crisis by additional topics for bargaining. Moreover, multiple-issue crises are more likely than single-issue cases to produce change in an international system and, therefore, to generate super-power involvement, given their systemwide concerns. There are no *a priori* reasons to expect issues to affect other severity indicators directly.
10. For example, an initial re-coding scheme might be as follows: (1) single crisis: no change in Severity; (2) sequences of two crises: one full point added after the initial calculation of Severity; (3) sequences of three or more crises: two full points added after the initial calculation of Severity. The limit of two additional Severity points is set in order to prevent the inflation of scores for especially long series, like the nine-case set which terminated with the Rhodesian Settlement. For a more detailed treatment of this re-coding scheme, see James, Brecher and Hoffman, 1988: pp. 80–81.
11. For example, empirical studies of conflict in Africa are diverse in methods, time frame, and states included in the analysis. (Some examples include Bender, Coleman and Sklar (1985); Collins (1973); McGowan and Puckitt (1979); and Morrison and Stevenson (1972).) The one seemingly constant finding is that political life in Africa "constitutes an almost institutionless arena with conflict and disorder as its most prominent features" (Zolberg, 1968: p. 70).

8 Structural Attributes and Outcome Characteristics of International Crises

Patrick James and Jonathan Wilkenfeld

Introduction

Perhaps the most significant problem for theorists of international relations is the explanation of conflict in the system. To date, we have been more successful in the description of international disputes than in the prediction or control of their occurrence. Certainly there is no shortage of information about international relations phenomena in general, and international conflict in particular. There exist data sets on foreign policy behavior (Azar, 1980; Azar and Sloan, 1975; East, Salmore and Hermann, 1978; Callahan, Brady and Hermann, 1982; Wilkenfeld, Hopple, Rossa and Andriole, 1980); the attributes of crises and their participants (Brecher and Wilkenfeld et al., 1988; Wilkenfeld and Brecher et al., 1988); relational features of members of the international polity (Rummel, 1979); and war in the system (Singer and Small, 1972; Small and Singer, 1982).[1]

Complementing the extensive range of data which exists is a set of interesting speculative analyses of international conflict. Some of these studies may be described as behavioral, whereas others have a structural orientation.

Theorists of behavior such as Bull (1977), Waltz (1959, 1979) and Young (1978) have conceptualized the international polity as an anarchical society, albeit one in which certain regularities of conduct may be identified. For example, compliance with the regulations of international regimes has been found to be high, relative to what might be expected under conditions of anarchy (Young, 1980). And there exist well-understood channels (such as the United Nations) for adjudication of disputes among members of the international polity, although these instrumentalities often are bypassed in favor of more direct means of settlement. Even in cases of violent international disputes, combatants still share certain expectations regarding the rules of warfare (Blainey, 1973). In sum, it seems accurate to say that, while students of international behavior have identified important regularities, a general theory of international political relations is still remote.

Unfortunately, despite the presence of such variegated behavioral approaches, existing analyses of the *structural* factors which induce or inhibit international conflict suffer from a relatively narrow focus. In order to clarify the nature of this criticism, it is essential to explain first what is meant by the term "structural."

For purposes of the present study, we need to differentiate between structural characteristics of the international system as a collectivity, and the structural characteristics of a more restricted set of states involved in an interactive process. The structural characteristics of the international system, often referred to as systemic factors, would include such aspects as the distribution of military capabilities among members of the international community, with terms like "bipolarity" and "balance of power" being used to describe various configurations of such capabilities. Another example of such a structural factor would be the degree of social integration, as measured through an index of communication among members of the global polity. Today's international "society" could be described as well-integrated by comparison to those of past centuries, within which interactions almost invariably occurred among members of a given geographic subsystem. With technological advances, greater opportunities for interaction among geographically distant states have developed, ranging from the telegraph to intercontinental ballistic missiles.[2]

This study proposes a more narrow approach to structure in the international system than the one outlined above. Our unit of analysis is a collectivity of states involved in a conflict situation, more specifically, an international crisis. As such, this collectivity exhibits various structural characteristics, quite apart from those characteristics of the entire international system of which it is a part. Thus, the power capabilities of the subset of interacting states becomes a factor of concern to the actors, as distinguished from the capability distribution of the entire global system. Similarly, the degree to which the members of an interacting set of states may exhibit common value structures and approaches to conflict and cooperation may be distinguished from prevailing norms at the level of the international system.

By focusing our attention on the structural characteristics of interacting groups of states, we move away from some of the more traditional paths which have been followed in the search for pattern and meaning in international behavior. Consider the concept of "power," as it commonly is used. Power almost invariably has been measured in terms of the material capabilities controlled by states (Singer *et al.*, (1979; Singer and Wallace, 1979; Waltz, 1979; and Gilpin, 1981). Unfortunately, this closed system of measurement has produced a tendency toward tautological explanations, such as attributing concessions made by a state in crisis to its relative lack of power. It may not be the case that the sociology of conflict can be explained entirely under the rubric of capability dispersion among group members. Instead, there may be other significant structural or systemic influences at work.

Once we have defined our unit of analysis as a collectivity of interacting states, our next task is to identify a meaningful set of structural factors which will help explain the behavior exhibited by that collectivity. We have already indicated that such groups can be identified by conflict interaction patterns. We will narrow our focus even more, and concentrate on groups of states interacting in crisis situations. We now turn to the explication of the notion of crisis in international politics.

International Crises

The task of identifying the significant structural factors is made somewhat easier by our decision to focus on those factors which impact on the behavior that groups of states exhibit in international crises. Thus, our starting point will be the definition of an international crisis underlying the ICB Project and employed exclusively in studies elsewhere in this volume. Three principal reasons may be given for selection of this particular class of events.

First, international crisis as defined here is a relatively frequent and thus empirically relevant phenomenon. Moreover, the crises in the data set have occurred in a variety of geographical settings, and have involved an extensive subset of system members. Hence there is a good reason to believe that international crises constitute a valid testing ground for structurally-based hypotheses about conflict behavior.

A second question about selection of evidence concerns the use of data on international, as opposed to foreign policy, crises. As will become apparent, the variables in the analysis focus on aggregations of crisis actors. This information about the characteristics of the collectivity of states within an international crisis is required in order to test the propositions.

Concern with extending and building upon previous research devoted to international and foreign policy crises is the third reason for examination of this class of events. The ICB Project is an ongoing research effort which has as one of its central purposes the identification of regularities in crisis behavior. The research conducted here will focus on crisis outcomes. It deals with the impact of structural factors, whereas the usual practice among scholars of conflict – within and outside the Project – has been to assess the impact of behavioral differences on crisis attributes.

Theory and Hypotheses

The theoretical underpinnings of this analysis of structural factors in international crises address three central characteristics of crises: the nature of the *trigger; group size* (or number of crisis actors); and *homogeneity of worldview* among the crisis actors. These structural factors will be postulated as having important effects on a range of crisis process and outcome variables, including: centrality of violence as a crisis management technique; duration of the crisis; form of and satisfaction with the outcome; and impact on conflict escalation or reduction. Figure II.8.1. presents the theoretical structure of the analysis. In the sections below, we will examine three sets of hypotheses (corresponding to the three structural factors to be examined), followed by the appropriate empirical analysis.

Trigger to Crisis

The trigger, or source of crisis, refers to the specific event or situational change that leads decision-makers to perceive a threat to basic values, time pressure for response, and likely involvement in military hostilities. The trigger, being a specific event for a particular actor, is not usually conceptualized as a structural characteristic

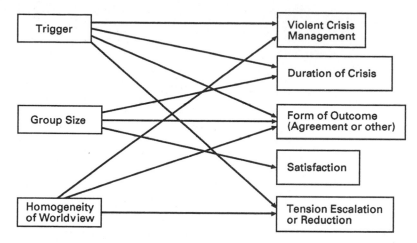

FIGURE II.8.1. Structural Factors and Crisis Outcomes

of a group. However, the trigger often sets the tone for the manner in which the participants pursue their goals during the course of the crisis. Certain triggers, by their very nature, may preclude outcomes satisfactory to all parties. Others may make the achievement of agreement among the parties difficult, while still others dictate outcomes which will necessitate compromise. Triggers range in severity from verbal, political and economic acts, to internal challenges to a regime, to non-violent military acts, and finally to indirect and direct military acts. For purposes of the present set of analyses, we will consider the trigger to be that event which triggered a crisis for the earliest actor in a particular international crisis. For example, the trigger for the 1973 October–Yom Kippur War cluster (in which ultimately Israel, Egypt, Syria, the US, and the USSR became crisis actors) was the movement of Egyptian forces toward the Suez Canal and a change from a defensive to an offensive posture, both non-violent military acts; this was the trigger for Israel on 5 October, 1973. International crises are classified according to whether they are characterized by an initial non-violent or violent trigger.

Hypothesis 1 expresses the link between the trigger as a structural factor and the outcome characteristics of crises.

> **Hypothesis 1: The more violent the trigger to an international crisis, the longer its duration and the more violent will be the crisis management techniques employed; the longer the duration of the crisis, the more likely it is that the crisis will terminate by explicit agreement among the principal parties, and the less likely it is that the underlying conflict level among the parties will be reduced.**

Concerning crisis management techniques, if we postulate that the nature of the trigger sets the tone for the entire crisis, then certainly we would expect that violent triggers will engender more violent crisis management techniques. This argument has been made for the conflict-begets-conflict process, in general, by Phillips (1973, 1978), Wilkenfeld (1975) and Ward (1982), and for crises, in particular, by Brecher, Wilkenfeld and Hill (Chapter 12 below). Violent triggers will restrict the range of choices available to decision-makers when they consider coping mechanisms, thus making pacific response patterns much less likely. Crises involving violent triggers will generally be longer in duration, measured from the date of initial trigger to the final termination for all actors. While the period of active violence may not necessarily be lengthy, the necessity for terminating such violent crises with some form of agreement among the parties will have the effect of lengthening the duration of the crisis period. Thus, we recognize here the explicit need for resolution once the crisis has occurred, or face the potential exacerbation of the existing conflict situation.

Finally, crises characterized by violent triggers (and, as hypothesized, violent crisis management techniques), will be less likely to reduce underlying tension among the participants. Such crisis terminations, often necessitating agreements involving compromise among the parties, prove to be less durable than the termination conditions for non-violent crises. Sadat's notorious characterization of the Arab–Israeli conflict as primarily psychological in nature supports the notion that violent strife has a pernicious dynamic which inhibits its permanent resolution. And this, of course, is but one from among many examples of seemingly interminable conflicts which might have been cited.

Group Size Group size is the second structural characteristic of international crises. The propositions which link the size of the group of crisis actors to outcome are derived from the theory of public choice. More specifically, they are hypotheses about the differences between large and small groups, and how these groups may be expected to obtain dissimilar outcomes from bargaining and negotiation. A brief exposition of the debate between Avaizian and Callen (1981) and Coase (1960, 1981) should clarify the basis of the group size variable.

Coase (1960) proposed that, regardless of the prevailing system of rules and property rights, parties to a bargaining situation could always obtain an outcome which allocated their resources optimally. This conjecture rapidly became known as the "Coase Theorem" and, until recently, met with general approval among scholars of bargaining and negotiation. But Avaizian and Callen (1981) have questioned the range of application of the Coase Theorem. In particular, they have asserted that bargaining among three or more individuals differs qualitatively from two-party interactions because of the potential for coalitions to form. Consequently, Avaizian and Callen believed that groups of three or more might not reach an optimal or stable allocation of resources, as the Coase Theorem would predict. And it is interesting that, in his response to this line of argument, Coase (1981) could do no better than observe that multiparty interactions have been studied inadequately, and hence generalizations about their outcomes must be speculative.

Hypothesis 2 summarizes the expected impact of group size on various outcome characteristics of crises.

> **Hypothesis 2: Crises involving three or more crisis actors will tend to be longer in duration, generate agreements among parties, and result in lower levels of satisfaction with the outcome.**

With regard to duration, the hypothesized relationship harks back to the notion of bargaining. Coalitional dynamics are expected to introduce complications which would not be present in two-party bargaining situations. Protracted sequences of interaction may result when there are three or more actors, because coalitions add a further element of complexity to an already difficult situation. It also follows that since compromise is a likely outcome in crises involving three or more parties, such crises are also likely to terminate with some form of agreement among the parties. That is, except in those rare cases where a compromise is derived through some form of tacit agreement, compromise generally necessitates some type of explicit agreement among the parties. In other words, the terms of the compromise usually need to be stated formally. Finally, in dealing with group satisfaction, our purpose is to discern whether or not groups of three or more actors are less likely to obtain an optimal crisis outcome. "Optimal" as used here means that all parties involved are satisfied with the outcome. It is expected that the Coase Theorem may break down when there are three or more participants in a bargaining process.

Homogeneity of World-view The third structural factor examined in this analysis is a measure of the composition of the group of crisis actors. Our assumption is that dissimilarities in élite images of international conflict and crisis (Bobrow, Chan and Kringen, 1977, 1979) will result in cognitive and behavioral differences. In fact, the term "crisis" itself may mean different things to different decisional élites. As a result, when a set of élites (each representing a different actor) involved in a crisis does (or does not) share a common image of crisis as a phenomenon, it is reasonable to expect that this may affect their interactions.

Fundamentally, the two images of crisis may be characterized by the terms "Western" and "non-Western." The standard definitions of crisis (including the one employed in this study) generally consider crises to be relatively brief aberrations which result from external threats (or internal threats with external origins and/or consequences), and which also increase the danger of military conflict. This can be largely classified as the Western image of crisis. It fits the Cold War notion that crises are infrequent, high-tension episodes which demand coordinated management from their participants.

Consider, in the context of the Western and non-Western dichotomy, the following set of conjectures: perhaps the leaders of non-Western states see conflict as a norm rather than as an aberration. Perhaps also it is the case that these decisional élites view crises as opportunities for issue-linkage in bargaining. Consequently, their interactions with adversaries favoring *status quo* arrangements may be expected to result in very different processes than those which characterize crises involving only Western states.

While a variety of rigorous taxonomies of states exist (Rosenau, 1966; Wilkenfeld, Hopple, Andriole and McCauley, 1978), they are not particularly useful when the objective is to probe the cultural differences among states. In the present analysis, we opt for a relatively straightforward approach, in which the less-developed states will be grouped together as non-Western, with membership in the "Group of 77" as the primary indicator to be used. While this system has its drawbacks, it also is fair to say that it has some potential for identifying major differences in outlook on international politics in general, and international crisis in particular. Less developed states presumably have an interest in pursuing revisionist policies, and may not see international conflict as too costly, given the point from which they begin. That is, those with little to lose may consider a crisis to be an opportunity, as opposed to a situation to be avoided. Conversely, highly industrialized states are expected to internalize a Western image of crisis, because they do not see such episodes as avenues toward structural change in the international political economy.

In operational terms, homogeneity of worldview will have two values: homogeneous and heterogeneous. A set of crisis actors is considered to be homogeneous when either all of the élites are Western, or none is Western; while a heterogeneous group is one in which both types of élites are represented. Hypothesis 3 presents the postulated relationships between homogeneity of world view and various outcome characteristics of crises.

> **Hypothesis 3: heterogeneous clusters of crisis actors will exhibit more violent crisis management techniques, agreement as the form of outcome, and an escalated level of post-crisis conflict.**

Heterogeneous clusters of crisis actors are expected to be more conflict-prone than are homogeneous groups. This follows from their different perceptions of and expectations from the crisis situation, resulting in an inability of the parties to communicate at anything but the most conflictual of levels. By contrast, a common image of the external environment should enable decisional élites to infer purpose much more readily from each other's actions. Therefore, homogeneous groups should exhibit less violent conflict. It also is anticipated that heterogeneous groups will generate greater agreement, since the disparities in perspectives will necessitate more formalized outcomes. Finally, it is expected that in a crisis involving Western and non-Western élites, these decision-makers will experience difficulties in establishing a mutually intelligible dialogue on the issues, because of differences in image. Thus it is anticipated that these interactions will create further post-crisis confrontations, because resolution of such crises will not be to the mutual satisfaction of the parties involved.

Analysis

We now turn to an analysis of the impact of three structural factors – trigger to crisis, group size, and homogeneity of worldview – on the outcome characteristics of crises. The analysis will encompass all international crises between 1929 and 1985, with the exception of World War II. Most of these crises comprise at least two crisis actors, whose decision-makers manifest the three perceptions of grave threat, finite time, and war likelihood. However, there is also a substantial number of international crises with but one crisis actor. These single actor crises will also include one or more adversarial actors, whose decision-makers may have initiated the crisis and, in any event, are involved, but do not perceive all three conditions noted earlier as applying to themselves (e.g., Dominican Republic in a 1947 crisis with Guatemala, with the latter as an adversarial actor; Egypt in its 1955 Baghdad Pact Crisis, with the UK, US, Iraq and Turkey as adversarial actors; Portugal in the Goa Crisis in 1955, with India as an adversarial actor). For purposes of the present analysis of structural factors, since we lack information on the adversarial (but non-crisis) actors, such single-actor clusters will be excluded.

In addition, several of the international crises constitute groups of crisis actors all of which were on the same side of a particular issue, with no adversarial actors as crisis actors (e.g., Turkey, Greece and the US in the Truman Doctrine Crisis of 1947; and Syria, Egypt, Lebanon and Iraq in the Palestine Partition Crisis of 1947). These cases are similar to the single actor cases noted above, since the adversary is only an involved actor. Such cases were also excluded from the current analysis, on the grounds that the structural factors could not be properly evaluated. After excluding the single actor and non-adversarial cases, the final data set for the present analysis was composed of 153 international crises for the 1929-1985 period.[3]

We turn first to the analysis of the relationships implicit in Hypothesis 1, in which we assess the impact of the nature of the crisis trigger on violence as a crisis management technique, the duration of the crisis, the form of outcome, and subsequent tensions. Tables II.8.1.a.-d. present the results of this analysis.

As expected, Table II.8.1.a. shows that the level of violence of the original crisis trigger was clearly associated with the subsequent use of violence as the preeminent or leading crisis management technique. Only a relatively few cases moved from non-violent triggers to a preeminent role for violence as a crisis management tech-

---

TABLE II.8.1.a.   Crisis Trigger and Centrality of Violence as Crisis Management Technique

	Low or no Violence	Violence Important	Violence Preeminent		
Non-Violent	35 50%	23 33%	12 17%	70	46%
Violent	12 15%	36 43%	35 42%	83	54%
	47 31%	59 38%	47 31%	153	100%

$X^2 = 24.45$; $p = .000$

TABLE II.8.1.b.   Crisis Trigger and Duration of Crisis

	0–60 days	61+ days		
Non-Violent	28 41%	40 59%	68	45%
Violent	26 32%	56 68%	82	55%
	54 36%	96 64%	150*	100%

$X^2 = 1.06$; $p = .302$

* Three cases with missing data on date of termination.

TABLE II.8.1.c.   Crisis Trigger and Form of Outcome

	Agreement	No Agreement		
Non-Violent	53 76%	17 24%	70	46%
Violent	48 58%	35 42%	83	54%
	101 66%	52 34%	153	100%

$X^2 = 4.64$; $p = .031$

Table II.8.1.d. Crisis Trigger and Escalation or Reduction of Tension

	Escalation	Reduction		
Non-Violent	28	40	68	
	41%	59%		45%
Violent	47	36	83	
	57%	43%		55%
	75	76	151*	
	50%	50%		100%

$$X^2 = 2.98; p = .084$$

* Two cases with missing data on tension.

nique. These cases included Hungary 1956 (demonstrations in Hungary with USSR military action as the response), Taiwan Straits II 1958 (Chinese military buildup in coastal areas, with all actors – US, China, Taiwan – ultimately employing violence) and Congo II 1964 (formation of a breakaway Revolutionary Council in the Congo, with the US and Belgium dispatching troops to Stanleyville). Similarly, only a small number of cases exhibited violent triggers and non-violent crisis management techniques. These cases included the Gaza Raid 1955 (Israeli retaliatory raid on Gaza; Egyptians respond by appealing to the USSR for arms), India/China Border I 1959 (Chinese dispatch troops into Indian territory; India responds with placement of police with army at border, but no violence), Cyprus II 1967 (Greek-Cypriot military action against Turkish-Cypriot villages, with Turkey responding with dispatch of troops and call for ousting of head of Greek forces), Cod War I 1973 (Icelandic patrol boats attempt to board UK trawlers inside 50 mile limit; UK responds by sending frigate into area), and Omdurman Bombing 1984 (Libya bombs Sudan outpost; Sudan responds with negotiation). Generally, the data show that the violence-begets-violence phenomenon is very much a part of the crisis situation as it was found in previous research to be part of the conflict dynamic in general.

Table II.8.1.b. indicates only a very weak tendency for violent triggers to be associated with crises of longer duration. While this type of trend would not indicate that violence itself is prolonged, it does point to the sometimes prolonged process of negotiating a settlement to such violent crises. The Middle East Wars of 1956, 1967 and 1973 are examples of relatively brief periods of active hostilities – 8 days, 6 days, and 21 days, respectively – followed by rather prolonged periods of negotiation – 4 months in 1956, 4 months in 1967, and 7 months in 1973.

Table II.8.1.c. examines the relationship between the extent of violence in the crisis trigger and the form of outcome. Here the data run counter to our expectations, indicating that while crises with non-violent triggers terminated in agreement in 76% of cases, only 58% of crises triggered by violence terminated in agreement.

Finally, Table II.8.1.d. assesses the relationship between the nature of the trigger and subsequent tension, in terms of whether or not the major parties were involved in another crisis within a five-year period. Here, we find that violent triggers were slightly more likely to be associated with conflict escalation than with conflict reduction, and non-violent triggers tended to engender conflict reduction. Eight of the 28 cases of non-violent triggers which nevertheless resulted in conflict escalation were among those that also showed violence as the preeminent crisis management technique in response to non-violent triggers: Austria *Putsch* 1934; Israel Independence 1948–49; Pushtunistan I 1949–50; Taiwan Straits I 1954–55; Six Day War 1967; Invasion of Cambodia 1970; Sahara 1975–76; and Chad/Libya IV 1979.

We turn now to the second hypothesis, which deals with the structural factor of group size. Specifically, we had proposed that crises involving three or more actors would be longer in duration, result in suboptimal outcomes and agreement, and produce lower levels of satisfaction with the outcome. The results of this analysis are presented in Tables II.8.2.a.–c.

Turning first to Table II.8.2.a., we note a strong tendency for crises involving three or more actors to be longer in duration than those involving only two actors. As Avaizian and Callen (1981) have argued, bargaining among three or more individuals differs qualitatively from two-party interactions because of the potential for

TABLE II.8.2.a. Group Size and Duration of Crisis

	0–60 Days	61+ Days		
2 Actors	45 46%	54 54%	99	66%
3+Actors	9 18%	42 82%	51	34%
	54 36%	96 64%	150*	100%

$$X^2 = 10.12; \ p = .002$$

* Three cases with missing data on date of termination.

TABLE II.8.2.b. Group Size and Form of Outcome

	Agreement	No Agreement		
2 Actors	66 66%	34 34%	100	65%
3+Actors	35 66%	18 34%	53	35%
	101 66%	52 34%	153	100%

$$X^2 = .00; \ p = 1.00$$

TABLE II.8.2.c. Group Size and Satisfaction with Outcome

	All Satisfied	Mixed		
2 Actors	40 41%	58 59%	98	65%
3+Actors	11 21%	42 79%	53	35%
	51 34%	100 66%	151*	100%

$$X^2 = 5.32; \ p = .021$$

* Two cases with missing data on satisfaction.

coalitions to form. Coalitional dynamics introduce complications which would not be present in two-party bargaining, with such complications resulting in more protracted sequences of interaction. Indeed, our data attest to the notion that three actors constitute a threshold in bargaining situations, since we find that crises with three actors are indistinguishable from larger clusters insofar as duration is concerned.

Table II.8.2.b. assesses the relationship between group size and the form of outcome. The data show virtually no relationship between group size and tendency to terminate in agreement.

The final table in this series, II.8.2.c., assesses the relationship between group size and satisfaction with the outcome. An optimal outcome is one in which all parties perceive satisfaction. As the table indicates, there is a relatively small proportion of the total cases (34%) in which all parties emerged as satisfied with the outcome. This generally low frequency of unanimous satisfaction should not be surprising, given that crises are often episodes in more protracted conflict situations, and under such circumstances satisfaction is a rare commodity. As expected, we do note a greater tendency for crises with only two actors to result in satisfaction for all parties than is the case for crises involving three or more actors (41% satisfaction as opposed to 21%). Among the 40 two-party crises with universal satisfaction with outcome are Leticia 1932; Changkufeng 1938; Poland Liberalization 1956; Malaysia Federation 1963; Kashmir II 1965; Beagle Channel 1977; US Hostages in Iran 1979; and Chad/Nigeria 1983. Among the 11 cases of satisfaction with outcome when three or more actors were involved were Taiwan Straits II 1958; Cyprus I 1963; Shaba II 1978; and Omdurman Bombing 1984.

The final portion of our analysis focuses on the impact of the cultural diversity of the actors in an international crisis on the outcomes of crises. Homogeneity of world-view is expected to impact on the extent of violence, the form of outcome, and on subsequent levels of tensions. As noted earlier, this variable differentiates between heterogeneous crises involving both Western and non-Western actors, and homogeneous crises involving only a single type of actor. Homogeneity, in turn, may be either all-Western or all-non-Western. Tables II.8.3.a–c. trichotomizes this variable, producing heterogeneous, homogeneous non-Western, and homogeneous Western categories.

Table II.8.3.a. exhibits considerable differences between non-Western and Western homogeneous crises. Western homogeneous crises were overwhelmingly non-violent (76%), compared to a 24.5% non-violence rate for non-Western homogeneous crises. In fact, among the crises in which violence played little or no role in crisis management, the non-Western homogeneous crises exhibited similar patterns to the heterogeneous crises. But among crises in which violence was preeminent in crisis management, the heterogeneous crises had a rate considerably higher than either homogeneous Western or homogeneous non-Western crises (38%, 24.5%, and 18%, respectively). Only three homogeneous Western crises employed violence as the preeminent crisis management technique: Austria *Putsch* 1934; Suez Nationalization 1955; and Hungarian Uprising 1956.

TABLE II.8.3.a. Homogeneity of Worldview and Centrality of Violence as Crisis Management Technique

	Low or No Violence		Violence Important		Violence Preeminent			
Heterogeneous	19	26%	27	36%	28	38%	74	50%
Homogeneous Non-Western	14	24.5%	29	51%	14	24.5%	57	38%
Homogeneous Western	13	76%	1	6%	3	18%	17	12%
	46	31%	57	39%	45	30%	148*	100%

$$X^2 = 22.68; p = .000$$

* Five cases with missing data on homogeneity.

Table II.8.3.b. examines the relationship between homogeneity of worldview and form of outcome. The results indicate that there was no meaningful difference between heterogeneous and homogeneous crises insofar as a tendency toward agreement is concerned.

Finally, Table II.8.3.c. examines the impact of homogeneity of world view on the escalation or reduction of tensions, i.e., whether or not there was an outbreak of another crisis among the adversaries within a five-year period. We find a considerable difference between homogeneous Western crises, on the one hand, and the heterogeneous and homogeneous non-Western crises, on the other. A substantial majority of the homogeneous Western crises yielded tension reduction (71%) – the five exceptions were Austria *Putsch* 1934; Spanish Civil War 1936–39; Czech May Crisis 1938; Marshall Plan 1947; and Berlin Deadline 1957–59. Tension reduction for the other two groups occurred at a considerably lower rate. The original hypothesis had expected the contrast we have found between heterogeneous and homogeneous Western crises, but the findings for the homogeneous non-Western crises diverge from our expectations.

TABLE II.8.3.b. Homogeneity of Worldview and Form of Outcome

	Agreement		No Agreement			
Heterogeneous	49	66%	25	34%	74	50%
Homogeneous Non-Western	39	68%	18	32%	57	38%
Homogeneous Western	11	65%	6	35%	17	12%
	99	67%	49	33%	148*	100%

$$X^2 = .11; p = .945$$

* Five cases with missing data on homogeneity.

TABLE II.8.3.c. Homogeneity of Worldview and Escalation or Reduction of Tension

	Escalation		Reduction			
Heterogeneous	43	58%	31	42%	73	50%
Homogeneous Non-Western	24	43%	32	57%	56	38%
Homogeneous Western	5	29%	12	71%	17	12%
	71	49%	75	51%	146*	100%

$$X^2 = 5.58; p = .061$$

* Seven cases with missing data on homogeneity or tension.

Summary

We began this analysis with the point that the structural characteristics of collectivities of states have been largely ignored in studies of conflict and crisis. The analysis was aimed at identifying, operationalizing, and examining the effects of a set of such structural factors on process and outcome characteristics of crises. While structural factors alone can hardly be expected to provide full explanations for the behavior of states in crises, our analysis has shown that in several key areas, such factors warrant greater attention on the part of the research community. At this point, it is appropriate to review the key findings for the three structural factors considered here.

(1) *Triggers to Crises*: Our expectation was that the trigger for the entire crisis would set the tone for the manner in which the participants would pursue their goals during the course of the crisis. Specifically, we found that crises which were triggered by violence had a far greater propensity to exhibit violent crisis management techniques than did crises triggered by non-violent acts. Also, crises with violent triggers were more likely than non-violent crises to result in an escalation of tensions, defined in terms of the recurrence of crisis among the parties during the subsequent five-year period.

Twenty-six international crises with violent triggers fit the profile for the first structural factor. That is, these cases exhibit a violent trigger, preeminent violence in crisis management, and escalation of tension. Among these are three pre-World War II crises (Ethiopian War 1935, Spanish Civil War 1936, Marco Polo Bridge 1937), nine Indo-China crises, and five African crises (War in Angola 1975, Operation Thrasher 1976, Cassinga Incident 1978, Chad/Libya II 1978 and Raid on ZIPRA 1979).

(2) *Group Size*: Consistent with the public choice literature on the effects of group size on the outcomes of bargaining and negotiation, it was our expectation that international crises with two actors would exhibit substantially different patterns

than would larger groups of crisis actors. More specifically, we found that the larger international crises (in terms of number of crisis actors) tended to be associated with longer duration. Larger crisis clusters tended to exhibit a lower tendency toward satisfaction with the outcome.

Thirty-one international crises fit the profile for the second structural factor: group size of three crisis actors or larger, long duration from trigger to termination, and dissatisfaction with outcome. Among these cases are two from the East/West protracted conflict (Berlin Blockade 1948 and Berlin Wall 1961), four from the Arab–Israeli protracted conflict (Israel Independence 1948, Suez-Sinai Campaign 1956, Jordan Waters 1963 and October–Yom Kippur War 1973), a cluster of four crises involving Yemen between 1962 and 1967, four Indo-China crises, and five diverse crises in Africa.

(3) *Homogeneity of Worldview*: It was our expectation that Western states would differ markedly from non-Western states in the way they view crises. Accordingly, we felt that international crises involving heterogeneous groups of states (mixed Western and non-Western) would exhibit different outcome patterns than either non-Western homogeneous clusters or Western homogeneous clusters. In fact, we found that the homogeneous Western crises were quite uniform in their characteristics, and differed markedly from the other two types. More specifically, the Western homogeneous crises were less likely than others to exhibit violence as the preeminent crisis management technique, and were more likely to lead to tension reduction. Ten international crises fit this homogeneous Western profile: Assassination of King Alexander 1934; *Anschluss* 1938; Communism in Hungary 1947; Communism in Czechoslovakia 1948; Berlin Blockade 1948; Trieste II 1953; Poland Liberalization 1956; Berlin Wall 1961; Cod War I 1973; and Cod War II 1975.

Clearly, our work constitutes only the beginning of what should be serious and systematic attention to the identification of the conditions under which structural characteristics of collectivities of interacting states impact on international behavior. Our exclusive focus on international crises makes problematical any generalization of the findings to the entire range of international behavior, or even to the more focused phenomenon of international conflict. Nevertheless, our discovery that the structural factors of crisis trigger, group size, and homogeneity of worldview are variously related to such process and outcome characteristics of crises as the use of violence, duration, satisfaction with, and durability of outcomes should encourage a wider examination of the role of these and other structural factors.

Notes

1. Efforts to integrate these and other data sets are relatively recent. Over the last few years, the Data Development in International Relations (DDIR) Project has been active in identifying points of convergence among existing sources of data and setting an agenda for further work. The DDIR Project also holds conferences and issues a newsletter to report on its progress.
2. Some earlier structural analyses include those of Coser (1957), E. Haas (1964), Kaplan (1957) and Merritt (1972).
3. Lists of included and excluded cases are available from the authors upon request.

Part III
International/Foreign Policy Crises: Combined Macro-Micro Analysis

9 Protracted Conflicts and Crises

Michael Brecher and Jonathan Wilkenfeld

Introduction

The concepts of "crisis," "conflict" and "war" were discussed briefly in Chapter 1. "Crisis," along with "system," were explored in depth in Chapter 2. And they served as conceptual foundations for a reexamination of the link between polarity and stability, in Chapters 3 and 4. Here and in the two chapters to follow, the relationships between two of these phenomena will be analyzed, more precisely, the effects of "protracted conflict" on crisis. A Protracted Conflict–Crisis Model will be specified, a proposition on the link framed, and hypotheses will be deduced. These will be tested: globally, using the ICB dataset for more than half of the twentieth century (this chapter); through a comparison of crises in the dominant (East/West) system and in two subsystems, the Middle East and South Asia (Chapter 10); and, finally, in a multi-stage comparison of crises within and outside protracted conflict, in different regions and in various conflicts (Chapter 11).

The point of departure for this analysis is the pioneering definition of "protracted conflict" in international relations by Azar *et al.* (1978: pp. 50, 53):

> Protracted conflicts are hostile interactions which extend over long periods of time with sporadic outbreaks of open warfare fluctuating in frequency and intensity. These are conflict situations in which the stakes are very high – the conflicts involve whole societies and act as agents for defining the scope of national identity and social solidarity. While they may exhibit some breakpoints during which there is a cessation of overt violence, they linger on in time and have no distinguishable point of termination. . . . Protracted conflicts, that is to say, are not specific events or even clusters of events at a point in time; they are processes.[1]

This definition was applied by Azar *et al.* to the Arab/Israel Conflict, now 40 years old, with a highly conflictual normal relations range punctuated by six major outbursts of violence (1948-49, 1956, 1967, 1969-70, 1973-74, 1982), with persistent hostility over political, cultural, economic and territorial issues, and a slow, painful process towards accommodation, highlighted by a formal peace agreement between one pair of adversaries, Egypt/Israel, in 1979. The Arab/Israel Conflict, however, is not unique in recent world politics. There are comparable conflicts between India and Pakistan, Ethiopia and Somalia, Greece and Turkey (over Cyprus), Afghanistan and Pakistan (over Pushtunistan), etc. All are lengthy, several decades or more. All have fluctuated in intensity, moving from war to near-accommodation and back to violence. All have aroused intense animosities among the actors, with spillover to a broad spectrum of issues. Marginal disputes have been highly salient to the adversaries. And conflict termination has yet to occur in most of them.

There are, moreover, several extended interstate conflicts in the twentieth century which manifest all but one of the specified conditions of the Azar *et al.* definition, namely, "sporadic outbreaks of open warfare." In some, notably the East/West Conflict since 1945, violence between the principal adversaries has been conspicuously absent. In others, violence was persistent and intense, notably the conflict between the Axis Powers and the Allies from 1939 to 1945, the Vietnam Conflict between North Vietnam, on the one hand, and South Vietnam and the United States, on the other, and the Iran–Iraq Conflict from 1980–88. These were/are protracted conflicts in every other respect – extended duration of hostile interaction, very high stakes, spillover to many domains, conflict processes over time rather than specific events. We therefore found it necessary to modify the definition by eliminating "sporadic warfare" as a necessary condition of a protracted conflict (PC).[2]

Some international crises, as noted in Chapter 1, take place within a protracted conflict. Others erupt outside that setting; that is, they emerge in an environment without the antecedent condition of prolonged dispute over one or more distinctive issues, and without the spillover effects of cumulative crises between the same adversaries on other domains of their relationship. This distinction in crisis setting between protracted conflict (PC) and non-protracted conflict (non-PC) provides the conceptual basis for the analysis in this chapter and two chapters to follow. Here, the guiding research questions can be formulated thus: are there differences between international crises within and outside of protracted conflicts and, if so, what are they? Specifically, does the (multiple) attribute of protractedness affect any or all of the crucial dimensions of crisis from onset to termination?

Protracted Conflict–Crisis Model   Underlying these questions about PCs is a general proposition about protracted conflict and crisis, and a set of specific hypotheses derived therefrom.

> **Proposition: International crises within a PC differ from those outside a PC along a number of dimensions, from type of trigger and values at stake, through the role of violence in crisis management, the extent of involvement by the superpowers and the global organization, and their effectiveness in crisis abatement, to the type of outcome, both content and form.**

The character of a PC generates a set of expectations about the process and management of crises. Specifically, it is postulated that international crises within a PC will be characterized by:

> **Hypothesis 1: The more visible presence of *violence* in crisis *triggers*;**
> **Hypothesis 2: Higher stakes, that is, a perceived threat to more *basic values*;**
> **Hypothesis 3: Greater reliance on *violence* in coping with crisis;**
> **Hypothesis 4: A resort to *more intense* types and levels of violence in crisis management;**
> **Hypothesis 5: A *primary role* for violence in crisis management;**
> **Hypothesis 6: *More political* and *less military activity* by the *superpowers*;**
> **Hypothesis 7: *Greater effectiveness* of superpower activity in *crisis abatement*;**
> **Hypothesis 8: *More involvement* by the *global organization*;**
> **Hypothesis 9: *More effectiveness* of global organization involvement in *crisis abatement*;**
> **Hypothesis 10: *More ambiguous* crisis *outcomes*, that is, stalemate or compromise; and**
> **Hypothesis 11: *Less formal* agreements to mark the *termination* of crises.**

The model which represents these hypotheses is presented in Figure III.9.1.

The first dependent variable in the Conflict–Crisis Model is *trigger*, that is, the

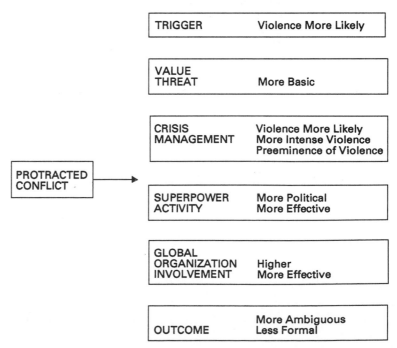

FIGURE III.9.1. Protracted Conflict-Crisis Model

act, event or situational change which catalyzes the basic conditions of an international and foreign policy crisis. The breakpoint or trigger ranges from: a verbal act (protest, accusation, etc.); through a political act (subversion, alliance of foreign adversaries, etc.); an economic act (embargo, nationalization of foreign property, etc.); a non-violent military act (show of force, mobilization, etc.); to an indirect violent act (violence directed at an ally or client state); and a violent act (sea-air incident, large-scale military attack, etc.).[3]

The postulate that international crises within a protracted conflict are more likely than others to be triggered by violence (Hypothesis 1) derives from a PC's distinctive characteristics. First, prolonged hostility between the same adversaries creates mutual mistrust and expectation of violent behavior. Moreover, the likely presence of several issues within an ongoing conflict strengthens this anticipation. Thirdly, the periodic resort to violence reinforces the belief that violence will occur. Finally, the importance of the values at stake creates a disposition to initiate a crisis by violent acts, as well as to expect a violent trigger from the adversary. In crises outside a setting of violence and hostility, by contrast, there is no logical reason to anticipate a violent rather than a non-violent trigger. The type of trigger will depend upon the specific configuration of a crisis – the attributes of the adversarial actors, the centrality of the issue(s) in dispute, the power balance, etc. However, the long-term effects of protractedness, especially intense mistrust, which spills over to perceptions and behavior are absent from these crises. Thus, while violence may be present in crisis triggers outside a PC, it is not necessarily more likely than non-violence; and it is less probable than violence in crises which are part of a PC.

The second dependent variable of the Conflict–Crisis Model is *value threat*, that is, the most serious threat during an international crisis perceived by any of the crisis actors. This ranges from a threat to: population and property; economic interests (trade restrictions, etc.); the political system (overthrow of a regime, intervention in domestic politics, etc.); territorial integrity (annexation of territory, partition, etc.); influence in the international system (diplomatic isolation, cessation of patron support, etc.); a threat of grave damage (mass bombing, large casualties in war, etc.); and to the most basic value, existence (total annexation, occupation, etc.).

As indicated in Hypothesis 2, it is postulated that crises within a protracted conflict are more likely than others to be characterized by a perceived threat to more basic values. The reason lies in a core strand of a PC, namely, a deep, abiding clash over multiple values, whether between ideologies, civilizations or belief systems. While a specific crisis in such a context may focus on a limited goal or issue, it is linked to the enduring values in conflict over a prolonged period. By contrast, threatened values in other crises are specific to the issues in immediate dispute, without the psychological baggage of ongoing conflict. Thus crises within a PC tend to involve more basic values. These are more likely to be threatened in an environment of mistrust of, and hostility toward, adversaries as a consequence of preceding clashes or crises.

Hypotheses 3, 4 and 5 relate to three closely-related aspects of violence: *crisis management technique* (CMT), that is, the primary method used by states to protect threatened values in a crisis, ranging from negotiation through mediation and non-violent pressure to violent military acts; *intensity of violence*, from none through minor or serious clashes to full-scale war; and *centrality of violence*, from none to the preeminent role in crisis management. It is postulated that crises within a PC are more likely than others to be characterized by: violence in the response of crisis actors (Hypothesis 3); a resort to more intense violence (Hypothesis 4); and the preeminent role for violence in crisis management (Hypothesis 5).

Violence, as noted, is a central and endemic attribute of a protracted conflict. As long as adversaries see no end to their PC, the dynamics of their relationship create a disposition to violence in crisis management. The fragility of conflict reduction, the persistence of value competition, and the expectation of violence, taken together, generate a reliance on violent crisis behavior. In non-PC crisis situations, by contrast, adversaries function in an environment relatively free from a history of violence. Crisis actors are as likely to rely on negotiation, third party intervention or some form of coercive diplomacy as on violence in coping with a crisis. Even in situations where violence is considered necessary, there is no *a priori* disposition to intense violence; rather, full-scale war and serious clashes may yield to less severe coercive activity. In short, a PC environment is more conducive to violence in crisis management. The "lessons of history" strengthen that tendency. Non-PC situations do not.

Hypothesis 6 concerns *superpower activity* in crises. This ranges from none, through low-level (political, economic and propaganda), to semi-military (covert support, dispatch of military aid or advisors), and direct military activity (dispatch of troops, naval assistance, etc.). This hypothesis postulates more political participation and less military involvement by superpowers in crises which are part of a protracted conflict.

The rationale for these expectations is that, given their greater disposition to violence, crises in a PC setting are likely to be more destabilizing. Superpowers have a vested interest in system stability (and equilibrium), in order to ensure their continued status at the apex of its hierarchy. Since crises within PCs are more dangerous to system stability, superpowers are more inclined to attempt to reduce the likelihood of violence and, if it occurs, to limit its intensity, scope and duration. Similarly, superpowers are more disposed to intervene politically so as to prevent destabilizing escalation. A crisis in a non-PC setting, by contrast, is more likely to be managed by the parties through non-violent techniques, thus reducing the pressure on superpowers to become militarily involved. Moreover, crises in a non-PC setting do not create the same concern for superpowers in crisis termination through minimal violence because they do not pose as much of a danger to international stability. PC crises pose a greater threat to stability and are therefore likely to attract more superpower political activity to minimize negative systemic consequences.

A closely-related variable of the Conflict–Crisis Model is *superpower effectiveness* in crisis abatement, ranging from the most important contribution, through an important impact, a marginal effect, no role, to (in negative terms) crisis escalation. Hypothesis 7 postulates that superpower activity will be more effective in crises within PCs than in other cases. The reasons are the "lessons of the past" syndrome and greater superpower concern, leading to more determined activity.

Superpowers fear being drawn into protracted conflicts by client states and, even more, confrontation with another superpower. Thus they are likely to commit resources in order to expedite crisis resolution. Greater commitment, in turn, increases the likelihood of effectiveness in crisis abatement. Moreover, the longer a PC continues, the more effective superpower activity is likely to be in its crises. Behavior by adversaries becomes known and predictable. Rules of the game are formulated, recognized and accepted by the adversaries and their patrons. The conditions under which superpower intervention will occur also become established; so too with its intensity, objectives and impact on crisis abatement. In sum, the process of crisis routinization, reinforced by their joint interest in system stability, increases the likelihood that superpower activity will be effective. Crises in a non-PC setting do not have the benefits of routinization or the same degree of superpower interest in crisis termination with minimal violence – for they do not pose as much of a danger to system stability. Stated differently, superpowers are more willing to allow non-PC crises to run their course without risking influence, status and resources. This is so because of the higher costs of crisis escalation within a protracted conflict and the greater pressure on superpowers to intervene.

Global organization (GO) involvement in crises ranges from low (discussion without passing a resolution, fact-finding, good offices), through medium activity (call for action by adversaries, mediation, etc.), to high involvement (observers, emergency military force, etc.). It is postulated that crises within PCs will be characterized by more active GO participation (Hypothesis 8) and more effectiveness (Hypothesis 9).

A protracted interstate conflict poses a continuing challenge to the global organization, as well as to the stability of the international system in which it occurs. Moreover, crises within such a conflict leave the parties dissatisfied and their tendency toward violence undiminished. Thus the GO is strongly disposed to intervene in such crises in order to achieve accommodation, if not resolution, of the underlying conflict. This tendency to intervention is reinforced by past experience: one or more parties seek(s) the involvement of the global organization; it responds positively; and a pattern of peace-oriented intervention develops within the PC.

More involvement does not generate strikingly greater effectiveness. PCs focus on core issues, with fundamental values at stake. While crises may be contained in their scope of action and consequences, they do not lend themselves to resolution as long as the underlying causes of the conflict remain. The global organization is likely to be less effective than superpowers in abating crises because it lacks the ability to coerce the adversaries. However, the benefits of routinization and a greater degree of interest by the global organization suggests more effectiveness within than outside PCs.

The last dimension of the Conflict-Crisis Model relates to *outcome*, both *content* and *form*. It is postulated that crises within PCs will terminate with less outcomes such as stalemate or compromise (Hypothesis 10) and formal agreements (Hypothesis 11) than non-PC crises.

Crises within protracted conflicts are phases in a multi-issue, continuing dispute. Whatever value is at stake in a particular crisis, the conflicting parties do not tend to identify its outcome in decisive terms. Regardless of outcome, the conflict over other values remains. Indecisive results symbolize an unresolved conflict. By contrast, crises which occur outside a PC have more autonomous starting and termination points. They are usually less threatening than crises within PCs. They are not affected by the legacy of an ongoing conflict; the actors can address the specific crisis. Outcomes therefore will be clearer and unlinked to other crises and outcomes. Victory or defeat can be more readily identified.

As for the form of outcome: because PC crises are viewed by the protagonists as interim stages, termination represents a decline in the intensity of threat perception and hostility, a pause between two phases of acute, ongoing conflictive interaction. The agreement to end a crisis is an acknowledgement by the parties at a point in time that the specific source of crisis has been overcome – but the conflict remains. Thus crisis termination is more likely to take the form of tacit understanding, an informal mutual acknowledgement that a specific threat to one or both parties has been overcome. By contrast, a crisis outside a PC lends itself to a more formal type of agreement, with less reference to residual disputes between the actors. It can be treated by the parties as an aberration from a normal relationship of cooperative or low conflictive interaction. In short, PCs spill over to the mode of crisis resolution, as with other crisis dimensions.

Operationalization

The task of analyzing the relationship between crises and conflicts in twentieth-century world politics required the integration of the ICB data set and the concept of protracted conflict. Applying the latter to the period 1929–85 generated 24 conflicts which meet the essential conditions of the modified definition noted above. All international crises which occurred within a protracted conflict were then grouped, along with their related actor–cases. Thus all crises in which the US and the USSR were adversarial crisis actors (e.g., Berlin Blockade 1948–49, Cuban Missiles 1962) were included in the set for the East/West protracted conflict.

"Mixed" international crisis, that is, those with pairs or clusters of adversaries belonging to different PCs, were assigned to the predominant protracted conflict (e.g., the Six Day War 1967 and the October–Yom Kippur War 1973–74 were primarily part of the Arab/Israel PC and were so designated). However, in classifying cases for conflict setting at the actor level, the US and the USSR, both of which were crisis actors in these two international crises, were grouped as cases within the East/West protracted conflict, while the actor-cases for Israel, Egypt, Jordan and Syria were incorporated into the set for the Arab/Israel protracted conflict.

Some of the components of crises specified above will be analyzed on the basis of unit-level data. Trigger, value and behavior are primarily actor variables. Other dimensions, however, superpower and international organization activity and effectiveness in crisis abatement, as well as outcome, apply to an international crisis as a whole, not to a specific actor. In short, the number of cases used to test hypotheses of the Protracted Conflict–Crisis Model will vary depending upon whether testing is at the foreign policy crisis (actor) level or the international crisis (system) level.

Overall: an aggregate set of 698 foreign policy crises from 1929 to 1985 grouped into 323 international crises, such as: Austria *Putsch* 1934, with four actor-cases (Austria, Czechoslovakia, Italy, Yugoslavia); Munich 1938, also with four actor-cases (Czechoslovakia, France, UK, USSR); Azerbaijan 1945–46, with five actor–cases [Iran (twice), UK, US, USSR]; Cuban Missiles 1962, with three actor-cases (US, USSR, Cuba); and War in Angola 1975–76, with seven actor-cases (Zambia, Zaire, South Africa, Angola, Cuba, US, USSR).

Crises within Protracted Conflicts: a subset of 375 actor-cases, 54% of the total. These 375 actor-cases occurred in 174 international crises: 109 PC international crises [e.g., Kashmir 1947–48, with two actor-cases (India, Pakistan), and Cyprus

III 1974–75, with three actor-cases (Cyprus, Greece, Turkey)]; and 65 long-war PC international crises [e.g., Fall of Western Europe 1940, with five actor-cases (Luxemburg, Netherlands, Belgium, France, UK), and Christmas Bombing 1972–73, with three actor-cases (South Vietnam, US, North Vietnam)]. These are presented in Table III.9.1.

Non-Protracted Conflicts: a subset of 323 actor-cases, 46% of the total. These 323 actor-cases occurred in 149 international crises [e.g., Amur River Incident 1937, with two actor-cases (Japan, USSR), Mali Federation 1960, with two actor-cases (Mali, Senegal)].

We turn now to the first set of tests of the postulated effects of protractedness on key dimensions of crisis, in the light of more than half a century of crisis data.

Conflict Protractedness and Crisis The first component of crisis to be explored is *trigger*. As will be recalled, it was postulated that crises within a protracted conflict are more likely than others to be catalyzed by violence, notably because of the deep-rooted mistrust and hostility.

The data on crisis triggers from 1929 to 1985 are presented in Table III.9.2. As evident, our expectation is supported. First, violence was present in 55% of the crisis triggers within PCs, compared to 35% of other cases (e.g., within a PC, the bombing of Quemoy and Matsu by the PRC on 3 September 1954, triggering the first US Taiwan Straits Crisis; and, for a non-PC setting, the attack by Moroccan irregulars against the Spanish enclave of Ifni on 23 November 1957, triggering a crisis for Spain). Moreover, the proportion of direct violent cases among PCs was almost double that in a non-PC setting – 44% to 24% (e.g., a Chinese ambush of Soviet forces on the Ussuri River on 2 March 1969, triggering a crisis for the USSR). Thus, in general, the postulated relationship between conflict protractedness and

TABLE III.9.1. Conflict Setting of International Crises

	First crisis/ conflict duration	Protracted Conflict	
		International Crisis	Foreign Policy Crisis
AFRICA			
Rhodesia	(1965–80)	11	17
Western Sahara	(1975–)	9	12
Angola	(1975–)	8	13
Chad/Libya	(1971–)	6	14
Ethiopia/Somalia	(1960–)	5	7
Ethiopia/Italy	(1934–45)	2	2
Rwanda/Burundi	(1963–)	1	2
AMERICAS			
Chaco	(1928–35)	2	4
Essequibo	(1968–)	2	2
ASIA			
Indo–China	(1953–)	18	39
Sino/Japanese	(1931–45)	11	20
Indo/Pakistani	(1947–)	7	15
PRC/Taiwan	(1948–)	4	11
Indonesia	(1945–49	3	6
Pushtunistan	(1949–)	3	7
Korea	(1950–)	3	12
Sino/Soviet	(1969–)	1	2
EUROPE			
World War II	(1939–45)	18*	49
Greece/Turkey	(1963–)	5	14
Trieste	(1945–53)	2	5
MIDDLE EAST			
Arab/Israel	(1947–)	25	53
Yemen	(1962–)	6	16
Iran/Iraq	(1980–)	3	6
MULTIREGIONAL			
East/West	(1945–)	19	47
Total		174**	375**

* Four of these crises occurred in North and East Africa and the Middle East.
** The other 149 international crises and 323 foreign policy crises occurred outside of protracted conflicts.

violence in the crisis trigger (Hypothesis 1) is strongly supported by the data for more than half a century of crises.

TABLE III.9.2. Crisis Triggers: Protracted vs. Non-Protracted Conflicts

	Non-Violent		Indirect Violent		Violent				
Non-Protracted Conflict	211	65%	36	11%	79	24%	326	47%	
Protracted Conflict	167	45%	40	11%	165	44%	372	53%	
	378	54%	76	11%	244	35%	698	100%	

$X^2 = 32.75$, p = .000

Code for Trigger:
Non-Violent Trigger = Verbal, political, economic, external change, internal verbal challenge.
Indirect Violent Trigger = Indirect violence in another state, internal physical challenge in another state.
Violent Trigger = Violent act, including internal physical challenge.

The second component of the crisis profile is *threatened value*, specifically, the tangible or intangible interest which is perceived by the principal decision-maker(s) of a crisis actor to be the object of gravest threat at any time during its foreign policy crisis. This ranges from a limited threat to population and/or territory to a threat to the most basic state value, its existence. It was postulated that crises within a PC are more likely than others to be characterized by higher stakes, that is, a perceived threat to more basic values. The reason, as noted, is that the stakes of a crisis are extensions or derivatives of fundamental cleavages over values.

The data relating to values are presented in Table III.9.3. On the value dimension of crisis, too, the evidence supports the Protracted Conflict–Crisis Model. For the three lowest categories of value threat – low, political system, territory – we find higher proportions of non-protracted than protracted conflict actors. For the three highest categories of value threat – influence, grave damage, existence – the proportions for protracted conflict actors are consistently higher than those for non-protracted conflicts. Among these latter cases exhibiting more serious threat, the differences for cases with grave damage as the value threat are particularly significant (e.g., in a PC setting, Taiwan's perception of the buildup of PRC forces in the coastal areas opposite Quemoy and Matsu on 17 July 1958, as a threat of grave damage in the Taiwan Straits II Crisis; and North Vietnam's perception of grave damage that might ensue from the US–South Vietnam invasion of Laos on 8 February 1971, which set in motion one of Hanoi's many crises during the Indo-China long-war PC).

Influence ranks first in the frequency of threatened values within PCs but only third in non-PC crises. This is primarily because it is pervasive in superpower crises, the core of the East/West protracted conflict. However, it is also present in other conflict settings (e.g., Pakistan's perceived threat to its influence in Central-South Asia, following Afghanistan's formal threat on 30 August 1962 to sever diplomatic relations and, by inference, move towards an alignment with the USSR unless Pakis-

TABLE III.9.3. Threatened Values in Crises: Protracted vs. Non-Protracted Conflicts

	Low		Political System		Territory		Influence		Grave Damage		Existence				
Non-Protracted Conflict	45	14%	79	24%	77	24%	68	21%	36	11%	21	6%	326	47%	
Protracted Conflict	41	11%	39	10%	67	18%	111	30%	74	20%	40	11%	372	53%	
	86	12%	118	17%	144	20%	179	26%	110	16%	61	9%	698	100%	

$X^2 = 40.96$, p = .000

tan withdrew its demand that Afghan consulates and trade agencies in Pakistan be closed because of their alleged subversive activities; and, in a non-PC setting, Egypt's nationalization of the Suez Canal on 26 July 1956, as a UK- and France-perceived threat to their global and regional influence, in the Suez Nationalization Crisis).

Another striking difference is the much greater frequency of threats to the *political system* in non-PC crises – 24% compared to 10% of all PC cases (e.g., Lebanon's perception of a threat to its political regime flowing from large-scale anti-government riots following the murder of a pro-Communist Beirut newspaper editor on 8 May 1958, in the Lebanon/Iraq Upheaval). In summary, whichever of these value indicators is used, the perceived stakes in crises within protracted conflicts are more basic than in other crises (Hypothesis 2).

A third (multiple) component of crisis relates to the place of *violence* in behavior, specifically, in terms of four aspects: the *primary crisis management technique* (CMT), that is, the *method* used to protect threatened values in a foreign policy crisis, ranging from negotiation to violence; the *major response*, that is, the *act* which captures the major thrust of its behavior during a crisis, such as the US "quarantine" of Cuba during the 1962 Missile Crisis; the *intensity of violence*, from none to full-scale war; and the *centrality of violence*, from none to the preeminent role in crisis management. It was postulated earlier that crises within a PC are more likely than others to be characterized by a primary role for violence in crisis management, a resort to more intense forms of violence, and a more central role for violence in crisis management. The rationale for these expectations, it will be recalled, is to be found in the essence of a protracted conflict.

What does the evidence indicate? The data on crisis behavior are presented in Tables III.9.4., III.9.5., III.9.6. and III.9.7.

TABLE III.9.4. Violence in Crisis Management: Protracted vs. Non-Protracted Conflicts

	Pacific Techniques		Non-Violent Military		Violence			
Non-Protracted Conflict	166	51%	53	16%	107	33%	326	47%
Protracted Conflict	109	29%	49	13%	213	58%	371	53%
	275	39%	102	15%	320	46%	697*	100%

$X^2 = 44.36$; $p = .000$

* 1 case missing data
Code for Crisis Management Technique:
Pacific Techniques = Mediation (by global or regional IO, ally, etc.);
   negotiation (formal or informal, bilateral,
   multilateral, international);
   multiple techniques excluding violence;
   arbitration, adjudication.
Non-Violent Military = Non-violent military act – maneuvers, mobilization, alerts;
   non-military pressure – withholding of military or economic aid.
Violence = Violence; multiple techniques including violence.

The differences are striking. As evident in Table III.9.4., violence was the primary CMT of states in more than half the foreign policy crises in PCs (58%), compared to 33% in non-PC cases (e.g., US resort to violence – air strikes against North Vietnam – as its primary CMT in the Pleiku Crisis of March 1965, in the Indo-China PC; and, in a non-PC setting, Costa Rica's reliance on OAS mediation in a 1955 crisis arising from Nicaragua's dispatch of military transports to Costa Rica's territory). There was little difference in the relative frequency of non-violent military acts as the primary CMT (e.g., an alert and military maneuvers by Yugoslav forces, in response to a Soviet ultimatum, in the Soviet Bloc/Yugoslavia Crisis 1949–   ). However, as the counter to greater disposition to violence in PC crises, more than half of non-PC crises (51%) were managed by pacific techniques, compared to 29% of all PC crises (e.g., negotiation between the parties, in the Poland Liberalization Crisis of October 1956; and, in a PC setting, mediation by the UK in the India/Pakistan Kutch Crisis, April-June 1965).

The findings are even more supportive for the major response by a crisis actor. As evident in Table III.9.5., the proportion of violent responsive acts in PC crises was almost double that in non-PC crises (44%–24%).

There was, too, more than four times the proportion of full-scale war cases in protracted conflicts than in a non-PC setting (34%–8%), (Table III.9.6.) (e.g., the Republic of (South) Yemen waged a full-scale war, in alliance with Egypt and against a coalition of Yemen royalists, Saudi Arabia and Jordan, in the first crisis of the protracted Yemen Conflict, which was catalyzed by a coup against the Yemen ruler on 26 September 1962; and, in a non-PC setting, the resort to full-scale war by Uganda and Tanzania in the Fall of Amin Crisis 1978–79). If war and serious clashes are combined as "high intensity" violence, the evidence is still strongly supportive of Hypothesis 4: 26% in non-PC cases, 55% in PC cases. Minor clashes, by contrast, were more than three times as frequent in non-PC crises than in PC crises.

As for the centrality of violence (Table III.9.7.), there were, proportionately,

TABLE III.9.5. Violence in the Major Response: Protracted vs. Non-Protracted Conflicts

	Non-Violent Acts		Non-Violent Military Acts		Violent Acts					
Non-Protracted Conflict	156	48%	92	28%	78	24%	326		47%	
Protracted Conflict	120	32%	87	24%	165	44%	372		53%	
	276	39%	179	26%	243	35%	698		100%	

$$X^2 = 33.10; \; p = .000$$

Code for Major Response:
Non-Violent = Compliance, verbal act, political act, economic act.
Non-Violent Military = Non-violent military act, non-military pressure.
Violence = Violence.

TABLE III.9.6. Intensity of Violence in Crisis Management: Protracted vs. Non-Protracted Conflicts

	No Violence		Minor Clashes		Serious Clashes		Full-Scale War					
Non-Protracted Conflict	176	54%	66	20%	57	18%	27	8%	326		47%	
Protracted Conflict	140	38%	26	7%	80	21%	126	34%	372		53%	
	316	45%	92	13%	137	20%	153	22%	698		100%	

$$X^2 = 86.76; \; p = .000$$

TABLE III.9.7. Centrality of Violence in Crisis Management: Protracted vs. Non-Protracted Conflicts

	No Violence		Minor Role		Important Role		Preeminent Role					
Non-Protracted Conflict	176	54%	44	14%	70	21%	36	11%	326		47%	
Protracted Conflict	140	38%	21	51%	104	28%	107	29%	372		53%	
	316	45%	65	9%	174	25%	143	21%	698		100%	

$$X^2 = 51.33; \; p = .000$$

Code for Centrality of Violence:
No Violence =
Minor Role = Relative to other crisis management techniques.
Important Role = Supported by other CMTs.
Preeminent Role = The dominant CMT.

considerably more crises within protracted conflicts in which violence was the preeminent CMT or had an important role (57%–32%) (e.g., the use of airstrikes against the China mainland by Taiwan, on 7 September 1954, as its preeminent CMT in the Taiwan Straits Crisis arising from the PRC's bombing of the offshore islands, Quemoy and Matsu, four days earlier; and, outside a PC, El Salvador's use of violence – full-scale war – in the Football War with Honduras in 1969).

The evidence on all three hypotheses related to crisis behavior (Hypotheses 3,4,5) is unmistakable: crises which occurred within protracted conflicts contained much more – and more intense – violence, with a more central role for violence as the primary CMT than did crises outside the setting of a protracted conflict.

We turn now to several macro-level variables, beginning with *superpower (SP) activity* in crises. Here we postulated more political and less military activity in crises which are part of a protracted conflict for, as noted, crises in that setting are likely to be more destabilizing for an international system.

The relevant data on SP activity are presented in Tables III.9.8.a. and b. The US was active in more crises within protracted conflicts, proportionately, than in other cases (74%–64%). The comparable proportions for the USSR are much sharper

TABLE III.9.8.a.   Superpower Activity in Crises: Protracted vs. Non-Protracted Conflicts: US

	No Activity		Low-Level		Semi-Military		Military			
Non-Protracted Conflict	41	36%	45	40%	21	18%	7	6%	114	45%
Protracted Conflict	37	26%	62	44%	26	19%	15	11%	140	55%
	78	31%	107	42%	47	18%	22	9%	254*	100%

$$X^2 = 3.72, p = .293$$

TABLE III.9.8.b.   Superpower Activity in Crises: Protracted vs. Non-Protracted Conflicts: USSR

	No Activity		Low-Level		Semi-Military		Military			
Non-Protracted Conflict	67	59%	26	23%	16	14%	5	4%	114	45%
Protracted Conflict	48	34%	53	38%	31	22%	8	6%	140	55%
	115	45%	79	31%	47	19%	13	5%	254*	100%

$$X^2 = 15.35, p = .002$$

* Cases prior to the end of World War II excluded in Tables III.9.8. and III.9.9.

(66%–41%). However, the data are less supportive on US semi-military and military activity: 30% in PC cases, 24% in non-PC cases (e.g., the US invasion of Cambodia on 21 April 1970, when Vietcong forces linked to North Vietnam cut the road to Phnom Penh). USSR political activity (low-level) was considerably more visible in PC than in non-PC cases, 38%–23%; but so too was Soviet combined military activity (28%–18%) (e.g., Soviet pilots flying combat missions in support of Egypt during the War of Attrition 1970, and a massive airlift–sealift of weapons to Egypt and Syria during the October–Yom Kippur War 1973–74). In short, the evidence on Hypothesis 6 is mixed.

The data about *superpower effectiveness* in crises from 1945 to 1985 (see Tables III.9.9.a. and b.) provide moderate support for a related postulate, namely, more effectiveness in the abatement of crises within than outside the setting of protracted

TABLE III.9.9.a. Superpower Effectiveness in Crises: Protracted vs. Non-Protracted Conflicts: US

	No Activity		Ineffective		Marginal		Important and Most Important			
Non-Protracted Conflict	41	36%	35	31%	10	9%	28	24%	114	45%
Protracted Conflict	37	26%	48	34%	8	6%	47	34%	140	55%
	78	31%	83	33%	18	7%	75	29%	254	100%

$X^2 = 4.66$, p = .198

TABLE III.9.9.b. Superpower Effectiveness in Crises: Protracted vs. Non-Protracted Conflicts: USSR

	No Activity		Ineffective		Marginal		Important and Most Important			
Non-Protracted Conflict	67	59%	38	33%	4	4%	5	4%	114	45%
Protracted Conflict	48	34%	66	47%	11	8%	15	11%	140	55%
	115	45%	104	41%	15	6%	20	8%	254	100%

$X^2 = 16.46$, p = .001

conflict (Hypothesis 7): there is minimal support for the US role, modest support for that of the USSR. In the high effectiveness category (important or most important contribution), the US record was 34% in PC crises, 24% in non-PC cases (e.g., successful US mediation of a 1967 crisis between Greece and Turkey, persuading the latter to cancel preparations for a large-scale invasion of Cyrpus; and, in a non-PC setting, indirect mediation (through the OAS) of a crisis between Venezuela and the Dominican Republic in the summer of 1960, over the latter's complicity in an assassination attempt on the Venezuelan President). More so than with the US, the combined effectiveness of Soviet activity is more visible in PC crises (19%–8%) (e.g., on 29 October 1957 the USSR succeeded in deescalating a US–Turkey military buildup by tacitly dropping its accusation that Turkey was about to attack Syria; and, in a PC setting, the Soviet threat on 5 November 1956 to intervene militarily in the Suez War if France, Israel and the UK did not cease operations against Egypt and withdraw their forces contributed to the abatement of that crisis).

Soviet ineffectiveness in crisis abatement was high in both groups of crises – and higher than that of the US in both categories (e.g., the Soviets contributed to escalation by providing arms and economic aid to Pathan tribesmen during a 1961–62 Afghanistan/Pakistan crisis over Pushtunistan; and the USSR exacerbated the 1956 Poland Liberalization Crisis, following Gomulka's return to power, by massing seven divisions on the Polish border). The US, by contrast, was ineffective almost as frequently in PC as in non-PC crises (e.g., it gave a green light to Turkey's invasion and occupation of the northern part of Cyprus in July 1974).

Turning to the role of the global international organization, it was postulated that crises within protracted conflicts will be characterized by more *involvement* (Hypothesis 8) and more *effectiveness* (Hypothesis 9) than other crises. The relevant data are presented in Tables III.9.10. and III.9.11.

The evidence strongly supports our expectation. First, from 1929 to 1939 (League of Nations) and 1945 to 1985 (United Nations) the global organization (GO) was strongly disposed to aloofness or low-level involvement in non-PC cases (84%), where the danger to international stability and major power interests was less, compared to 60% in PC crises. In the latter, by contrast, the League and the UN were

TABLE III.9.10. Global Organization Involvement in Crises: Protracted vs. Non-Protracted Conflicts

	None	Low-Level	Medium-Level	High-Level		
Non-Protracted Conflict	82	37	19	4	142	
	58%	26%	13%	3%		49%
Protracted Conflict	46	44	51	9	150	
	31%	29%	34%	6%		51%
	128	81	70	13	292*	
	44%	28%	24%	4%		100%

$$X^2 = 27.08, p = .000$$

* Six cases missing data; includes only post-World War II cases.
Code for Global Organization Involvement:
Low-Level Activity = Fact-finding, good offices, discussion without resolution, general – other.
Medium-Level Activity = Mediation, resolution calling for action, condemnation.
High-Level Activity = Arbitration, sanctions, observer group, emergency military force.

TABLE III.9.11. Global Organization Effectiveness in Crises: Protracted vs. Non-Protracted Conflicts

	No GO Involvement	GO Ineffective	GO Marginally Effective	GO Effective Important + Most Important		
Non-Protracted Conflict	82	43	4	13	142	
	58%	30%	3%	9%		49%
Protracted Conflict	46	63	19	22	150	
	31%	42%	13%	14%		51%
	128	106	23	35	292*	
	44%	36%	8%	12%		100%

$$X^2 = 25.80, p = .000$$

* Six cases missing data; includes only post-World War II cases.

much more active – 34% to 13%, medium-level activity. Overall, medium- and high-level GO activity was much more evident in PC crises (40%–16%) (e.g., the formation of an emergency military force (UNEF I) during the Sinai–Suez Crisis 1956–57; and, in a non-protracted conflict setting, the dispatch of UN observers to Lebanon in 1958 by the Security Council, in the Lebanon/Iraq Upheaval).

As for effectiveness, there are similarities and differences in global organization performance within PC and non-PC settings (Table III.9.11.). The proportion of cases with "an important" or "the most important" GO role in crisis abatement is only slightly higher in PC crises (14%–9%). Moreover, the League/UN "marginal" role was somewhat more conspicuous in PC cases (13%–3%). Finally, the combined data for GO contribution to crisis abatement support Hypothesis 9: non-PC – 12%, PC – 27% (e.g., the UN was the most important contributor to abatement of a South Africa/Zambia crisis in October 1971, through a Security Council resolution calling upon the former to respect the latter's sovereignty, following a military incursion into Zambia; and a UN recommendation of a plebiscite in Indonesia was incorporated into the Renville Agreement of 17 January 1948 which terminated the second of three Netherlands/Indonesia crises following the latter's proclamation of independence in August 1945).

The most striking finding on this dimension, however, is the preeminence of UN ineffectiveness in both settings for crisis (e.g., a Security Council discussion had no effect on the abatement of a March 1968 Arab/Israel crisis over PLO intrusions from Jordan and an Israeli retaliation raid on the village of Karameh; nor did discussions in the General Assembly have an effect on the UK crisis over Guatemala's threat to seize the British colony of Belize in November 1975). In fact, positive

TABLE III.9.12. Substance of Crisis Outcome: Protracted vs. Non-Protracted Conflicts

	Ambiguous Outcome		Definitive Outcome			
Non-Protracted Conflict	65	44%	84	56%	149	46%
Protracted Conflict	97	56%	77	44%	174	54%
	162	50%	161	50%	323	100%

$$X^2 = 4.25, p = .039$$

Code for Crisis Outcome: Substance:
Ambiguous = All stalemate, all compromise, victory/stalemate, defeat/stalemate, victory/compromise, defeat/compromise.
Definitive = Victory/defeat, all victory, all defeat.

effectiveness by the global organization – marginal, important and most important – is evident in only 20% of the 292 crises for which data are available.

The last dimension of the crisis profile relates to outcome, both *substance* and *form*. It was postulated that crises within protracted conflicts will terminate with more ambiguous outcomes (Hypothesis 10) and less formal agreements (Hypothesis 11). The data on outcomes are presented in Tables III.9.12. and III.9.13.

As for the substance of outcome, there is considerable support: ambiguous outcomes account for a higher proportion of crises within PCs (56%–44%) (e.g., within a protracted conflict, the Soviet-initiated Tashkent Agreement between India and Pakistan on 10 January 1966, a compromise outcome of their second crisis-war over Kashmir; and the division of Trieste between Yugoslavia (northern zone) and Italy (southern zone) on 5 October 1954, as a compromise between conflicting claims in a major South European crisis).

The evidence on form of outcome (see Table III.9.13.) is also supportive of our expectation: agreements in PC crises were, proportionately, fewer (40%–50%). And non-agreement in the form of unilateral acts was more evident in PC crises (38%–25%) (e.g., a cease-fire agreement between Cyprus and Turkey on 10 August 1964, terminating one of several crises within that protracted conflict; among semi-formal agreements, the termination of the first Taiwan Straits Crisis in 1955 with Prime Minister Chou En-Lai's offer to negotiate with the US; in a non-PC setting, a joint communiqué issued by Dahomey and Niger on 4 January 1964 ending a 15-day crisis over the disputed ownership of the tiny island of Lete; and, as for tacit understandings, an informal acceptance by India and China in December 1962 that no forces would be stationed in the disputed areas straddling their frontier).

The findings from this overall inquiry into the relationship between crises and protracted conflicts are summarized in Table III.9.14. In general, the data on 698 actor-cases in 323 international crises from 1929 to 1985 provide considerable or moderate support for the postulated character of five of six dimensions encompassing 10 of 11 hypotheses about crises within protracted conflicts.

In short, the Protracted Conflict-Crisis Model and the hypotheses deduced therefrom have considerable support from the evidence of crises during more than half

TABLE III.9.13. Form of Crisis Outcome: Protracted vs. Non-Protracted Conflicts

	Agreement		Tacit		Unilateral Act		No Agreement			
Non-Protracted Conflict	74	50%	15	10%	38	25%	22	15%	149	46%
Protracted Conflict	69	40%	15	9%	67	38%	23	13%	174	54%
	143	44%	30	9%	105	33%	45	14%	323	100%

$$X^2 = 6.31, p. = .097$$

TABLE III.9.14. Summary of Findings: Protracted vs. Non-Protracted Conflicts

Crisis Dimension	Protracted Conflict	Non-Protracted Conflict
Trigger	prominent presence of violence – 55% of cases;	predominance of non-violence – 65%
Value	perception of higher stakes (existence, grave damage, influence) – 61%;	perception of lower stakes – 62%
Behavior	prominence of violence in crisis management – 58%; violent major response – 44%;	prominence of pacific and other non-violent CMTs – 67%; non-violent major response – 76%; much less intense violence – 54%; no violence – 26%;
	full-scale war and serious clashes (high intensity) – 55%; and important/preeminent role of violence – 57%;	War or serious clashes 26%; and no/minor role for violence – 68%
SP Effectiveness	important/most important contribution by US and USSR to crisis abatement higher in PC than in non-PC crises – 34%–24%, 11%–4%, respectively;	
GO Involvement	medium – and high-level – 40%;	non-involvement or low level – 84%;
GO Effectiveness	contribution to abatement – 27%;	no/negative contribution to abatement – 88%
Outcome: Substance	prominence of ambiguous outcomes – 56%;	prominence of definitive outcomes – 56%
Outcome: Form	prominence of non-agreements – 51%	prominence of agreements – 60%

of the twentieth century. Two further tests of this linkage (Chapters 10 and 11) offer even stronger support for the basic contention that protractedness of conflict is a crucial determinant of the configuration of international and foreign policy crises.

Notes

1. These properties resemble those identified by Rapoport (1974: Chap. 17) with endogenous conflicts which he distinguishes from exogenous conflicts. The former involve members of the same social system; the latter are between two autonomous systems. The only other explicit reference to "protracted conflict" is the title of the book by Strausz-Hupé *et al.* (1958), which applied the term exclusively to the US/Soviet struggle for global mastery. For an exploration of other aspects of "protracted conflict," see Azar (1979), Azar and Farah (1981) and Azar (1985).
2. A list of protracted conflicts from 1929 to 1985, and the international and foreign policy crises within each, are to be found in Table III.9.1.
3. The values for this and all other dependent variables in the conflict–crisis model are elaborated in Brecher and Wilkenfeld, *et al.*, *op. cit.*, I.Part III.

10 Conflicts, Crises and Systems

Michael Brecher and Jonathan Wilkenfeld

Introduction

The second strand of our inquiry into crisis and conflict relates to the effects of system level on crises within protracted conflicts. Here too we are guided by a general proposition which specifies a crisis profile.

> **Proposition: International and foreign policy crises which occur within dominant system protracted conflicts will differ from crises within subsystem protracted conflicts along a number of dimensions, from type of trigger and value threat to the substance and form of outcome.**

Specifically, it is postulated that dominant system PC crises are more likely to be characterized by:

Hypothesis 1: predominantly non-violent triggers;
Hypothesis 2: the pervasiveness of influence as the perceived value under threat;
Hypothesis 3: a lesser role for violence in the major response to crisis;
Hypothesis 4: a prevalent resort to non-violent techniques of crisis management;
Hypothesis 5: a reliance on less intense violence to manage crises;
Hypothesis 6: the primacy of political activity by the superpowers in subsystem crises;
Hypothesis 7: a positive contribution by superpower activity to crisis abatement;
Hypothesis 8: less involvement by the global international organization;
Hypothesis 9: less effectiveness by the global organization, in terms of crisis abatement;
Hypothesis 10: indecisive non-zero-sum outcomes; and
Hypothesis 11: the preeminence of unilateral acts among the forms of crisis outcome.

This proposition is presented in Figure III.10.1.

We begin with the difference in *triggers*. It is postulated that crises within the

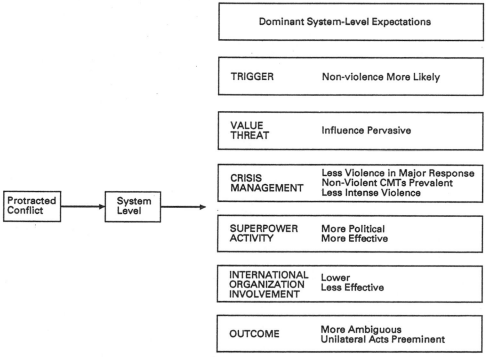

FIGURE III.10.1. System-Level Protracted Conflict–Crisis Model

141

East/West dominant system Conflict are more likely than those in subsystem conflicts (e.g., Arab/Israel, India/Pakistan) to be characterized by non-violent triggers. The reason lies in the special constraints on superpower behavior.

The protracted conflict in the dominant international system since 1945 is essentially a struggle between the superpowers (SPs) for global hegemony. Other states have participated in crises within the East/West Conflict (France, the UK, FRG and GDR in crises over Berlin, South and North Korea and the PRC in the Korean War, Cuba in the Missile Crisis, etc.); but they have done so as allies or clients of the US or the USSR whose behavior determines the outcome in most crises within this conflict. Both superpowers, as well as their lesser adversaries, are aware of the US and Soviet capability to cause great damage while responding to a crisis, along with the danger of uncontrollable escalation of violence. Thus all actors in the dominant system protracted conflict tend to be prudent in the type of act chosen to catalyze a crisis. Violent triggers are eschewed whenever possible because of the risk and costs that may ensue.

By contrast, subsystem actors do not generally function under these constraints. For one thing, neither superpower is a direct continuing participant in subsystem protracted conflicts: full-scale war between Chad and Libya, Ethiopia and Somalia, Greece and Turkey, or Israel and Syria, with one or both SPs actively engaged on the battlefield, is highly unlikely. For another, as a consequence of, at most, indirect superpower participation, the destructiveness of violent subsystem crises, even with full-scale war, is qualitatively less than intense violence between the superpowers would be in the East/West Conflict. Prudence regarding a violent trigger is less essential at the subsystem level and is therefore a less effective self-restraint. If a crisis trigger contains violence, marginal or central, and even if it heightens the likelihood of greater violence, the costs are less serious. Thus subsystem actors are likely to be less cautious in the use of violent acts to catalyze a crisis within their protracted conflict.

The relevant data for the trigger dimension of a system-level crisis profile are presented in Tables III.10.1.a. and b.

As evident, the data strongly support the expected differences in crisis triggers. Overall, non-violence was more frequent in dominant system triggers; and, if long-war PC cases are excluded, the gap is much larger – 73%–48%. Stated in terms of proneness to violent triggers, subsystem PC crises outside a war setting exhibit more than double the proneness to direct violence of their counterpart at the dominant system level – 44%–17%.

Violent triggers were sparse in the East/West Conflict; and they were just as likely to be experienced first by a client or an ally, that is, indirect violence (e.g., the landing of US and Belgian paratroops in Stanleyville, the Congo (Zaire), on 24 November 1964, triggering a Soviet crisis over Katanga). By contrast, violent acts

---

TABLE III.10.1.a.   Crisis Triggers: System Level and Protracted Conflicts

Dominant System	Non-Violent		Indirect Violent		Violent			
Non-long-war PC	48		7		11		66	
		73%		10%		17%		49%
Long-war PC	23		15		30		68	
		34%		22%		44%		51%
	71		22		41		134	
		53%		16%		31%		100%

$X^2 = 20.49$, p = .000

Subsystem	Non-Violent		Indirect Violent		Violent			
Non-long-war PC	78		12		71		161	
		48%		8%		44%		68%
Long-war PC	18		6		53		77	
		23%		8%		69%		32%
	96		18		124		238	
		40%		8%		52%		100%

$X^2 = 14.24$, p = .001

TABLE III.10.1.b. Crisis Triggers: Systems and Protracted Conflicts

East/West	Non-Violent		Indirect Violent		Violent			
Non-long-war PC	39	86.7%	3	6.7%	3	6.7%	45	96%
Long-war PC	2	100%	0	0%	0	0%	2	4%
	41	87%	3	6.5%	3	6.5%	47	100%
Arab/Israel								
Non-long-war PC (Total)	28	52%	1	2%	25	40%	54	100%
India/Pakistan								
Non-long-war PC (Total)	8	53.3%	2	13.3%	5	33.3%	15	100%

Code for Triggers:
Non-Violent = external verbal, political, economic, non-violent military acts, external change, or internal challenge to a regime, verbal or physical.
Indirect Violent = Violence directed at ally, friendly state, vassal.
Violent = Border clash, invasion of air space, sinking of ship, military attack – limited or large-scale, etc.

were prominent as catalysts to crisis in the Arab/Israel and India/Pakistan conflicts. In the Middle East (e.g., Egypt's crisis at the onset of the Six Day War, triggered by Israel's preemptive air strike on 5 June 1967), they comprised 46% of the total, and in South Asia, one-third of the cases. Even if the two violent trigger categories are combined, violence was conspicuously more frequent in subsystem crises: almost double those at the dominant system level overall for non-long-war cases; with Arab/Israel and India/Pakistan cases each more than triple the frequency of East/West violent triggers. In summary, there is strong support for Hypothesis 1: violence is much more visible in the triggers to crises within subsystem conflicts; dominant system PC crises began mainly with political, verbal or other non-violent acts.

Threatened *values* are a second component of the crisis profile for protracted conflicts at different system levels. It is anticipated that superpowers will be predominantly concerned with status and influence in the international system while crisis actors within subsystem conflicts will perceive primary threats to more tangible values such as territory. The reason lies in the character of the East/West Conflict.

Dominant system crises, with the US and the USSR as direct or indirect adversaries, for the most part, focus primarily on relative influence in world politics. The predominance of that value is a consequence of the core issue in superpower relations, namely, their competition for global hegemony or, at least, primacy in the hierarchy of power and status among states. Existence would be perceived to be threatened only if one superpower became convinced that the other was about to launch a nuclear first-strike; this is unlikely as long as deterrence is an effective constraint on SP behavior, based on the expectation of mutual assured destruction in the event of nuclear war. The same constraint prevents a frequent perception of grave damage, for this would result only from direct superpower war or, as in the Cuban Missile Crisis, the image of one superpower's willingness to risk such a war. Prudence by both the US and the USSR means that either of these basic values is likely to be a rare object of perceived threat.

Lesser values, too, will not often be the primary object of superpower concern. Geographic distance makes a direct physical threat to each other's territorial integrity remote. Mutual respect for their military capability to repel such a danger reinforces the low salience of territory among superpower values in crisis. And lesser powers cannot, by themselves, threaten the territory of either superpower. The same reasoning applies to political system as a value in crises. Neither the rival superpower nor weaker international actors can undermine the political system of the US or the USSR. And while other values such as economic interests may be at stake in a crisis, they are usually accompanied by a much higher intangible value, namely, their relentless struggle to enhance or at least to maintain their relative influence in the global system.

Subsystem conflicts, by contrast, focus mainly on tangible values, notably territory and political regime. This tendency is enhanced by the fact that the regional subsystems comprise many new, underdeveloped states whose national integration is incomplete as ethnic and other sources of disunity prevail.

The relevant data for the value dimension of crisis are presented in Tables III.10.2.a. and b.

TABLE III.10.2.a.   Threatened Values in Crises: System Level and Protracted Conflicts

Dominant System	Low		Political System		Territory		Influence		Grave Damage		Existence			
Non-long-war PC	1	1%	5	8%	9	14%	35	53%	13	20%	3	4%	66	49%
Long-war PC	6	9%	1	1%	0	0%	14	21%	26	38%	21	31%	68	51%
	7	5%	6	4%	9	7%	49	37%	39	29%	24	18%	134	100%

$$X^2 = 42.05, p = .000$$

Subsystem	Low		Political System		Territory		Influence		Grave Damage		Existence			
Non-long-war PC	21	13%	17	11%	52	32%	39	24%	20	12%	12	8%	161	68%
Long-war PC	13	17%	16	21%	6	8%	23	30%	15	19%	4	5%	77	32%
	34	14%	33	14%	58	24%	62	26%	35	15%	16	7%	238	100%

$$X^2 = 20.09, p = .001$$

TABLE III.10.2.b.   Threatened Values in Crises: Systems and Protracted Conflicts

East/West	Low		Political System		Territory		Influence		Grave Damage		Existence			
Non-long-war PC	1	2%	4	9%	3	7%	31	69%	6	13%	0	0%	45	96%
Long-war PC	0	0%	1	50%	0	0%	1	50%	0	0%	0	0%	2	4%
	1	2%	5	11%	3	6%	32	68%	6	13%	0	0%	47	100%

Arab/Israel	Low		Political System		Territory		Influence		Grave Damage		Existence			
Non-long-war PC (Total)	12	22%	2	4%	10	18%	14	26%	14	26%	2	4%	54	100%

India/Pakistan	Low		Political System		Territory		Influence		Grave Damage		Existence			
Non-long-war PC (Total)	1	7%	0	0%	11	73%	0	0%	2	13%	1	7%	15	100%

Code for Values:

Low Values = Threat to economic interests, limited threat to population and property.

Political System = Threat of: overthrow of regime, change of political institutions, intervention in domestic politics, etc.

Territory = Threat of partial annexation, separatism, etc.

Influence = Threat of diplomatic isolation or, generally, to one's capacity to affect policies of other states in global and/or regional systems.

= (for superpowers) threat of adverse change in global military balance between SPs or decline in SPs' influence: within its bloc; within non-bloc client state; with non-aligned group, or within adversary bloc.

Grave Damage = Threat of large casualties in war, mass bombing, etc.

Existence = Threat of genocide or threat to existence of entity through occupation or colonial rule, etc.

Here, too, our expectation is clearly supported. External influence was the most frequently perceived threatened value in dominant system crises as a whole (53% of non-long-war PC cases, more than double the frequency in the corresponding subsystem category). The prominence of influence is even more evident in East/West crises (69%) (e.g., the Azerbaijan Crisis in 1945–46 as a threat to US and UK influence in the Middle East and in the global system generally; and, for the USSR, the threat posed to its influence with clients and adversaries alike by the US quarantine in the Cuban Missile Crisis). By contrast, the protection or acquisition of territory was the most frequently perceived value threat in subsystem non-long-war PC crises (32%), more than double the dominant system territory cases.

Hypothesis 2 is even more strongly supported by the evidence on specific systems. Crises in the East/West Conflict exhibit a perceived threat to influence more than twice as often as in Arab/Israel crises; and there were no influence cases in the India/Pakistan Conflict. In the latter, territory was the preeminent value threat (73%). The coming of independence to India and Pakistan in 1947 was accompanied by several residual territorial disputes, notably over Kashmir, the central issue in major crises in 1947–48 and 1965–66. In the Arab/Israel Conflict there was a much more even distribution of threatened values in crises, the three most frequent being grave damage, influence, and limited damage to persons and/or property (e.g., respectively, the threat of grave damage to Egypt, including heavy casualties, created by the France–Israel–UK attack on Sinai and the Suez Canal Zone beginning 29 October 1956; and the limited threat to Jordan posed by Israel's retaliation against the village of El-Samu in November 1966).

Violence was examined in Chapter 9 as a crucial component of profiles of crises within – and outside the setting of – protracted conflicts. For reasons to be indicated below, it is expected that, compared with crises in subsystem conflicts, those in the dominant system conflict will manifest: a lesser role for violence in the actors' *major response* (Hypothesis 3); less resort to violent *techniques of crisis management* (Hypothesis 4), and reliance on *less intense* violence to manage crises (Hypothesis 5). The fundamental reason for the different attitude to, and role of, violence in crisis behavior is similar to that noted for triggers, namely, the awareness of relative danger and cost.

Violent behavior by states in any foreign policy crisis carries the risk of value loss because of the anarchic character of international systems. However, the potential cost of violence used by superpowers is vastly greater than the resort to violence by small and middle powers in subsystem conflicts. The superpowers (and their allies) become increasingly aware of the danger of unleashing violence, for their military capability has grown astronomically during their protracted conflict. A learning process after the successful management of each major East/West crisis – Iran (1945–46), the Berlins (1948–49, 1957–59,1961), Cuban Missiles (1962), etc. – is expected to reinforce their caution, acting as an effective self-restraint on their use of violence in crisis management; and when violence seems necessary, to avoid the most severe type, namely, full-scale war (Nye, 1987).

This constraint is likely to be less in the behavior of actors within subsystem conflicts. Few if any of the adversaries have second-strike nuclear capability. The scale of destructiveness is limited, though potentially considerable and growing over time. Thus the awareness of danger to survival from a nuclear war, which was evident in the perceptions of superpower decision-makers during most of the post-World War II era, could not act as a constraint at the subsystem level. At the same time, intense hostility between subsystem adversaries could be expected to reinforce a disposition to use full-scale war as a primary technique of crisis management. In short, there are few – and weak – constraints on the resort to violence in managing crises within subsystems, whether from the UN or the superpowers. This combination of negative factors – the absence of effective constraints, and positive factors – the intense adversarial animosity, operated very early in these conflicts. One could therefore anticipate much greater violence – and full-scale war – in the management of Middle East, South Asia and other subsystem PC crises.

The data pertaining to crisis behavior and violence at different system levels are presented in Tables III.10.3.a. and b.; III.10.4.a. and b.; III.10.5.a. and b.; and III.10.6.a. and b.

Conflict in the dominant system has been a central feature of world politics since the end of the Second World War. Caution regarding the use of violence was the norm, much more so than in crises within subsystem protracted conflicts. The con-

TABLE III.10.3.a. Major Response in Crises: System Level and Protracted Conflicts

Dominant System	Non-violent		Non-Violent Military		Violent				
Non-long-war PC	30	45%	25	38%	11	17%	66	49%
Long-war PC	25	37%	11	16%	32	47%	68	51%
	55	41%	36	27%	43	32%	134	100%

$X^2 = 16.13$, p = .000

Subsystem	Non-violent		Non-Violent Military		Violent				
Non-long-war PC	49	30%	43	27%	69	43%	161	68%
Long-war PC	16	21%	8	10%	53	69%	77	32%
	65	27%	51	22%	122	51%	238	100%

$X^2 = 15.11$, p = .000

TABLE III.10.3.b. Major Response in Crises: Systems and Protracted Conflicts

East/West	Non-Violent		Non-Violent Military		Violent				
Non-long-war PC	25	56%	20	44%	0	0%	45	96%
Long-war PC	1	50%	1	50%	0	0%	2	4%
	26	55%	21	45%	0	0%	47	100%
Arab/Israel								
Non-long-war PC (Total)	15	28%	14	26%	25	46%	54	100%
India/Pakistan								
Non-long-war PC (Total)	3	20%	2	13%	10	67%	15	100%

Code for Major Response:
Non-Violent = Compliance, verbal, political, economic act.
Non-Violent Military = Non-Violent military act, non-military pressure.

trast in *major response* is striking. First, it was a violent military act in more than half of the crises within subsystem conflicts (51%), compared to 32% in the dominant system; and, if the long-war PC category is excluded, the contrast is much sharper (43%–17%); that is, violence was 2½ times more frequent in the major response of subsystem crisis actors (e.g., Pakistan's response in kind on 8 April 1965 to an attack by Indian forces the same day on a Pakistani police station in the disputed Rann of Kutch; and, in the dominant system, the PRC's dispatch of thousands of "volunteers" across the Yalu River beginning on 16 October 1950, in response to the crossing of the 38th Parallel in Korea by UN forces under MacArthur following authorization by the UN General Assembly on 7 October).

The data on specific protracted conflicts at the two system levels provide even stronger support for Hypothesis 3. There was not a single case in which violence was the major response in East/West crises, compared to 46% in Arab/Israel crises and 67% in India/Pakistan cases. Actor behavior in East/West crises reveals a prominent role for non-violent military responses (mobilization, alert, etc.) (44%), considerably more than in the Arab/Israel Conflict, and much more than in the India/Pakistan Conflict.

Violence at the subsystem level was also more visible as the primary *crisis management technique* (CMT) (Tables III.10.4.a. and b.): it was present in 63% of subsystem PC cases, 48% of crises in the dominant system; and, if long-war PC cases are omitted (since violence is expected), the difference is stark – 52% violent CMTs versus 23%. There is even stronger support for Hypothesis 4 in the data on specific conflicts. Actors in East/West crises resorted to violence as their primary CMT in 2% of 45 cases, compared to 54% in the Arab/Israel Conflict, and 60% in the India/Pakistan Conflict (e.g., Syria's primary reliance on violence to manage its crisis created by Israel's attack on the Golan Heights on 9 June during the 1967 Six Day War; and India's invasion of East Pakistan in December 1971 as its principal CMT in the crisis over Bangladesh). East/West crises were characterized by a much

TABLE III.10.4.a.   Violence in Crisis Management: System Level and Protracted Conflicts

Dominant System	Pacific Techniques		Non-Violent Military		Violence				
Non-long-war PC	40	60%	11	17%	15	23%	66		50%
Long-war PC	9	13.5%	9	13.5%	49	73%	67		50%
	49	37%	20	15%	64	48%	133*		100%

$$X^2 = 37.86, p = .000$$

Subsystem	Pacific Techniques		Non-Violent Military		Violence				
Non-long-war PC	54	33%	24	15%	83	52%	161		68%
Long-war PC	6	8%	5	6%	66	86%	77		32%
	60	25%	29	12%	149	63%	238		100%

$$X^2 = 26.43, p = .000$$

TABLE III.10.4.b.   Violence in Crisis Management: Systems and Protracted Conflicts

East/West	Pacific Techniques		Non-Violent Military		Violence				
Non-long-war PC	36	80%	8	18%	1	2%	45		96%
Long-war PC	1	50%	1	50%	0	0%	2		4%
	37	79%	9	19%	1	2%	47		100%
Arab/Israel									
Non-long-war PC (Total)	12	22%	13	24%	29	54%	54		100%
India/Pakistan									
Non-long-war PC (Total)	5	33%	1	7%	9	60%	15		100%

Code for Crisis Management Technique:
Negotiation and other Pacific CMTs = Mediation, negotiation, multiple techniques excluding violence, arbitration, adjudication.
Non-Violent Military CMT = Non-violent military act, non-military pressure.
The apparent discrepancy among Non-Violent Major Responses and Non-Violence in the Intensity of Violence as CMTs is due to the following: two South Asia cases, coded Minor Clashes (intensity) are included in the Non-Violent Major Response category precisely because the *major response* of the crisis actor was not of a violent character.
* One case with missing data.

greater resort to multiple CMTs excluding violence (e.g., US diplomatic messages and political activity, reaffirming its commitment to Turkey's security, during the latter's territorial crisis with Syria from 18 August to 29 October 1957).

The pattern of violence in subsystem crisis behavior is also evident in the prevalence of the most intense type of violence, full-scale war (Tables III.10.5.a. and b.). Full-scale war occurred almost three times as frequently in subsystem non-long-war PCs as in corresponding dominant system cases (26%–9%); and, if war and serious clashes are combined, the gap is still very large (48%–23%); (long-war PC cases can be excluded from this analysis since they can be expected to exhibit a high incidence of intense violence and they did, 84% in subsystem cases, 72% in dominant system cases).

Whereas the East/West PC has been spared a full-scale war in which both super-

---

TABLE III.10.5.a. Intensity of Violence in Crisis Management: System Level and Protracted Conflicts

Dominant System	No Violence	Minor Clashes	Serious Clashes	Full-Scale War		
Non-long-war PC	50 76%	1 1%	9 14%	6 9%	66	49%
Long-war PC	14 21%	5 7%	8 12%	41 60%	68	51%
	64 48%	6 4%	17 13%	47 35%	134	100%

$X^2 = 49.02$, p = .000

Subsystem	No Violence	Minor Clashes	Serious Clashes	Full-Scale War		
Non-long-war PC	68 42%	16 10%	36 22%	41 26%	161	68%
Long-war PC	8 11%	4 5%	27 35%	38 49%	77	32%
	76 32%	20 8%	63 27%	79 33%	238	100%

$X^2 = 30.07$, p = .000

TABLE III.10.5.b. Intensity of Violence in Crisis Management: Systems and Protracted Conflicts

East/West	No Violence	Minor Clashes	Serious Clashes	Full-Scale War		
Non-long-war PC	44 98%	0 0%	1 2%	0 0%	45	96%
Long-war PC	2 100%	0 0%	0 0%	0 0%	2	4%
	46 98%	0 0%	1 2%	0 0%	47	100%

Arab/Israel	No Violence	Minor Clashes	Serious Clashes	Full-Scale War		
Non-long-war PC (Total)	24 44%	3 6%	7 13%	20 37%	54	100%

India/Pakistan	No Violence	Minor Clashes	Serious Clashes	Full-Scale War		
Non-long-war PC (Total)	4 27%	2 13%	2 13%	7 47%	15	100%

Code for Intensity of Violence:
Minor Clashes = Clashes involving few or no deaths or injuries.
Serious Clashes = Fighting short of full-scale war.

Conflicts, Crises and Systems 149

powers were actively engaged in direct military operations against each other, subsystem conflicts have experienced a plethora of wars: Arab/Israel – in 1948–49, 1956, 1967, 1969–70, 1973–74 and in 1982; India/Pakistan – in 1947–48, 1965 and 1971. All have been conventional wars. More generally, actors in these two subsystem protracted conflicts have resorted to war or serious clashes in 50% of Arab/Israel crises and in 60% of India/Pakistan crises. In short, Hypothesis 5, too, is strongly supported by the evidence of half a century of crises and conflicts.

As for *superpower activity* in crises within protracted conflicts, where the US and the USSR are not crisis actors, we expect the primacy of political activity in subsystem crises, military activity in dominant system crises. The reason is essentially the same as that indicated to explain the lesser role for violence in crisis management by the superpowers generally.

There is a disposition to superpower prudence in other states' disputes – beyond their bloc – because of their awareness of several risks: catalyzing military involvement by the other superpower; crisis escalation triggering direct superpower confrontation; and the potential high cost of superpower violence to their basic values. Within dominant system crises, however, these risks are overcome by the perceived direct threat to values, especially their influence in international systems if an ally or client suffers great defeat in a crisis. Political activity is often insufficient to ensure key values. The result is a greater willingness to direct or indirect military activity in support of a bloc member. Threats to more basic values induce military activity by the superpowers in crises within their own system, even those once-removed from their direct interests.

The relevant data on superpower activity in crises at different system levels of protracted conflict are presented in Tables III.10.6.a. and b.

The evidence in support of our expectation is clear. First, the most frequent type of activity by both superpowers in subsystem crises from 1945 to 1985 was low-level, that is, verbal or political: the US, 44%, compared to 16% (semi-military), 7% (military); the USSR, 35%, compared to 21% (semi-military), 2% (military). In Arab/Israel crises, US political or verbal activity was overwhelming – 79%; and Soviet low-level activity, too, was prominent in those crises (42%) (e.g., the US condemnation of Israel at the UN and elsewhere for its Beirut Airport raid on 28 December 1968, along with an American offer of aid to Lebanon). Secondly, both superpowers resorted to semi-military or direct military activity more frequently in dominant system than in subsystem crises: the US – 54%–23%; the USSR – 46%–23%.

Parenthetically, both superpowers were much less active in subsystem than in

TABLE III.10.6.a. Superpower Activity in Crises: System Level and Protracted Conflicts

Dominant System	No Activity US	USSR	Low-Level US	USSR	Semi-Military US	USSR	Military US	USSR		
Non-long-war PC	0	1	13	13	7	5	4	5	24	24
	0%	4%	54%	54%	29%	21%	17%	21%	86%	86%
Long-war PC	0	0	0	1	1	2	3	1	4	4
	0%	0%	0%	25%	25%	50%	75%	25%	14%	14%
	0	1	13	14	8	7	7	6	28	28
	0%	4%	46%	50%	29%	25%	25%	21%	100%	100%

US X² = 6.85, p = .032; USSR X² = 1.94, p = .584

Subsystem	No Activity US	USSR	Low-Level US	USSR	Semi-Military US	USSR	Military US	USSR		
Non-long-war PC	26	32	37	29	15	15	0	2	78	78
	33%	41%	48%	37%	19%	19%	0%	3%	70%	70%
Long-war PC	11	15	12	10	3	9	8	0	34	34
	32%	44%	35%	29%	9%	27%	24%	0%	30%	30%
	37	47	49	39	18	24	8	2	112	112
	33%	42%	44%	35%	16%	21%	7%	2%	100%	100%

US X² = 20.75, p = .000; USSR X² = 1.92, p = .590

TABLE III.10.6.b. Superpower Activity in Crises: Systems and Protracted Conflicts

East/West	No Activity US	No Activity USSR	Low-Level US	Low-Level USSR	Semi-Military US	Semi-Military USSR	Military US	Military USSR		
Non-long-war PC	0	0	8	9	6	5	4	4	18	18
	0%	0%	45%	50%	33%	28%	22%	22%	95%	95%
Long-war PC	0	0	0	0	1	1	0	0	1	1
	0%	0%	0%	0%	100%	100%	0%	0%	5%	5%
	0	0	8	9	7	6	4	4	19	19
	0%	0%	42%	47%	37%	32%	21%	21%	100%	100%
Arab/Israel										
Non-long-war PC (Total)	4	7	19	10	1	6	0	1	24	24
	17%	29%	79%	42%	4%	25%	0%	4%	100%	100%
India/Pakistan										
Non-long-war PC (Total)	3	4	3	3	1	0	0	0	7	7
	43%	57%	43%	43%	14%	0%	0%	0%	100%	100%

Code for Superpower Activity:
Low-Level = Political (mediation, etc.); economic (dispatching, suspending economic aid, etc.).
Semi-Military = Covert aid; military aid; advisors.
Military = Direct military intervention.

dominant system PC crises – US inactivity, 33% and 0%, respectively; USSR inactivity, 42% and 4%. Moreover, in both subsystems under inquiry, the US was more active than the USSR – 83%–71% in Arab/Israel crises, 57%–43% in India/Pakistan cases.

To the extent that superpower military activity occurred in protracted conflicts, several findings are noteworthy. First, the frequency of semi-military and direct military activity by the US and the USSR was virtually identical in the dominant system, in non-long-war PCs at the subsystem level, and in the East/West Conflict. Secondly, the Soviets were much more active militarily in Arab/Israel crises than was the US – 7 cases – 1 (e.g., the Soviet large-scale supply of arms, via Czechoslovakia, to Egypt and Syria in the aftermath of Egypt's Gaza Raid Crisis, beginning 28 February 1955). Thirdly, the US engaged in much more direct military activity in subsystem long-war PC cases, the USSR in semi-military activity, 24%–0%, 27%–9%, respectively. Finally, both superpowers resorted to semi-military activity much more frequently than direct military activity in subsystem PC crises generally; this is especially evident in non-long war PC cases – the US, 19%–0%, the USSR, 19%–3%.

Several reasons may be suggested to explain superpower behavior in other states' crises. For one thing, many early post-World War II Soviet crises occurred on the geographic periphery of the USSR, with vassals or clients as adversaries – Poland 1946, Hungary 1947 and Czechoslovakia 1947–48. With them, in contrast to Hungary 1956 and Czechoslovakia 1968, a "show of force" was sufficient for effective crisis management; that is, there was no need for direct Soviet military activity in such cases. For another, in more distant crises and conflicts, such as Korea 1950–51, Vietnam 1964–75, Angola 1975 ff. and the Middle East 1967, 1973, military aid was the preferred technique of Soviet involvement, in order to assist clients but to reduce the danger of confrontation with the US. Moreover, when direct military intervention was considered necessary to protect or enhance Soviet values, Moscow tended to use proxies (e.g., Cuba in Angola 1975 ff.; Somalia in the Horn of Africa 1964). As for US military activity, there were several US crises in its immediate security zone (Guatemala 1954, Cuba 1961 and 1962, and Dominican Republic 1965). Moreover, direct military activity was often necessary to achieve US goals in more distant regions, as in Korea (1950–53) and the long-war protracted conflict over Indo-China, with many crises from 1964 to 1975.

Superpower activity, whatever the type, may be expected to make a more positive *contribution to crisis abatement* within the dominant system protracted conflict than in crises at the subsystem level. Several reasons may be adduced. First, in East/West crises, especially those in which only one superpower is a crisis actor, its activity can determine the outcome, including abatement of the crisis; often unilateral activity by the US or the USSR leads to effective termination of a crisis. Moreover, in East/West crises with the two superpowers as adversarial crisis actors, their combined activity will lead to crisis abatement.

In subsystem conflicts superpowers can influence client states' behavior but cannot determine crisis outcomes when important values for subsystem actors are at stake. An attempt by one superpower – or both – to impose an outcome may lead to more active superpower involvement, including confrontation with the other superpower. Both try to avoid confrontation because it is more threatening to their values than the possible benefits of a superpower-imposed outcome on recalcitrant clients. Thus, ironically, superpower activity will be more effective in terms of crisis abatement within the dominant system conflict, where the US and the USSR are the principal and continuing adversarial crisis actors, than in crises within subsystem conflicts, where they are usually active peripherally and unable or unwilling to control the behavior of their clients.

The data on superpower effectiveness in crisis abatement are presented in Tables III.10.7.a. and b.

The findings are strongly supportive of Hypothesis 7. As expected, there was a much more positive US contribution to crisis abatement in dominant system crises than in those within subsystem conflicts – 61%–27% for the important/most important category. The same obtains for Soviet activity, the corresponding figures being 25%–7%. In specific subsystem conflicts the data on US effectiveness reinforce the general findings; that is, a much lower effectiveness rate in Arab/Israel crises (33%) and India/Pakistan crises (14%) than in the dominant system, almost all East/West (72%), for the important/most important category of non-long-war PC crises. The data on USSR effectiveness reveal much less difference – Arab/Israel crises, 17% effectiveness, India/Pakistan cases, 14% compared to 25% for non-long-war PC crises at the dominant system, mostly East/West, level.

There are other noteworthy results. The effectiveness of US activity was far greater than that of the USSR in dominant system crises (71%–25%) (e.g., Washington persuaded Moscow to attend a Foreign Ministers Conference on Berlin during the Deadline Crisis, December 1957–September 1959). Correspondingly, the ineffective performance of the superpowers is reversed for crises in the East/West Con-

TABLE III.10.7.a. Superpower Effectiveness in Crises: System Level and Protracted Conflicts

Dominant System	No Activity US	USSR	Ineffective US	USSR	Marginal US	USSR	Important and Most Important US	USSR	US	USSR
Non-long-war PC	0	1	7	15	0	2	17	6	24	24
	0%	4%	29%	63%	0%	8%	71%	25%	86%	86%
Long-war PC	0	0	4	2	0	1	0	1	4	4
	0%	0%	100%	50%	0%	25%	0%	25%	14%	14%
	0	1	11	17	0	3	17	7	28	28
	0%	3%	39%	61%	0%	11%	61%	25%	100%	100%

US X² = 4.55, p = .033; USSR X² = 1.14, p = .766

Subsystem	No Activity US	USSR	Ineffective US	USSR	Marginal US	USSR	Important and Most Important US	USSR	US	USSR
Non-long-war PC	26	32	22	32	6	8	24	6	78	78
	33%	41%	28%	41%	8%	10%	31%	8%	70%	70%
Long-war PC	11	15	15	17	2	0	6	2	34	34
	32%	44%	44%	50%	6%	0%	18%	6%	30%	30%
	37	47	37	49	8	8	30	8	112	112
	33%	42%	33%	44%	7%	7%	27%	7%	100%	100%

US X² = 3.45, p = .327; USSR X² = 4.09, p = .252

TABLE III.10.7.b. Superpower Effectiveness in Crises: Systems and Protracted Conflicts

East/West	No Activity US	No Activity USSR	Ineffective US	Ineffective USSR	Marginal US	Marginal USSR	Important and Most Important US	Important and Most Important USSR		
Non-long-war PC	0 0%	0 0%	5 28%	12 67%	0 0%	1 5%	13 72%	5 28%	18 95%	18 95%
Long-war PC	0 0%	0 0%	1 100%	0 0%	0 0%	0 0%	0 0%	1 100%	1 5%	1 5%
	0 0%	0 0%	6 32%	12 63%	0 0%	1 5%	13 68%	6 32%	19 100%	19 100%
Arab/Israel										
Non-long-war PC (Total)	4 17%	7 29%	9 38%	10 42%	3 12%	3 12%	8 33%	4 17%	24 100%	24 100%
India/Pakistan										
Non-long-war PC (Total)	3 43%	4 57%	3 43%	1 14.3%	0 0%	1 14.3%	1 14%	1 14.3%	7 100%	7 100%

Code for Superpower Effectiveness:
No Activity =
Ineffective = Superpower activity did not contribute to crisis abatement or escalated crisis.
Marginal = Marginal contribution.
Important or Most Important = Superpower activity had an important impact on or was the most important factor in crisis abatement.

flict (28%–67%) (e.g., active Soviet support for the *Tudeh* Party and its unwillingness to evacuate military forces from Iran escalated the Azerbaijan Crisis 1945–46).

The *global organization* is likely to be less active in crises within the dominant system conflict than in those at the subsystem level. Moreover, its involvement is likely to be less effective in abating major power crises. The reason for this expectation lies in the structure and functioning of the global organization (League of Nations, United Nations), which was designed primarily to manage international conflicts and crises. That role, in the UN, was given to the Security Council, in which the major powers have a formal veto. (In the League, all Council members had a veto). In terms of the "rules of the game," the US and the USSR have a *de facto* veto as well; that is, their agreement or acquiescence has always been a *sine qua non* of effective UN crisis management through the Security Council. Thus dominant system crises, in which at least one superpower is a key actor, are less likely to be considered actively by the (Security) Council. Moreover, the UN/League will be less effective in crises where the US and the USSR (or two great powers, in the League) are direct or even indirect adversaries.

By contrast, subsystem crises, in regions where the major powers are less directly involved, will attract more global organization activity. And because the crisis actors in the two subsystem conflicts under inquiry are middle or small powers, the UN has a greater potential for effective crisis management. Another reason for the contrast in global organization effectiveness is that the superpowers view it as a neutral forum through which they can achieve effective crisis management while, at the same time, satisfying their interests.

The data on global organization involvement and effectiveness are presented in Tables III.10.8.a. and b. and III.10.9.a. and b.

As expected, the global organization was much less active in dominant system crises – 53%, compared to 73% in subsystem PC cases. In terms of specific conflicts, there was no UN activity in half of the East/West cases. And this inactivity was, proportionately, more than twice as much as in Arab/Israel crises and even more relative to the South Asia Conflict. The most frequent UN activity in East/West crises was a resolution, usually by the Security Council, but without a call for action by UN members (e.g., a Security Council resolution during the Guatemala Crisis,

TABLE III.10.8.a. Global Organization Involvement in Crises: System Level and Protracted Conflicts

Dominant System	None		Low-level		Medium-level		High-level			
Non-long-war PC	13	52%	6	24%	4	16%	2	8%	25	83%
Long-war PC	1	20%	2	40%	1	20%	1	20%	5	17%
	14	47%	8	27%	5	16%	3	10%	30	100%

$X^2 = 1.95$, $p = .582$

Subsystem	None		Low-level		Medium-level		High-level			
Non-long-war PC	23	28%	24	29%	33	40%	3	3%	83	69%
Long-war PC	9	24%	12	33%	13	35%	3	8%	37	31%
	32	27%	36	30%	46	38%	6	5%	120	100%

$X^2 = 1.39$, $p = .707$

TABLE III.10.8.b. Global Organization Involvement in Crises: Systems and Protracted Conflicts

East/West	None		Low-level		Medium-level		High-level			
Non-long-war PC	9	50%	5	28%	4	22%	0	0%	18	95%
Long-war PC	0	0%	1	100%	0	0%	0	0%	1	5%
	9	47%	6	32%	4	21%	0	0%	19	100%

Arab/Israel	None		Low-level		Medium-level		High-level			
Non-long-war PC (Total)	5	21%	4	17%	13	54%	2	8%	24	100%

India/Pakistan	None		Low-level		Medium-level		High-level			
Non-long-war PC (Total)	1	14.3%	4	57.1%	1	14.3%	1	14.3%	7	100%

Code for Global Organization Involvement:
None =
Low-Level = Discussion without resolution, fact-finding, good offices, general – other.
Medium-Level = Condemnation, call for action by adversaries, mediation.
High-Level = Arbitration, sanctions, observers and emergency military forces.

December 1953–June 1954, against UN intervention until the OAS completed its investigation). In the Middle East Conflict, there were many cease-fire resolutions as on 11 June 1967, directed to Israel, Egypt, Jordan and Syria during the Six Day War. In South Asia crises, the most frequent activity was discussion without a resolution (e.g., the UN General Assembly discussion of the Bangladesh issue in March 1971, without a resolution, on the grounds that it was a domestic problem for Pakistan). High UN involvement, such as sanctions, observers, emergency military forces, etc., was rare, in only 3 of 49 PC crises within the three specific conflicts under inquiry.

As for IO effectiveness (Tables III.10.9.a. and b.), the evidence from 40 years of UN involvement in PC crises provides strong support for our expectation: the combined figures for most important, important and marginal effectiveness in sub-

TABLE III.10.9.a. Global Organization Effectiveness in Crises: System Level and Protracted
Conflicts

Dominant System	No Involvement		Ineffective		Marginal		Important and Most Important			
Non-long-war PC	13	52%	7	28%	2	8%	3	12%	25	83%
Long-war PC	1	20%	4	80%	0	0%	0	0%	5	17%
	14	47%	11	37%	2	6%	3	10%	30	100%

$X^2 = 4.99$, p = .173

Subsystem	No Involvement		Ineffective		Marginal		Important and Most Important			
Non-long-war PC	23	28%	32	39%	12	14%	16	19%	83	69%
Long-war PC	9	24%	20	54%	5	14%	3	8%	37	31%
	32	27%	52	43%	17	14%	19	16%	120	100%

$X^2 = 3.56$, p = .313

TABLE III.10.9.b. Global Organization Effectiveness in Crises: Systems and Protracted
Conflicts

East/West	No Involvement		Ineffective		Marginal		Important and Most Important			
Non-long-war PC	9	50%	7	39%	0	0%	2	11%	18	95%
Long-war PC	0	0%	1	100%	0	0%	0	0%	1	5%
	9	47%	8	42%	0	0%	2	11%	19	100%

Arab/Israel										
Non-long-war PC (Total)	5	21%	12	50%	3	12%	4	17%	24	100%

India/Pakistan										
Non-long-war PC (Total)	1	14.3%	3	42.9%	1	14.3%	2	28.6%	7	100%

Code for Global Organization Effectiveness:
No Involvement =
Ineffective = Did not contribute to crisis abatement or escalated.
Marginal = Marginal contribution.
Important or Most Important = Important impact on or the most important factor in crisis abatement.

system cases are almost double those for dominant system crises (30%–16%). The
gap is even larger between specific conflicts: Arab/Israel, 29%, India/Pakistan,
43%, East/West, 11%. Another – negative – finding is no less noteworthy. Non-
effectiveness was clearly the most frequent consequence of UN activity in dominant
system and subsystem PC cases as a whole, and specifically in East/West and Arab/
Israel crises (e.g., a Security Council resolution on 5 October 1948 placing the Berlin
issue on its agenda had no effect on abating the Blockade Crisis; and, in the Middle

East, a UN fact-finding mission into the Jordan Waters dispute between Israel and four Arab neighbors in 1963–64 was not effective).

The last dimension of our crisis profile relates to *outcome*, both content and form. It is postulated that *substantive* outcomes are more likely to be indecisive in dominant system crises than in those at the subsystem level. There are several reasons for this expectation.

First, the key value perceived to be threatened in superpower crises is, as noted, influence in international systems, the least tangible among actor values. Thus the outcome – more or less influence – tends to fall into the ambiguous category. Stated differently, a victory-defeat outcome is more difficult to identify in crises over relative influence than in crises over territory, change in political system, economic benefits or losses, etc. Moreover, when superpowers are in direct adversarial crisis roles the substantive outcomes are likely to be blurred, for a decisive victory-defeat outcome would mean, and would be interpreted as, a basic shift in the global balance of power. Neither superpower is prepared to acknowledge such a change in world politics. At the same time, the outcomes of dominant system crises in which only one superpower is a crisis actor are almost certain to be stark and unambiguous, for major powers do not allow lesser powers to share the benefits of a crisis outcome, i.e., compromise. They regard it as "natural" to obtain their goals unqualifiedly in an unequal power relationship, namely, victory for themselves, defeat for their weaker adversaries.

The data on the content of outcomes are found in Tables III.10.10.a. and b.

On this component, our expectation is not supported by the evidence from 1945 to 1985. A majority of crises within the dominant system (53%) ended in decisive, zero-sum terms, whereas a larger majority of subsystem crises (62%) reveal an ambiguous outcome. The pattern for crisis outcomes in the three specific PCs is the same: East/West, 78% definitive outcomes, compared to 42% for Arab/Israel and 43% for India/Pakistan cases (e.g., the withdrawal of Soviet forces from Azerbaijan in May 1946, under persistent US–UK pressure, a victorious outcome to that crisis in 1945–46 for the Western Powers, a defeat for the USSR).

The *form* of outcome, too, may be expected to differ in crises at the two system levels. Crises within the dominant system conflict are more likely to be characterized by the preeminence of unilateral acts, those at the subsystem level by agreement. The reason lies in the difference of constraints on superpower and lesser power behavior.

Many East/West crises, as noted, involve less powerful actors as adversaries, for example, the Soviet Union's Communism in Poland Crisis in 1947 and the US Communism in Guatemala Crisis in 1954. In these unequal power relationships, superpowers are able and are disposed to determine a crisis outcome by a threat of use (show of force) or an actual use of superior strength to compel a favorable

TABLE III.10.10.a. Substance of Crisis Outcome: System Level and Protracted Conflicts

Dominant System	Ambiguous Outcome		Definitive Outcome			
Non-long-war PC	9	36%	16	64%	25	83%
Long-war PC	5	100%	0	0%	5	17%
	14	47%	16	53%	30	100%

$X^2 = 4.53$, p = .033

Subsystem						
Non-long-war PC	49	59%	34	41%	83	69%
Long-war PC	26	70%	11	30%	37	31%
	75	62%	45	38%	120	100%

$X^2 = .94$, p = .332

TABLE III.10.10.b. Substance of Crisis Outcome: Systems and Protracted Conflicts

East/West	Ambiguous Outcome		Definitive Outcome			
Non-long-war PC	4	22%	14	78%	18	95%
Long-war PC	1	100%	0	0%	1	5%
	5	26%	14	74%	19	100%
Arab/Israel						
Non-long-war PC (Total)	14	58%	10	42%	24	100%
India/Pakistan						
Non-long-war PC (Total)	4	57%	3	43%	7	100%

Code for Substance of Outcome:
Ambiguous Outcome = At least one actor coded as stalemate or compromise.
Definitive Outcome = All actors coded as either victory or defeat.

outcome acquiesced in by the lesser power. Nor do the global or regional organizations have the capacity to prevent a superpower resort to a unilateral act. The global system's lack of effective constraining institutions or rules gives the superpowers a free hand to impose outcomes by unilateral acts, military, political or economic. Conversely, subsystem actors are constrained by one or both superpowers acting as patron or adversary, as well as by the UN and, often, a regional organization, from resort to a unilateral act as the form of crisis outcome. Moreover, the superpowers have learned the necessity – and the techniques – to prevent the termination of subsystem crises by unilateral acts. The UN is a less effective constraint on the behavior of less powerful states. Nonetheless, because they are middle or small powers, the UN, supported by the superpowers, has more leverage in these subsystem crises.

The data on this component of our crisis profile are presented in Tables III.10.11.a. and b.

TABLE III.10.11.a. Form of Crisis Outcome: System Level and Protracted Conflicts

Dominant System	Agreement		Tacit		Unilateral Act		No Agreement			
Non-long-war PC	11	44%	3	12%	11	44%	0	0%	25	83%
Long-war PC	2	40%	1	20%	1	20%	1	20%	5	17%
	13	43.3%	4	13.3%	12	40%	1	3.3%	30	100%

$X^2 = 5.82$, p = .121

Subsystem	Agreement		Tacit		Unilateral Act		No Agreement			
Non-long-war PC	31	37%	11	13%	27	33%	14	17%	83	69%
Long-war PC	12	32%	0	0%	19	52%	6	16%	37	31%
	43	36%	11	9%	46	38%	20	17%	120	100%

$X^2 = 7.45$, p = 0.59

TABLE III.10.11.b. Form of Crisis Outcome: Systems and Protracted Conflicts

East/West	Agreement		Tacit		Unilateral Act		No Agreement				
Non-long-war PC	6	33%	1	6%	11	61%	0	0%	18		95%
Long-war PC	0	0%	1	100%	0	0%	0	0%	1		5%
	6	32%	2	10%	11	58%	0	0%	19		100%
Arab/Israel											
Non-long-war PC (Total)	7	29%	5	21%	8	33%	4	17%	24		100%
India/Pakistan											
Non-long-war PC (Total)	4	57%	1	14%	2	29%	0	0%	7		100%

Code for Form of Outcome:
Formal and Semi-Formal Agreement = Treaty, armistice, cease-fire, exchange of letters, oral statements by adversaries.
Tacit Agreement = Mutual understanding by adversaries, neither stated nor written.
Unilateral Act = Act imposed by crisis actor on adversary.
Crisis Faded/No Agreement = No known termination date, no known agreement between adversaries.

The findings are mixed. The anticipated differences are not supported for the two sets of system-level crises as a whole: the proportion of agreements and unilateral acts are almost identical for all dominant system and subsystem cases. However, the hypothesis is supported for two specific protracted conflicts: East/West crises (61% unilateral acts, 33% agreements); South Asia, the reverse (29%–57%). In both subsystem conflicts, initial UN intervention led to the termination of crises by formal agreement – the armistice agreements of 1949 in the Arab/Israel War of Independence and the Kashmir Cease-Fire between India and Pakistan on 1 January 1949, followed by extended mediation and an Observer Group. This reinforced pressures from external powers for agreement, along with subsystem crisis actors' expectation of UN-assisted formal agreements to restore "normal relations" between periods of acute crisis and widespread violence in these protracted conflicts.

In the two subsystem PCs, the adversaries have often been prevented by one or both of the superpowers from determining their crisis outcomes. This was especially so when these crises involved full-scale war containing the potential of escalation and the danger of sucking the SPs into an adversarial confrontation neither wishes, as in the 1967 and 1973–74 Middle East crisis-wars. It was also true of the second India/Pakistan War over Kashmir in 1965-66, with the USSR mediating a formal agreement at Tashkent.

Conclusion

The findings from this inquiry into the relationship between crises and different system levels of protracted conflict may be summarized.

The data from more than half a century of international and foreign policy crises (1929-85) support our postulated profile for seven components of crises within dominant system and subsystem conflicts.

	Dominant System	*Subsystem*
Triggers	predominantly non-violent	mainly violent
Behavior	mainly non-violent response	mainly violent military response
	mainly pacific CMTs	violence most visible CMT
	full-scale war infrequent	full-scale war most frequent
SP Effectiveness	much more positive	less positive
IO Role	less active	more active
IO Effectiveness	less effective	more effective

There is partial support for two other dimensions of the crisis profile:

(1) influence is the most frequent threatened value at the dominant system level, as postulated; but it is also prominent at the subsystem level, second to territory among threatened values; and

(2) superpower activity in subsystem crises is most frequently low-level (political) – but this primacy is also evident in dominant system crises.

In sum, this profile has substantial support from more than half a century of data on crises and conflicts.

11 Conflicts and Crisis Management

Michael Brecher and Patrick James

Introduction

The stimuli to this inquiry into patterns of conflict and crisis management are two-fold. One is skepticism about a widely-held belief among area specialists that conflict in their region (whatever it may be) is unique; although frequently asserted, that contention has not been explored comparatively or tested rigorously. The other catalyst is increasing concern about the danger of crisis escalation in the nuclear era, particularly in a "grey zone" of superpower competition.

This chapter focuses on the relationship between crisis and conflict, with special reference to the Middle East. The specific research questions are as follows: Are there differences between international crises within the Arab/Israel protracted conflict (PC) and other, non-PC cases in the Middle East? How do Middle East crises, as a whole, compare with crises in the rest of the global system? Do Arab/Israel crises differ from all other international crises? Do PC cases in the Middle East (Arab/Israel) differ from PC crises elsewhere? More generally, as an extension of the analysis in Chapters 9 and 10, are the dimensions of crisis affected by the attribute of protractedness and, if so, how?

Of course, it could be – and is – argued that the highly unusual character of the Arab/Israel conflict is self-evident; why bother to compare it to other conflicts? Babbie (1983: p. 19) provides the rationale for such an investigation:

> documenting the obvious is a valuable function of any science, physical or social. All too often, the obvious turns out to be wrong, and apparent triviality is not a legitimate objection to any scientific endeavor. (Darwin coined the phrase *fool's experiment* in ironic reference to much of his own research – research in which he tested things that everyone else already knew.)

Thus it may be valuable to "document" the character of the Arab/Israel conflict. While the findings may simply verify that the Arab/Israel conflict is unique or unusual, the reason(s) behind that result may be instructive.

Crisis management, the point of departure for this study, has two distinct meanings in the literature on world politics. One refers to the behavior of *participants* and identifies the mechanisms which states employ to cope with stress. The other is concerned with the behavior of *intermediaries*, especially major powers and international organizations, to prevent crisis escalation and/or to hasten crisis abatement among states.

Research on crisis management has generated a large body of findings on participant behavior, from single case studies and comparative analysis.[1] The literature on the foreign policies of the superpowers is vast, although less so on their crisis management role.[2] Research on the intermediary role of the global organization is less extensive.[3]

In a careful appraisal of the various strands within the crisis literature until the late 1970s, Tanter (1979: pp. 361–364) described the scholarship in general as "diffident," although he acknowledged that "a body of propositions relevant to crisis management has emerged from the literature on decision-making. . . ." The areas of theorizing include (1) "the impact of crisis management experiences;" (2) "conflicts between achieving crisis management, on the one hand, and coercive diplomacy and deterrence goals on the other . . . ;" (3) "strategies for manipulating crisis components . . .;" and (4) "aggregate comparisons across cases. . . ."

The primary empirical domain of this inquiry is the Middle East from 1945 to 1985.[4] Although that region has been analyzed by a wide range of scholars, studies of crisis management are infrequent, except for single state case studies (Brecher, 1974, 1975, 1980; A. I. Dawisha, 1980; Dowty, 1984; Stein and Tanter, 1980) and an occasional events data analysis (Rasler, 1984). No comparison across the region as a whole over the course of several decades has been attempted, except as part of a much larger, globally-oriented inquiry into crises in the twentieth century (Brecher and Wilkenfeld *et al.*, 1988; Wilkenfeld and Brecher *et al.*, 1988).

Further study of crisis management can adopt a narrow focus, namely, actor behavior in coping with stress, or third party intervention to prevent escalation or to assist in crisis abatement. Crisis management also can be explored in a broader context, from the onset of crisis to termination. The latter path will be followed here, as in Chapter 5, using the strategy of aggregate comparison across cases in the quest for greater knowledge about both dimensions of crisis management – participant behavior and intermediary roles, specifically, intervention by the super-powers and the global organization. The ultimate purpose is to acquire a reliable basis for anticipating the likely profile of future crises in the Middle East – in the Arab/Israel protracted conflict and elsewhere.

The concepts of crisis and conflict have been discussed at length earlier in this volume (Chapters 1 and 2). Similarly, protracted conflict has been delineated and elaborated above (Chapter 9). Suffice it to recall the essence of a protracted conflict as: ". . . hostile interactions which extend over long periods of time. . . . The stakes are very high. . . . Protracted conflicts . . . are not specific events . . . , they are processes." (Azar *et al.*, 1978: pp. 50, 53).

In Chapter 9, as well, a Protracted Conflict–Crisis Model was specified (Figure III.9.1 and p. 128), along with a set of expectations about the characteristics of crises within protracted conflicts, and their collective rationale. Since these hypotheses serve as the focal points of this chapter's multi-stage analysis of Arab/Israeli crises, other Middle East crises, and various other clusters of international crises in the global system, it is appropriate to restate here our expectations about international crises within a protracted conflict:

Hypothesis 1: The more visible presence of *violence* in crisis *triggers*;
Hypothesis 2: Higher stakes, that is, a perceived threat to more *basic values*;
Hypothesis 3: Greater reliance on more *violence* in coping with crisis;
Hypothesis 4: A resort to *more intense* types and levels of violence in crisis management:
Hypothesis 5: A *primary role* for violence in crisis management;
Hypothesis 6: *More political* and *less military activity* by the *superpowers*;
Hypothesis 7: *Greater effectiveness* of superpower activity in *crisis abatement*;
Hypothesis 8: *More involvement* by the *global organization*;
Hypothesis 9: *More effectiveness* of global organization involvement in *crisis abatement*;
Hypothesis 10: *More ambiguous* crisis *outcomes*, that is, stalemate or compromise; and
Hypothesis 11: *Less formal* agreements to mark the *termination* of crises.

Operationalization   For the period, 1929–1985, the ICB Project has uncovered 63 international crises in the Middle East, incorporating 145 actor-cases, that is, a foreign policy crisis for an individual state, according to the definitions indicated in Chapter 1 above. Six international crises occurred before the end of World War II, beginning with a Saudi Arabia/Yemen crisis in 1933–34. Of the 57 cases from mid-1945 to the end of 1985, from Kars-Ardahan to Basra/Kharg Island, 25 are part of the Arab/Israel protracted conflict (category "A" in Table III.11.1.); 32 fall into the "other Middle East" group (category "B"). Six of the "other Middle East" category are part of the Yemen protracted conflict and are excluded from the testing of hypotheses derived from the Protracted Conflict-Crisis Model. They are, however, included in the comparison of Middle East international crises and all others after World War II, 57 and 203, respectively, in the total ICB data set of 323 international crises (comprising 698 actor-cases) from 1929 to 1985. These Yemen crises appear in Table III.11.1. under category "F". Categories "C" through "E" in Table III.11.1. will be clarified during the discussion of Figure III.11.1.

Each dependent variable comprises an ordinal scale of values.[5] For purposes of aggregate analysis in this chapter, the number of categories per variable has been reduced, for two reasons. Greater precision in classification would be inappropriate for an exploratory data analysis; regularities in the data should prove useful in refinement of the variable configuration at a later point. The more practical consider-

TABLE III.11.1. Selected List of International Crises 1945–85[1], with Actors[2] and Duration[3]

A	B	C	D	E	F	Crisis Actors	Duration[4]
	Kars-Ardahan					Turkey	07/06/45–05/04/46
	Azerbaijan					Iran, UK, USA, USSR	23/08/45–09/05/46
			East/West				1945–
				Marshall Plan		USSR, Czechoslovakia	04/07/47–10/07/47
		Dominican Republic/Cuba				Dominican Republic	26/07/47–28/09/47
	Turkish Straits					Turkey, USA	07/08/45–26/10/46
			India/Pakistan				1947–
			Arab/Israel				1947–
				Junagadh		India, Pakistan	17/08/47–24/02/48
Palestine Partition						Egypt, Iraq, Lebanon, Syria	29/11/47–17/12/47
Israel Independence						Iraq, Egypt, Lebanon, Jordan, Israel, Syria	15/05/48–20/07/49
Sinai Incursion						Egypt, UK, Israel	25/12/48–10/01/49
Tel Mutillah						Syria, Israel	15/03/51–14/05/51
Qibya						Jordan	14/10/53–
	Baghdad Pact					Egypt	24/02/55—/10/55
Gaza Raid						Egypt, Israel	28/02/55–23/06/56
Qalqilya						Jordan, Israel	13/09/56—/10/56
Suez–Sinai Campaign						USSR, Egypt, France, UK, USA, Israel	29/10/56–12/03/57
	Jordan Regime					Jordan	04/04/57–03/05/57
	Syria/Turkey Border					Turkey, USA, Syria	18/08/57–29/10/57
		Ifni				Spain	23/11/57–
	Formation of UAR					Iraq, Jordan	01/02/58–14/02/58
	Lebanon/Iraq Upheaval					Lebanon, USA, Jordan, UK	08/05/58—/10/58
	Shatt-al-Arab I					Iraq, Iran	28/11/59–04/01/60
Rottem						Egypt, Israel	15/02/60–08/03/60
	Kuwait Independence					Kuwait, UK	25/06/61–13/07/61
	Breakup of UAR					Egypt	28/09/61–05/10/61
					Yemen War I	Jordan, Saudi Arabia, Egypt, Yemen	26/09/62–15/04/63
	Jordan Internal Challenge					Israel	21/04/63–04/05/63
Jordan Waters						Egypt, Jordan, Lebanon, Syria, Israel	11/12/63–05/05/64
		Panama Canal				Panama, USA	09/01/64–12/01/64
					Yemen War II	Egypt, Yemen, Saudi Arabia	—/05/64–08/11/64
					Yemen War III	Egypt, Yemen, Saudi Arabia	03/12/64–25/08/65
				Rann of Kutch		Pakistan, India	08/04/65–30/06/65
					Yemen War IV	Saudi Arabia, Egypt, Yemen	14/10/66–26/09/67
El Samu						Israel, Jordan	12/11/66–15/11/66
Six Day War						Israel, Egypt, Jordan, USA, Syria, USSR	15/05/67–11/06/67
Karameh						Israel, Jordan	18/03/68–22/03/68
Pre-War of Attrition						Israel	07/09/68–07/11/68
Beirut Airport						Lebanon	28/12/68—/01/69

TABLE III.11.1. (cont.)

A	B	C	D	E	F	Crisis Actors	Duration[4]
War of Attrition I						Israel	08/03/69–28/07/69
	Shatt-al-Arab II					Iran, Iraq	15/04/69–30/10/69
	Cairo Agreement					Lebanon	22/10/69–03/11/69
War of Attrition II						Egypt, USSR, Israel	07/01/70–07/08/70
	Black September					Syria, USA, Israel, Jordan	15/09/70–29/09/70
					North/South Yemen I	North Yemen, South Yemen	26/09/72–28/11/72
Libyan Plane						Israel	21/02/73–21/02/73
	Iraq Invasion–Kuwait					Kuwait	20/03/73–08/06/73
Israel Mobilization						Israel	10/04/73——/06/73
October–Yom Kippur War						Israel, Syria, USA, Egypt, USSR	05/10/73–31/05/74
	South Yemen/Oman					Oman	18/11/73–11/03/76
	Lebanon Civil War I					Syria	18/01/76–30/09/76
	Iraqi Threat					Syria	09/06/76–17/06/76
Syria Mobilization						Israel	21/11/76–13/12/76
	Lebanon Civil War II					Syria	07/02/78–13/06/78
Litani Operation						Lebanon	14/03/78–13/06/78
					North/South Yemen II	North Yemen, South Yemen	24/02/79–30/03/79
	US Hostages in Iran					USA, Iran	04/11/79–20/01/81
	Onset Iran/Iraq War					Iran	17/09/80–19/11/80
	Jordan/Syria Confrontation					Jordan	25/11/80–14/12/80
Biqa Valley Missiles						Syria, Israel	28/04/81–24/07/81
Iraqi Nuclear Reactor						Iraq	08/06/81–19/06/81
	Bahrain Coup Attempt					Bahrain, Saudi Arabia	13/12/81–08/01/82
	Khoramshar					Iraq	22/03/82–30/07/82
Lebanon War						Lebanon, Syria, Israel	05/06/82–01/09/82
	Basra/Kharg Island					Iraq, Iran, Kuwait, Saudi Arabia	21/02/84–11/07/84

Notes to Table III.11.1.

1. Constraints of space make it impossible to include all instances of categories C through E. However, three examples from each category are provided.
2. Crisis Actor: a sovereign state whose decision-maker(s) perceive(s) a high threat to one or more basic values, finite time for response to the value threat, and a high probability of involvement in military hostilities; all three perceptions derive from a change in the state's external or internal environment.
3. Duration: the time between the first breakpoint (the date on which the earliest crisis actor perceived threat, time pressure and war likelihood) and the last exitpoint (the date on which the last actor perceived crisis termination).
4. Other attributes of international crises – triggering entity, triggering act, highest value threat, intensity of violence, superpower activity, global organization involvement, form of outcome – are specified in Brecher and Wilkenfeld et al., op. cit., Table II.7 and in Appendix A below.

ation is the problem of near-empty scale points in a disaggregated coding scheme; that is, a more economical set of categories will facilitate an initial statistical analysis.

Eight types of *trigger* have been combined to form three categories: (1) violent act; (2) non-violent military; and (3) non-violent, comprising internal verbal or physical challenge to regime or élite, external change, economic act, political act, and verbal act. The basis for aggregation is the presence or absence, and degree, of violence, which is qualitatively different across the categories.[6]

A dichotomous classification is used for the six types of threatened *values*: (1) threat to existence or of grave damage; and (2) political, territorial, influence, and low threat. Once again, the basis for aggregation is largely intuitive, as opposed to a taxomony reflecting an interval or ratio scale.

Crisis management technique is differentiated by three scale points: (1) violence; (2) multiple, including violence; and (3) pacific, combining non-violent military, non-military pressure, mediation, and negotiation. A primary reliance upon violent actions is judged to be more intense than diverse tactics including violence, which in turn stand above non-violent management techniques.

Intensity of violence encompasses: (1) full-scale war or serious clashes; and (2) minor clashes or no violence.

Centrality of violence is accorded a twofold categorization: (1) preeminent or important role as crisis management technique; and (2) minor role or no violence.

Superpower (US and USSR) activity has identical, dichotomous categories: (1) none or low (political, economic); and (2) covert, semi-military or direct military. Military action is the distinguishing criterion.

Superpower (US and USSR) effectiveness, too, is collapsed into two categories: (1) most important or important contributor to crisis abatement; and (2) not active, marginal contribution to abatement, or escalating a crisis.

Global organization involvement and effectiveness are dichotomous variables as well. The categories are: for the former, (1) not involved; and (2) involved; and, for the latter, (1) most important or important to crisis abatement; and (2) uninvolved, ineffective, marginal to abatement, and escalating.

Substance of outcome has two categories: (1) ambiguous – compromise, stalemate; and (2) definitive – victory, defeat.

Form of outcome is trichotomous: (1) formal and semi-formal agreement; (2) tacit understanding; and (3) termination through a unilateral act or no agreement.

This completes the presentation of categories for the configuration of variables in the analysis.

Aggregate Analysis

Although the basis of evidence in this inquiry is the set of international and foreign policy crises within a specific region, the ultimate purpose is to test hypotheses on a global scale. To this end, an aggregate analysis will be conducted in five stages, beginning with the PC and non-PC clusters of crises in the Middle East, and ending with Middle East PC cases versus all other international crises within PCs elsewhere in the global system.

Table III.11.2. displays the coefficients from 65 bivariate measures of association, 13 for each of the five stages of the analysis.[7] Constraints of space make it impossible to complement these aggregate findings from each phase with tables showing categorical distributions. As a middle ground between comprehensiveness and economy, tables will be provided for the first stage only, *Intra-region*, that which focuses exclusively on the Middle East. However, at each stage the descriptive analysis will include references to specific crises.

1. Arab/Israel (PC) Versus Other Middle East (non-PC) Crises

All of the tau-b coefficients listed in Table III.11.2. for *Intra-region* are in the expected direction. Protractedness therefore can be used to reduce the errors in predicting categories of the dependent variables. For example, once it is known whether or not a crisis occurs within the Arab/Israel PC, there will be a 21% reduction in error with regard to anticipating the centrality of violence. Eight of the coefficients indicate at least a 20% reduction in error, and two are above 30%.

Two sets of data for the years 1945–1985 will be used to test the 11 hypotheses specified earlier: for the actor-oriented Hypotheses 1–5, the evidence from 145 Middle East foreign policy crises; and for the system-oriented Hypotheses 6–11, the evidence from 63 Middle East international crises. There are 33 foreign policy and 12 international crises that occurred within the Yemen War cluster or terminated prior to the end of World War II. Since these cases will be excluded from the analysis, the tables to appear later contain 112 foreign policy and 51 international crises, respectively.

Turning now to the distribution of cases across categories and examples, the evidence on Middle East crises strongly supports Hypothesis 1, as evident in Table III.11.3. Violence was present in 39% of the 64 crisis *triggers* within the Arab/Israel protracted conflict, compared to 21% of the 48 other, non-PC, Middle East cases from 1945 to 1985 (e.g., within a PC setting, the Israeli invasion of Sinai on 29 October 1956, triggering Egypt's Suez Crisis; and, in a non-PC setting, the intrusion of Iraqi troops into Kuwait on 20 March 1973, with a view to annexing part of the disputed territory along their 99-mile border, triggering a crisis for Kuwait). If the

TABLE III.11.2. Bivariate Measures of Association*

Stages	Independent Variables	Crisis Subsets	Trigger	Values	Crisis Management Technique	Intensity of Violence	Centrality of Violence	USA Activity	USSR Activity	USA Effectiveness	USSR Effectiveness	Global Organization Involvement	Global Organization Effectiveness	Substance of Outcome	Form of Outcome
I.	Intra-region	Arab/Israel vs. other Middle East	0.20 (0.02)**	0.25 (0.01)	0.23 (0.01)	0.20 (0.02)	0.21 (0.02)	0.45 (0.01)	0.07	0.06	0.20	0.38 (0.01)	0.06	0.18	0.01
II.	Inter-region	Middle East vs. other regions	−0.03	0.03	−0.03	0.01	−0.02	0.05	−0.11 (0.04)	0.00	0.01	0.00	−0.00	0.05	−0.02
III.	Context	Arab/Israel vs. non-Middle East	−0.00	0.13 (0.01)	0.01	0.01	−0.02	0.18 (0.01)	−0.05	0.04	0.08	0.12 (0.04)	0.03	0.06	0.03
IV.	Protracted/Non-Protracted Conflict	Arab/Israel vs. crises outside of protracted conflicts	0.22 (0.02)	0.19 (0.03)	0.27 (0.01)	0.26 (0.01)	0.27 (0.01)	0.19 (0.03)	−0.08	0.10	0.19 (0.02)	0.23 (0.01)	0.09	0.12	0.07
V.	Protractedness	Arab/Israel vs. crises within other protracted conflicts	−0.01	0.04	0.01	−0.04	−0.02	0.27 (0.01)	−0.04	0.02	0.06	0.10	0.01	0.04	−0.01

Independent variables for Stages I–V, with corresponding subsets of International Crises

* Kendall's tau-b has been used to generate these coefficients.

** The numbers in parentheses correspond to the significance level for cases in which $p < 0.05$.

TABLE III.11.3. Intra-Region and Triggers

	Violent		Non-Violent Military		Non-Violent				
Arab/Israel	25	39%	5	8%	34	53%	64		57%
Other Middle East	10	21%	3	6%	35	73%	48		43%
	35	31%	8	7%	69	62%	112		100%

non-violent military triggers are added, the difference is just as notable: 47% of all Arab/Israel cases were initiated by a military act, as opposed to 27% of other Middle East crises. Finally, while 69% of the Middle East crises from 1945 to 1985 were catalyzed by a non-violent act, event or challenge, the postulated relationship between conflict protractedness – or its absence – and the likelihood of violence in the crisis trigger is clearly supported by the data for post-World War II crises in that region.

On the *value* dimension of the Conflict–Crisis Model (Hypothesis 2), the evidence in Table III.11.4. also provides strong support. There is no difference in the number of cases with existence as the value under threat – two each in the Arab/Israel cluster and in other Middle East cases, 3% and 4%, respectively (e.g., within the Arab/Israel PC, Israel's decision-makers perceived Egypt's actions in the last half of May 1967 – closure of the Tiran Strait, massing of troops in Sinai, etc. – as a threat to its existence; and, outside the Arab/Israel PC setting, Kuwait perceived a threat to its existence when Baghdad claimed all of its territory on 23 June 1961, one week after the UK granted independence to Kuwait). The Middle East PC/non-PC difference with respect to the threat of grave damage, by contrast, is glaring: 16 cases, or 25% of the total, within the Arab/Israel protracted conflict, two in the other Middle East cluster (e.g., the perception by Israel of a threat to vital water supplies, in the Jordan Waters Crisis of 1963–64, following an Arab Summit decision in January 1964 to divert the three tributaries of the Jordan River and prevent Israel's completion of its National Water Carrier Project). In sum, one of these two basic values was perceived to be threatened in 28% of Arab/Israel crises, as compared to 8% in other Middle East cases. Thus support for this hypothesis is overwhelming.

TABLE III.11.4. Intra-Region and Values

	Threat to Existence or of Grave Damage		Other Values Threatened				
Arab/Israel	18	28%	46	72%	64		57%
Other Middle East	4	8%	44	92%	48		43%
	22	20%	90	80%	112		100%

What does the evidence indicate regarding crisis management in the sense of coping with crises? In general, differences are noteworthy for all three *violence* variables. Violence as the *primary* CMT (Hypothesis 3) was more visible in the Arab/Israel conflict, 28% to 10% (Table III.11.5.). Even when the mixed category, "multiple, including violence" is added, Arab/Israel crises show almost double the frequency of violence, 47% to 25% (e.g., Egypt's appeal to the UK on 31 December 1948 to press for a Security Council resolution demanding the withdrawal of Israeli troops from Sinai, along with use of the Egyptian Army, as its multiple CMT including violence, in the Sinai Incursion Crisis from 25 December 1948 to 10 January 1949; and, in a non-PC setting, Lebanon's resort to diplomacy – complaints to the Arab League and the UN against massive UAR interference in its internal affairs,

TABLE III.11.5. Intra-Region and Crisis Management Technique

	Violence		Multiple Including Violence		Pacific				
Arab/Israel	18	28%	12	19%	34	53%	64	57%	
Other Middle East	5	10%	7	15%	36	75%	48	43%	
	23	20.5%	19	17%	70	62.5%	112	100%	

and an appeal for US assistance – along with violence, to cope with the Lebanon Upheaval of 1958).

As for the *intensity* of violence (Hypothesis 4), there was much more frequent resort to full-scale war or serious clashes in Arab/Israel crises, 42% to 23% (Table III.11.6.) (e.g., full-scale war by Israel, Egypt, Jordan and Syria in the crisis of 1967; and, in a non-PC Middle East setting, the resort to war by Syria and Jordan to manage the Black September Crisis of 1970). Regarding the *centrality* of violence (Hypothesis 5), there were, proportionately, more than twice as many Arab/Israel crises in which violence was the preeminent CMT as in other Middle East cases (Table III.11.7.) (45%–21%) (e.g., the preeminence of violence by the principal adversaries in the Arab/Israel crisis-wars of 1956, 1967 and 1973). The conclusion on the violence dimension is unmistakable: crises which occurred within the Arab/Israel protracted conflict were characterized by much more violence, more intense violence, and a more central role for violence in crisis management than in other, non-PC Middle East crises.

TABLE III.11.6. Intra-Region and Intensity of Violence

	Serious Clashes or War		No Violence or Minor Clashes				
Arab/Israel	27	42%	37	58%	64	57%	
Other Middle East	11	23%	37	77%	48	43%	
	38	34%	74	66%	112	100%	

TABLE III.11.7. Intra-Region and Centrality of Violence

	Violence Preeminent or Important		Minor or No Violence				
Arab/Israel	29	45%	35	55%	64	57%	
Other Middle East	10	21%	38	79%	48	43%	
	39	35%	73	65%	112	100%	

The evidence on *superpower activity* strongly supports Hypothesis 6 for the US: its involvement was political almost three times as often in Arab/Israel crises as in other Middle East cases (80% to 27%); and it was involved (semi-) militarily in only one Arab/Israel crisis (4%), compared to 11 cases (42%) in the other Middle East cluster, two with direct military activity and nine in the semi-military category (e.g., US pressure on Israel to delay a preemptive attack, in May 1967, and then support for Israel against Soviet threats, in the Six Day War Crisis; and, in the non-PC setting, strong US pressure on the Soviet Union to withdraw its troops from Iran, during the 1945–46 Azerbaijan Crisis). The overall low/high US activity is presented in Table III.11.8.

As for the USSR (Table III.11.9.), there is virtually no difference in the two clusters: 72% low activity, 28% military activity, in Arab/Israel crises; 65% low, 35% military activity, in other Middle East cases (e.g., Soviet direct military participation – air power – in support of Egypt during the 1970 War of Attrition Crisis; and, in the non-PC setting, the massing of Soviet forces on the Turkish frontier during the 1945–46 Kars-Ardahan Crisis). The US was more frequently involved than the USSR in Arab/Israel crises, and more active politically overall, but was much less active militarily than the other superpower.

The Middle East data are mixed for Hypothesis 7. The US role as the "most important" or "an important" contributor to crisis abatement was similar in Arab/Israel and other Middle East crises, 36% and 31%, respectively (Table III.11.10.); and it accounted for less than a third of all crises in that region (e.g., the dispatch of US Marines to Beirut on 14 July 1958 played an important role in abating that segment of the Lebanon/Iraq Upheaval; and, in the Arab/Israel PC, US pressure on Israel on 7 November 1956 to agree to withdraw from Sinai was an important contribution to abating the Suez Crisis).

The Soviet Union was less *effective* than the US in an overall sense (Table III.11.11.), but it showed a difference between Arab/Israel and other Middle East crises – 16% and 4%, respectively, as the "most important" or "an important"

TABLE III.11.8. Intra-Region and US Activity

	Low*		High**			
Arab/Israel	24	96%	1	4%	25	49%
Other Middle East	15	58%	11	42%	26	51%
	39	76%	12	24%	51	100%

* Low = Political, economic, propaganda and no activity.
** High = Covert, semi-military and direct military activity.

TABLE III.11.9 Intra-Region and USSR Activity

	Low*		High**			
Arab/Israel	18	72%	7	28%	25	49%
Other Middle East	17	65%	9	35%	26	51%
	35	69%	16	31%	51	100%

* Low = (See Table III.11.8. * note.)
** High = (See Table III.11.8.** note.)

TABLE III.11.10. Intra-Region and US Effectiveness

	High*		Low**			
Arab/Israel	9	36%	16	64%	25	49%
Other Middle East	8	31%	18	69%	26	51%
	17	33%	34	67%	51	100%

* High = Most important or important contributor to crisis abatement.
** Low = Marginal or no contribution to crisis abatement, escalation of crisis, or no activity.

TABLE III.11.11. Intra-Region and USSR Effectiveness

	High*	Low**		
Arab–Israel	4 16%	21 84%	25	49%
Other Middle East	1 4%	25 96%	26	51%
	5 10%	46 90%	51	100%

* High = (See Table III.11.10.* note.)
** Low = (See Table III.11.10. ** note.)

contributor to crisis abatement (e.g., on 29 October 1957 the USSR succeeded in deescalating a US–Turkey military buildup by tacitly dropping its accusation that Turkey was about to attack Syria; and, in the Arab/Israel PC setting, the Soviet threat on 5 November 1956 to use force, if Britain, France and Israel did not cease military operations against Egypt and withdraw their forces, contributed to the "winding down" of the Suez–Sinai Crisis).

The evidence on global IO *involvement* supports Hypothesis 8. The UN was involved in 76% of the crises in the Arab/Israel PC, in only 38% of other Middle East crises (Table III.11.12.) (e.g., the UN was not involved in the 1960 Rottem Crisis over the dispatch of Egyptian troops to Sinai and Israeli forces to the Negev; and, in a non-PC setting, it was inactive in the Baghdad Pact Crisis of 1955). Moreover, medium- and high-level UN activity (call for action by members, condemnation, arbitration, observers and emergency military forces) was, proportionately, much more frequent in Arab/Israel cases than in others, (e.g., the dispatch of an emergency military force (UNEF/I) by the global IO during the Suez–Sinai Crisis of 1956–57; and, in a non-protracted conflict setting, the Security Council's call for an agreement by Moscow and Teheran in March 1946 on the withdrawal of Soviet forces from Iran, during the Azerbaijan Crisis).

As for IO *effectiveness* (Hypothesis 9), the UN was not effective or exhibited little effectiveness in the overwhelming majority of both clusters of Middle East crises (Table III.11.13.) – in 84% (Arab/Israel), (or 72% if "marginal" contribution to

TABLE III.11.12. Intra-Region and Global Organization Involvement

	Not Involved	Involved		
Arab/Israel	6 24%	19 76%	25	49%
Other Middle East	16 62%	10 38%	26	51%
	22 43%	29 57%	51	100%

TABLE III.11.13. Intra-Region and Global Organization Effectiveness

	High*	Low**		
Arab/Israel	4 16%	21 84%	25	49%
Other Middle East	3 12%	23 88%	26	51%
	7 14%	44 86%	51	100%

* High = Most important or important contributor to crisis abatement.
**Low = Marginal or no contribution to crisis abatement; escalation of crisis, or no involvement.

crisis abatement is added to "most important" and "important" contribution); and 88% (other Middle East) (e.g., a Security Council discussion had no effect on the abatement of a March 1968 Arab/Israel crisis over PLO intrusion from Jordan and an Israeli retaliation raid on the village of Karameh; nor did discussions in the General Assembly have an effect on the Syria/Turkey Border Crisis of 1957). In fact, UN effectiveness is evident in only 14% of the 51 (non-Yemen War) Middle East international crises from 1945 to 1985.

The evidence does support expectations regarding the *content of outcome* (Hypothesis 10): ambiguous outcomes – stalemate and compromise – account for a higher proportion of Arab/Israel crises, 60% to 42% (Table III.11.14.) (e.g., within the Arab/Israel protracted conflict, a compromise between Egypt and Israel in the 1970 War of Attrition, as expressed in the US' Rogers-mediated cease-fire agreement; and, in a non-PC setting, a stalemate between Iraq and Syria in the 1976 Iraqi Threat Crisis, with the troops of both states withdrawing from the border and resuming their defensive posture). Moreover, victory/defeat (definitive) was the outcome of 58% of the crises outside a protracted conflict setting (e.g., a victory for Jordan – and defeat for Syria – in the Black September Crisis of 1970).

As for the *form of outcome* (Hypothesis 11), there was a formal or semi-formal agreement in 28% of Arab/Israel cases, compared to 38% of other Middle East crises (Table III.11.15.) (e.g., separate armistice agreements between Israel and four Arab states ending the Israel Independence Crisis of 1948–49; and, in a non-PC setting, an agreement between Iran and the Soviet Union, announced on 24 March 1946, providing for the withdrawal of Soviet forces within five to six weeks, ending the Azerbaijan Crisis). Tacit understandings, by contrast, are relatively more frequent in Arab/Israel cases, 24% as compared to 8%.

The findings on the relationship between international crises and protracted conflict in the Middle East are summarized in Table III.11.16.

(1) The categorical distributions from 51 Middle East international crises from 1945 to 1985, comprising 112 crisis actors, support 7 of 11 hypotheses – with two others supported partially – on seven dimensions of crisis within PCs, compared with other crises;

(2) Four expectations regarding crises within and outside a PC are either weakly or not supported: USSR activity, US and IO effectiveness and form of outcome; that is, knowledge about protractedness does not greatly facilitate the

TABLE III.11.14. Intra-Region and Substance of Outcome

	Ambiguous*	Definitive**		
Arab/Israel	15 60%	10 40%	25	49%
Other Middle East	11 42%	15 58%	26	51%
	26 51%	25 49%	51	100%

* Ambiguous = Stalemate or compromise.
** Definitive = Victory/defeat.

TABLE III.11.15. Intra-Region and Form of Outcome

	Formal/Semi-Formal	Tacit	Unilateral/No Agreement		
Arab/Israel	7 28%	6 24%	12 48%	25	49%
Other Middle East	10 38%	2 8%	14 54%	26	51%
	17 33%	8 16%	26 51%	51	100%

TABLE III.11.16. Crises and Protracted Conflict in the Middle East: Summary of Findings

Dimension	Focus of Hypothesis	PC Setting (%)	Non-PC Setting(%)
Trigger:	Violence	39	21
Value:	Threat to existence or of grave damage	28	8
Behavior:	Violence as primary CMT	28	10
	Intense violence	42	23
	Violence preeminent or important CMT	45	25
SP Activity (US):	Political	80	27
SP Effectiveness (USSR):		16	4
IO Involvement:		76	38
Outcome (Content):	Ambiguous	60	42

prediction of Soviet activity, effectiveness by the US or the UN with regard to abating crises in the Middle East, or form of outcome.

This completes the first stage of the aggregate analysis.

The link between crisis and protracted conflict is not, as noted, confined to the Middle East region. Rather, it is a global phenomenon. Thus we now broaden the inquiry to four other domains. Conceptually, the independent variables for these domains – Inter-region, Context, Protracted/Non-Protracted Conflict and Protractedness – can be explained through reference to Table III.11.1., which displays the 57 international crises in the Middle East from 1945 to 1985.[8] Three subsets of cases, 25 Arab/Israel crises, 26 non-PC crises in the region and six Yemen War cluster cases, are distinguished in that table and in Figure III.11.1. as A, B and F, respectively.

Intra-region, the independent variable in Stage I, distinguishes crises in Subset A from those in B. With respect to *Inter-region*, the cases in Table III.11.1. include the full set of Middle East crises (i.e., A, B and F together). All other international crises in the era, 1929–85, are viewed as non-Middle East, and comprise Subsets C and E in Figure III.11.2. Thus Stage II of this analysis compares the Middle East as

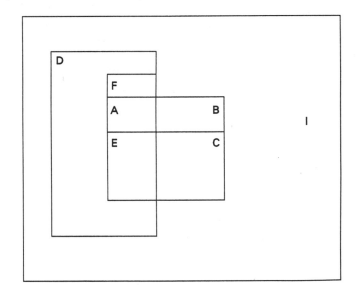

I = International conflict.
A = Arab/Israel crises.
B = Non-protracted conflict Middle East crises.
C = Non-Middle East crises outside of protracted conflict.
D = Protracted conflicts.
E = Non-Middle East crises within protracted conflict.
F = Yemen War cluster.

FIGURE III.11.1 International Conflict, Crisis and Protracted Conflict

a region (A, B and F) to the rest of the world (C and E, with C comprised of crises outside PCs and E crises within PCs). In Stage III, the *Context* variable distinguishes Arab/Israel crises from those who have occurred outside the Middle East (i.e., A versus C and E). In Stage IV, *Protracted/Non-Protracted Conflict* as the independent variable distinguishes Arab/Israel crises (Subset A) from crises outside the region which have not occurred within PCs (Subset C). In Stage V, the independent variable, *Protractedness*, has two categories: Arab/Israel crises (Subset A) and all other crises within PCs (Subset E). All of these subsets of crises (and D, the full subset of protracted conflicts, which includes some instances of conflict that do not meet the definition of a crisis), belong to I, the overall set of international conflicts. Examples of cases from categories C through E appear in Table III.11.1.

Each of the independent variables in Stages II–V will be correlated with the relevant members of the set of dependent variables. This extension of the analysis is guided by two theoretical considerations. First, it is not logically possible to draw inferences from strictly Middle East findings for crises in any other region and in the global system as a whole. In other words, a valid test of the Protracted Conflict–Crisis Model requires an extension of the analysis beyond a single region. This purpose is served by the second, third and fourth stages of the analysis. If the model is valid, it is not enough to discover differences between Subsets A and B. Dissimilarities also should emerge when Arab/Israel crises are compared to others outside the region (Stage III). These differences should be even more dramatic at Stage IV, when *all* of the crises in the comparison group have occurred outside of PCs. By contrast, Stage II is not expected to produce significant differences, because each group contains crises within and outside of PCs.

A second reason to extend the analysis is that differences between Arab/Israel crises and others which have occurred outside of PCs would not, *per se*, demonstrate that protracted conflict is the primary explanatory factor for the disparity. At Stage V, crises within PCs outside of the Middle East will be compared to the Arab/Israel subset. These two subsets of cases should manifest the same pattern with respect to crisis management, if the Model is valid.

II. Middle East Crises Versus Rest of the World

A general proposition about crisis dimensions for the Middle East region relative to the rest of the world emerges logically from the first stage of the analysis. The hypothesized differences between Arab/Israel crises and others in the Middle East were based upon the concept of protracted conflict. If PC is what distinguishes Arab/Israel crises from others, then the Middle East as a region should be no different than other regional clusters of crisis along the dimensions under investigation. This is because some Middle East crises have occurred within a PC (i.e., Arab/Israel and Yemen), while others have not, and the same mixture is true of the other regions. Differences based upon protractedness thus should not emerge through a comparison of regions. In other words, this *null hypothesis* declares that there should be *no difference between international crises which occur in a specific region and those in the world at large*.

The evidence from Table III.11.2. strongly indicates that Middle East crises as a group are virtually the same as those in the rest of the world: there is no coefficient for *Inter-region* cases with a magnitude higher than 0.11 across the crisis dimensions. In the context of the point of departure for this investigation, the preceding result is especially striking. To be more specific, area specialists almost certainly would have expected regional uniqueness along at least some crisis dimensions. Yet the comparative analysis of the Middle East with the rest of the world is more consistent with the perspective of social science. In other words, geographic location does not seem to be a decisive factor in explaining patterns of crisis management.

III. Arab/Israel Crises Versus Rest of the World

The general proposition relating to the *Context* of a crisis is somewhat more complicated. When comparing Arab/Israel crises to those in the world beyond the Middle East, the protractedness of the former would be expected to produce a contrast with the latter. However, a significant number of crises outside the Middle East, too, have occurred *within* protracted conflicts. Hence the comparison is not a pure one. PCs outside the Middle East may create "white noise" and thus reduce the amount of variation observed. Propositions matching those for protractedness can be tested, but with less expectation that sharp differences will emerge between Arab/Israel crises and *all* those of other regions.

As evident in Table III.11.2., there are noteworthy relationships. Value threats in Arab/Israel cases are of a higher gravity than in crises outside the Middle East. The earlier pattern of US activity in crises receives further support. And the more extensive role of the global organization in Arab/Israel crises also is reaffirmed. These results are consistent with the expectation that differences would emerge but not to the degree evident in Stage I.

IV. Arab/Israel Crises Versus Those Outside of Protracted Conflicts

The guiding proposition is an extension of the one from Stage III. The differences between the two sets of cases are expected to be more extensive. Since the comparison group consists entirely of crises outside of PCs, it is natural that Arab/Israel crises should stand out even more, as they do from non-PC crises in the Middle East (Stage I).

Each of the three differences which appeared at Stage III has been reaffirmed, and additional contrasts have emerged. The patterns concerning value threat, US activity, and global organization involvement continue to hold true. Several other linkages also have found some degree of support: trigger, crisis management technique, intensity of violence, centrality of violence, USSR effectiveness, and substance of outcome, ranging from 12% to 27% reduction in error. These results provide further support for the Protracted Conflict–Crisis Model.

V. Arab/Israel Crises Versus Other Protracted Conflict Crises

If the Model is to be regarded as valid, then these two sets of cases should not differ along the various dimensions of crisis. Crises within PCs are hypothesized to be similar across regions. In other words, Arab/Israel crises should not be distinguishable from crises which have taken place in other PCs.

There are few deviations (Table III.11.2.) from the anticipated pattern of similarity. Arab/Israel crises feature a lower level of US military activity than do crises in the comparison group. Involvement by the global organization also is somewhat higher in the Arab/Israel subset of cases. However, the two sets of crises are virtually identical when the dimensions of crisis are considered as a whole.

The most salient patterns within Table III.11.2. may now be summarized:

(1) for the dimensions of crises in the Middle East, protracted conflict is the determining attribute;
(2) virtually no regional variation is evident regarding the Middle East (as a whole) and the rest of the world;
(3) Arab/Israel crises differ in several respects from crises outside the Middle East which have occurred outside of protracted conflicts;
(4) Arab/Israel crises strongly resemble those within other protracted conflicts; and
(5) taken together, the results support the overarching propositions corresponding to the five domains of analysis.

Conclusion

Evidence from four decades of international crises in the post-World War II era has demonstrated the distinctiveness of the Arab/Israel conflict within the Middle East. But on what basis has that conflict been distinguished? The comparison of crises across regions suggest that the concept of *protractedness* is the key. Arab/Israel crises are different from crises outside the region *and* from crises in the Middle East which have not occurred within PCs. At the same time, Arab/Israel crises are very similar to others which have taken place in PCs.

Given these findings, the "fool's experiment" – to use Darwin's terminology once again – has been worthwhile. The character of the Middle East as a unique setting for conflictual interaction is "obvious" to the area specialist, yet the results of the aggregate analysis have suggested otherwise. As for "documenting" conventional wisdom, Arab/Israel crises have indeed turned out to be different, but not because of geographic setting, a standard explanation.

Assuming that the conditions of a protracted conflict continue to hold true in cases such as Arab/Israel, the aggregate findings are also of some practical import. The statistical patterns that have emerged provide a basis for anticipating the likely profile of future crises in a given protracted conflict.

Notes

1. For the former, see Allison, 1969, 1971; A. I. Dawisha, 1980; K. Dawisha, 1984, O. R. Holsti, 1965; Holsti, Brody and North, 1964; Paige, 1968, Shlaim, 1983; Stein and Tanter, 1980; Vertzberger, 1984; and Whiting, 1960. For the latter, consult Bell, 1971; Brecher with Geist, 1980; Butterworth, 1976; Chan, 1978; Dowty, 1984; George and Smoke, 1974; O. R. Holsti, 1972, 1980; Howe, 1971; Lebow, 1981; Leng and Gochman, 1982; Milburn, 1972; Paige, 1972; Snyder, 1972; Snyder and Diesing, 1977; Tanter, 1974; Whiting, 1975; Williams, 1976; Winham, 1988; and Young, 1967, 1968b.

2. Studies of superpower crisis management include: Abolfathi *et al.*, 1979; Allison, 1969, 1971; Blechman and Kaplan, 1978; Butterworth, 1978; K. Dawisha, 1984; Dowty, 1984; George, 1983; George and Smoke, 1974; George *et al.*, 1971; Hazlewood *et al.*, 1977; Horelick, 1964; S. S. Kaplan, 1981; Lebow, 1987; Paige, 1968; Shlaim, 1983; Stein, 1988; Valenta, 1979; and Wilkenfeld and Brecher, 1982.

3. Some examples are: E. Haas, 1983; E. Haas, Butterworth and Nye, 1972; M. Haas 1986; Wilkenfeld and Brecher, 1984; and Zacher, 1979.

4. The reason for confining the time frame of this analysis to the post-World War II period, unlike most chapters in this volume, is that almost all Middle East territories and peoples had a dependent status before 1945, mostly League of Nations Mandates held by the UK and France, with the result that there were very few international crises in that region from 1929 to 1945 (6 of 63).

5. Inter-coder reliability for the data on these variables was greater than 85%. For an extensive discussion of ICB coding procedures consult Brecher and Wilkenfeld *et al.*, *op. cit.*, Part II.

6. The categories for this variable and for the others to follow are explained in detail in *ibid.*, Part III.

7. This data analysis relies upon a bivariate measure of association, as opposed to more elaborate techniques. Since a "population" of cases is used, the significance levels reported in Table III.11.2. are intended to be used in an advisory manner, not to make inferences about samples.

8. The classification of international crises within or outside of protracted conflicts is explained in Chapter 9 above.

Part IV
Foreign Policy Crises

12 Threat and Violence in State Behavior

Jonathan Wilkenfeld, Michael Brecher and Stephen R. Hill

Conflict Begets Conflict

Among the most venerable theories of human behavior is that based on the notion of stimulus-response. In this formulation, behavior is seen as a response to an environmental stimulus, and that response is congruent with the stimulus in terms of both substance and intensity. Indeed, branches of science from zoology through psychology have relied on this theory to explain behavior in a wide range of situations. In the literature of international politics, this approach is best illustrated by the Stanford Studies of the 1914 crisis (for example, Holsti, Brody and North, 1964; Zinnes, 1966, 1968; Holsti, 1972; Zinnes, Zinnes and McClure, 1972).

A segment of the literature which can be broadly classified as focusing on the stimulus-response process has been concerned with the notion that "conflict begets conflict." In a series of studies relying heavily on events data, researchers such as Phillips (1973, 1978), Ward (1982), Wilkenfeld (1975), Wilkenfeld, Hopple, Rossa and Andriole (1980) and Zinnes and Wilkenfeld (1971) probed the conditions under which the external behavior of states was systematically related to the behavior they received from the environment. These studies typically focused on conflict behavior, and the reasoning behind them was summarized by Wilkenfeld (1975: p. 177):

> . . . It is assumed that state X ought to exhibit toward state Y an amount of conflict which is roughly proportional to the amount of conflict which state Y has directed towards it, or, to expand the notion somewhat, total conflict sent to all conflict partners ought to roughly equal total conflict received.

Ward (1982: p. 97) formalizes the action-reaction dynamic as follows:

> . . . The action-reaction dynamic is comprised of three major components: (1) a historical propensity toward a certain level of interaction (that is, long-term memory), (2) the impact of recent behavior upon present behavior (short-term memory), and (3) the impact of the behavior of other states upon present behavior of the initiator state.

Indeed, the findings of these studies were rather startling in terms of the degree of explanatory power such a model generates. Thus, Wilkenfeld, Hopple, Rossa and Andriole (1980: p. 198) found that "the reception of behavior is directly and strongly linked to foreign behavior. . . . Behavioral stimuli constitute universal determinants of action while other factors vary in importance by state type." Phillips (1973: p. 146) found that "military initiative on the part of a specific nation is met with a military response from the environment. Thus, violence begets violence and warnings and defensive acts are the response to warnings and defensive acts." Finally, in a study which focused in part on conflict interactions between the US and the USSR, Ward (1982: p.107) found that "most of the dynamic explaining conflict patterns between these two major powers is accounted for by their relatively strong and significant reaction to the amount of conflict received from one another." This finding is also confirmed by Ward (1982: p. 11) for Israeli/Egyptian behavior.

Clearly, then, these studies all point to a rather well-established interactive dynamic in the conflict realm. Yet, Wilkenfeld (1975: pp. 177–178) warned against wholesale acceptance of the behavior-begets-behavior notion.

> The functions of policy makers in the foreign policy realm would be greatly simplified were the above partial model of conflict behavior (conflict-begets-conflict) to apply universally. In fact, one might envision the elimination of policy makers entirely under this rather mechanistic scheme. It is readily apparent, however, that only a portion, albeit a rather large portion, of conflict behavior sent can be explained by conflict behavior received.

177

It is these other factors which intervene in the conflict process and thus make this area of inquiry such a maze of imponderables.

One of the major innovations in stimulus-response theory has been the notion of mediation as a crucial intervening variable. Thus, the mediated stimulus-response approach posits that perception mediates the direct relationship between stimulus and response, and that as social scientists we need to gain a greater understanding of the circumstances under which differences in perception "distort" the straight-forward stimulus-response mechanism (for example, North, Brody and Holsti, 1964). In addition to perception, other variables, such as societal cohesion, type of government, and domestic instabiliy, are posited as mediating the stimulus-response mechanism.

This chapter proposes to add two new dimensions to the analysis of stimulus-response in the realm of state behavior. First, we will be concerned with conflict situations which can be characterised as international crises. Second, we will argue that in crisis situations the key mediating factor in the stimulus-response dynamic is the stress experienced by decision-makers at the time that responses to incoming stimuli are formulated. In the process, we hope to shed further light on the behavioral dynamics of crisis situations. Since the notion of stress plays a pivotal role in the analysis to follow, we turn first to an exploration of this concept.

Stress in State Behavior

What is the meaning of *stress*? The breadth of this concept is indicated by Lazarus (1968: pp. 337–338):

> As in the use of the term in engineering, where it is applied to forces exerted on inorganic objects, "stress" suggests excessive demands made on men and animals, demands that produce disturbances of physiological, social and psychological systems. . . . The term "stress" is thus loose, in that it is applied to a host of phenomena related only by their common analogy with the engineering concept and, at the same time, exceedingly broad, in that it covers phenomena at the physiological, social, and psychological levels of analysis.

According to Holsti and George (1975: p. 257): "It is customary to regard stress as the anxiety or fear an individual experiences in a situation which he perceives as posing a severe threat to one or more values. . . . Psychological stress occurs either when the subject experiences damage to his values or anticipates that the stimulus situation may lead to it." In a similar vein, Janis and Mann (1977: p. 50) observe:

> *Psychological stress* is used as a generic term to designate unpleasant emotional states evoked by threatening environmental events or stimuli. A "stressful" event is any change in the environment that typically induces a high degree of unpleasant emotion (such as anxiety, guilt, or shame) and affects normal patterns of information processing.

In the study of foreign policy behavior, stress refers to a state of mind among decision-makers brought on by an environmental challenge requiring a response within a limited time; that is, stress is a psychological condition usually associated with anxiety and/or frustration produced by crisis and threat. Through the 1960s and most of the 1970s the consensual view of a foreign policy crisis was the Hermann definition (1969: p. 414): a situation characterized by threat to high priority goals; short time for response; and surprise. This was later revised, as noted in Chapter 1, fn. 15 above, by: the omission of "surprise" as a necessary condition; the replacement of "short" time by "finite" time for response; the addition of "internal" environmental change as a source of threat; the focus on "basic values" rather than the narrower "high-priority goals"; and the addition of perceived "high probability of involvement in military hostilities" (Brecher 1977: pp. 42–44).

In this volume, a foreign policy crisis for a state is identified with three necessary and sufficient perceptual conditions, namely, a threat to (one or more) basic values, finite time for response, and a heightened expectation of military hostilities as a consequence of environmental change. The pivotal component of the stress experienced by foreign policy decision-makers is threat. It is the precondition of time pressure and the likelihood of violence, both of which follow the anticipation of harm. Thus, O. R. Holsti, in an extensive discussion of "Crises, Stress, and Decision-Making" (1972: p. 11), defined stress as "the result of a situation that threatens important goals or values." He also pointed out the dependence of time perspectives on perceptions of high stress (1972: p. 14): "the ability to judge time is impaired in situations which increase anxiety" – i.e., those of high stress. Holsti and George (1975: p. 257) noted the consensus view that "the perception of threat is regarded as the central intervening variable in psychological stress." Finally, Lazarus (1968: p. 343) emphasized the sequence: "threat is more intense when harm is more imminent."[1]

The analysis below will be guided by the following general proposition:

The violence-begets-violence dynamic which underlies the interactions of states in crisis will be strengthened under conditions of high stress for decision-makers.

Our assumption is that interactions among states in crisis are governed by the same dynamic present in more routine interactive processes. Nevertheless, it is our contention that under conditions of high stress – as expressed in grave threat to basic values – the behavior-begets-behavior linkage is considerably strengthened. Underlying this view is the premiss that stress evokes greater attentiveness on the part of decision-makers to both the content and intensity of incoming actions as the proper responses are formulated; that is, decision latitude is circumscribed by the greater need to respond meaningfully and accurately. Conversely, under conditions of lower stress, such matching is not as critical, since the dangers inherent in the situation are not viewed by the decision-makers as grave. As a consequence, greater decision latitude exists, and we can expect to find some breakdown in the behavior-begets-behavior linkage.

While the impact of stress on behavior has been the subject of extensive scholarly attention at the individual level, it has remained relatively unexplored at the nation-state level. In a landmark study, Holsti (1965) examined the effect of stress on the patterns of communication among decision-makers in the 1914 crisis leading to World War I. Among the hypotheses he examined was the following: "As stress increases, decision-makers will perceive the range of alternatives open to themselves to be narrower." (Holsti, 1965: p. 365). It is this limiting of the range of alternatives which forms the basis for the hypothesis under examination in the present study; that is, as the level of stress increases, the range of alternatives narrows, and the choice of violence as an appropriate response to a violent trigger becomes more probable. At lower levels of stress, we would expect a less clearcut relationship between violence in the trigger and violence in the response, while such a relationship should be stronger at high levels of stress.

A second line of reasoning converges with the above to lend credence to the hypothesized impact of stress on crisis behavior. Wilkenfeld, Hopple, Rossa and Andriole (1980) found that the impact of psychological factors on nation-state behavior is maximized in less routine, more crisis-like situations. More specifically, their findings indicate that psychological factors have their greatest impact in situations typified by force, the highest level of conflict behavior. Here again, then, we have evidence of the intervention of psychological factors such as stress in behavioral sequences.

This analysis of the impact of stress on crisis behavior focuses on the periods 1929–39 and 1945–85.[2] Data on 621 crisis actors during that time frame will be examined in the ensuing analysis.

Operationalization

Thus far we have dealt generally with the notion that stress intervenes in a mechanistic process identified as "conflict-begets-conflict." In this section, we will discuss the specific indicators of crisis interaction and stress.

Independent Variable: Crisis Trigger

By *trigger*, as noted earlier in this volume, we refer to the act(s), event(s), or change(s) which generate(s) a perception of threat to basic values among the decision-makers of a state. In the present context, a trigger embodies the act(s), event(s) or change(s) which set(s) in motion the behavior-begets-behavior dynamic. For purposes of this analysis, triggers to crises are grouped into three broad categrories:

(1) *Non-violent* (N = 239), including *verbal* (e.g., protests), *political* (e.g., alliance of adversaries), *economic* (e.g., embargo), *external change* (e.g., in weapon system(s)), and *non-violent internal challenge* (e.g., proclamation of new regime);

(2) *Non-violent military* (N = 93), (e.g., mobilization); and

(3) *Violent* (N = 289), including *direct* (e.g., border clashes), *indirect* (e.g., violence against a client state), and *violent internal change*.

Dependent Variables: Crisis Behavior

The first of four dependent variables indicates the *major response* to the act, event or change which triggers the crisis period. This variable, as noted earlier, attempts to capture the major thrust of the behavior of a state in crisis, such as the US quarantine of Cuba in the 1962 Missile Crisis. Three broad categories of response will be examined: (1) *Non-violent* (N = 249); (2) *Non-violent military* (N = 164); and (3) *Violent* (N = 208).[3]

The second indicator of behavior refers to the primary *crisis management technique* (CMT) utilized by a crisis actor in the crisis as a whole. Three categories of crisis management were defined: (1) *Negotiation and other pacific CMTs* (N = 252); (2) *Non-violent military* (N = 96), (e.g., threat to use violence); and (3) *Violence* (N = 273), including multiple techniques involving violence.

The third indicator of behavior in crisis addresses the *intensity of violence* used as a crisis management technique. Intensity is classified as: (1) *Full-scale war* (N = 114); (2) *Serious clashes* (N = 128); and (3) *Minor* or *no* violence (N = 379).

The fourth indicator of crisis behavior is the *extent of violence* employed as a crisis management technique, that is, the relative importance decision-makers attach to their use of violence to attain their goals in a particular crisis. Thus, extent of violence is classified as: (1) *Pre-eminent* (N=110); (2) *Important*, but supported by other CMTs (N=160); and (3) *Marginal* role or *no* violence (N=351).

Mediating Variable: Stress

Stress is operationalized in terms of a *threat to values*, as perceived by the principal decision-maker(s) of a crisis actor. Value threats are classified as follows

(1) *High threat* (N = 416), including threat to *existence*, threat of *grave damage*, threat to *influence* (for the superpowers), threat to *territorial integrity*, and threat to *political system*,[4] and
(2) *Low threat* (N = 205), including threat to *influence* (of non-superpowers), threat to *economic interests*, and limited danger to *population* and *property*.

Analysis

The focus of inquiry in this chapter, as indicated, is the impact of a crisis trigger on subsequent behavior, as mediated by the stress experienced by the decision-maker(s). Figure IV.12.1. provides a schematic representation of the research design. The results of the analysis of trigger, threat and violence are presented in a set of contingency tables.

We begin with an examination of the direct effect of trigger on behavior, unmediated by a control for stress. These results can be seen in the first matrices of Tables IV.12.1.–4. In all four cases, the data clearly show that, as one moves from less to more violence in the trigger, the proportion of non-violent behavior decreases, and the proportion of violent behavior increases. For example, in Table IV.12.1.a., non-violent triggers produced non-violent major responses in 52% of the cases, and violent triggers did so in 30% of the cases. Conversely, non-violent triggers produced violent responses in only 17% of the cases, compared to 52% of the cases with

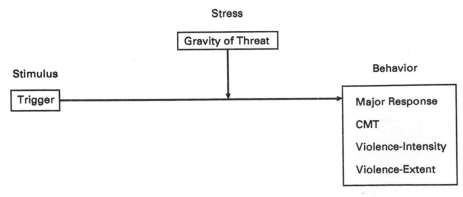

FIGURE IV.12.1. Research Design on Threat and Violence

TABLE IV.12.1. Crisis Trigger and Major Response 1929–39, 1945–85

a. Total (N = 621)

Major Response

Trigger		Non-Violent	Non-Violent Military	Violence		
	Non-Violent	124 / 52%	75 / 31%	40 / 17%	239	38%
Trigger	Non-Violent Military	39 / 42%	36 / 39%	18 / 20%	93	15%
	Violence	86 / 30%	53 / 18%	150 / 52%	289	47%
		249 / 40%	164 / 26%	208 / 34%	621	100%

$X^2 = 85.58$, p = .000

b. High Threat (N = 416)

Trigger		Non-Violent	Non-Violent Military	Violence		
	Non-Violent	89 / 55%	56 / 35%	16 / 10%	161	39%
Trigger	Non-Violent Military	26 / 41%	24 / 37%	14 / 22%	64	15%
	Violence	58 / 30%	31 / 16%	102 / 54%	191	46%
		173 / 41%	111 / 27%	132 / 32%	416	100%

$X^2 = 81.97$, p = .000

c. Low Threat (N = 205)

Trigger		Non-Violent	Non-Violent Military	Violence		
	Non-Violent	35 / 45%	19 / 24%	24 / 31%	78	38%
Trigger	Non-Violent Military	13 / 45%	12 / 41%	4 / 14%	29	14%
	Violence	28 / 29%	22 / 22%	48 / 49%	98	48%
		76 / 37%	53 / 26%	76 / 37%	205	100%

$X^2 = 15.69$, p = .004

violent triggers. Similarly, Table IV.12.3.a. indicates that, while non-violent triggers resulted in intense violence (i.e., serious clashes or full-scale war, columns 2 plus 3) as the primary crisis management technique in only 21% of the cases, violent triggers produced intense violent responses in 59% of the cases. Overall, the findings strongly support the behavior-begets-behavior assumption implicit in our basic hypothesis.

Let us now explore the impact of stress, in the form of high or low threat to basic values, on the trigger to behavior transition. Tables IV.12.1.b.–IV.12.4.b. show that the underlying relationship between trigger and behavior is significantly strengthened under conditions of high threat. As one moves up the level of violence in the trigger, the probability of violent response by a crisis actor increases sharply under conditions of high threat – from 10% for non-violent triggers to 22% for non-violent military triggers and 54% for violent triggers. The progressions for the other three behavior variables are even more pronounced: violent crisis management technique – 19%–27%–71%; intense form of violence (serious clashes and full-scale war) – 14%–28%–64%; and extent of violence (violence as important or preeminent CMT – 19%–26%–71%.

Examination of the cases of low threat to basic values (Tables IV.12.1.c. through IV.12.4.c.) reveals a very different picture. No basic trend is evident; the overall results signify that, under conditions of low stress, the presence or absence of violence in the trigger does not assist us in understanding the level, intensity, and extent of violence in subsequent crisis behavior.

Closer examination of the low threat data reveals the major reason for the sharp

TABLE IV.12.2. Trigger and Crisis Management Technique 1929–39, 1945–85

a. Total (N = 621)

Crisis Management Technique

		Pacific	Non-Violent Military	Violence	
	Non-Violent	131 55%	46 19%	62 26%	239 38%
Trigger	Non-Violent Military	45 48%	26 28%	22 24%	93 15%
	Violence	76 26%	24 8%	189 66%	289 47%
		252 41%	96 15%	273 44%	621 100%

$X^2 = 105.62$, p = .000

b. High Threat (N = 416)

		Pacific	Non-Violent Military	Violence	
	Non-Violent	93 58%	37 23%	31 19%	161 39%
Trigger	Non-Violent Military	27 42%	20 31%	17 27%	64 15%
	Violence	48 25%	8 4%	135 71%	191 46%
		168 40%	65 16%	183 44%	416 100%

$X^2 = 112.40$, p = .000

c. Low Threat (N = 205)

		Pacific	Non-Violent Military	Violence	
	Non-Violent	38 49%	9 11%	31 40%	78 38%
Trigger	Non-Violent Military	18 62%	6 21%	5 17%	29 14%
	Violence	28 29%	16 16%	54 55%	98 48%
		84 41%	31 15%	90 44%	205 100%

$X^2 = 17.12$, p = .002

contrast between low and high threat situations. For the low gravity of threat cases, there is one cell which is consistently out of line with the rest of the findings. We refer to the cell which indicates a major imbalance between non-violent triggers and high levels of violence in behavior. For example, in Table IV.12.2., non-violent triggers produce violent crisis management responses in 40% of the low-threat cases, contrasting with only 19% violent responses for high-threat cases.

This split is apparent in all four relationships and points to a noteworthy underlying process. *The seriousness of the situations defined by high stress* (in the form of high threat to basic values) *dictates a closer matching of behavior to initial conditions.* Decision-makers feel under pressure not to overreact or underreact to incoming stimuli, since the gravity of the situation can easily result in dangerous escalation. In low-threat situations, on the other hand, decision-makers feel less constrained by initial conditions, since the level of threat is low enough so that the danger of escalation is more remote. In a sense, they can afford the luxury of deviant behavior and can defy the straight stimulus-response dynamic which we find in many other international exchanges. It is interesting to note that in these low-threat cases with non-violent triggers, the deviations are in the direction of higher-than-projected violence in behavior; that is, states are more prone to over-reaction than to under-reaction when uncertain about the appropriate intensity or extent of violence in coping with value threats.

Thus, differing stimuli serve to create differing levels of stress. Grave threats to basic values evoke high stress. High stress evokes greater attentiveness to both the

TABLE IV.12.3. Crisis Trigger and Intensity of Violence 1929–39, 1945–85

a. Total (N = 621)

		Intensity of Violence				
		No Violence or Minor	Serious Clashes	Full-Scale War		
Trigger	Non-Violent	190 79%	23 10%	26 11%	239	38%
	Non-Violent Military	71 76%	13 14%	9 10%	93	15%
	Violence	118 41%	92 32%	79 27%	289	47%
		379 61%	128 21%	114 18%	621	100%

$X^2 = 93.68$, p = .000

b. High Threat (N = 416)

		No Violence or Minor	Serious Clashes	Full-Scale War		
Trigger	Non-Violent	138 86%	14 9%	9 5%	161	39%
	Non-Violent Military	46 72%	10 16%	8 12%	64	15%
	Violence	69 36%	57 30%	65 34%	191	46%
		253 61%	81 19%	82 20%	416	100%

$X^2 = 95.33$, p = .000

c. Low Threat (N = 205)

		No Violence or Minor	Serious Clashes	Full-Scale War		
Trigger	Non-Violent	52 67%	9 11%	17 22%	78	38%
	Non-Violent Military	25 86%	3 10%	1 4%	29	14%
	Violence	49 50%	35 36%	14 14%	98	48%
		126 61%	47 23%	32 16%	205	100%

$X^2 = 23.50$, p = .000

content and intensity of incoming actions in order to formulate meaningful and accurate responses in dangerous situations. Fundamental to this characterization of international behavior are decision-makers' perceptions of threat created by incoming stimuli. Implicit in this explanation is the environmental context in which these perceptions are formed.

Controls

It has been postulated that, when high stress among decision-makers is present, the relationship between the extent of violence in a crisis trigger (from verbal threat to full-scale military attack) and the extent of violence in a state's response (from compliance to war) will be tighter than in situations where stress is absent or low. The question arises: do other attributes affect the trigger-behavior relationship in conditions of high stress? As outlined below, three control variables will be explored in this context: polarity, level of power, and protractedness of conflict.

Polarity In a bipolar system all states which are associated with a bloc leader as ally or client are constrained in their foreign policy behavior by the needs of the bloc and/or the pressure of the bloc leader. In crisis situations the constraints will be even greater because of the danger perceived by bloc leader and crisis actor alike that resort to violence could escalate to confrontation between the bloc leaders or direct inter-bloc violent conflict, with uncertain and potentially grave consequences. Bloc leaders, too, will feel constrained by the structure of the global system regarding the

---

TABLE IV.12.4. Crisis Trigger and Centrality of Violence 1929–39, 1945–85

a. Total (N = 621)

Centrality of Violence

		No Violence or Marginal		Violence Important		Violence Preeminent			
	Non-Violent	179	75%	32	13%	28	12%	239	38%
Trigger	Non-Violent Military	71	76%	17	18%	5	5%	93	15%
	Violence	101	35%	111	38%	77	27%	289	47%
		351	56%	160	26%	110	18%	621	100%

$X^2 = 104.55$, p = .000

b. High Threat (N = 416)

		No Violence or Marginal		Violence Important		Violence Preeminent			
	Non-Violent	131	81%	19	12%	11	7%	161	39%
Trigger	Non-Violent Military	47	74%	13	20%	4	6%	64	15%
	Violence	56	29%	85	45%	50	26%	191	46%
		234	56%	117	28%	65	16%	416	100%

$X^2 = 106.08$, p = .000

c. Low Threat (N = 205)

		No Violence or Marginal		Violence Important		Violence Preeminent			
	Non-Violent	48	61%	13	17%	17	22%	78	38%
Trigger	Non-Violent Military	24	83%	4	14%	1	3%	29	14%
	Violence	45	46%	26	26%	27	28%	98	48%
		117	57%	43	21%	45	22%	205	100%

$X^2 = 14.53$, p = .006

---

use of violence in crisis management. The same reason – structural constraints as perceived by crisis actors' decision-makers – will lead to less intense and less extensive violence by crisis actors in response to a violent trigger. This expectation does not apply directly to non-bloc states, though they too will be affected in their crisis behavior by the overall structure of the international system.

Multipolarity, as noted earlier in this volume (Chapter 3), is characterized by a diffusion of power and decision among several relatively equal units within an international system, at least three, usually more. In general, multiple centers of power and decision lead to uncertainty about the behavior of the other major powers and, therefore, flexible alliances. This, in turn, is likely to influence the behavior of crisis actors, whether strong or weak: they will perceive more opportunities to gain support from one or more major powers, along with the danger that their adversary will do the same. In that context of changing and changeable alliances, crisis actors perceive greater freedom of choice among crisis management techniques, especially whether or not to employ violence, its intensity and centrality. Thus the effect of multipolarity is likely to be a strengthening of the association between type of trigger and type of behavior, including the relationship between the extent of violence in the trigger (stimulus) and the several components of behavior in a crisis – major response, primary CMT, and the degree and centrality of violence used in crisis management.

In a polycentric system, too, states will act with greater freedom in a crisis situation. Neither a bloc nor a bloc leader will exert the restraining influence present in a bipolar, especially tight bipolar system. Concerns about escalation of violence, that is, the cost of escalation relative to the benefits of victory in a crisis, are qualitatively less in a system where military capability, decision-making, goal-definition, diplomacy, and economic power are much more diffuse. Thus the impact of bipolarity is likely to be a weakening of the association between the extent of violence in a crisis trigger and response by a crisis actor, even where high stress is present; the effect of polycentrism, as of multipolarity, may be anticipated as the reverse. Similarly, bipolarity will be expected to undermine the association between violence in crisis triggers and proportionately intense and extensive violence in the response.

Tables IV.12.5.a.–d. present a summary of the data on the impact of stress on the trigger-behavior dynamic when a control for polarity is introduced. The percentage figures which are reported in the three main columns of the tables refer to the percent of cases falling in the three categories of the trigger variable – non-violent (N-V), non-violent military (N-V-M), and violent (V) – which exhibit violence in crisis behavior. Thus, for the total group, for the bipolar period (Table IV.12.5.a.), 15% of the non-violent triggers, 22% of the non-violent military triggers, and 29% of the violent triggers resulted in a violent major response.

At first glance, polarity does not seem to affect the stimulus-stress-response link in the pre- and post-World War II eras; that is, as one moves from no violence to violence in the crisis trigger, the proportion of violent behavior increases – in all

---

TABLE IV.12.5.a. Control for Polarity: Trigger/Violent Major Response

Polarity	Total			High Threat			Low Threat		
	N–V(%)	N–V–M(%)	V(%)	N–V(%)	N–V–M(%)	V(%)	N–V(%)	N–V–M(%)	V(%)
Multipolar	11	5	47**	9	0	46**	25	50	50
Bipolar	15	22	29	9	27	35*	28	10	6
Polycentric	22	26	62**	12	36	64**	34	12	58**

TABLE IV.12.5.b. Control for Polarity: Trigger/Violent Crisis Management Technique

Polarity	Total			High Threat			Low Threat		
	N–V(%)	N–V–M(%)	V(%)	N–V(%)	N–V–M(%)	V(%)	N–V(%)	N–V–M(%)	V(%)
Multipolar	14	9	53**	11	5	50**	50	50	67
Bipolar	27	28	57**	22	32	69**	36	20	19
Polycentric	31	28	71**	23	41	76**	42	13	62*

TABLE IV.12.5.c. Control for Polarity: Trigger/Intense Violence (Serious Clashes and Full-Scale War)

Polarity	Total			High Threat			Low Threat		
	N–V(%)	N–V–M(%)	V(%)	N–V(%)	N–V–M(%)	V(%)	N–V(%)	N–V–M(%)	V(%)
Multipolar	15	9	44*	11	5	42*	50	50	50
Bipolar	22	28	49*	14	32	59**	36	20	12
Polycentric	22	28	66**	17	46	71**	29	6	58**

TABLE IV.12.5.d. Control for Polarity: Trigger/Extensive Violence (Important and Preeminent

Polarity	Total			High Threat			Low Threat		
	N–V(%)	N–V–M(%)	V(%)	N–V(%)	N–V–M(%)	V(%)	N–V(%)	N–V–M(%)	V(%)
Multipolar	15	9	53**	11	5	50**	50	50	67
Bipolar	27	28	57**	22	32	69**	36	20	19
Polycentric	29	28	70**	21	41	77**	40	12	60**

* p ≤ .01
** p ≤ .001

three systems. This is evident in the total set of cases, as well as in those characterized by high threat, for all four indicators of behavior. For example, the probability of resort to intense violence in crisis management (Table IV. 12.5.c.) increases from 22% for non-violent triggers to 28% for non-violent military triggers and 49% for violent triggers for all cases in the bipolar system, and from 14% to 32% to 59% in the high-threat subset within that system. The progression is similar in the polycentric system – 22% to 28% to 66% for the total set of cases, 17% to 46% to 71% for the cases in which high threat was present. And, while there is a dip from non-violent to non-violent military in the multipolar system, the essential thrust is the same; from non-violence (15% or 9%) to intense violence (44%); and, for cases with high threat, from 11% or 5% to 42%.

A more careful examination of the data in Table IV.12.5. indicates several striking differences in the mediated stimulus-response relationship within the three international systems.

1. The probability of violent behavior is highest in crises occurring within a polycentric system, regardless of the type of trigger (Table IV.12.5.a.).

    The systemic contrast is even sharper for the subset of low-threat cases involving violent triggers, with a wide disparity in the probability of violent behavior. The data for the polycentric and bipolar systems (Tables IV.12.5.a., b., c. and d.) are, respectively: trigger-major response, 58%–6%; trigger-CMT, 62%–19%; trigger-intensity of violence, 58%–12%; and trigger-extent of violence, 60%–19%. The same sharp contrast is evident for multipolarity and bipolarity cases – 50%–6%, 67%–19%, 50%–12% and 67%–19%, respectively.

    This strongly suggests that, where the power of decision is more broadly distributed in an international system – a trait of both multipolarity and polycentrism – state actors are more likely to use violence in an attempt to manage a crisis. Since the volume of violence in a system is an indicator of the degree of stability, this segment of the crisis data for 1929–39 and 1945–85 indicates that, as noted in Chapter 4, a bipolar system is more stable than multipolar or polycentric systems.

2. There is, too, a conspicuous difference between bipolarity and the other two systems in the probability of a violent response to a violent trigger in high-threat and low-threat crises. In bipolarity, the distribution, for the four indicators of behavior, is 35%–6% (major response), 69%–19% (CMT), 59%–12% (intensity) and 69%–19% (extent). The comparable figures for crises in the polycentric system are 64%–58%, 76%–62%, 71%–58% and 77%–60%. They are also less sharp for multipolarity cases, and in the opposite direction.

    Thus, in a bipolar system the gravity of threat (stress) has a much greater mediating effect on the stimulus-response link. In substantive terms, states in a bipolar system tend to use violence in crises when they perceive a high value threat, but not when the threat to values is low. By contrast, the disposition to violent behavior in crises within polycentric and multipolar systems is little affected by the level of threat; it is high in all cases. A plausible explanation is that, in a bipolar system, constraints by bloc leaders on violent crisis behavior by lesser actors, as well as by themselves, are much more effective than the constraints of major powers in multipolar and polycentric systems.

    These data also shed light on the controversial issue of relative stability discussed in Chapters 3 and 4 above: the weaker tendency to violence in a bipolar system provides further evidence of its greater stability than interactions within multipolar or polycentric systems.

In sum, the polarity configuration of an international system has a considerable impact on the trigger-stress-behavior dynamic, especially on the proneness to violence in crisis management.

Level of Power   When high stress is present, that is, a basic value (existence, territory, etc.) is perceived to be threatened, the response of crisis actors, as has been noted, is highly associated with the triggering event(s) or act(s): a non-violent trigger is likely to induce a non-violent response; and a violent trigger can be expected to call forth a response of proportionately severe and extensive violence. This linkage, it may be argued, will also be affected by the power status of the crisis actor concerned. Major powers (superpowers and great powers) are less likely than minor powers (middle and small powers) to behave in a direct reciprocal manner, and are more likely to use violence when confronted by a non-violent trigger.

If stress is high because of the importance of a threatened value, major powers can be expected to be more likely to respond with violence than non-violence in order to overcome a threat. This tendency flows from their assumption of a right as key members of the international system to use violence whenever this is considered essential to their interests. Minor powers are likely to be more aware of the risks and costs of a violent response to a non-violent trigger.

If a trigger is violent and a basic value is threatened, major powers are likely to respond in kind and with at least proportional violence, in terms of intensity and extent, lest the triggering entity interpret non-violence or less violence by the crisis actor as an indicator of weakness in military capability, resolve or both. A proportionately violent response will be the minimum where a triggering entity is perceived to be a minor power or at least not more powerful, that is, the vast majority of triggering entities in crises for major powers.

Minor powers cannot always be expected to behave with reciprocal intensity and extent of violence. If a triggering entity is more powerful, prudence will dictate the use of crisis management techniques other than violence, from compliance to arbitration. Where a triggering entity is perceived to possess relatively equal capability, minor powers will be less cautious in resorting to violence in a crisis. On the one hand, they have a greater fear of intervention by one or more major powers, either as allies of their adversary, or when a patron major power is likely to abort the full benefit of a client's victory in a violent crisis between two minor powers. On the other hand, minor powers will perceive the need to use violence in response to a violent trigger, often of a very severe and extensive kind, particularly when fundamental values are perceived to be threatened. However, in general, one may hypothesize that the stronger a crisis actor, the less tight will be the association between the extent of violence in the trigger and in crisis behavior.

In general, the data in Tables IV.12.6.a.–d. indicate that the level of power does affect the stimulus-response dynamic for states in international crises. Minor powers had a higher rate of violent behavior resulting from virtually all types of triggers, regardless of the level of threat.

Several specific findings are noteworthy:

1. While minor powers consistently exhibited higher rates of violence in crisis behavior than did major powers, this difference was most pronounced when the trigger was violent and threat was at a high level. Thus, the middle column of Tables IV.12.6.a.–d. reveals that, for high-threat cases, violent triggers produced violent major responses in 56% of the minor power cases, compared to 33% for major powers. The comparable figures are 74% versus 48% violence for crisis management technique, 66% versus 43% for intensity of violence, and 74% to 48% for extent of violence.

2. It is also clear that crisis actors confronted with a low value threat exhibited similar patterns of behavior, regardless of the power of the actor (right column of Tables IV.12.6.a.–d.): there is only a very slight tendency for less powerful states to exhibit more violence than more powerful states. While minor powers which experienced low threat were somewhat less inclined to respond with violence to violent crisis triggers than were their high-threat counterparts, the opposite was true for major powers. For this latter group, low threat had a much less dampening effect on their propensity to use violence in crisis behavior.

3. Crises with non-violent military triggers present something of an anomaly, in that these cases show the least variation as we move from high to low threat. Non-violent and violent triggers show considerable variation across levels of threat.

4. The proposition that major powers would be less likely than minor powers to behave in a direct reciprocal manner is strongly supported by the evidence for the high threat cases (middle column). Although minor and major powers exhibited similar rates of violent response to non-violent triggers, major powers showed a consistent trend toward much greater violence in response to violent triggers.

TABLE IV.12.6.a. Control for Level of Power: Trigger/Violent Major Response

Power	Total			High Threat			Low Threat		
	N–V(%)	N–V–M(%)	V(%)	N–V(%)	N–V–M(%)	V(%)	N–V(%)	N–V–M(%)	V(%)
Major Powers	15	11	42**	9	11	33	24	14	47
Minor Powers	17	22	54***	10	27	56***	35	14	50**

TABLE IV.12.6.b. Control for Level of Power: Trigger/Violent Crisis Management Technique

Power	Total			High Threat			Low Threat		
	N–V(%)	N–V–M(%)	V(%)	N–V(%)	N–V–M(%)	V(%)	N–V(%)	N–V–M(%)	V(%)
Major Powers	21	23	54**	14	26	48	31	14	59
Minor Powers	28	24	68***	21	27	74***	45	18	53*

TABLE IV.12.6.c. Control for Level of Power: Trigger/Intense Violence (Serious Clashes and Full-Scale War)

Power	Total			High Threat			Low Threat		
	N–V(%)	N–V–M(%)	V(%)	N–V(%)	N–V–M(%)	V(%)	N–V(%)	N–V–M(%)	V(%)
Major Powers	18	19	44**	12	21	43*	28	14	44
Minor Powers	22	25	63***	15	31	66***	37	14	53**

TABLE IV.12.6.d. Control for Level of Power: Trigger/Extensive Violence (Important and Preeminent)

Power	Total			High Threat			Low Threat		
	N–V(%)	N–V–M(%)	V(%)	N–V(%)	N–V–M(%)	V(%)	N–V(%)	N–V–M(%)	V(%)
Major Powers	19	23	53***	14	26	48*	28	14	56*
Minor Powers	28	24	68***	20	27	74***	45	18	53*

* $p \leqslant .05$
** $p \leqslant .01$
*** $p \leqslant .001$

In sum, as we found with polarity, the level of power has a meaningful impact on the stimulus-stress-response dynamic in international crises.

Protracted Conflict Many international crises occur within the context of protracted conflicts, that is, conflicts characterized by: lengthy duration; generally, fluctuation in the intensity and frequency of interaction – from violence to near-accommodation, and back to violence; intense animosities among the participants; spillover to a broad spectrum of issues, and the absence of a distinct and final termination (see Chapters 9, 10 and 11 above). Protracted conflicts exist at the dominant system level (East/West or US- and USSR-led blocs) and at the subsystem level (e.g., Arab/Israel, India/Pakistan), as well as in more limited regional domains (Greece/Turkey over Cyprus, Ethiopia/ Somalia over Ogaden, etc.).[5] Other crises occur outside such a setting of persistent and pervasive conflict. Does the attribute of protractedness impinge upon the trigger-behavior linkage when high stress is present?

Two interrelated postulates are germane to this question: first, international crises within a protracted conflict are more likely than others to be catalyzed by violence; and second, crises within a protracted conflict are more likely than others to be characterized by violence in the major response of crisis actors, a primary role for violence in crisis management, and a resort to more intense forms of violence, including full-scale war.

The evidence for crises from 1929 to 1939 and 1945 to 1985 clearly supports these expectations: in crises within protracted conflicts, a striking presence of violent triggers and the preeminence of violence in crisis management, notably full-scale war; in crises outside protracted conflicts, the predominance of verbal-political triggers and the preeminence of pacific crisis management techniques, with much less intense violence (see Chapter 9 above).

At first glance, this suggests no effect of protracted conflict – its presence or absence – on the trigger-behavior linkage: violence in both trigger and behavior within, and non-violence in both trigger and behavior outside, a protracted conflict setting. However, there are reasons to expect a tighter link between trigger and behavior in crises outside a protracted conflict.

As long as adversaries see no finite end to their conflict, the dynamics of their relationship create a disposition to violence in crisis management. In non-protracted conflict situations, by contrast, the behavior of the actor is not as closely linked to that of its adversaries. They are just as likely to rely on negotiation or some type of third party intervention – good offices, mediation, arbitration or adjudication – or even some form of coercive diplomacy or non-violent pressure.

In the absence of a cumulative burden of violence, the crisis actor is more likely to respond in kind – non-violent behavior when the trigger is non-violent, violent behavior to cope with a violent threat to values. And even in situations where violence is considered necessary, there is no *a priori* disposition to intense forms of violence. In general, it may be argued, protracted conflicts create an environment conducive to the use of violence in crisis management. Thus we expect a protracted conflict setting for crises to undermine the association between the extent of violence in the crisis trigger and the behavior of the crisis actor when high stress is present.

The data in Tables IV.12.7.a.–d. indicate that the presence or absence of a protracted conflict has effects on the trigger-stress-behavior dynamic in international crises.

TABLE IV.12.7.a. Control for Protracted Conflict: Trigger/Violent Major Response

Conflict	Total			High Threat			Low Threat		
	N–V(%)	N–V–M(%)	V(%)	N–V(%)	N–V–M(%)	V(%)	N–V(%)	N–V–M(%)	V(%)
Non-Protracted Conflict	13	14	41*	6	16	40*	29	10	42
Protracted Conflict	22	27	59*	14	32	61*	35	17	53

TABLE IV.12.7.b. Control for Protracted Conflict: Trigger/Violent Crisis Management Technique

Conflict	Total			High Threat			Low Threat		
	N–V(%)	N–V–M(%)	V(%)	N–V(%)	N–V–M(%)	V(%)	N–V(%)	N–V–M(%)	V(%)
Non-Protracted Conflict	21	17	56*	14	19	57*	38	10	52
Protracted Conflict	33	33	73*	26	36	80*	45	25	59

TABLE IV.12.7.c. Control for Protracted Conflict: Trigger/Intense Violence (Serious Clashes and Full-Scale War)

Conflict	Total			High Threat			Low Threat		
	N–V(%)	N–V–M(%)	V(%)	N–V(%)	N–V–M(%)	V(%)	N–V(%)	N–V–M(%)	V(%)
Non-Protracted Conflict	13	17	44*	8	19	49*	24	10	35
Protracted Conflict	30	32	71*	22	36	76*	45	25	61

TABLE IV.12.7.d. Control for Protracted Conflict: Trigger/Extensive Violence (Important and Preeminent)

Conflict	Total			High Threat			Low threat		
	N–V(%)	N–V–M(%)	V(%)	N–V(%)	N–V–M(%)	V(%)	N–V(%)	N–V–M(%)	V(%)
Non-Protracted Conflict	20	17	56*	14	19	57*	35	10	52
Protracted Conflict	32	32	73*	25	36	80*	45	25	59

* $p \leqslant .001$

1. There is, as suggested, a much greater tendency to violent behavior by states in crises within protracted conflicts, especially in response to violent triggers. The probability of a violent major response to a violent trigger, in protracted and non-protracted conflict cases, is, respectively, 59% to 41% for the total set of cases, and 61% to 40% for the high-threat subset (trigger-major response) (Table IV.12.7.a.). The comparable figures for the other behavioral indicators are 73%–56%, and 80%–57% (trigger-CMT – Table IV.12.7.b.); 71%–44%, and 76%–49% (trigger-intensity – Table IV.12.7.c.); and 73%–56%, and 80%–57% (trigger-extent – Table IV.12.7.d.). In the low-threat subset of cases (right column), while protracted conflict cases also show a greater propensity to violence, the difference between them and the non-protracted conflict cases is much less sharp.

2. The expectation of a tighter link between trigger and behavior in crises outside a protracted conflict setting is not supported. A sharp increase in the probability of violent behavior with a shift from non-violent to violent trigger is evident in the data for the total set and high-threat subset of cases within *both* non-protracted and protracted conflicts – *for all four behavioral indicators*. Among the low-threat cases, the data show a more modest increase in the probability of violent behavior resulting from an increase in violence in the trigger, for both non-protracted and protracted crisis actors. However, while the violence-begets-violence linkage is generally weaker for both types of crisis actors in low threat situations, the non-violence-begets-violence linkage is stronger. Thus, for the non-protracted conflict cases, non-violent triggers in high threat situations resulted in violent major responses in 6% of the cases, compared to 29% for low-threat crises (Table IV.12.7.a.). The comparable figures are 14% versus 38% for CMT (Table IV.12.7.b.), 8% versus 24% for intensity of violence (Table IV.12.7.c.), and 14%–35% for extent of violence (Table IV.12.7.d.). As noted, a similar pattern was in evidence for the protracted conflict crisis actors.

Profiles

The aggregate data on polarity as a control variable (Table IV.12.5.) indicate greatest violence in crisis behavior within a polycentric system. Similarly, the data on level of power (Table IV.12.6.) reveal that minor powers were more prone than major powers to use violence in international crises. And the data on protracted conflict (Table IV.12.7.) point to more violent behavior in crises within than outside protracted conflicts. Thus the most pronounced tendency to violent behavior in international crises is evident in the behavior of *minor powers* in crises within *protracted conflicts* in a *polycentric* system. A group of 100 actor-cases fits this profile.

Within the group of 100 crisis actors which fit the polycentric, minor power, protracted conflict profile, 71 are high-threat cases, while 29 are low-threat cases. Full-scale war characterized 24 or 34% of the high-threat crisis actors fitting the profile, but only 2 or 7% of the low-threat crises. The substance of several cases fitting the high-threat and low-threat profiles will be discussed below, with emphasis on the trigger, value threat, and violence dimension of state behavior for one or more crisis actors.

Profile A: High Threat
*Turkey (Cyprus),
November-December
1963*

The conflict between Greece and Turkey over the island of Cyprus began more than a century ago. Although Greece regained its independence in 1829, Cyprus remained a part of the Ottoman Empire until the transfer of control to Great Britain in 1878. A struggle for Cypriot independence achieved success in the Zurich–London Accords of 1959, which recognized and tried to safeguard the interests of both Greek and Turkish communities in Cyprus through a republican form of government. Suspicion between the two Cypriot communities was – and continues to be – rampant.

The first post-independence international crisis over Cyprus lasted from 30 November 1963 to 10 August 1964 and encompassed three foreign policy crises for Turkey, two for Greece, and one for Cyprus. The initial crisis *trigger* for Turkey occurred on 30 November 1963, in the form of a memorandum from the President of Cyprus, Archbishop Makarios, to Vice-President Kutchuk, leader of the Turkish minority, proposing 13 amendments to the constitution; these would have transformed Cyprus into a unitary state, with guarantees for the Turkish Cypriots, approximately 20% of the island's population. The three guarantor states, Great Britain, Greece and Turkey, also received the memorandum. Turkey perceived a *high threat* to a basic value, namely, grave damage to the security and interests of its kinsmen on the island. Following the outbreak of fighting between Greek and Turkish Cypriots in the capital, Nicosia, and elsewhere, and an appeal by the latter for aid, Turkey's *major response*, on 25 December 1963, was a mobilization of forces, the dispatch of naval units towards the island, overflights of the capital of Cyprus, etc. A cease-fire, arranged under the aegis of Great Britain four days later, along with the creation of neutral zones, marked the *termination* of Turkey's first crisis in this continuing conflict.

Egypt, Jordan, Syria (Six Day War), May-June 1967 As in the eastern Mediterranean, there has been a protracted conflict in the Middle East during the past forty years, between Israel and a group of front-line Arab states, Egypt, Iraq, Jordan, Syria and Lebanon, supported with weapons, finance, diplomacy and rhetoric by Saudia Arabia, Libya and others. There, too, the roots of the conflict are deep, at least a century, when the Jewish "Return to the Land of Israel" began. And as in the crisis over Cyprus, collective violence has been frequent and intense, with full-scale wars in 1948–49, 1956, 1967, 1969–70, 1973 and 1982.

Within the protracted Arab/Israel Conflict there has been a plethora of crises, one of which culminated in the Six Day War of 1967. The pattern of trigger, threat and violence identified with Profile A applied to three of the six crisis actors, namely, Egypt, Jordan and Syria. The link between trigger and major response for the three Arab states was immediate, in contrast to the considerable time which elapsed between Israel's crisis trigger and major response – from the UN Secretary-General's acceptance on 18 May of President Nasser's demand to withdraw UNEF from Sinai until the decision to preempt militarily, on 4 June. It was the implementation of that Israeli decision the next day which *triggered* a crisis for Egypt and Jordan, both of which *responded* with (unsuccessful) counter-attacks. Similarly, Israel's assault on the Golan Heights on 9 June *triggered* a crisis for Syria, which *responded* on the same day by bombarding Israeli border settlements. For all three Arab states the *value threat* was high, namely, the loss of territory – Sinai, the West Bank, and the Golan Heights. The war – and the specific 1967 crisis – *terminated* for Egypt, Jordan and Syria, as well as for Israel, with their acceptance of a UN-arranged cease-fire on 10-11 June. The protracted conflict continues unabated, except for the Egypt/Israel bilateral segment since the peace treaty of 1979.

North Vietnam, South Vietnam, US (Ports Mining), March–July 1972 The interstate conflict over Vietnam, too, dates to the 1940s. Unlike the others discussed above, however, its predominant form was the long war, at first between North Vietnam and France from 1946 to 1954, and then, from 1964 to 1975, between Hanoi and the US in alliance with South Vietnam. Many other states were involved, the USSR and China providing material assistance to North Vietnam, several Asian and Commonwealth countries supporting Saigon.

There were many international crises prior to, during and between, the long wars in this protracted conflict, as well as since 1975. Among them was the Ports Mining Crisis of 1972. While the pattern of trigger-threat-violence identified with Profile A applies to South Vietnam only, the US and North Vietnam, too, were crisis actors. The *trigger* for South Vietnam – and for the US – was Hanoi's Spring Offensive which was launched on 30 March 1972. Saigon perceived a *threat* to its existence and responded the same day by defending its positions wherever possible. The US, perceiving a grave *threat* to its influence in Indo-China and elsewhere, renewed B-52 bombing of the Hanoi-Haiphong industrial complex. The North Vietnamese escalated the ground fighting on 24 April and forced the Saigon troops to withdraw from the strategically important Central Highlands. The US *major response*, on 8 May, was a presidential order to mine and blockade North Vietnamese ports. This *triggered* a crisis for Hanoi which perceived a serious *threat* to its economy and military capability. It *responded* the next day with a statement at the Paris peace talks rejecting the US ultimatum and appealing to Communist states to press the US to make concessions. The crisis – but not the war or the conflict – can be said to have *terminated* on 19 July 1972, when the peace talks renewed in an atmosphere of anticipated compromise, following the US/USSR Moscow Summit in May and intense Soviet and Chinese pressure on North Vietnam soon thereafter. The stress for all three crisis actors abated until the next intra-war crisis, the Christmas Bombing of North Vietnam in December 1972.

Profile B: Low Threat

Israel (War of Attrition I), March–July 1969

In the aftermath of the June 1967 War, there was tranquillity along the *de facto* Egypt/Israel frontier, the Suez Canal. The lull was broken in September 1968 when Egyptian artillery bombarded Israeli positions east of the Canal, the "Bar-Lev Line." This turned out to be a prelude to the War of Attrition, which began as a serious crisis for Israel.

The *trigger* was a massive Egyptian artillery barrage across the Canal beginning on 8 March 1969. Increasing Israeli casualties through May, June and July, as always a basic value *threat*, led to Israel's *major response*, namely, a decision on 20 July to launch deep penetration air raids into Egypt. This had the desired effect, namely, Egypt's reappraisal of the strategic balance and an indefinite postponement of its plan to cross the Canal in force. Israel's air attacks were suspended on 28 July, an indication of reduced stress and the *termination* of its crisis, which was coterminous with the first phase of the War of Attrition. Once more, there was relative calm and normal stress – until a new Israeli crisis arose as a result of direct Soviet intervention in the resumed War of Attrition, in March–April 1970.

South Vietnam, North Vietnam, Cambodia, US (Cambodia), March–July 1970

The pattern of violent trigger, low value threat and violent major response (Profile B) applies to South Vietnam as a crisis actor in the complex 1970 struggle over Cambodia (Kampuchea). Despite its proclaimed neutrality in the second Vietnam War, Cambodian territory was used as a Vietcong and North Vietnam base for military operations against South Vietnam, leading to US bombing of enemy sanctuaries in Cambodia from March 1969 onwards. Persistent penetration of Cambodia led to its formal demand, on 13 March 1970, that all Vietcong and North Vietnamese troops be withdrawn from its territory within forty-eight hours. This *triggered* an intra-war crisis for Hanoi. Its *major response* was an invasion of Cambodia beginning 31 March, along with Vietcong forces and troops loyal to Prince Sihanouk, who had been deposed as Head of State by Cambodia's National Assembly thirteen days earlier.

A crisis for South Vietnam was *triggered* on 10 April, when Cambodian forces were compelled to evacuate border positions in "Parrots Beak," which was surrounded by South Vietnamese territory on three sides. Its *major response* was to send troops into Cambodia on 29 April. Cambodia, now under the leadership of Lon Nol, *responded* to its invasion crisis by appealing to the US for aid on 11 April and again on the 20th. The next day, the US experienced a crisis when Cambodia's capital, Phnom Penh, was isolated by the advance of North Vietnamese and Vietcong forces. It *responded* on the 29th by dispatching American troops to Cambodia. Their withdrawal on 30 June *terminated* the crisis for North Vietnam and the US. And the crisis ended for South Vietnam and Cambodia on 22 July with the beginning of the withdrawal of South Vietnamese forces. The stress level had declined for all the crisis actors, though the Vietnam War was to continue another five years, and the struggle for Cambodia even longer.

Summary of Findings

The point of departure in this chapter was the stimulus-response dynamic in international politics, in particular, the conflict-begets-conflict notion as it relates to state behavior. The focus of our inquiry was the conditions under which states are likely to resort to violence in crisis management. We postulated that the mediating effect of stress – more precisely, threat – will influence the trigger-behavior relationship and that the presence of high threat will strengthen the violence-begets-violence linkage.

The empirical domain was a set of 621 actor-cases, that is, crises for individual states, from 1929 to 1939 and 1945 to 1985. To enhance our understanding of the violence component in state behavior, we introduced three controls in the analysis of the trigger-threat-violence causal chain, namely, polarity of an international system (multipolar/bipolar/polycentric), level of power (minor/major), and protracted conflict (crises within/outside this setting).

The principal findings from this inquiry may now be summarized.

1. The tendency for states to match violence in behavior to violence in the trigger is significantly strengthened when decision-makers perceive a high threat to

values. By contrast, there is no pattern when the stimulus-response linkage is mediated by low threat.

2. The likelihood of violence in crisis behavior is greater in a polycentric system than in multipolar or bipolar systems, regardless of the type of trigger. This provides further evidence of the greater instability of a polycentric international system.

3. The level of threat has a much greater effect on the violence-begets-violence dynamic in a bipolar system.

4. Minor powers display a greater proneness to violent crisis behavior than do major powers, regardless of trigger.

5. Major powers tend to respond to a violent trigger with violence, especially under conditions of high value threat.

6. There is a much greater tendency to violent behavior in crises within than outside protracted conflicts.

7. International crises with the following profile have the highest proneness to violence and war: *minor powers* in crises within a *protracted conflict* in a *polycentric system*, with the presence of a *violent trigger* and a *high threat* to values.

Notes

1. The authors are aware of the difficulty of determining the salient indicators of stress in crisis decision-making. As Lazarus (1968: p. 347) noted: "The dilemma posed here is that the measurement of stress-relevant processes is exceedingly complex, and no simple, single class of measurement device can solve the problem adequately."

2. Since virtually all intra-war crises of the World War II period were characterized by high levels of stress, due to the unique characteristics of global conflict, that period is excluded from the present analysis.

3. One case with missing data.

4. A subset of cases where the perceived value threat was influence in the international system was included in the high-threat group, namely crises in which one or both superpowers perceived a threat of: 1) adverse change in the global balance between them (e.g., the USSR in the Cuban Missile Crisis of 1962); or 2) a decline in superpower influence within its own bloc (e.g., the USSR in the Prague Spring Crisis of 1968).

5. For an extended treatment of the concept of protracted conflict and its impact on international crises, see Chapters 9, 10 and 11 in this volume.

13 Superpower Crises: Trigger, Behavior, Outcomes

Jonathan Wilkenfeld and Michael Brecher

Introduction

There are many ways of exploring US and Soviet behavior in international crises. One is to compare their behavior in a single case, as in the Berlin Blockade of 1948–1949 or the Cuban Missile Crisis of 1962.[1] Another is to examine their perceptions of each other's goals, strategies and tactics.[2] A third is to analyze their activity in crises in a specific region, whether a gray geopolitical zone, such as the Middle East, sub-Saharan Africa, or Southern Asia, or within their own bloc.[3] One may focus on their decision-making styles in crisis and non-crisis situations[4], their use of international organizations, negotiations, or violence in crisis management[5], the role of alliance partners[6], or the consequences of a particular crisis for their power, status, behavior, and attitudes to each other in a subsequent phase of their relationship. The number of possible approaches is large. Each can illuminate a limited aspect of a crucial domain in world politics, namely, superpowers in international crises.

The approach in this chapter differs from all of these. Its *scope* is global and long-term – US and Soviet crises throughout the international system from the end of World War II to the end of 1985. Its *method* is statistical analysis of aggregate data. Its *focus* is on five dimensions of crisis: triggers or sources; actor behavior, that is, superpower responses to triggers and their crisis management techniques, including the role of violence; outcomes, their substance, form and degree of satisfaction among the parties; the duration of crises; and crisis legacy. The 46 US and 22 Soviet actor-cases pertaining to the period 1945–1985 derive from the ICB global set of 698 actor-cases for the entire 1929–1985 period.

Tables IV.13.1.a. and b. present chronological lists of US and USSR crises for the 1945–1985 period. Also listed are the trigger and termination dates for each crisis, as well as indicators pertaining to the crisis outcome. (The trigger date for a superpower may differ from the trigger date for other actors in a particular international crisis.)

The superpowers differed in the *location* of their crises. US crises occurred in all regions of the global system, though with a concentration in Asia – 22 cases; there were also 10 in the Middle East, 8 in Central America, 3 in Europe, and 3 in Africa. USSR crises were heavily focused on the Eurasia Heartland – Europe, 11, Asia, 3, and 5 in the Middle East, with 2 in Africa, and 1 in the Americas.

Perhaps the most striking difference between superpower crises is their distribution by *type*. The largest group of United States crises (19) falls within the protracted *East/West inter-bloc conflict*, from Azerbaijan in 1946, through the Truman Doctrine and Marshall Plan crises in 1947, along with Korean War I, the 3 Berlin crises, Cuban Missiles, Pueblo, Cienfuegos, and Afghanistan Invasion, among others. A second cluster comprises 11 US crises in the prolonged *struggle over Indo-China*, from Dien Bien Phu in 1954 through Pathet Lao I and II in the early sixties, 6 intra-war crises in the Vietnam War until the Mayaguez Crisis of 1975. (The first and last of these crises were also related to the inter-bloc conflict, but their primary focus was the ideological and political systems in the former French colonial empire in Indo-China). A group of 10 US crises occurred in *gray Third World zones*, from the Suez-Sinai War of 1956 through the Syria/Turkey Border in 1957, the Lebanon/Iraq Upheaval in 1958, the Six Day War, Black September, the October-Yom Kippur War, and the US Hostages in Iran Crisis 1979–81, all in the Middle East, and Congo II 1964, Angola 1975–76, and Shaba II 1978, in Africa. (Four of these cases, too, spilled over to the East/West conflict). A fourth group of 6 cases dealt with the *US sphere of influence in Central America* (e.g., Guatemala 1954, Dominican Republic 1965, Nicaraguan MIG-21s 1984).

Most Soviet crises fall into three types, and they differed fundamentally in content. One is *hegemony* over a self-proclaimed security zone in *Eastern and Central Europe*,

TABLE IV.13.1.a. Superpower Crises, 1945–85*: US Cases

Case number and name	Duration for US as crisis actor	Substance of outcome	Form of outcome	Satisfaction with outcome	Crisis legacy-tension level
1 (0491) Azerbaijan	04/03/46-09/05/46	Victory	Semi-Formal Agreement	Satisfied	Reduction
2 (0480) Turkish Straits	07/08/46-26/10/46	Victory	Unilateral Act	Satisfied	Escalation
3 (0485) Truman Doctrine	21/02/47-22/05/47	Victory	Unilateral Act	Satisfied	Reduction
4 (0644) Berlin Blockade	24/06/48-12/05/49	Victory	Formal Agreement	Satisfied	Reduction
5 (0660) China Civil War	23/09/48-26/10/48	Defeat	Unilateral Act	Not Satisfied	Escalation
6 (0710) Korean War I	25/06/50-29/09/50	Victory	Unilateral Act	Satisfied	Escalation
7 (0715) Korean War II	31/10/50-10/07/51	Compromise	Semi-Formal Agreement	Satisfied	Escalation
8 (0716) Korean War III	16/04/53-27/07/53	Victory	Formal Agreement	Satisfied	Escalation
9 (0820) Guatemala	10/02/54-29/06/54	Victory	Tacit Agreement	Satisfied	Reduction
10 (0880) Dien Bien Phu	20/03/54-08/05/54	Defeat	Unilateral Act	Not Satisfied	Reduction
11 (0830) Taiwan Straits I	03/09/54-02/12/54	Victory	Formal Agreement	Satisfied	Escalation
12 (0830) Taiwan Straits I	10/01/55-23/04/55	Stalemate	Semi-Formal Agreement	Satisfied	Escalation
13 (0970) Suez-Sinai Campaign	05/11/56-08/11/56	Victory	Tacit Agreement	Satisfied	Reduction
14 (1030) Syria/Turkey Border	18/08/57-29/10/57	Victory	Tacit Agreement	Satisfied	Reduction
15 (1080) Lebanon/Iraq Upheaval	14/07/58-14/10/58	Victory	Formal Agreement	Satisfied	Reduction
16 (1120) Taiwan Straits II	23/08/58-14/09/58	Victory	Semi-Formal Agreement	Satisfied	Reduction
17 (1135) Berlin Deadline	27/11/58-30/03/59	Victory	Formal Agreement	Satisfied	Escalation
18 (1350) Pathet Lao Offensive	09/03/61-16/05/61	Victory	Formal Agreement	Satisfied	Escalation
19 (1270) Bay of Pigs	15/04/61-24/04/61	Defeat	Unilateral Act	Not Satisfied	Escalation
20 (1320) Berlin Wall	13/08/61-17/10/61	Compromise	Unilateral Act	Not Satisfied	Reduction
21 (1351) Vietcong Attack	18/09/61-15/11/61	Victory	Unilateral Act	Satisfied	Escalation
22 (1352) Pathet Lao Offensive II	06/05/62-12/06/62	Victory	Tacit Agreement	Satisfied	Escalation
23 (1400) Cuban Missiles	16/10/62-20/11/62	Victory	Semi-Formal Agreement	Satisfied	Reduction
24 (1530) Panama Canal	10/01/64-12/01/64	Compromise	Semi-Formal Agreement	Satisfied	Reduction
25 (1638) Gulf of Tonkin	02/08/64-07/08/64	Stalemate	Unilateral Act	Satisfied	Escalation
26 (1570) Congo II	26/09/64-29/11/64	Victory	Unilateral Act	Satisfied	Reduction
27 (1639) Pleiku	07/02/65-02/03/65	Stalemate	Unilateral Act	Not Satisfied	Escalation
28 (1680) Dominican Republic	24/04/65-31/08/65	Victory	Formal Agreement	Satisfied	Reduction
29 (1690) Six-Day War	06/06/67-11/06/67	Victory	Formal Agreement	Satisfied	Reduction
30 (1730) Pueblo	22/01/68-23/12/68	Defeat	Semi-Formal Agreement	Not Satisfied	Reduction
31 (1720) Tet Offensive	27/02/68-31/03/68	Victory	Unilateral Act	Not Satisfied	Escalation
32 (1829) Vietnam Spring Offensive	22/02/69-18/03/69	Victory	Unilateral Act	Satisfied	Escalation
33 (1805) EC-121 Spyplane	15/04/69-26/04/69	Stalemate	Unilateral Act	Satisfied	Reduction
34 (1850) Invasion of Cambodia	21/04/70-30/06/70	Stalemate	Unilateral Act	Satisfied	Escalation
35 (1860) Black September	15/09/70-29/09/70	Victory	Formal Agreement	Satisfied	Escalation
36 (1865) Cienfuegos Base	16/09/70-23/10/70	Victory	Semi-Formal Agreement	Satisfied	Reduction
37 (1930) Vietnam-Ports Mining	30/03/72-19/07/72	Compromise	Semi-Formal Agreement	Satisfied	Escalation
38 (1931) Christmas Bombing	04/12/72-27/04/73	Compromise	Formal Agreement	Satisfied	Escalation
39 (2030) October-Yom Kippur War	12/10/73-31/05/74	Victory	Formal Agreement	Satisfied	Reduction
40 (2080) Mayaguez	12/05/75-14/05/75	Victory	Unilateral Act	Satisfied	Reduction
41 (2070) War in Angola	01/09/75-19/12/75	Defeat	Unilateral Act	Not Satisfied	Reduction
42 (2570) Shaba II	14/05/78-22/05/78	Victory	Unilateral Act	Satisfied	Reduction
43 (2860) US Hostages in Iran	04/11/79-20/01/81	Compromise	Formal Agreement	Satisfied	Reduction
44 (2900) Afghanistan Invasion	24/12/79-28/02/80	Stalemate	Faded	Not Satisfied	Escalation
45 (3230) Invasion of Grenada	19/10/83-28/10/83	Victory	Unilateral Act	Satisfied	Reduction
46 (3320) Nicaragua MIG-21s	06/11/84-09/11/84	Stalemate	Tacit	Satisfied	—

*See note at the bottom of Table IV.13.1.b.

a cluster of 4 crises in Poland, Hungary and Czechoslovakia in 1946–48, along with the East Berlin Uprising in 1953, and a second round in 1956 – Poland Liberalization and the Hungarian Uprising – and, in 1968, the Prague Spring. A second type was *support of client states and allies*, such as North Korea in the second Korean Crisis 1950–51, Egypt and Syria in 4 crises during the protracted Arab/Israel conflict –

TABLE IV.13.1.b. Superpower Crises, 1945–85*: USSR Cases

Case number and name	Duration for USSR as crisis actor	Substance of outcome	Form of outcome	Satisfaction with outcome	Crisis legacy-tension level
1 (0491) Azerbaijan	09/03/46-09/05/46	Defeat	Unilateral Act	Satisfied	Reduction
2 (0565) Communism in Poland	30/06/46-19/01/47	Victory	Unilateral Act	Satisfied	Reduction
3 (0570) Communism in Hungary	10/02/47-01/06/47	Victory	Unilateral Act	Satisfied	Reduction
4 (0576) Marshall Plan	04/07/47-10/07/47	Victory	Unilateral Act	Satisfied	Escalation
5 (0577) Communism in Czechoslovakia	13/02/48-25/02/48	Victory	Formal Agreement	Not Satisfied	Reduction
6 (0644) Berlin Blockade	07/06/48-12/05/49	Defeat	Unilateral Act	Satisfied	Reduction
7 (0715) Korean War II	07/10/50-26/12/50	Victory	Unilateral Act	Satisfied	Reduction
8 (0781) East Berlin Uprising	17/06/53-11/07/53	Victory	Semi-Formal Agreement	Satisfied	Reduction
9 (0930) Poland Liberalization	—/10/56-22/10/56	Compromise	Unilateral Act	Satisfied	Reduction
10 (0960) Hungarian Uprising	23/10/56-14/11/56	Victory	Semi-Formal Agreement	Satisfied	Reduction
11 (0970) Suez-Sinai Campaign	29/10/56-08/11/56	Victory	Formal Agreement	Satisfied	Reduction
12 (1135) Berlin Deadline	15/12/57-15/09/59	Compromise	Unilateral Act	Satisfied	Escalation
13 (1320) Berlin Wall	29/07/61-17/10/61	Victory	Semi-Formal Agreement	Not Satisfied	Reduction
14 (1400) Cuban Missiles	22/10/62-20/11/62	Defeat	Unilateral Act	Not Satisfied	Reduction
15 (1570) Congo II	24/11/64-17/12/64	Defeat	Formal Agreement	Not Satisfied	Reduction
16 (1690) Six Day War	09/06/67-11/06/67	Defeat	Formal Agreement	Not Satisfied	Escalation
17 (1750) Prague Spring	27/06/68-18/10/68	Victory	Formal Agreement	Satisfied	Reduction
18 (1790) Ussuri River	02/03/69-20/10/69	Stalemate	Semi-Formal Agreement	Satisfied	Reduction
19 (1800) War of Attrition II	22/01/70-07/08/70	Compromise	Formal Agreement	Satisfied	Escalation
20 (2030) October-Yom Kippur War	22/10/73-31/05/74	Compromise	Formal Agreement	Satisfied	Reduction
21 (2070) War in Angola	15/08/75-24/02/76	Victory	Unilateral Act	Satisfied	Escalation
22 (2900) Invasion of Afghanistan	13/03/79-27/12/79	Victory	Unilateral Act	Satisfied	Escalation

*The ICB set of 68 superpower actor-cases from 1945 to 1985 is much smaller than other lists of crises for the US or the USSR. For example, the CACI study of USSR crisis management experience contains 386 'crises of concern to the Soviet Union,' which it terms incidents, from the beginning of 1946 to the end of 1975 (1978: Chap. 3). Similarly, Blechman and Kaplan (1978: App. A) explore US military behavior in 215 political, diplomatic, and military 'incidents'. These two sets are not comparable with the 68 ICB military-security crises in which the US or the USSR was a *direct participant* crisis actor. The CACI and Blechman-Kaplan sets are similar to, but not strictly comparable with, the overall set of 519 ICB actor-cases from 1945 to 1985, in more than 90% of which the superpowers were involved to some extent.

Suez–Sinai War 1956, Six Day War 1967, War of Attrition II 1970 and October-Yom Kippur War 1973–74, Afghanistan 1979 and 2 Africa-located crises, Congo II and Angola. The third group centered on the enduring *East/West inter-bloc conflict* over Berlin – Blockade 1948–49, Deadline 1957–59 and Wall 1961 – and the Cuban Missile Crisis 1962. One Soviet case, Ussuri River 1969, focused on *territory and frontiers*.

It is our intention to provide both a description of, and an explanation for, various observable trends in US and Soviet crisis behavior since 1945. We begin by specifying a general model of crisis outcomes and its variables.

Model and Variable Specification

From the array of actor attributes and crisis dimensions (see Figures I.1.1. and I.1.2. in Chapter 1) we postulate that the following variables are useful in explaining US and Soviet crisis outcomes during the period 1945–1985: trigger, issue-area, value threat, technique of crisis management, and extent of violence. Interacting with these are two systemic variables: degree of superpower confrontation and structure of the international system. The crisis outcome variables to be explained are substance, form and satisfaction with outcome, duration of crisis and crisis legacy. Figure IV.13.1. presents a crisis outcome model, specifying the linkages among these variables. The variables will be discussed in turn and comparative frequencies provided for the US and the USSR on the various categories of each variable.

Independent Variables *Trigger*. The trigger to a crisis, as noted earlier in this volume, refers to the specific act, event or situational change that leads decision-makers to perceive a threat to basic values, time pressure for response, and likely involvement in military hostilities. The trigger often sets the tone for the manner in which the participants pursue

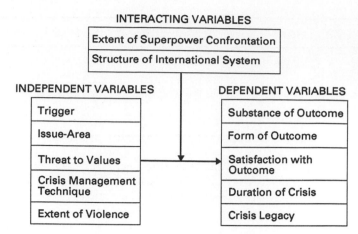

FIGURE IV.13.1. Model of Superpower Crisis Outcomes

their goals during the course of a crisis. Certain triggers, by their nature, may preclude outcomes in which all parties are satisfied. Others may make it difficult to achieve formal or even semi-formal agreements. Finally, some may make compromise difficult to attain. Table IV.13.2. presents the basic data for the US and Soviet cases on the trigger variable.

TABLE IV.13.2. Trigger to Crises: US and USSR

Type of Trigger	US Cases Frequency	%	USSR Cases Frequency	%
Verbal	8	17	3	13.5
Political	9	20	4	18
External Change	3	6	5	23
Other Non-Violent	0	0	1	4.5
Non-Violent Military	4	9	1	4.5
Indirect Violent	13	28	7	32
Violent	9	20	1	4.5
Total	46	100	22	100

An examination of the distribution of cases for the US and the USSR reveals both converging and contrasting patterns. For both superpowers, triggers resulting from indirect violent military action, that is, military action not directly involving the United States or the Soviet Union initially, constitute the largest category. For the United States, the vast majority of these indirect violence cases involved interests in Asia, such as the China Civil War 1948, the onset of the Korean War 1950, Taiwan Straits 1954 and 1958, and crises associated with Vietnam 1961, 1962, 1968 (Tet) and 1970 (Cambodia). For the USSR, the indirect violence cases were geographically more dispersed and included the escalation of the Korean War (October) 1950, East Berlin Uprising 1953, Suez 1956, Congo II 1964, Six Day War 1967, October War 1973 and Afghanistan Invasion 1979.

Strikingly, the USSR perceived a crisis for itself in only one of the US indirect violence cases, October-Yom Kippur War, whereas the United States was a crisis actor in six of the seven Soviet indirect violence cases. In five of these six cases, US crisis participation was not triggered by violence, as it was for the USSR, the exception being Korea II 1950. The United States was more prone than the USSR to direct violent triggers, including Korea I and II, June and October 1950; Gulf of Tonkin 1964; Pleiku 1965; Pueblo 1968; Spyplane 1969; Vietnam Spring Offensive 1969; Vietnam 1972; and Mayaguez 1975. Finally, five Soviet crises (23%) were triggered by external change of a political or military nature, four in the Eastern European regional system, i.e., Hungary 1947, Poland 1956, Hungary 1956 and Berlin 1961.

Issue. Here, the focus is on the most important initial issue-area of a foreign policy crisis as perceived by a crisis actor. Generally, it is our expectation that the issue-area for a crisis actor will significantly affect the nature of the outcome. More specifically, we differentiate between crises involving military-security and political-diplomatic issues. Table IV.13.3. presents the basic issue-area data for the US and Soviet cases.

TABLE IV.13.3. Issue-Area of Crises: US and USSR

Issue	US Cases Frequency	%	USSR Cases Frequency	%
Military-Security	18	39	5	23
Political-Diplomatic	28	61	17	77
Total	46	100	22	100

There is little difference between the two superpowers on this variable. For both, a large majority of cases falls in the political-diplomatic category. As expected, the (more serious) military-security cases generally involved system clusters in which both superpowers, or one superpower and China, were direct participants: Berlin Blockade 1948–49, Korea 1950, Berlin Wall 1961, Cuba 1962, Six-Day War 1967, Ussuri River 1969 and October War 1973–74. A number of Vietnam-related cases for the US constituted exceptions to this rule. The preponderance of political-diplomatic issues attests to the general role of superpowers in the international system since the end of World War II and their tendency to be active at a political or diplomatic level in crises which for other participants often directly involved more threatening military-security issues.

Threat to Values. The gravity of values threatened identifies what a crisis actor perceives to be the object of gravest threat at any time during a specific crisis. While crisis actors reveal a range of threatened values, such as threat to existence, influence, territorial integrity, political system, economic interests, and so forth, the data for the two superpowers indicate that the threat to their influence is overwhelming.[7] The severity of a threat to influence is assumed to impact significantly on the outcome characteristics of a crisis. Table IV.13.4. presents the distribution of cases for this variable.

The data reveal diversity for each superpower, as well as considerable differences between them. For the USSR, there is a striking centrality of concern for potential decline in influence within its own bloc (41%) whereas this is only a peripheral concern for the United States (4%). The relevant Soviet cases included the early Communist takeovers immediately following the end of World War II, and the later cases of liberalization in Poland 1956, Hungary 1956 and Czechoslovakia 1968. For the United States, the Korean War and the Syria/Turkey Border Crisis of 1957 were the only cases of within-bloc concern. This suggests that the USSR has been much less secure in its control over its bloc than the United States. By contrast, the United States is primarily concerned with potential decline in its influence among non-bloc clients and non-aligned states (54%), whereas the USSR perceived this type of threat in only 32% of its cases. Interestingly, less than a fourth of the cases fall into the category of the most serious threat to values – adverse change in the global balance between the superpowers – (26% for the United States, 18% for the USSR), the only cases in this category common to both superpowers being the Berlin Blockade and the Arab/Israel wars of 1967 and 1973–74.

Crisis Management Technique. It is our expectation that the choice of crisis management technique by a crisis actor will affect the nature of the outcome, particularly

TABLE IV.13.4. Threat to Values: US and USSR

Threat to Values	US Cases Frequency	%	USSR Cases Frequency	%
Adverse Change in Global Balance between Superpowers	12	26	4	18
Decline in Superpower Influence in Own Bloc	2	4	9	41
Decline in Superpower Influence over Non-Bloc Clients	12	26	3	14
Decline in Superpower Influence with Non-Aligned Group	13	28	4	18
Decline in Superpower Influence in Adversary Bloc	3	7	0	0
Value other than Influence Gravest Threat	4	9	2	9
Total	46	100	22	100

as regards the degree of compromise and the extent to which agreement is achieved, as well as the duration of a crisis. Table IV.13.5. presents the basic US and Soviet data on this variable.

Several significant differences are evident in patterns of superpower crisis management techniques. The United States has been somewhat more inclined than the USSR to employ negotiation as the primary technique (20% versus 9%). Moreover, negotiation was used by the United States in diverse types of crises, ranging from direct superpower confrontations such as Azerbaijan 1946, Berlin 1958 and Berlin 1961, to single superpower crises such as China Civil War 1948, Dien Bien Phu 1954, Taiwan Straits II 1958, Panama 1964 and Pueblo 1968. For the Soviet Union, the dominant crisis management technique was nonviolent military action, with 41% of its cases falling in this category (compared with only 20% for the United States). The bulk of these Soviet cases involved the efforts immediately following the end of World War II to establish and solidify Communist regimes in Eastern Europe. In terms of resort to violence (violence and multiple techniques involving violence), the two states are relatively equal, the United States with 30%, the USSR with 27%. Yet only half of the 14 US cases of violence as the primary crisis management technique were responses to direct violent triggers: Korea, October 1950 and 1953; Gulf of Tonkin 1964; Pleiku 1965; Vietnam Spring Offensive 1969; Vietnam Ports Mining 1972; and Mayaguez 1975. This contrast is even more pronounced for the USSR, where only one of six cases of violence as the primary crisis management technique was a response to a direct violent trigger – Ussuri River 1969. This lack of a strong direct relationship between trigger and the crisis management technique points to the existence of a complex process with a number of intervening factors, such as the type of initiating state, region, period, and extent of threat.

Extent of Violence. This variable assesses the degree to which violence was employed as a crisis management technique by a superpower, that is, whether it was exclusive, central, or minor. The distribution of cases is reported in Table IV.13.6.

Overall, the superpowers resorted to extensive violence (exclusive or central) infrequently as their primary crisis management technique (30% for the United States, 23% for the Soviet Union). Violence as the exclusive crisis management technique was employed on only eight occasions by the US – Korea I and II June and October 1950; five Indo-China cases – Gulf of Tonkin 1964, Pleiku 1965, Vietnam Spring Offensive 1969, Cambodia 1970 and Mayaguez 1975; and Grenada 1983 – and only three times by the USSR – uprising in East Berlin 1953, Hungary 1956 and Afghanistan Invasion 1979. This is not to say that violence was avoided in other

TABLE IV.13.5. Crisis Management Technique: US and USSR

Crisis Management Technique	US Cases Frequency	%	USSR Cases Frequency	%
Negotiation	9	20	2	9
Multiple not Involving Violence	13	28	5	23
Non-Military Pressure	1	2	0	0
Non-Violent Military	9	20	9	41
Multiple Involving Violence	6	13	3	13.5
Violence	8	17	3	13.5
Total	46	100	22	100

TABLE IV.13.6. Extent of Violence as Crisis Management Technique: US and USSR

Extent of Violence	US Cases Frequency	%	USSR Cases Frequency	%
Violence Exclusive	8	17.5	3	14
Violence Central	6	13	2	9
Violence Minor	1	2	1	4
No Violence as Crisis Management Technique	31	67.5	16	73
Total	46	100	22	100

cases. Rather, what sets these cases apart is the exclusive reliance on violence in crisis management.

Dependent Variables *Substance of Outcome.* This variable relates to the content of crisis outcome from the perspective of a crisis actor. Thus the focus is on the degree to which its articulated goals were achieved. Victory signifies the successful protection or enhancement of threatened values, while compromise means partial attainment of objectives. Stalemate indicates no clear outcome, that is, no change in the situation or restoration of the *status quo*. Finally, defeat means that a crisis actor yielded when its basic values were threatened. For purposes of subsequent analysis the following categories will be utilized: (1) goal achievement (victory and compromise), and (2) non-achievement of goals (stalemate and defeat). Table IV.13.7. presents the distribution of cases for the United States and the Soviet Union.

The pattern for the two superpowers is similar. Overall, both were successful crisis managers: the US achieved victory in 61% of its crises, the USSR in 54%.[2] The comparable figures for defeat were 23% and 11%. Interestingly, among the five cases of US defeat – China Civil War 1948, Dien Bien Phu 1954, Bay of Pigs 1961, Pueblo 1968 and Angola 1975 – the USSR was a crisis actor only in the Angola crisis. The US, by contrast, was a direct participant in all five cases of USSR defeat – Azerbaijan 1946, Berlin Blockade 1948, Cuba 1962, Congo II 1964 and Six Day War 1967. Clearly, the United States has had the upper hand in the crisis confrontations between the two superpowers.

Another way of looking at the data is in terms of decisive outcomes (victory and defeat) as opposed to ambiguous outcomes (stalemate and compromise). From this perspective, too, the US and the USSR are similar, with 72% and 77.5% decisive outcomes, respectively. Thus, there is striking evidence of goal achievement and finality in the US and USSR cases, both important characteristics of superpower crisis behavior and outcomes.

Form of Outcome. The form of outcome variable is dichotomous: formal agreement (such as a treaty, armistice or cease-fire); or less formal outcome, comprising semi-formal agreements (such as letters or oral declarations); tacit understandings by adversaries; and unilateral acts. The distribution of US and Soviet cases on this variable is reported in Table IV.13.8.

Overall, the results show a remarkable similarity between the two superpowers. For both, almost half the cases terminated through agreement – 46% for the US, 50% for the USSR, and almost half through a unilateral act – 41% for the US, 50% for the USSR. Tacit understandings were rare for the superpowers in crises, with none for the USSR and only five for the US – Guatemala 1954, Suez 1956,

TABLE IV.13.7. Substance of Outcome: US and USSR

Substance of Outcome	US Cases Frequency	%	USSR Cases Frequency	%
Victory	28	61	12	54.5
Compromise	6	13	4	18
Stalemate	7	15	1	4.5
Defeat	5	11	5	23
Total	46	100	22	100

TABLE IV.13.8. Form of Outcome: US and USSR

Form of Outcome	US Cases Frequency	%	USSR Cases Frequency	%
Formal Agreement	12	26	7	32
Semi-Formal Agreement	9	20	4	18
Tacit Understanding	5	11	0	0
Crisis Faded	1	2	0	0
Unilateral Act	19	41	11	50
Total	46	100	22	100

Syria/Turkey Border 1957, Pathet Lao Offensive II 1962 and Nicaragua MIG-21s 1984. The category, "crisis faded," which accounted for nearly 20% of the outcomes for all other actors, is represented by only one US case: Afghanistan Invasion 1979.
Satisfaction with Outcome. This variable assesses the extent to which a crisis actor is satisfied with the outcome, relative to the other actors in the crisis. Satisfaction can be perceived by all parties or by only one. Dissatisfaction, too, can be universal or one-sided. The distribution of US and USSR cases on the satisfaction variable is presented in Table IV.13.9.

The pattern for the US and the USSR is almost identical. In the vast majority of cases (81% for the US, 77% for the USSR), the superpower crisis actor was satisfied with the outcome. Dissatisfaction was evident in nine US cases – China Civil War 1948, Dien Bien Phu 1954, Bay of Pigs 1961, Berlin Wall 1961, Pleiku 1965, Tet Offensive 1968, Pueblo 1968, Angola War 1975, Afghanistan Invasion 1979 – and five USSR cases – Azerbaijan 1946, Berlin Blockade 1948–49, Cuban Missiles 1962, Congo II 1964, Six Day War 1967.
Duration of Crisis. The duration of a crisis is measured in terms of elapsed time between trigger and termination. Crisis termination is that point when there is an observable decline toward pre-crisis norms in the intensity of the three perceptual conditions of a foreign policy crisis: threat, time pressure, and war likelihood. It is our expectation that duration is determined by critical characteristics of the crisis itself, such as trigger and crisis management technique. Table IV.13.10. presents the US and Soviet frequency distribution for this variable.

TABLE IV.13.9. Satisfaction with Outcome: US and USSR

Satisfaction with Outcome	US Cases Frequency	%	USSR Cases Frequency	%
All Parties Satisfied	11	24	4	18
Actor Satisfied, Adversary Dissatisfied	26	57	13	59
Actor Dissatisfied, Adversary Satisfied	7	15	5	23
All Dissatisfied	2	4	0	0
Total	46	100	22	100

TABLE IV.13.10. Crisis Duration: US and USSR

Crisis Duration	US Cases Frequency	%	USSR Cases Frequency	%
0–31 Days	14	30	9	41
32–90 Days	17	37	3	14
91–180 Days	9	20	2	9
Over 180 Days	6	13	8	36
Total	46	100	22	100

There is a considerable dispersion of cases for both superpowers. A higher proportion of the Soviet cases terminated within one month, 41% to 30% for the US. US crises, on the other hand, show a much higher propensity to one–three months duration (37%–14%). And a high proportion of USSR cases (36%) lasted more than half a year, compared to only 13% for the US. The longest US cases, each more than six months, were the Berlin Blockade 1948–49, Korea 1950–51, Berlin Deadline 1958–59, Pueblo 1968, October War 1973–74 and US Hostages in Iran 1979–81. For the USSR, the crises of longest duration were Poland 1946–47, Berlin Blockade 1948–49, Berlin Deadline 1957–59, Ussuri River 1969, War of Attrition 1970, October War 1973–74, Angola 1975–76 and Afghanistan Invasion 1979.
Crisis Legacy. A crucial attribute of crisis outcome from the perspective of an international system is the extent to which crisis termination led to a reduction or escalation of tension among the principal adversaries. The indicator of reduction or escalation of tension used here assesses whether or not the principal actors are adversarial crisis actors during the subsequent five years. Table IV.13.11. reports the frequencies for the legacy of superpower cases.

TABLE IV.13.11. Crisis Legacy: US and USSR

Crisis Legacy	US Cases Frequency	%	USSR Cases Frequency	%
Escalation of Tension	21	47	6	27
Reduction of Tension	24	53	16	73
Total	45*	100	22	100

*1 case with missing data.

The pattern exhibited by the US and the USSR is considerably different. US cases are almost equally divided between tension escalation and reduction, whereas only 27% of Soviet cases resulted in tension escalation. Protracted conflicts account for most of the tension escalation cases for the US: the conflicts relating to China's Civil War, the Korean War and the Taiwan Straits account for seven US cases; and Indochina an additional ten. For the USSR, the six crises leading to tension escalation were the Marshall Plan 1947, Berlin Deadline 1957–59, Six Day War 1967, War of Attrition II 1970, Angola 1975–76 and Afghanistan Invasion 1979.

Interacting Variables   The model of crisis outcomes also assesses the interactive effects of two factors, the seriousness of superpower confrontation in a crisis, and the structure of the international system at the time of a crisis. While other interacting factors are both plausible and relevant (such as triggering entity and stability of the international system), superpower confrontation and structural factors are of particular interest. Due to the relatively small number of Soviet cases (22), the impact of these interacting variables will be assessed only for the US (46 cases).
Extent of Superpower Confrontation. An underlying assumption is that US crisis behavior will be affected by the extent of USSR involvement in a crisis. Thus, we differentiate US cases in which there was a serious confrontation with the USSR from those in which no confrontation occurred. Confrontation with the other superpower is defined as a situation in which the USSR engaged in covert activity, semi-military activity (military aid or advisors, without participating in actual fighting), or direct military intervention (dispatch of troops, aerial bombing, or naval assistance to a state in a war). Non-confrontation cases are those in which the USSR was either not involved at all or those where its involvement was limited to the political, economic, or propaganda spheres. The 19 cases of US/USSR confrontation are: Azerbaijan 1946; Berlin 1948–49; Korea, June and October 1950; Guatemala 1954; Lebanon/Iraq 1958; Quemoy 1958; Berlin 1961; Vietcong Attack 1961; Cuban Missiles 1962; Congo II 1964; Pleiku 1965; Tet 1968; Cienfuegos 1970; October War 1973–74; Angola 1975; Shaba II 1978; Afghanistan Invasion 1979; and Nicaragua MIG-21s 1984.
Structure of International System. As noted in Chapters 3 and 4 above, it is commonly argued that the structure of an international system will have a profound effect on types of behavior exhibited by entities within the system. Crisis behavior should be no exception. Thus, our task is to identify breakpoints in the structure of the post-World War II international system and to observe the impact of system transformation on the relations being investigated in the model of crisis outcomes. The breakpoints are: 1945–1962 – bipolarity (23 US cases) and 1963–1985 – polycentrism (23 US cases).

Findings on Superpower Crisis Outcomes

A number of relationships pertaining to US and Soviet crisis outcomes will now be examined. Specifically, our approach will analyze the impact of each of the independent variables on the five dependent variables specified in the model: substance, form and satisfaction with outcome, duration and legacy. Wherever appropriate, we will also discuss the interactive effect on US crises of superpower confrontation and structure of the international system. Although a large number of relationships are analyzed in this chapter, the voluminous tabular material is omitted, due to space restrictions. Summary statements will pull together the findings for the US and the USSR and compare their modes of behavior.

Trigger to Superpower Crisis

The first set of findings relates to the association between crisis trigger and outcome, duration, and crisis legacy. Triggers are grouped into three categories: *non-violent* (verbal, political, economic, non-violent military, external change, and internal challenge); *indirect violent* (military action initially involving third parties only); and *violent*. It is assumed that indirect violent triggers occupy a middle ground on a non-violence to violence scale.

For the United States, several points are noteworthy. First, the less violent a crisis trigger, the greater was the probability of goal achievement (83% for non-violent triggers, 56% for cases triggered by violence). This trend is particularly apparent during polycentrism, and is attributable in part to the Vietnam-era crises, which posed unusual problems for the US. Moreover, the less violent a trigger, the more likely it was that agreement among adversaries would result. Again, this finding is accentuated during polycentrism. Third, the less violent a crisis trigger, the shorter the duration, although confrontation with the USSR tended to lengthen a crisis, regardless of trigger. In polycentrism, the trend is reversed: violent triggers are associated with short crises. Finally, US crises characterized by non-violent triggers showed a low rate of subsequent tension among the parties (30%), while violent triggers tended to produce escalation (64%). In sum, the less violent a US crisis trigger, the more its goals were achieved, agreements reached, and tensions reduced, and the shorter a US foreign policy crisis.

For the USSR, goal achievement was generally the rule, regardless of the extent of violence in the trigger. Unlike the US, crises with more violent triggers tended to be of shorter duration – the exceptions being Ussuri River 1969 (the lone Soviet case of a direct violent trigger), October–Yom Kippur War 1973–74, Angola 1975–76 and Afghanistan Invasion 1979. And, finally, USSR crises generally led to tension reduction, regardless of trigger.

Issue-Area and Superpower Crisis

The issue-areas of crisis are considered in two broad categories, military-security and political-diplomatic. As indicated in Table IV.13.3., the latter was the preponderant issue-area for both superpowers.

For the United States, goal achievement was uniformly high, although the structure of the international system had an important impact. During bipolarity, US goal achievement was more closely associated with military-security crises (100%–75%), while for polycentrism, goal achievement was much more closely associated with crises over political-diplomatic issues (92%–36%). These findings attest to the basic change in the US role in the international system, from power dominance to parity with the USSR. The early preponderance of US power also led to a higher probability of termination in agreement in military-security cases involving confrontation with the USSR than in political-diplomatic crises (75%–40%). Finally, in bipolarity, tension reduction was more likely to result from military-security crises, while political-diplomatic crises during polycentrism were more likely to lead to tension reduction. In sum, goal achievement, while generally high, was accentuated in military-security crises with superpower confrontation. And those cases were considerably more likely than others to terminate in agreement.

The USSR exhibited a higher rate of goal achievement among political-diplomatic than among military-security crises (82%–40%). This apparent USSR inability to manage military-security crises to its advantage contrasts with that of the US, and constitutes an important characteristic of superpower relations in the post-World War II era. It conforms with the Soviet perception of US military superiority during most of the period under consideration. Nonetheless, USSR military-security crises did exhibit a strong tendency to terminate in agreement (80%). They also tended to be longer than political-diplomatic crises (60%–29%). In short, agreement was the more likely outcome of longer Soviet military-security crises, as was tension reduction.

Threat to Values and Superpower Crisis

In this section we explore the extent to which gravity of perceived value threat is related to crisis outcome, duration, and legacy. For both superpowers, the highest threat was an adverse change in the global balance between them. For the US, a middle level of threat was a decline in influence among non-bloc and non-aligned states. The counterpart for the USSR was a decline in influence within its bloc.

For the United States, the higher the level of value threat the greater was the probability of goal achievement and termination in agreement among the adversaries. Higher threat levels also meant longer crises, a trend which was accentuated in cases involving confrontation with the USSR. Generally, too, crises with the lowest level of threat exhibited the highest rate of tension escalation. This finding reflects an overwhelming trend in this direction among superpower confrontation cases, and for cases occurring during polycentrism. In sum, the higher the threat, the higher was the probability of goal achievement, agreement, tension reduction and longer duration in US crises.

For the USSR, goal achievement was highest in cases with medium threat, and lowest among high-threat cases, once again pointing to an international system dominated by the US and its interests. Similarly, satisfaction with outcome was highest for the USSR, as with the US, among those crises with medium threat. However, these cases tended to terminate without agreement, most often through Soviet unilateral acts (i.e., crises in Eastern Europe). In short, goal achievement, termination without agreement and satisfaction with outcome were highest for Soviet crises exhibiting a medium threat.

Crisis Management Technique and Superpower Crisis This section focuses on the link between the primary superpower crisis management technique (CMT) and crisis outcome. We differentiate among *negotiation*, *non-violence* (other than negotiation), and *violence*. In particular, we report differences in the patterns of superpower crises when negotiation is the primary CMT.

For the United States, negotiation as the primary crisis management technique in USSR confrontation cases was found to be associated with goal achievement, termination in agreement, less satisfaction with outcome and reduction in tension levels. For example, all four cases of negotiation in superpower confrontation resulted in US goal achievement – Azerbaijan 1946 (victory), Quemoy 1958 (victory), Berlin 1961 (compromise) and Cienfuegos 1970 (victory). On the other hand, less than half of the US cases involving negotiation in non-confrontation crises resulted in goal achievement. Similarly, among confrontation cases, negotiation was more likely than violence to be associated with satisfaction with outcome, the reverse of the trend among non-confrontation cases. In sum, negotiation, particularly under conditions of superpower confrontation, was found to be associated with goal achievement, satisfaction with outcome, shorter crises and reduction in tension levels.

Among the USSR cases, goal achievement was enhanced when violence was employed in crisis management. In addition, negotiation resulted in the lowest satisfaction rate, violence in the highest. Crises in which negotiation was employed tended to be shortest in duration.

Extent of Violence in Crisis Management Here we focus on the extent of violence as the primary crisis management technique and its effect on outcome, duration, and legacy. The categories for this variable are extreme *violence* (exclusive or central) and *minor or no violence*.

The United States was most likely to achieve its goals in cases in which violence was employed in crisis management and when a confrontation with the USSR was involved. This tendency was strongest during bipolarity. No violence or the employment of minor violence were more conducive to reaching agreement than were more extreme forms of violence. This again is strengthened in cases of US/USSR confrontation. When no confrontation existed, extreme violence in crisis management overwhelmingly resulted in satisfaction with outcome. However, superpower confrontation cases showed violence and satisfaction to be unrelated. Extreme violence was highly associated with long duration in bipolarity, but with short duration in polycentrism. Finally, superpower confrontation cases exhibited no tension reduction when extreme violence was employed, but considerable tension reduction with minor and no violence. In sum, in superpower confrontations, goal achievement, agreement and satisfaction with outcome were enhanced when minor or no violence was employed, while tension levels escalated.

For the USSR, goal achievement was at a high level, and was unrelated to the extent of violence. At the same time satisfaction with outcome tended to be associated with high levels of violence in crisis management. Unlike the US, extreme violence was more likely to result in tension reduction than escalation (67%–33%).

CONCLUSION

There are considerable points of convergence and divergence in the crisis behavior of the two superpowers. First, the findings point to a global system dominated by the United States and its interests. Thus, in terms of goal achievement, the United States was less likely than the USSR to experience defeat; the US experienced defeat in only one case in which the USSR was also a crisis actor (Angola 1975–76), whereas all USSR defeats were direct confrontations with the United States. US crises terminated in agreement more than did Soviet cases. US resort to extreme violence in crisis management, particularly in cases of confrontation with the USSR, tended to enhance its goal achievement.

Along with the findings that point to US domination of the international system are signs that a significant shift began to occur in the transition from bipolarity (1945–1962) to polycentrism (1963–1985). US goal achievement resulting from direct and indirect violent triggers decreased during the polycentric period. US crises in polycentrism were generally longer. Military-security crises were strongly associated with goal achievement during bipolarity, but not during polycentrism. Finally, the United States achieved its objectives when extreme violence was employed during the bipolar period, but not during polycentrism.

Turning to the USSR, an outstanding feature is the identification of threat of decline in its influence within its bloc as being of overwhelming importance for its crisis behavior. Interestingly, these crises of intra-bloc threat to influence were uniformly associated with USSR goal achievement. Generally, the USSR exhibited a singular inability to manage military-security crises to its advantage, in sharp contrast to the findings for the United States.

Finally, a word is in order concerning the role of violence as the primary superpower crisis management technique: violence accounts for 30% of US and 27% of Soviet crisis responses. Overall, violent triggers are not necessarily associated with violent crisis management techniques. Nevertheless, violence was employed with considerable success by both superpowers, particularly as regards goal achievement. This finding is consistent with that of an earlier study which focused on superpower actors (Brecher and Wilkenfeld, 1982), to the effect that "violence paid in crisis situations;" that is, when a state responded to overt threat with violence, it was likely to achieve its goals.

It should not be at all surprising that considerable diversity exists in the patterns of US and Soviet crisis outcomes. There is a large number of factors in crisis situations, that, when operating in concert, combine to produce unique effects on the behavior of participants. Furthermore, we have not as yet controlled for several critical factors. Nevertheless, this analysis has uncovered considerable regularity in the manner in which the United States and the Soviet Union have approached crises during the 1945–1985 era.

Notes

1. The literature on these two direct confrontation crises is vast. For the 1948–1949 Berlin crisis, see especially Acheson (1969), Bohlen (1973), Davison (1962), George and Smoke (1974), Gottlieb (1960), Murphy (1964), Shlaim (1983), Tanter (1974), Truman (1956), Ulam (1971, 1974), Windsor (1963) and Young (1968a, 1968b). For the Cuban Missile Crisis, see especially Abel (1966), Allison (1971), Chayes (1974), Crankshaw (1966), Dinerstein (1976), Garthoff (1987), George, Hall, and Simons (1971), George and Smoke (1974), Hilsman (1967), Horelick (1964), Kennedy (1962, 1964, 1969), Khrushchev (1970), Knorr (1964), Kolkowicz (1967), Schlesinger (1965), Sorensen (1965), Steinberg (1981), Tatu (1969), Ulam (1974), Wohlstetter and Wohlstetter (1965), and Young (1968a).
2. For American and Soviet élite attitudes toward each other, see Angell (1964), Horelick (1964), Singer (1964), Welch (1970) and Zimmerman (1970). On superpower goals, strategies and tactics, see, for example, Brzezinski and Huntington (1964), Horelick and Rush (1964), Kaufmann (1964), Mackintosh (1963), and Triska and Finley (1968).
3. Studies of this *genre*, too, are numerous. See, for example, Barnet (1968), Blechman and Kaplan (1978), Borisov and Koloskov (1975), CACI (1978), Confino and Shamir (1973), Golan (1977), Kolko and Kolko (1972), Rubinstein (1978), Ro'i (1979), Shaked and Rabinovich (1980), Sheehan (1976) and Wolf (1967).
4. See, for example, Hoffmann and Fleron (1980).
5. See Bloomfield (1967), Dallin (1962), Henkin (1959), Ikle (1964) and Schick (1965).
6. See, for example, Osgood (1968) and Zagoria (1962).
7. The US exceptions were Suez 1956, Cuban Missiles 1962, Cienfuegos 1970, and the USSR exception was Korea 1950.
8. Their record as crisis managers in other states' crises during those 40 years was assessed in Chapter 6 above.

Part V
Conclusion

14 Toward a Theory of Crisis in World Politics

Michael Brecher

Most of this volume on twentieth-century crises has taken the form of "islands of analysis:" a new approach to the unresolved debate over polarity and stability (Chapters 3 and 4); a reexamination of enduring topics in the world politics literature, such as third party intervention in crises by international organizations and superpowers (Chapters 5 and 6), threat and violence in crisis behavior (Chapter 12), and crisis management by the US and the USSR (Chapter 13); an attempt to measure the intensity and consequences of crises in two Third World regions, the Middle East and Africa (Chapter 7); a study of structural determinants of international crises (Chapter 8), and an inquiry into the conflict-crisis linkage at several levels of analysis (Chapters 9-11).

The final chapter will focus on the foundations of a theory of crisis, building upon concepts (system and crisis) and linkages (macro and micro) discussed in Chapters 1 and 2. The fundamental question can be phrased simply: what does one seek to explain about crises in world politics? This encompasses an array of specific questions. Under what conditions is a crisis most likely to erupt? Why do some crises escalate to war (e.g., Entry into World War II 1939), while others do not (e.g., Cuban Missiles 1962)? What are the conditions in which a crisis is most likely to "wind down"? What are the effects of stress on the ways in which decision-makers cope with crisis? When are states likely to resort to violence in crisis management (e.g., the UK in the Falklands/Malvinas Crisis 1982)? What are the procedures leading to choice in situations of high stress? Why do some crises terminate in agreement (e.g., Berlin Blockade 1948-49), while others do not (e.g., Berlin Wall 1961)? And what are the consequences of crises: for the adversarial actors (e.g., reduction of tension between Egypt and Israel after the October–Yom Kippur War 1973); and for the system or subsystem in which they occur (e.g., the creation of a new actor in South Asia, and a basic change in the India/Pakistan balance of power, following the Bangladesh War 1971)?

The answers to these questions lie in a logical sequence of four interrelated domains – onset, escalation, deescalation and impact. In search of theory we present for each domain: (1) operational definitions of concepts; (2) independent, dependent and intervening variables; (3) models of an international crisis and of state behavior in a foreign policy crisis; (4) propositions deduced from these models; and (5) an integrated model for crisis as a whole. To close the circle, ICB evidence will be used – later – to test the validity of specific hypotheses and the theory as a whole.

Concepts

At the outset, it is well to recall the definitions of crisis set out in Chapter 1:

> An *international crisis* is a situational change characterized by two necessary and sufficient conditions: (1) a change in the type or an increase in the intensity of disruptive interactions between two or more adversaries, with a high probability of military hostilities or, during a war, an adverse change in the military balance; and (2) the higher-than-normal conflictive interactions destabilize the existing relationship of the adversaries and pose a challenge to the structure of an international system – global, dominant and/or subsystem.

Every international crisis, as noted, contains one or more foreign policy crises for states (e.g., Entry into World War II 1939, with 21 crisis actors; Taiwan Straits I 1954-55, with three actors; and Falklands/Malvinas 1982, with two actors).

> A *foreign policy crisis*, that is, a crisis viewed from the perspective of an individual state, is a situation with three necessary and sufficient conditions deriving from a change in a state's external or internal environment: (1) a threat to basic values; (2) an awareness of finite time for response to the value threat; and (3) a high

probability of involvement in military hostilities. All three are perceptions held by the highest level decision-makers of the state concerned.

In sum, a crisis can be addressed in both system and actor terms. As for the link between the two levels, which is crucial to an integrated theory, suffice it to note at this point: an international crisis requires behavioral change by adversaries, leading to more intense conflictual interaction; such change always triggers a foreign policy crisis for a state and can be traced to its perceptual origin. Here lies the structural link between the two levels.

Turning to the domains of crisis, *onset* is characterized at the system level by more intense conflictive interaction among adversaries than the non-crisis norm, but not yet encompassing war likelihood. At the actor level, onset designates the pre-crisis period of an emerging foreign policy crisis, characterized by a change from no (or low) perceived threat (non-crisis norm) to low (or higher) threat from an external adversary, that is, low stress.

Onset does not refer to any phase of disruptive interaction (macro) or any period of threat perception (micro), for conflict and stress are pervasive in a global system of fragmented authority and unequal distribution of power and resources. Rather, the onset of a crisis refers to a qualitative change in the intensity of disruption between two or more state actors and of threat perception by one of them (e.g., a verbal statement by A threatening to attack B unless it complies with some demand by A; a politically hostile act, such as the severance of diplomatic relations; an economic boycott of B's exports by A).

Escalation is generally treated as synonymous with a crisis. At the macro-level, it denotes more intense distortion than the onset phase, including the presence of a high probability of war. At the micro-level, the trigger to escalation (e.g., placing forces on alert, mobilization of troops, change of force posture from defense to offense, a military attack) leads to the crisis period for a state, in which perceptions of time pressure and war likelihood are added to more acute threat perception. The escalation phase, in short, marks the peak of a crisis and maximum stress.

Deescalation is the conceptual counterpart to escalation, the "winding-down" of a crisis compared to the "spiral" process. At the system level, this domain is characterized by a reduction in the volume and intensity of conflictive interactions. At the micro-level, it denotes a decline in perceptions of value threat, time pressure and war likelihood, that is, a decline in stress, towards the pre-existing non-crisis norm. The latter, when reached, signifies the end of the post-crisis period and of a foreign policy crisis. The conflict/crisis/war literature has devoted much less attention to deescalation than to escalation. This is a natural, given the danger of crises "getting out of hand", that is, escalating to war. At the same time, no theory of crisis would be complete without an explanation of accommodation and crisis termination. Moreover, in policy terms, the reduction of disruptive, often violent, interaction to a non-crisis norm is a goal of many states including major powers, and international organizations; and the graver the challenge to system stability posed by a crisis, the graver the concern among system actors.

The concept of crisis begins with onset and ends with *impact*, that is, the effects of a crisis. All crises have consequences at one or more levels: for the relationship between adversarial actors; and, possibly, for one or more international systems – the subsystem of which they are members, other subsystems, the dominant system of world politics, and, in the widest sense, the global system. The task of a theory of crisis, in this domain, is to describe and explain the legacy of crises.

The behavioral (macro/system) and perceptual (micro/actor) linkages among the four crisis domains over time are set forth in Figure V.14.1.:

Variables

Within each domain of an international crisis – onset, escalation, deescalation, impact – the *dependent* variable comprises nominal-level dichotomies:

Onset – eruption/non-eruption of an international crisis;
Escalation – war/no war;
Deescalation – short/long duration;
       agreement or other form of termination;
Impact – reduction/increase of tension among adversaries; no system change/system change, regarding actors/regimes, power, alliances and/or rules.

The principal goal of a theory of crisis is to explain onset, escalation, deescalation and impact in all of these meanings. In operational terms, one seeks to uncover the

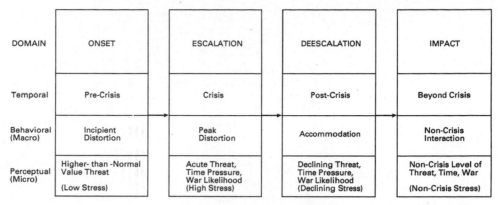

DOMAIN	ONSET	ESCALATION	DEESCALATION	IMPACT
Temporal	Pre-Crisis	Crisis	Post-Crisis	Beyond Crisis
Behavioral (Macro)	Incipient Distortion	Peak Distortion	Accommodation	Non-Crisis Interaction
Perceptual (Micro)	Higher- than -Normal Value Threat (Low Stress)	Acute Threat, Time Pressure, War Likelihood (High Stress)	Declining Threat, Time Pressure, War Likelihood (Declining Stress)	Non-Crisis Level of Threat, Time, War (Non-Crisis Stress)

FIGURE V.14.1. Crisis Domains: Linkages

conditions in which a crisis is likely to erupt, to escalate to war, to wind down, to transform an international system, etc.? As indicated, models will be specified, and explanations offered, in the form of testable hypotheses about each of these core questions.

There are three types of *explanatory* or *independent* variables in this complex analysis (Model 1 below). One comprises *system* attributes, which define the context in which a crisis breaks out and unfolds through the onset (pre-crisis), escalation (crisis), and deescalation (post-crisis) phases, leading to impact:

> Structure of system authority (polarity) – hegemonial (unipolar), polarized (bi-polar, multipolar), diffuse (polycentric);
> Conflict environment – protracted conflict (PC), non-PC, long-war-PC.

Another group consists of *crisis* attributes, that is, components of the crisis proper:

> Trigger – political, economic, non-violent military act, violent act, external/internal change;
> Number of crisis actors – n = 1. . . . . . ;
> Major power involvement – none, low, high;
> Geostrategic salience – to subsystem(s), dominant system, global system;
> Heterogeneity – none, minimal, extensive, total;
> Issues – military, political, economic, cultural;
> Violence – none, minor, serious clashes, war;
> Substance of Outcome – definitive, ambiguous;
> Form of Outcome – agreement, tacit, unilateral act.

A third cluster incorporates actor attributes;

> Threatened values for adversaries – limited, economic, political, territory, influence, existence.
> Capability gap – no, low, high power discrepancy between adversaries;
> Domestic stability/instability – decreasing, same, increasing;
> Territorial distance – contiguous, same sub-region, same continent, elsewhere;
> Regime divergence – democratic/non-democratic (civil or military);

In the foreign policy crisis model (Model 2 below), the *dependent* variable is choice. Viewed in terms of a foreign policy crisis as a whole, the decision options may be designated along a scale – do nothing, delay, comply, negotiate, fight. Within each phase, however, the options are dichotomous:

> Onset – initiate/do not initiate a crisis;
> Escalation – increase or maintain low level of hostility;
> Deescalation – accommodate/sustain a crisis.

The *independent* variable for this model is perception of crisis, for choice derives from "decision-makers" images of their environment. How they view the setting of structure and conflict, and their relative power *vis-à-vis* an adversary will predispose initial choices. Similarly, their perception of issues, major power involvement, and other attributes of a crisis *per se*, along with system and/or actor attributes, will shape their decisions in later phases – whether or not to escalate, whether or not to "wind down" a crisis and, if so, how to terminate it. In operational terms, there are three separate but closely-related perceptual variables:

Threat – no, low, high, declining;
Time pressure – no, low, high, declining;
War likelihood – no, low, high, declining.

The *intervening* variable in Model 2 is coping with crisis, through four mechanisms: information search, consultation, decisional forums, and consideration of alternatives. These will be elaborated in the exposition of the crisis behavior model.

The rationale for specific explanatory variables is provided in the discussion of models and propositions below. As for external validity, two observations are pertinent. First, the structure and environment variables reflect one major strand in the literature – the emphasis on the systemic level of analysis in explaining all phenomena in world politics (e.g., Kaplan, 1957; Modelski, 1974; and Waltz 1979). Actor variables reflect another – the unit-level or decision-making approach (e.g., Snyder *et al.*, 1962; East, Salmore and Hermann, 1978; and Bueno de Mesquita, 1981). And the crisis variables reflect the importance attached to the dynamics of the adversarial relationship in influencing crisis behavior and outcome (e.g., Snyder and Diesing, 1977). All are necessary to an understanding of crisis. Secondly, the choice of independent variables was reinforced by the persausive evidence of more than a decade of empirical research on twentieth-century crises. In the largest sense, the set of variables specified above reflects two theoretical concerns – parsimony and comprehensiveness, that is, maximal explanatory power.

Models and Hypotheses

A theory must address different levels of analysis and define properties at each level. It must also relate inputs (or independent variables) to processes (or changes over time) and to outputs (dependent variables). The primary objective, as noted, is to explain the phenomenon of crisis. To that end, three models will be delineated, along with hypotheses for each domain.

Model 1: International Crisis

A path model of crisis is presented in Figure V.14.2. In essence, it depicts a four-phase process, in which an international crisis – its eruption, acute distortion, accommodation and legacy over time – is shaped by system, actor and crisis attributes. The process begins with a triggering act, event or environmental change, that is, a breakpoint, which is conditioned by several system and actor attributes, to be specified below. Once in motion, a crisis continues at a low level of conflictive interaction – the onset phase – until other attributes escalate it to a more intense level of distortion.

The escalation phase persists until another configuration of attributes sets in motion accommodation among the adversaries, the deescalation phase, which culminates in crisis termination. Although extinguished, an international crisis has spillover effects for the adversaries and, often, for one or more of the systems of which they are members – global, dominant, subsystems; that is, the "earthquake" enters the impact phase beyond the crisis (see Chapter 7 above). In elaborating this model, we will specify the causal links between system, actor and crisis attributes, on the one hand, and on the other, the four phases of an international crisis as a macro-level phenomenon in world politics. The four phase models to be discussed below are integral parts of Model 1. Some variables are common to several of the phase models, while others are specific to one or another of these models.

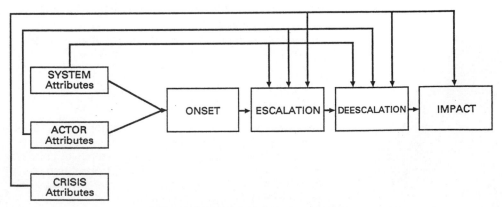

Figure V.14.2. Model of International Crisis

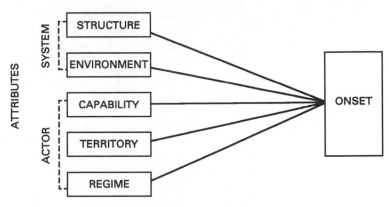

FIGURE V.14.3. Crisis Onset Model

Onset   A phase model of crisis onset in presented in Figure V.14.3. As evident, the outbreak of a crisis and the onset phase are postulated to be the result of system and actor attributes. The former are type of international structure and type of conflict setting. The latter comprise extent of power discrepancy, territorial distance and regime divergence among the adversaries. Our expectations regarding their role in generating a crisis will now be stated briefly.

We begin with *system structure. A priori*, the larger the number of autonomous decisional centers, the larger will be the number of dyads. Assuming that any pair of states has a fixed probability (p) of involvement in a crisis in any year, an increase in the number of states will lead to an increase in the number of expected crises, without a change in p.[1] Further, in a system of limited, unevenly distributed resources the dyads are likely to be competitive (adversarial). And the fewer the system constraints on actor behavior, the more likely will there be more-than-normal conflictive interaction and the eruption of an international crisis.[2]

An *ongoing conflict* between a pair of states or coalitions may also be expected to increase the likelihood that a crisis will break out. The reason, as noted in the analysis of conflicts and crises earlier (Chapter 9), is that, all other things being equal, previous hostility between the same adversaries creates a higher probability of intense conflictive interaction in the future. Moreover, in a setting of non-protracted conflict among states, there is no logical basis for expecting a crisis, let alone a violent trigger, whereas crisis onset and violent catalyst are more likely in a setting of cumulative conflict. And the longer, the more intense and the more violent a conflict, the more likely the eruption of a crisis.

One actor attribute which helps to determine whether or not a crisis will erupt is *capability*, more precisely, the balance of capability. Assuming rational actor behavior, a large power gap (e.g., a major power vs. a minor power) makes it unnecessary for the former to protect or enhance its interests by triggering a crisis for a weaker state. Similarly, that discrepancy make it less likely (because it is less rational) that the latter will initiate a crisis for a much stronger adversary: the possibility of violence and the probability of non-achievement of goals are likely to constrain a weaker state from provoking a stronger one. By contrast, the smaller the power gap between an adversarial pair, the less the constraint on crisis initiation by either and the greater the cost if an adversary acts first; therefore, the more likely the outbreak of a crisis.[3]

Territorial proximity, too, increases the likelihood of crises, for the possibility of conflictive interaction is greater between a contiguous than a physically separate dyad. It may arise from undemarcated borders or wider competitive claims to territory, often a residue of past relationships. There is also the greater possibility of ethnic spillovers from one state to another. Where the bilateral power gap is large, it is likely to depreciate the effect of proximity. However, contiguity, *per se*, generates more sources of competition than does distance and, therefore, a higher probability of hostile interaction leading to an international crisis.[4]

A third actor attribute which is expected to induce more disruption is *political regime* divergence. More specifically, democratic/non-democratic regimes are hypothesized as more likely to experience international crises than democratic adversaries. One reason is that decision-makers in a pluralist polity and economy are more constrained by diverse interest groups from initiating – or becoming involved in – external crises, with their attendant human and material costs.[5] Another is that divergence in type of political regime accentuates the differences between, and mistrust of, potential crisis adversaries; when, as often, regime difference also expresses ideological differences, it contributes to more intense hostility, increased fear, and a greater willingness to initiate a crisis lest values be threatened by a preemptive act on the part of an adversary.

This discussion of crisis onset is summarized as:

> **Proposition 1: An international crisis is more likely to occur when :**
> a) **decisional authority in an international structure is diffuse;**
> b) **the environment of the potential adversaries is one of ongoing conflict;**
> c) **the power gap between them is small or non-existent;**
> d) **the dyadic states are territorially contiguous; and**
> e) **their regimes are divergent along a democratic/non-democratic axis.**

Two closely-related questions arise about this proposition and all others to follow. First, what is the relative weight of the attributes specified in the models for crisis onset, escalation, deescalation and impact? Second is the question of necessary and sufficient conditions.

The point of departure for the former is a discussion of *clusters* of attributes. The relationship of *system* and *actor* (as well as, for later phases, *crisis*) attributes can, *a priori*, be viewed as analogous to substructure and superstructure. The polarity configuration of a system, that is, the number of decisional centers, clearly shapes the potential scope for outbreak of crises by determining the number of dyads and, therefore, the number of possible conflicting dyads. Similarly, the presence or absence of one or more protracted conflicts in the system determines the likelihood of more or less frequent crises – for reasons noted above and elaborated in Chapter 9. Thus these systemic attributes must be accorded the highest weight among the clusters of attributes in explaining onset, escalation, deescalation and impact. Stated differently, they are the preconditions or substructure in the analysis of crisis occurrence or any of its phases.

Actor attributes, by contrast, are specific to an actor or an adversarial pair. The balance of military capability or territorial contiguity or regime divergence may lead to the outbreak of a crisis in various polarity configurations and/or conflict environments. What is argued here is that the *likelihood* of their so doing will be greater with a more diffuse authority structure in an international system in which protracted conflicts abound; that is, the likelihood that an interstate dispute will lead to a crisis will vary with the type of structure and context. Thus actor attributes must be given less weight than system attributes in the explanation of crisis onset.

Turning to the second question: are all five attributes specified in Proposition 1 necessary to crisis onset? For example, what are the implications for onset if a, b, c, d hold true but there is little or no divergence in the regimes of the adversaries? Or what if a, b, d, e hold true but the power gap between the adversaries is large? Put simply, these are not *necessary* conditions, for crises can and do occur in bipolar and multipolar, as well as polycentric, structures, in an environment in which protracted conflicts do not exist, where the power gap between adversaries is large, they are territorially distant, and they share a regime type. Rather, the five attributes specified in Figure V.14.3. are *sufficient* conditions for crisis onset. More precisely, they are the conditions in which a crisis is *most likely* to erupt.

The accuracy of the discussion concerning relative potency of variables will be assessed – elsewhere – through statistical analysis. Initially, the bivariate relationship between each attribute and crisis onset will be examined. For example, structure will appear as a trichotomous independent variable – multipolarity, bipolarity, polycentrism, with the number of crises (crisis onsets) as the dependent variable. Thereafter a multivariate factor analysis will be employed to test the relative potency of system and actor attributes as clusters in explaining the onset of crises, following the procedure discussed at length in Chapter 9 above.

Escalation   Whereas the analysis of crisis onset concentrated on the catalyst, the focus here will be on the dynamic of escalation. Specifically, we identify which type of interstate crises tend to war or, more precisely, the conditions in which a crisis is likely to escalate to war.

A phase model of crisis escalation is presented in Figure V.14.4. As evident, the

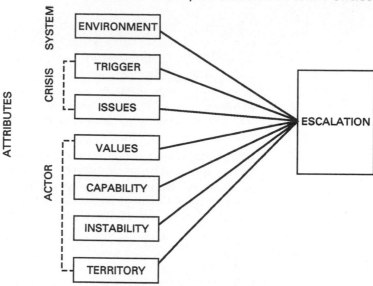

FIGURE V.14.4. Crisis Escalation Model

escalation process is postulated to be the result of factors from each of the three clusters of attributes: a protracted conflict setting (systemic); a violent trigger and several issues in dispute (crisis); and threatened values, large power discrepancy, domestic instability and territorial contiguity between the adversaries (actor).

The rationale for this expectation can first be stated in general terms. War is the most disruptive type of interaction among states: it is most likely to ensue when crucial crisis and actor attributes – type of trigger, issues at stake, threatened values, relative capability, domestic instability, and territorial distance – manifest the most acute conflictual point on their respective scales, namely, the most violent catalyst, the largest number of issues in dispute, the most basic value threatened, etc. When all of these attributes are at the extreme, and when a crisis erupts within an ongoing conflict, the likelihood of escalation to war will be highest.

The pivotal role of *protracted conflict* (PC) must be emphasized at the outset. One of its effects, the greater likelihood that a crisis will erupt in violence, was noted in the rationale for Proposition 1. There are others, all pointing to crises within such a conflict as more destabilizing and more prone to war than others.

First, while a PC crisis may focus on a limited issue, it its linked to values in dispute over a prolonged period; that is, the stakes of a specific PC crisis are extensions of fundamental cleavages. Threatened values in non-PC crises, by contrast, are unencumbered with the psychological baggage of an ongoing conflict. In short, PC crises generate more basic value threats.

Secondly, as long as adversaries do not see a finite end to their conflict, the persistence of value competition and the expectation of recurrent violence generate a continuing reliance on violence in crisis management, including full-scale war. In non-PC situations, by contrast, adversaries may or may not resort to violence; and even when they do so, there is no *a priori* disposition to use the most severe form of violence. In short, if the "lessons of history" strengthen the tendency to intense violence in a PC crisis, non-protracted conflict situations do not.

Thirdly, crises within protracted conflicts are more likely to escalate to war because of what may be termed the paradox of major power involvement in crises. On the one hand, except for revolutionary regimes much of the time, they generally have a strong interest in global system stability and are therefore inclined to act to reduce the likelihood of violence in a crisis or to limit its severity and duration lest destabilization feed back to major power relations. On the other hand, violence, as noted earlier, is more likely to occur in a PC than in a non-PC crisis; and so inter-vention tends to stimulate escalation.

Overall, the expected effects of a protracted conflict point to a higher likelihood that crises within that setting will escalate to war.

Turning to the rationale for the choice of individual explanatory variables in the crisis escalation model:

Violent trigger – when a catalyst is violent, the target is likely to respond in kind; when it resorts to violence to manage a crisis, the adversary is likely to reciprocate

– the conflict-begets-conflict syndrome (Wilkenfeld, 1975 and Ward 1982); the consequent "spiral" effect is more likely than the effects of a non-violent trigger to escalate to the most intense form of violence, namely, war;

Several *issues* – the more – and more serious – the issues in contention, the more intense will be the hostile behavior between adversaries, the greater the reinforcing effects on other sources of conflictive interaction, including a willingness to expend more resources to defend threatened values with violence and, if necessary, war;

Basic value threats – the more fundamental the values at stake, ranging from limited threat to property, to existence, the higher the price crisis actors will be willing to pay to protect them and the more extreme will be their crisis management (value-protecting) technique, with violence as the most extreme CMT and war as the most costly form of violence;

Large power discrepancy – when adversaries are relatively equal in military power, crisis *escalation* to war is unlikely, because of the uncertain outcome and high cost; this is the reverse of the logic relating to power equality and crisis *initiation* (Proposition 1); when a large power gap exists, by contrast, the stronger actor will be more inclined to use its superior capability, including escalation to war;

Domestic instability – when crisis actors are confronted with internal turmoil, escalation to war is more likely, for political élites attempt to overcome domestic malaise by diverting the attention of their mass public to an external rival, enemy or adversary; and the greater the turmoil, the greater the disposition to violence, including war; reciprocity by the target provides another source of escalation; and when both adversaries are afflicted with domestic instability, the likelihood of escalation to war is even greater, for either may set the escalation in motion and contribute to the spiral.[6]

The rationale for the inclusion of *territorial proximity* as likely to affect crisis escalation builds upon the argument made earlier regarding crisis onset. Territory is linked to the escalation process because the geographic proximity of the adversaries is likely to increase state A's perceptions of threat, time pressure, and military hostilities, the conditions of a foreign policy crisis, given the proximity of state B's military forces – and vice-versa. Moreover, a major power is likely to be more inclined to escalate a crisis to violence in order to protect a geographically close ally: "For reasons of prestige and strategic value as a buffer state, or as a valuable ally in the regional balance of power, the loss of an adjacent protege is much more costly than the loss of a distant one." (Huth and Russett: 1988, 35).

The discussion of the factors contributing to crisis escalation is summarized as:

Proposition 2: An international crisis is more likely to escalate to war when:
a) **it occurs within a protracted conflict;**
b) **the crisis is triggerd by violence;**
c) **several issues are in dispute;**
d) **basic values are threatened;**
e) **large power discrepancy exists between the adversarial actors;**
f) **one or more crisis actors are faced with domestic turmoil; and**
g) **the adversaries are geographically contiguous.**

Proposition 2, if strongly supported, would facilitate a prediction of a configuration of future crises most likely to escalate to war. And such prediction would have considerable policy relevance, namely, to help abate a crisis or to prevent the destabilizing spread of such crises in the future. Thus a rigorous research strategy would have benefits for the emergent global society.

Deescalation   There are several ways in which the third domain of crisis can be analyzed. The most creative thus far has been in terms of bargaining among adversaries (Snyder and Diesing, 1977; Leng *et al.*, 1979, 1982, 1983). A prior question, however, is pertinent: what leads adversaries to choose to bargain, with the goal of a mutually-satisfactory agreement? Stated differently, another approach, as with the "spiral" or escalation process discussed above, is to seek the conditions in which crises are

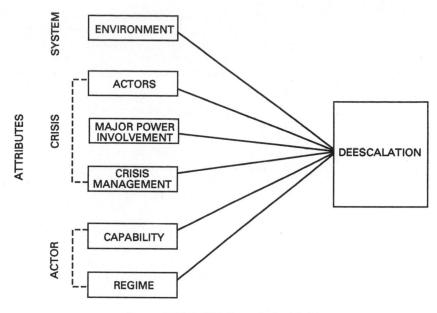

FIGURE V.14.5. Crisis Deescalation Model

more likely to wind down to a non-crisis norm of interaction. These are set out in Figure V.14.5.

Deescalation is not exactly analogous to escalation, for almost all crises wind down and terminate, whereas many crises do not escalate to war (e.g., Berlin Blockade 1948-49, Cuban Missiles 1962).[7] Nevertheless, one can indicate a cluster of factors to explain the shift from acute distortion to accommodation. One is a system attribute, namely, a non-protracted conflict setting. Three crisis attributes also help to induce deescalation: a small number of crisis actors; non-military activity by the major powers, and non-violent techniques of crisis management. So too do two actor attributes: power equality and regime convergence.

The rationale for the choice of three of these explanatory variables – *conflict setting*, *capability* and *regime* – is the obverse of their expected effects in the onset and escalation phases, respectively. Suffice it to summarize the argument, briefly. A crisis outside of an ongoing conflict is not burdened by cumulative hostility and mistrust, thereby reducing a major psychological obstacle to the pursuit of accommodation by the adversarial actors. Relatively equal power among them makes compromises more acceptable, once escalation has reached its peak, often in war, with its attendant high cost and a likely stalemate, because low – or no – power discrepancy means that neither is likely to triumph. And democratic regimes reduce the likelihood of miscommunication and misunderstanding in the bargaining process because mutual familiarity with, and acceptance of, the formal and tacit rules, principles, norms and institutions of the political system facilitates mutual understanding of signals and verbal exchanges between adversaries.

As for the *number of participants*, fewer crisis actors means fewer adversarial pairs, a less complex set of issues and disruptive interactions, even during the escalation phase; these make accommodation less difficult and less time-consuming.

The paradox of *major power activity* in crisis has already been noted: interest in system stability dictates behavior to reduce crisis severity and duration; but commitment to clients tends to foster high involvement, that is, military or semi-military intervention, which stimulates escalation. Low (political and/or economic) involvement, by contrast, generates less intense disruption among adversarial clients and facilitates a shift from distortion to accommodation.

Non-violent *crisis management*, too, eases the deescalation process. It is less disruptive than violence. It is less likely to induce reciprocal violence by an adversary. And it reduces the time required to achieve accommodation and crisis termination.

In the light of this discussion, the conditions of deescalation may be integrated into:

Proposition 3: An international crisis is more likely to wind down when:
a) it occurs outside of an ongoing conflict;

     b) there are few adversarial crisis actors;
     c) major power involvement is low-level, that is, non-military;
     d) the adversaries rely on non-violent crisis management techniques;
     e) they are relatively equal in military power; and
     f) the principal adversaries have democratic political regimes.

A related question in the domain of deescalation is the duration of crises. Some are very short, one less than a day (shooting down of a Libyan plane by Israel on 21 February 1973). Some are very long, a year or more (e.g., Berlin Deadline from 15 December 1957 to 15 September 1959). Is duration a product of chance, or can one discover a group of factors which shape the length of crises? As an extension of Proposition 3, it may be argued that, all other things being equal, the fewer the crisis actors, the less involved the major powers, the fewer the issues, and the less violent a crisis, the shorter it is likely to be.

Impact As noted in the discussion of concepts, the consequences (or importance) of crisis unfold at two levels: first, for the relationship between adversaries beyond a crisis; and, secondly, for one or more international systems. The factors which explain the direction of crisis impact are specified in Figure V.14.6.

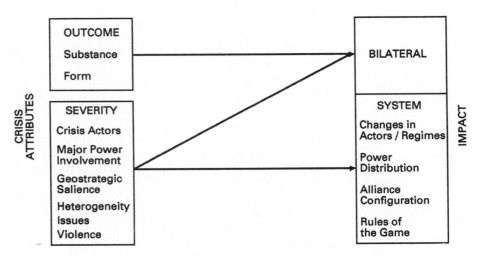

FIGURE V.14.6. Crisis Impact Model

    The *bilateral* effects of a crisis depend primarily upon the content and form of outcome; that is, who wins, who loses, or whether it ends in a draw; and whether or not it terminates through an agreement. It is expected that a disharmonious definitive outcome (victory/defeat) is more likely than an ambiguous outcome (compromise, stalemate) or a harmonious definitive outcome (victory/victory) to bequeath higher tension and instability beyond the crisis. Moreover, if a crisis terminates in agreement, the bilateral effect is more likely to be mutual satisfaction and, therefore, more stability than if a crisis is ended by a unilateral act or tacit understanding, or if it fades. In sum, a definitive outcome, formalized as an agreement, is most likely to generate less tension in subsequent interaction between adversaries.

    Bilateral effects are also shaped by the overall severity of a crisis, the composite independent variable which determines *systemic* impact. As will be recalled, severity (intensity) is measured by six indicators (actors, involvement, geostrategy, heterogeneity, issues and violence), while impact (importance), the dependent variable, is measured by four types of change (in actors/regimes, power, alliances and rules).

    The concept of severity and its impact on crises in two regions, the Middle East and Africa, were examined in Chapter 7; and the variables were operationalized above. Suffice it here to recall that severity and impact are postulated to have a cause-effect relationship and to state the reasons for the choice of severity and its components as explanatory variables to illuminate impact. In the largest sense, the rationale is that destabilizing effects during a crisis (severity) can be expected to penetrate the structure of international systems and, over time, to generate change (impact), large or small. The specific linkages will now be clarified:

Actors – the larger the number of direct participants, the more widespread will be embryonic change during a crisis; that is, more actors are likely to generate more hostile interactions, requiring more time for accommodation, leading to more dissatisfaction with a crisis outcome and, therefore, more negative "fallout" or the international system in which a crisis takes place and, possibly, others;

Major power involvement – their confrontation as crisis actors indicates more intense disruption and incipient structural change than any other type of involvement in a crisis; similarly, direct or semi-military intervention or covert activity is more destabilizing than political or economic involvement; thus more active support by major powers for a client or ally engaged in a crisis, or stronger opposition to its adversary, makes crisis accommodation more complex and termination more difficult, thereby enlarging the crisis legacy of unresolved issues and intra-system tension;

Geostrategic salience – a broader salience indicates more incipient structural change during a crisis; specifically, the more proximate a crisis to major power centers, such as central Europe during most of the twentieth century, and intense conflict zones, such as the Arab/Israel Near East core since 1948, the greater will be the spillover to non-crisis major powers and the more destabilizing will the crisis be for the dominant system, as well as the system in which it occurs;

Heterogeneity – the wider the divergence between adversaries, regarding military capability, economic development, political regime and culture, the more difficult it is to achieve accommodation, leaving a larger residue of unresolved issues, and thus extending the negative impact of a crisis outcome;

Issues – more issues in dispute complicate the process of crisis accommodation, make it less likely that all will be resolved, with destabilizing consequences for the system in which a crisis occurs, as well as for the adversaries; and

Violence – more intense violence leads to more mistrust, more dissatisfaction, and higher post-crisis tension within the system.

This discussion of systemic impact may now be framed as

> **Proposition 4: The impact of an international crisis for one or more international systems, measured in terms of change in actors/regimes, power, alliances and rules, is likely to be greater when a crisis is characterized by:**
> a) **a large number of actors;**
> b) **military or semi-military activity by the major powers;**
> c) **geostrategic salience to the dominant system and/or major power centers;**
> d) **cleavages among adversaries on several attributes;**
> e) **multiple issues in dispute; and**
> f) **intense violence.**

Thus far this approach to theory construction has focused on *intra*-phase models of crisis, in an attempt to explain onset, escalation, deescalation and impact. However, these four domains of crisis were linked in an *inter*-phase path model, in Figure V.14.2. Through the inter-phase model one can answer the crucial question: what combination of structure, crisis and actor attributes leads to system transformation (e.g., Entry into World War II 1939) or lesser consequences: system stabilization (e.g., Cuban Missiles 1962); substantial system change (e.g., Six Day War 1967), or minor change (e.g., Bizerta 1958)? In that context, the next propositoin can be deduced from this model:

> **Proposition 5: The more extreme a catalyst, the more intense the violence in crisis management, the longer its duration, and the less formal the outcome of a crisis, the more likely will the legacy be far-reaching.**

The rationale for these expectations will now be presented:

Trigger – a hostile physical act is generally more threatening than a verbal act, and a scale of intensity is clearly evident among the former, from non-military pressure through non-violent military to indirect military to military triggers to crisis; the more extreme a catalyst, the more mistrustful will the target be of the triggering entity, even after the termination of a specific crisis;

Crisis management technique – violent behavior generates more fear and mistrust than does negotiation, mediation or other pacific CMTs; and more intense violence – full-scale war – creates more hostility for a longer period than does minor clashes; and when the adversaries resort to war, the ensuing legacy beyond a crisis will be higher tension;

Duration – the longer a crisis lasts, the deeper will be mutual hostility between adversaries and mistrust of each other's intentions; and, if a lengthy crisis is also characterized by intense violence, in the trigger, in crisis management or both, the adverse effect will be even more profound;

Form of outcome – if a crisis ends through a mutually-accepted formal agreement, its legacy will be one of greater trust than crisis termination through a unilateral act, usually hostile, such as invasion, military defeat, occupation, etc.; similarly, a tacit understanding will generate less trust than a semi-formal agreement, and the latter less good faith than a formal agreement.

Aggregate ICB data to test this hypothesis are available for each international crisis from 1929 to 1985, in terms of: a) its legacy of escalation or reduction of tension between the adversaries; and b) the importance of a crisis, measured by changes in actors/regimes, power distribution, alliance configuration, and rules of the game.

Model 2: Foreign Policy Crisis

The path model of international crisis and its phase models (Model 1) indicate direct linkages between attributes (inputs or independent variables), on the one hand, and on the other, crisis onset, escalation, deescalation and impact (outputs or dependent variables). However, system, actor and crisis attributes do not *cause* the eruption, peak distortion, accommodation or legacy of a crisis. Each of these phases of the crisis process is the product of decisions and actions by states, and they, in turn, are the result of perceptions of relevant attributes by the foreign policy decision-makers of crisis actors. Stated differently, Model 1, like all macro models, treats actor-level phenomena as irrelevant givens, a "black box" which need not be explored in order to illuminate system-level phenomena, such as conflict, crisis and war.

As a first approximation to reality, such models are valuable, in fact, necessary, for they specify the salient inputs and outputs of the process to be explained. But they are incomplete analytical expressions of reality, for they ignore a crucial intervening role, namely, the "black box" of images and behavior by the participants. For example, crisis initiation is a function of a decision by state A to trigger a crisis for B, and possibly others; and that decision results from perceptions of salient attributes by A's decision-makers. They may view diffuse authority within an international system as an opportunity to achieve goals by triggering a crisis. A protracted conflict, sometimes reinforced by other sources of uncertainty, often generates an image that one's adversary of long-standing will initiate a crisis, with a consequent calculus that preemption is desirable. In short, opportunity or threat perceptions or both are likely to lead to a decision to trigger a foreign policy crisis for a state.

That trigger, whether a verbal statement or a military, political or economic act, generates a perception of threat among the decision-makers of state B and, possibly, C, D, . . . , and, in so doing, causes the onset of an international crisis. The target state may comply with A's demand or action, leading to abrupt crisis termination, with A's victory and its adversary's defeat. More often, B will respond with one or more hostile acts, leading to more conflictive interaction between the crisis adversaries, with the onset phase evolving through a spiral process to higher levels of distortion. In short, the macro model of international crisis must be complemented by a micro model of foreign policy crisis.

A model of state behavior in crisis (Model 2) is based upon three assumptions: 1) every foreign policy crisis can be dissected systematically through time in terms of a foreign policy system; 2) there are universal categories to classify relevant data; and 3) comparable findings can be used to assess the utility of a model, as well as to generate hypotheses about the crisis behavior of different types of states.

Model 2 is presented in Figure V.14.7. As evident, it postulates causal links among its variables and a time sequence. The triggering event, act or environmental change

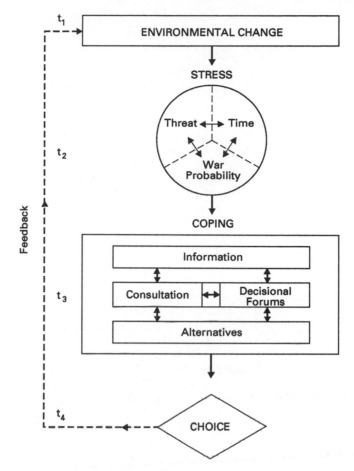

FIGURE V.14.7. Model of State Behavior in Crisis

occurs at time t_1. This is the prerequisite for a foreign policy crisis; that is, it necessarily precedes – and stimulates changes in – decision-makers' perceptions of threat and, later, of time pressure and high war likelihood as well. Perceptions of crisis, the composite independent variable, are generated – and often expressed – at time t_2. Decision-makers respond to threatening developments by adopting one or more coping strategies.[8] Whichever is selected, coping occurs within the time frame t_3. Changes in perceptions of crisis affect not only coping mechanisms; they also influence the content of decisions.

In terms of this micro-level path model, perceptions of crisis-induced stress (independent variable) at t_2 are mediated through coping (intervening variable at t_3 and shape decisions (dependent variable) at t_4. The direct link to choice is from the decisional forum, which selects one option after evaluation of alternatives in accordance with a set of decision rules.[9]

The interrelations among the three independent variables of Model 2, which were specified earlier in this chapter, may now be elaborated. *Threat* "refers to the anticipation of harm of some kind" and "concerns harms or losses that have not yet taken place but are anticipated" (Lazarus, 1968: p.340; Lazarus and Folkman, 1984: p.32). Threat perception may be active or passive, strong or weak, and central or peripheral to one's values.

Time pressure is closely related to uncertainty. Decision-makers may be uncertain, for example, about their adversaries' intentions and capabilities or the scope of information to be processed. Time pressure refers to the gap between available time and the deadline of choice; that is, crisis time cannot be equated with clock time; it depends on available time in relation to time pressure for decision (Robinson, 1972: pp.24–25). And when decision-makers are uncertain, the pressure of time is likely to be greater.

The *probability of war*, more precisely, of involvement in military hostilities, too, is related to uncertainty. If war is perceived to be certain or as certain not to occur, the situational change which generates that image is the source of something other than a crisis: there must be some uncertainty about involvement in war. A sharp change in perceived war likelihood, as noted (Chapter 1), for example, from 10% to 30%, may be just as, or more, salient to crisis perceptions of high probability, that is, over 50%, especially if that is the norm, as so often in a protracted conflict. Moreover, in the post-World War II context, the saliency of changes in war likelihood may also be a function of whether decision-makers are confronted with nuclear as opposed to conventional war. Whatever the context, it is uncertainty about war, value threat and time pressure that makes a situation a foreign policy crisis and leads to crisis-type decision-making.

The three independent variables of Model 2 are logically separate: threat refers to values, time to temporal constraint, and war to means of goal attainment. However, one expects to find interrelations among the three perceptual components of crisis. It may be argued that the more active and stronger the threat and the more central the value(s) threatened, the higher will be the perceived probability that military hostilities will ensue. That, in turn, would lead to a more intense perception of crisis. Similarly, the more active, the stronger, and the more central (basic) the threatened value(s), the more limited will be the perceived time for response. Moreover, the greater the time pressure, the higher will be the perceived probability of war, and the more intense the perception of threat. The reverse relationship also obtains: the higher the perceived probability of war, the more central, active and strong will be the perceived value threat, and the more limited will be the time perceived to be available for response to that threat.

Two of these linkages, between environmental change and threat, and between threat and time, were summarized by Lazarus (1968: pp. 340, 343): "The immediate stimulus configuration resulting in threat merely heralds the coming of harm. Threat is thus a purely psychological concept, an interpretation of the situation by the individual. . . . Another, less emphasized factor in the stimulus configuration is the imminence of the confrontation with harm. Threat is more intense when harm is more imminent."

The general postulate is that the three perceptual components of a foreign policy crisis are mutually-interacting. Moreover, as the cognitive reaction to the environmental stimulus, they induce a feeling of psychological *stress* which is "a generic term to designate unpleasant emotional states evoked by a threatening stimulus situation . . . " (Janis and Mann, 1977: p. 50). Stress has also been defined as "a particular relationship between the person and the environment that is appraised by the person as taxing or exceeding his or her resources and endangering his or her well-being" (Lazarus and Folkman, 1984: p.19). These definitions are no less applicable to decision-makers faced with foreign policy crises than to individuals in private life.

The same applies to *coping*, a process of "constantly changing cognitive and behavioral efforts to manage specific external and/or internal demands that are appraised as taxing or exceeding the resources of the person" (Lazarus and Folkman, 1984: p.141). The first reactive (coping) step by decision-makers is to seek information about the threatening event(s) or act(s): threat-induced stress generates a felt need for information and a consequent quest. The probe may be through ordinary or special channels. It will be marginal, modest or thorough, depending on the level of stress. The information may be received with an open mind or through a lens biased by ideology, memories of past experience or other factors; and it will be processed by n persons in small, medium or large groups. The kind of receptivity and size of the absorbing group, too, will vary with the level of stress. As indicated in Figure V.14.7., changes in crisis-induced stress at t_2 cause changes in information-processing at t_3.

The initial acquisition of information leads to a process of consultation – with peer members of the high-policy élite, bureaucratic and military subordinates, and possibly others from competing élites and interest groups. Consultation, as noted, may be frequent or infrequent, *ad hoc* or institutional in form, within a large or small circle, comprising one or more groups and n persons. Coping requires, too, the activation of a decisional forum which varies in size and structure. As with the other aspects of information processing, changes in the intensity of crisis-induced stress will have effects on the pattern of consultation and on the size, type and authority pattern of the decisional unit, as well as on the search for and evaluation of alternatives. Once more, the model specifies a causal link between perceptions of crisis at t_2 and the processing of alternatives at t_3. Finally, the model posits that different patterns of choice will be associated with different levels of stress.

Figure V.14.7. specifies a model of state behavior in a foreign policy crisis as a whole. However, several, perhaps many, choices will be made during a crisis. Moreover, stress changes, beginning with a more intense-than-normal perception of threat on the part of decision-makers and ending with a reduction toward normal perceptions of threat, time pressure and war likelihood. Thus a three-stage model of crisis behavior was designed to specify the changes that take place during a crisis, from its inception, with low stress (pre-crisis period), through rising, higher and peak phases of stress (crisis period), to a moderating, declining phase (post-crisis period).

The three-stage model, presented in Figure V.14.8., follows the integrated micro model in its central postulates: first, a time sequence from the trigger event, act or change (t_1) to perceived threat (t_2 – and later, to time pressure and war likelihood), to coping (t_3), to choice (t_4), with feedback to the environment; and second, a causal link from crisis-induced stress, mediated through coping, to choice, or decision. The three-stage model, however, goes further in trying to incorporate the pivotal concept of periods within a crisis, each with explicit indicators as noted above. Thus, whereas Figure V.14.7. presents behavior in a crisis as a total, integral phenomenon, Figure V.14.8. monitors change from the beginning to the end of a crisis through each period.

Viewed in this frame, the sequence from trigger to choice is replicated three times: t_1-t_4 in the pre-crisis period, t_5-t_8 in the crisis period; and t_9-t_{12} in the post-crisis period. Among the independent variables, perceived threat alone is present in the pre-crisis period, as indicated. Stress will therefore be at its lowest level, with minimal effects on coping mechanisms and choice. Their implementation will generate feedback to the environment. As long as this does not induce a sharp increase in threat, the flow from trigger to choice will be repeated. The essentially unchanged – and low – level of crisis-induced stress will lead to n decisions by a state during the pre-crisis period. It is only when feedback from decisions to the environment or some other situational change (or both) trigger a sharp rise in threat and, with it, an awareness of time pressure and the likelihood of war that the onset of the crisis period can be identified.

As evident in Figure V.14.8., threat perception in the crisis period is conspicuously

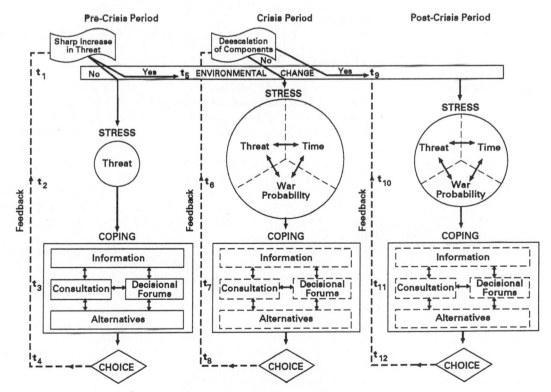

FIGURE **V.14.8.** Three-Stage Model of Crisis Behavior

larger than in the pre-crisis period. Moreover, time and the probability of war become salient. Therefore, crisis-induced stress escalates, with consequences for both coping and choice. As long as the perceived crisis components do not reveal declining intensity, the flow from t_5 to t_8 will be replicated within a crisis period encompassing rising, higher and peak crisis phases. Just as the model predicts a distinctive pattern of choice in the low-stress, pre-crisis period, so too it posits different choice patterns in the higher stress phases of the crisis period.

When a situational change or feedback from one or more choices triggers a decline in intensity among the perceptual components of crisis, another threshold has occurred, namely, a transition from crisis period to post-crisis period. As indicated, stress will lessen and that, in turn, will affect coping and choice in forms and extent hypothesized as different from those in the crisis and pre-crisis periods. In short, the model predicts at least three patterns of choice. Ultimately, a decision or cluster of choices in the post-crisis period will lead to a situational change which is perceived as no more threatening, time constraining, or likely to confront a state with war than events or acts in non-crisis periods. At that point, a foreign policy crisis ends.

The model of crisis behavior presented here focuses on two linkages: first, between different levels of crisis-induced stress and coping mechanisms; and, second, between stress and choice. The central question which the model seeks to answer is as follows: what are the effects of changing stress, derived from changes in perceptions of threat, time pressure and war likelihood, on the mechanisms through which decision-makers cope with crisis and on their choices? Following the model, case studies of crisis behavior address clusters of specific questions concerning the two linkages.

Nine questions focus on the effects of escalating and deescalating stress on coping: for example, on the perceived need and consequent quest for information; on the type and size of consultative units; on the size and structure of decisional forums; and on the search for and evaluation of alternatives. Similarly, a set of questions relating to the stress-choice linkage is explored: the core inputs into each decision problem; the perceived cost of the selected option, and the gravity of the choice; its complexity, in terms of the breadth of issue-areas involved; its systemic domain, that is, the perceived scope of reverberations across systems, domestic and external; the procedure of choice; the type of activity called for, and whether or not the decision is novel.[10]

This model and these research questions guided a series of in-depth case studies, which reported the findings about stress, coping and choice.[11] Unlike the hypotheses deduced from the macro-level model on international crisis (Model 1), it was the findings derived from the operationalization of Model 2 which led to the generation of more than 30 new hypotheses about state behavior in crises.[12]

Model 3: Crisis

Earlier it was argued that Model 1 is necessary but insufficient for a comprehensive analysis of crisis. This applies as well to Model 2. Opening the "black box" of images and decisions can illuminate how states perceive, cope and choose under crisis-induced stress. There is an added potential policy benefit, namely, contributing to more creative crisis management in the future. However, the theoretical value of micro analysis, like the macro model, is limited, for crisis encompasses much more than the behavior of a single state in a foreign policy crisis. The logical conclusion – and the critical task – is to integrate the two models in order to capture the insights provided by each and to simulate more accurately the complex reality of crises in world politics. Such a holistic model is the indispensable foundation for a theory of crisis.

Model 3, presented in Figure V.14.9., flows logically from the macro- and micro-level models delineated earlier. It recognizes that:
1) the concepts of international and foreign policy crisis denote dynamic processes over time, with separate phases – onset (pre-crisis), escalation (crisis), and deescalation (post-crisis);
2) the distinguishing trait of each phase – incipient distortion (low stress), peak distortion (high stress), and accommodation (normalization), or declining distortion (declining stress) can be explained by a set of factors – system, actor and crisis attributes for the macro phases, decision-makers' perceptions of threat, time pressure and war likelihood for the micro phases;
3) the two levels of crisis are analytically distinct but necessarily interrelated processes, each helping to explain the other, and both integral parts of a larger unified whole;

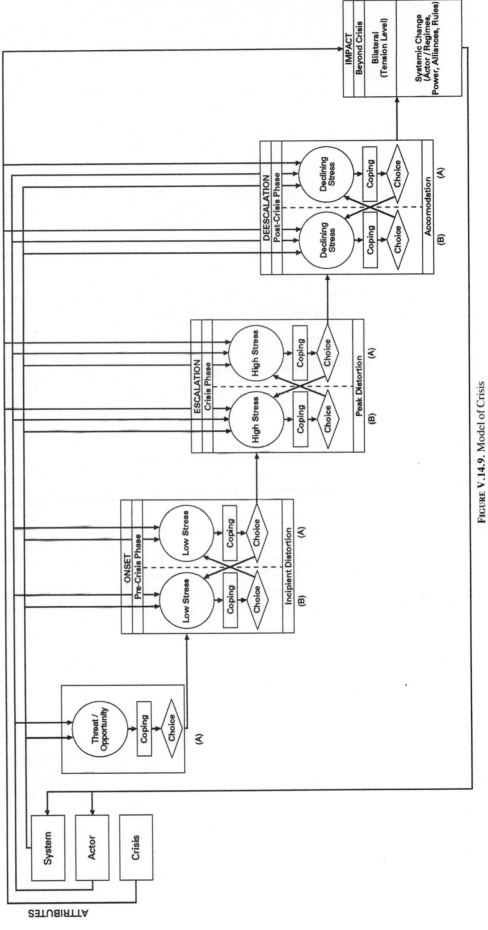

FIGURE V.14.9. Model of Crisis

4) Models 1 and 2 capture parts of a multi-layered reality, through the linkages between independent and dependent variables;

5) an explanation of cause-effect relationships in an international crisis requires the addition of an intervening variable, the "black box" of images and behavior by the crisis actors, for eruption, distortion and accommodation can only occur as a result of choices made by their decision-makers; and that

6) a synthesis of the two models sacrifices parsimony to achieve comprehensive explanatory power for the phenomenon of crisis in world politics.

Model 3 will not be elaborated at length, for it is a formal integration of Models 1 and 2, which have been discussed extensively in this chapter. Suffice it to "read" Figure V.14.9., that is, to translate the graphic skeleton into words. Perhaps the most important point to observe is that Model 3 incorporates the "black box" of actor perceptions, coping and behavior as the intervening variable in each of the first three phases of an international crisis – onset, escalation, deescalation. Impact, the fourth phase, is modelled as the product of two clusters of crisis attributes, namely, outcome, to explain the bilateral effects, and severity, to explain the systemic and, in part, the bilateral legacy.

The eruption of an international crisis and, with it, the onset phase, is postulated to be the product of several system and actor attributes, as these are filtered through the perceptual lens of the decision-makers of state A. Whether viewed as an opportunity to achieve a goal or as a response to an image or more-than-normal value threat, A copes with the situational change, decides and acts, thereby triggering a crisis for state B. With that input of higher-than-normal conflictive interaction, the onset phase is set in motion. The adversaries may make and implement several decisions without altering the initially low level of distortion and crisis-induced stress. During that phase, however, a new constellation of system and actor attributes, strengthened by some traits of the crisis itself, generate for at least one of the adversaries an image of more acute value threat, along with the perception of time pressure and the likelihood of involvement in military hostilities before the disruptive challenge is overcome. A response by that actor, following its attempt to cope with the new situation, leads to escalation of conflictive interaction with its adversary.

The escalation phase, too, continues until still another cluster of system, actor and crisis attributes is perceived by A or B as presaging reduced value threat, time pressure and war likelihood. If it decides and acts so as to lessen the intensity of the three perceptual components for its adversary, conflictive interaction declines, that is, the deescalation or post-crisis phase begins. Accommodation may be brief or lengthy, and there may even be escalation points within this phase. But once more, another group of system, actor and crisis attributes penetrates the psychological environment of the decision-makers, leading to crisis termination.

The process is not linear, as implied in this summary. Nevertheless, the central thrust of Model 3 is logically consistent: an international crisis is a four-phase dynamic process which unfolds through the perceptual interpretation by decision-makers of salient system, actor and crisis attributes, followed by coping, choice and behavior, which triggers a similar process for the decision-makers of state B; the phases are intertwined and follow the sequence suggested, though not always without deviations, sometimes substantial and lengthy.

Three general models (and four intra-phase models) have been presented, one for international crisis, another for state behavior in a foreign policy crisis, and a third, integrating the two levels into a holistic representation of reality. Five multi-part propositions were deduced from Model 1, and the rationale for the choice of independent variables was set forth. A larger group of hypotheses has been generated from the application of Model 2 in case studies. (These models and hypotheses will be further developed and tested in a subsequent volume on the meaning of crises in the twentieth century, using ICB aggregate data for 70 years of crises, 1918–88, as well as the findings from 30 case studies of how states perceived, coped with, and made choices in foreign policy crises since the 1930s.[13] This analysis also serves as the foundation of a scientific research program on crisis which integrates deductive theorizing with empirical investigation, both necessary elements in creating a valid theory of crisis in world politics.

Notes

1. For example, assume p = 0.1:

No. of States	2	3	4	5	6	7	8	9
No. of Days	1	3	6	10	15	21	28	36
Expected No. of Crises	0.1	0.3	0.6	1	1.5	2.1	2.8	3.6

Maoz (1987: p. 5) doubts that "these associations carry any significant theoretical implications," citing three reasons: first, increasing size "may cause increased interdependence," reducing the number of conflicts; second, it "increases the complexity of calculations" by states, reducing a tendency to initiate conflicts; and third, size and conflict may be a false correlation, concealing "a hidden process which is only partly tapped by the change in the number of states."

2. In this connection, there is a large but inconclusive literature on the notion of the addiction of states to conflict and war (though not to crisis *per se*). Those who contend that conflict or war spreads in a random manner include Richardson (1960), Singer and Small (1972), Small and Singer (1982), Levy (1983) and Levy and Morgan (1986). Others discern evidence of a contagious spread of war and lesser conflicts: Davis *et al.* (1978), Most and Starr (1980), Bremer (1982), Gochman and Maoz (1984). See also Beer (1981).

3. There is a continuing controversy, too, over the relationship between power discrepancy and *war*-proneness. For summaries of this debate, see Bueno de Mesquita (1980), Singer (1981) and Vasquez (1987).

4. On territorial proximity and *war*-proneness, see Most and Starr (1980), and Siverson and Tennefoss (1984).

5. The most extreme formulation of this hypothesis, applied to *war* initiation and involvement, is found in Rummel (1975–81, 1983, 1985). After extensive multiple tests with war data, Maoz and Abdolali (1989: p. 31) concluded: ". . . the answer to the question of whether democracies are more or less conflict prone than non-democratic regimes depends on which level of analysis one examines, what period is covered . . . and – to a lesser extent – on how regime types and conflict involvement are measured. The results . . . are generally mixed."

6. Other attributes can be postulated as likely to contribute to the escalation of an international crisis. For example, *number of actors* could be included, for more actors generate more hostile interactions, with a consequent greater likelihood of violence, escalating to war. So too with *major power activity*: intense support by the powers for clients engaged in a crisis is likely to generate escalation to war. It can also be argued that the more divergent the adversaries regarding level of economic development, type of political system, and culture, the more complex will be the process of deescalation; in fact, this point about *heterogeneity* is alluded to in the discussion of impact below. There may also be a link between the *geostrategic salience* of a crisis and the processes of escalation and deescalation, though its relevance would seem to be greatest for the "fallout" of a crisis for the relations between the adversaries and/or the system or subsystem of which they are members. Thus heterogeneity and geostrategic salience are incorporated into the crisis impact model but not elsewhere.

   The crucial criterion for the choice of independent variables in all the crisis models presented here is the tradeoff between parsimony and maximal explanatory power. Thus we specify only those variables which, *a priori*, seem to be the most salient *sufficient conditions* for the outbreak, escalation, deescalation, and impact of a crisis.

7. A few fade or merge into other crises, usually between the same adversaries (e.g., the Indonesia/Netherlands crisis over West Irian in 1957, merging into a second crisis over that disputed territory four years later).

8. Among these the most likely are:
   a) a "satisficing" rather than an "optimizing" decision strategy;
   b) the strategy of incrementalism;
   c) deciding what to do on the basis of "consensus politics";
   d) avoidance of value tradeoffs;
   e) use of historical models to diagnose and prescribe for the present;
   f) reliance on ideology and general principles as a guide to action; and
   g) reliance on "operational code" beliefs (Holsti and George, 1975: p. 264).

9. On the link between coping and choice, a pioneer definition by Snyder *et al.* (1962: p. 90) remains apt: "Decision-making is a process which results in the selection from a . . . limited number of . . . alternative (options) of one . . . intended to bring about the particular future state of affairs envisaged by the decision-makers."

10. A more elaborate version of Model 2 and the research questions may be found in Brecher (1979).

11. Brecher with Geist (1980); A. I. Dawisha (1980); Shlaim (1983); Dowty (1984); K. Dawisha (1984); Jukes (1985); Hoffmann (forthcoming); Anglin (forthcoming); and Geist (forthcoming).

12. The new hypotheses are elaborated in Brecher with Geist, *op cit.*, and Dowty, *op cit.* ICB scholars (see n. 11) tested these hypotheses and others which had accumulated in the literature (Paige, 1968; Hermann, 1972).

13. Two illustrations of the scope of evidence available for testing these models and hypotheses may be noted.

   Our aggregate data on the extent of violence during an international crisis range from no violence, through minor clashes, serious clashes, to full-scale war for all cases. Thus one can generate dichotomous distributions for protracted/non-protracted conflict, violent/non-violent trigger, one/several issue(s), basic/non-basic values, small/large power discrepancy, and domestic stability/instability to see whether there is a clear configuration of "more likely to lead to war" cases, as postulated in Proposition 2. Similarly, every international crisis has been coded for conflict environment, as well as for the number of crisis actors, combined involvement by the major powers, primary crisis management technique, relative power, and political regime. And the ICB Project has amassed summaries of each crisis, including the deescalation phase. These qualitative findings, including the in-depth case studies already noted, supplement our aggregate data with the human dimension of crisis behavior. In short, we can uncover the extent of support for each sub-hypothesis on deescalation and for Proposition 3 as a whole.

Appendix A

Code for Appendix A

Crisis actor = a sovereign state whose decision-maker(s) perceive(s) a high threat to one or more basic values, finite time for response to the value threat, and a high probability of involvement in military hostilities; all three perceptions derive from a change in the state's external or internal environment.

Duration = the elapsed time in days between the first breakpoint (the date on which the earliest crisis actor perceived threat, time pressure and war likelihood) and the last exitpoint (the date on which the last actor perceived crisis termination).

Triggering entity = the state(s) or non-state actor which triggered the crisis.

Triggering act = the specific event or situational change which catalyzed the three crisis perceptions noted above:

Political (verbal) act – protests, threats, accusations, demands, etc.

Political act – subversion, alliance of adversaries, diplomatic sanctions, severance of diplomatic relations, violation of treaties, etc.

Economic act – embargo, dumping, nationalization of property, withholding of economic aid, etc.

External change – intelligence reports, change in specific weapon, weapon system, offensive capability, change in global system or regional subsystem, challenge to legitimacy by international organization, etc.

Other non-violent

Internal verbal or physical challenge to regime or élite – incitement by media, proclamation of new regime, fall of government, *coup d'état*, sabotage act, terrorism, assassination, riot, demonstration, strike, arrest, martial law, execution, mutiny, revolt.

Non-violent military – show of force, war games or maneuvers, mobilization, movement of forces, change of force posture to offensive.

Indirect violent act – revolt in another country, violent act directed at ally, friendly state, or client state.

Violent act – border clash, border crossing by limited forces, invasion of air space, sinking of ship, sea-air incident, bombing of large target, large-scale military attack, war.

Highest value threat = the gravest threat perceived by the decision-maker(s) of any of the crisis actors during the course of an international crisis.

Low threat – limited threat to population and property, threat to the social system such as forced emigration, change of ethnic equilibrium, challenge to legitimacy of belief system, threat to economic interest such as control of another actor's economy, requisition of resources, loss of markets, blocked access to resources or markets.

Threat to political system – threat of overthrow of regime, change of institutions, replacement of élite, intervention in domestic politics, subversion.

Threat to territorial integrity – threat of integration, annexation of part of a state's territory, separatism.

Threat to influence in the international system or regional subsystem – threat of declining power in the global system and/or regional subsystem, diplomatic isolation, cessation of patron aid.

Threat of grave damage – threat of large casualties in war, mass bombings.

Threat to existence – threat to survival of population, genocide, threat to existence of entity, of total annexation, colonial rule, occupation.

Intensity of violence = the intensity of hostile physical interaction in the crisis as a whole.

No violence.

Minor clashes involving few or no deaths or injuries.

Serious clashes short of full-scale war.

Full-scale war.

Superpower activity = any substantive verbal or physical activity during an international crisis by the US and/or the USSR.

No activity.

Political – statements of approval or disapproval by authorized government officials.

Economic – financial aid, or the withholding of aid from an actor, etc.

Covert – support for anti-government forces, etc.

Semi-military – military aid or advisors, without participation in actual fighting.

Direct military – dispatch of troops, aerial bombing of targets or naval assistance to a party in a war.

Global organization involvement = the substance of activity by the United Nations during the course of an international crisis.

General.

Discussion without resolution.

Fact-finding.

Good offices – minimal involvement in both the content and the process of resolving the dispute.

Condemnation – includes implied or explicit demand to desist, request for member aid to victim of hostile activity.

Call for action by adversaries – includes call for cease-fire, withdrawal, negotiation, member action to facilitate termination.

Mediation – includes proposing a solution, offering advice, and conciliation of differences.

Arbitration – formal binding settlement by arbitral body.

Sanctions.
Observers.
Emergency military force.

Form of outcome = the form in which an international crisis ends.

Agreement – treaty, cease-fire, semi-formal agreement including letter, oral declaration.
Tacit – mutual understanding by adversaries, neither stated nor written.
Unilateral act.
Other/no agreement – crisis fades with no known termination date and no known agreement among the adversaries.

The numbers within brackets and the numbers beside each state are internal ICB code numbers. The former refer to the international crisis, the latter to the crisis actors.

APPENDIX A. List of International Crises 1979–85, with Select Attributes

Case and crisis actors	Duration	Triggering entity	Triggering act	Highest value threat	Intensity of violence	Superpower activity USA	Superpower activity USSR	Global organization involvement	Form of outcome
269									
(2666) Tan Tan	28/01/79–00/03/79	Non-state actor	Violent	Territory	Serious clashes	None	None	None	No agreement
9337 Morocco	28/01/79–00/03/79								
270									
(2729) Raids on ZIPRA	12/02/79–31/05/79	Zambia	Violent	Low threat	Serious clashes	None	None	Condemnation	Unilateral
9427 Rhodesia	12/02/79–31/05/79								
9426 Angola	26/02/79–10/05/79								
9425 Zambia	13/04/79–12/05/79								
271									
(2600) North/South Yemen II	24/02/79–30/03/79	North and South Yemen	Violent	Territory	War	Semi-military	Semi-military	None	Agreement
9270 North Yemen	24/02/79–30/03/79								
9265 South Yemen	24/02/79–30/03/79								
272									
(2730) Raids on SWAPO	06/03/79–28/03/79	South Africa	Violent	Low threat	Minor clashes	None	None	Condemnation	No agreement
9430 Angola	06/03/79–28/03/79								
273									
(2900) Afghanistan Invasion	15/03/79–28/02/80	Non-state actor	Violent	Influence	Serious clashes	Semi-military	Military	Condemnation	No agreement
9401 USSR	15/03/79–27/12/79								
9400 Afghanistan	15/07/79–25/12/79								
9402 Pakistan	24/12/79–02/02/80								
9403 USA	24/12/79–28/02/80								
274									
(2731) Chad/Libya IV	12/04/79–10/11/79	Chad	Political	Influence	War	None	None	General	Unilateral
9373 Libya	12/04/79–10/11/79								
9375 Chad	25/06/79–10/11/79								
9376 France	25/06/79–10/11/79								
275									
(2725) Goulimime-Tarfaya Road	01/06/79–25/06/79	Non-state actor	Violent	Territory	Serious clashes	None	None	Discussion	Unilateral
9371 Morocco	01/06/79–25/06/79								
9372 Algeria	06/06/79–25/06/79								
276									
(2726) Soviet Threat to Pakistan	01/06/79–03/07/79	USSR	Political (Verbal)	Low threat	No violence	Political	Political	None	Agreement
9374 Pakistan	01/06/79–03/07/79								
277									
(2780) Rhodesian Settlement	15/07/79–04/03/80	Internal Rhodesia	Internal challenge	Political regime	Serious clashes	Political	Semi-military	Condemnation	Agreement
9436 Rhodesia	15/07/79–04/03/80								
9437 Botswana	08/08/79–21/12/79								
9438 Mozambique	05/09/79–21/12/79								
9435 Zambia	17/11/79–31/01/80								
278									
(2735) Raid on Angola	28/10/79–02/11/79	South Africa	Violent	Low threat	Minor clashes	None	None	Condemnation	Tacit
9380 Angola	28/10/79–02/11/79								

Case and crisis actors	Duration	Triggering entity	Triggering act	Highest value threat	Intensity of violence	Superpower activity USA	USSR	Global organization involvement	Form of outcome
279 (2860) US Hostages in Iran	04/11/79–20/01/81	Iran	Political	Political regime	Minor clashes	Military	Political	Call for action	Agreement
9335 USA	04/11/79–20/01/81								
9340 Iran	24/04/80–20/01/81								
280 (2910) Nicaragua/ Colombia	12/12/79–08/07/81	Nicaragua	Political (Verbal)	Territory	No Violence	Political	None	Good offices	Unilateral
9410 Colombia	12/12/79–08/07/81								
281 (2920) Raid on Gafsa	27/01/80–00/04/80	Internal Tunisia	Internal challenge	Influence	Serious clashes	Semi-military	None	None	Unilateral
9460 Tunisia	27/01/80–00/04/80								
9461 Libya	28/01/80–27/02/80								
282 (2925) Operation Iman	01/03/80–09/05/80	Non-state actor	Violent	Territory	Serious clashes	None	None	None	Unilateral
9465 Morocco	01/03/80–09/05/80								
283 (2930) Operation Smokeshell	07/06/80–02/07/80	South Africa	Violent	Territory	Serious clashes	None	None	Condemnation	Unilateral
9470 Angola	07/06/80–02/07/80								
284 (2940) Libyan Threat-Sadat	11/06/80–	Libya	Political (Verbal)	Grave damage	No violence	None	None	General	No agreement
9475 Egypt	11/06/80–								
9476 Libya	16/06/80–								
285 (2950) Malta/Libya Oil Dispute	20/08/80–15/09/80	Libya	Non-violent military	Low threat	No violence	None	None	Discussion	Unilateral
9480 Malta	20/08/80–15/09/80								
286 (2960) Onset Iran/Iraq War	17/09/80–00/11/80	Iraq	Political (Verbal)	Territory	Full-scale war	Political	Semi-military	Mediation	No agreement
9486 Iran	17/09/80–00/11/80								
287 (2970) Libyan Intervention/Gambia	27/10/80–07/11/80	Internal Gambia	Internal challenge	Political	No violence	None	None	None	Unilateral
9490 Gambia	27/10/80–07/11/80								
288 (2990) Jordan/Syria Confrontation	25/11/80–14/12/80	Syria	Non-violent military	Territory	No violence	Semi-military	Political	None	Unilateral
9497 Jordan	25/11/80–14/12/80								
289 (2995) East Africa Confrontation	05/12/80–29/06/81	Ethiopia and Kenya	Political	Territory	Minor clashes	None	None	None	Agreement
9498 Somalia	05/12/80–29/06/81								
290 (3000) Chad/Libya V: Merger	06/01/81–16/11/81	Libya	Political	Political	No violence	Political	None	General	Unilateral
9500 France	06/01/81–16/11/81								
291 (3010) Peru/Ecuador	22/01/81–02/02/81	Ecuador	Violent	Territory	Minor clashes	Political	None	None	Agreement
9504 Peru	22/01/81–02/02/81								
9505 Ecuador	22/01/81–02/02/81								
292 (3020) Mozambique Raid	30/01/81–00/03/81	South Africa	Violent	Territory	Minor clashes	None	Semi-military	General	No agreement
9510 Mozambique	30/01/81–00/03/81								
293 (3035) Essequibo II	04/04/81–00/03/83	Venezuela	Political (Verbal)	Territory	No violence	None	None	Mediation	No agreement
9513 Guyana	04/04/81–00/03/83								
294 (3040) Biqa Missiles	28/04/81–24/07/81	Israel	Violent	Influence	Minor clashes	Political	Political	None	Tacit
9516 Syria	28/04/81–24/07/81								
9517 Israel	29/04/81–24/07/81								

APPENDIX A. – *continued*

Case and crisis actors		Duration	Triggering entity	Triggering act	Highest value threat	Intensity of violence	Superpower activity USA	USSR	Global organization involvement	Form of outcome
295 (3050)	Nigeria/Cameroon Border	16/05/81–24/07/81	Cameroon	Violent	Influence	Minor clashes	None	None	None	Agreement
9520	Nigeria	16/05/81–24/07/81								
9521	Cameroon	17/05/81–24/07/81								
296 (3060)	Iraqi Nuclear Reactor	08/06/81–19/06/81	Israel	Violent	Influence	Minor clashes	Economic	Political	Condemnation	Unilateral
9524	Iraq	08/06/81–19/06/81								
297 (3070)	Coup Attempt-Gambia	30/07/81–31/01/82	Gambia	Indirect violent	Influence	Serious clashes	Political	None	None	Agreement
9527	Senegal	30/07/81–31/01/82								
298 (3080)	Gulf of Syrte	12/08/81–01/09/81	USA	Political (Verbal)	Territory	Minor clashes	Military	None	None	Unilateral
9529	Libya	12/08/81–01/09/81								
299 (3090)	Operation Protea-Angola	23/08/81–30/09/81	South Africa	Violent	Territory	Serious clashes	Political	Political	Discussion	Unilateral
9532	Angola	23/08/81–30/09/81								
300 (3095)	Polisario Attack	13/10/81–09/11/81	Non-state actor	Violent	Territory	Serious clashes	Political	Political	None	Unilateral
9535	Morocco	13/10/81–09/11/81								
301 (3120)	Coup Attempt-Bahrain	13/12/81–08/01/82	Non-state actor	Internal challenge	Influence	No violence	None	None	None	No agreement
9546	Bahrain	13/12/81–08/01/82								
9547	Saudi Arabia	13/12/81–19/12/81								
302 (3130)	Khoramshar	22/03/82–30/07/82	Iran	Violence	Grave damage	Full-scale war	None	Semi-military	Call for action	Unilateral
9549	Iraq	22/03/82–30/07/82								
303 (3135)	Falklands/Malvinas	31/03/82–14/06/82	Argentina	Non-violent military	Territory	Full-scale war	Political	Political	Call for action	Agreement
9551	UK	31/03/82–14/06/82								
9552	Argentina	05/04/82–14/06/82								
304 (3150)	Lebanon War	05/06/82–17/05/83	Israel	Violent	Influence	Full-scale war	Political	Semi-military	Condemnation	Agreement
9554	Lebanon	05/06/82–17/05/83								
9555	Syria	07/06/82–01/09/82								
9556	Israel	09/06/82–01/09/82								
305 (3155)	Ogaden III	30/06/82–00/08/82	Ethiopia	Violent	Territory	Serious clashes	Semi-military	Political	None	No agreement
9557	Somalia	30/06/82–00/08/82								
306 (3170)	Lesotho Raid	09/12/82–15/12/82	South Africa	Violent	Territory	Minor clashes	Political	None	Condemnation	No agreement
9564	Lesotho	09/12/82–15/12/82								
307 (3180)	Libya Threat-Sudan	11/02/83–22/02/83	Libya	Non-violent military	Influence	No violence	Semi-military	None	Discussion	Unilateral
9567	Sudan	11/02/83–22/02/83								
9568	Egypt	11/02/83–22/02/83								
9569	Libya	17/02/83–22/02/83								
308 (3190)	Chad/Nigeria Clashes	18/04/83–02/07/83	Nigeria	Violent	Territory	Serious clashes	None	None	None	Agreement
9573	Chad	18/04/83–02/07/83								
9574	Nigeria	18/04/83–02/07/83								

Case and crisis actors	Duration	Triggering entity	Triggering act	Highest value threat	Intensity of violence	Superpower activity USA	Superpower activity USSR	Global organization involvement	Form of outcome
309 (3210) Chad/Libya VI	24/06/83–11/12/84	Libya	Violent	Existence	Minor clashes	Semi-military	Political	Discussion	Agreement
9580 Chad	24/06/83–10/10/84								
9581 France	31/07/83–11/12/84								
9582 Libya	09/08/83–10/11/84								
310 (3230) Invasion of Grenada	19/10/83–28/10/83	Grenada	Indirect violent	Influence	Serious clashes	Military	Political	Discussion	Unilateral
9585 USA	19/10/83–28/10/83								
9586 Grenada	22/10/83–28/10/83								
311 (3250) Botswana/ Zimbabwe Border	08/11/83–21/12/83	Zimbabwe	Violent	Low threat	Minor clashes	None	None	None	Agreement
9597 Botswana	08/11/83–21/12/83								
312 (3260) Sudan/Ethiopia Border	20/11/83–20/02/84	Ethiopia	Non-violent military	Political	Minor clashes	None	Semi-military	None	Unilateral
9599 Sudan	20/11/83–20/02/84								
313 (3270) Operation Askari	06/12/83–16/02/84	South Africa	Violent	Territory	Serious clashes	Political	Political	Condemnation	Agreement
9600 Angola	06/12/83–16/02/84								
314 (3275) Basra/Kharg Island	21/02/84–11/07/84	Iran	Violent	Grave damage	Full-scale war	Semi-military	Political	Condemnation	Agreement
9601 Iraq	21/02/84–00/03/84								
9602 Iran	01/03/84–10/06/84								
9603 Kuwait	13/05/84–11/07/84								
9604 Saudi Arabia	16/05/84–20/06/84								
315 (3280) Aegean Naval Crisis	08/03/84–09/03/84	Turkey	Violent	Low threat	Minor clashes	None	None	None	Agreement
9605 Greece	08/03/84–09/03/84								
316 (3290) Omdurman Bombing	16/03/84–	Libya	Violent	Influence	Minor clashes	Semi-military	None	Discussion	No agreement
9608 Sudan	16/03/84–								
9609 Egypt	16/03/84–								
9610 Libya	18/03/84–								
317 (3292) Thai Border Incident	25/03/84–17/04/84	Vietnam	Violent	Low threat	Minor clashes	Semi-military	None	General	No agreement
9611 Thailand	25/03/84–17/04/84								
318 (3295) Sino/Vietnam Clashes	02/04/84–00/06/84	PRC	Violent	Influence	Serious clashes	Political	Semi-military	General	Agreement
9612 Vietnam	02/04/84–00/06/84								
319 (3310) Village Border Clashes	05/06/84–00/10/84	Laos	Non-violent military	Territory	Minor clashes	None	None	Discussion	Tacit
9620 Thailand	05/06/84–17/07/84								
9621 Laos	06/06/84–00/10/84								
320 (3320) Nicaragua MIG-21s	06/11/84–12/11/84	USSR	Non-violent military	Influence	No violence	Semi-military	Semi-military	Discussion	Tacit
9625 USA	06/11/84–09/11/84								
9626 Nicaragua	07/11/84–12/11/84								
321 (3440) Botswana Raid	14/06/85–21/06/85	South Africa	Violent	Territory	Minor clashes	Political	None	Condemnation	Unilateral
9660 Botswana	14/06/85–21/06/85								
322 (3480) Expulsion/ Tunisians	21/08/85–26/09/85	Libya	Non-violent military	Political	No violence	Political	None	None	Unilateral
9680 Tunisia	21/08/85–26/09/85								
323 (3510) Burkina Faso/Mali Border	20/12/85–18/01/86	Burkina Faso	Non-violent military	Territory	Serious clashes	None	None	General	Agreement
9686 Mali	20/12/85–18/01/86								
9687 Burkina Faso	25/12/85–18/01/86								

Appendix B

Code for Appendix B

Crisis actor = a sovereign state whose decision-maker(s) perceive(s) a high threat to one or more basic values, finite time for response to the value threat, and a high probability of involvement in military hostilities; all three perceptions derive from a change in the state's external or internal environment.

Duration = for the international crisis: the elapsed time in days between the first breakpoint (the date on which the earliest crisis actor perceived threat, time pressure and war likelihood) and the last exitpoint (the date on which the last actor perceived crisis termination); for a foreign policy crisis: the elapsed time between a crisis actor's perception of a triggering act and the termination of its crisis, that is, the decline of the three perceptual foci – high threat, time pressure and war likelihood – to non-crisis norms.

Power status (system level) = the status of a crisis actor in the power hierarchy – super, great, middle, small – within the dominant or specific subordinate international system in which its foreign policy crisis occurs.

Triggering act = the specific event, act, or situational change which catalyzes the three crisis perceptions noted above.

Political (verbal) act – protests, threats, accusations, demands, etc.

Political act – subversion, alliance of adversaries, diplomatic sanctions, severance of diplomatic relations, violation of treaties, etc.

Economic act – embargo, dumping, nationalization of property, withholding of economic aid, etc.

External change – intelligence reports, change in specific weapons, weapon system, offensive capability, change in global system or regional subsystem, challenge to legitimacy by international organization, etc.

Other non-violent.

Internal verbal or physical challenge to regime or élite – incitement by media, proclamation of new regime, fall of government, *coup d'état*, sabotage act, terrorism, assassination, riot, demonstration, strike, arrest, martial law, execution, mutiny, revolt.

Non-violent military act – show of force, war games or maneuvers, mobilization, movement of forces, change of force posture to offensive.

Indirect violent act – revolt in another country, violent act directed at ally, friendly state or client state.

Violent act – border clash, border crossing by limited forces, invasion of air space, sinking of ship, sea-air incident, bombing of large target, large-scale military attack, war.

Gravity of threat = the gravest threat perceived by the decision-maker(s) of a crisis actor during the course of its foreign policy crisis.

Low threat – limited to population and property, threat to the social system such as forced emigration, change of ethnic equilibrium, challenge to legitimacy of belief system, threat to economic interest such as control of another actor's economy, requisition of resources, loss of markets, blocked access to resources or markets.

Threat to political system – threat of overthrow of regime, change of institutions, replacement of élite, intervention in domestic politics, subversion.

Threat to territorial integrity – threat of integration, annexation of part of a state's territory, separatism.

Threat to influence in the international system or regional subsystem – threat of declining power in the global system and/or regional subsystem, diplomatic isolation, cessation of patron aid.

Threat of grave damage – threat of large casualties in war, mass bombings.

Threat to existence – threat to survival of population, genocide, threat to existence of entity, of total annexation, colonial rule, occupation.

Source of threat = the state perceived by the decision-maker(s) of a crisis actor as the source of threat to its values in a crisis, usually – but not always – the entity which triggers its foreign policy crisis.

Crisis management technique = the principal technique of crisis management, as distinct from a specific act (major response), of a state actor in a foreign policy crisis.

Negotiation – formal, informal, bilateral, multilateral, international, diplomatic exchange.

Mediation – by global or regional organization, ally, or alliance personnel.

Multiple not including violence.

Non-military pressure – withholding of promised economic aid.

Military non-violent – physical acts, verbal acts

Multiple including violence.

Violence.

Intensity of violence = the intensity of violence used by a crisis actor in the management of its foreign policy crisis.

No violence.

Minor clashes involving few or no deaths or injuries.

Serious clashes short of full-scale war.

Full-scale war.

Substance of outcome = the content of a crisis outcome in terms of the achievement/non-achievement of a crisis actor's basic goal(s), in the context of a specific foreign policy crisis.

Victory – achievement of basic goal(s); the crisis actor defeated a threatening adversary by counter-threats.

Compromise – partial achievement of basic goal(s).

Stalemate – no effect on basic goal(s); no clear outcome to a crisis; no change in the situation.
Defeat – non-achievement of basic goal(s); the crisis actor yielded or surrendered when an adversary threatened basic values.

The numbers within brackets and the numbers beside each state are internal ICB code numbers. The former refer to the international crisis, the latter to the crisis actors.

APPENDIX B. List of Foreign Policy Crises 1979–85, with Select Attributes

Case and crisis actors		Duration	Power status (system level)	Trigger	Gravity of threat	Source of threat	Crisis management technique	Intensity of violence as CMT	Substance of outcome
269									
(2666)	Tan Tan	28/01/79–00/03/79	(Subsystem)						
9337	Morocco	28/01/79–00/03/79	Middle	Violent	Territory	Algeria	Mult. inc. viol.	Serious clashes	Victory
270									
(2729)	Raids on ZIPRA	12/02/79–31/05/79	(Subsystem)						
9427	Rhodesia	12/02/79–31/05/79	Middle	Violent	Limited	Zambia	Violence	Serious clashes	Stalemate
9426	Angola	26/02/79–10/05/79	Middle	Violent	Limited	Rhodesia	Non-viol. mil.	No violence	Stalemate
9425	Zambia	13/04/79–12/05/79	Small	Violent	Limited	Rhodesia	Non-viol. mil.	No violence	Stalemate
271									
(2600)	North/South Yemen II	24/02/79–30/03/79	(Subsystem)						
9270	North Yemen	24/02/79–30/03/79	Small	Violent	Territory	S. Yemen	Mult. inc. viol.	Full-scale war	Compromise
9265	South Yemen	24/02/79–30/03/79	Small	Violent	Territory	N. Yemen	Mult. inc. viol.	Full-scale war	Compromise
272									
(2730)	Raids on SWAPO	06/03/79–28/03/79	(Subsystem)						
9430	Angola	06/03/79–28/03/79	Middle	Violent	Limited	S. Africa	Negotiation	Minor clashes	Stalemate
273									
(2900)	Afghanistan Invasion	15/03/79–28/02/80	(Dominant)						
9401	USSR	15/03/79–27/12/79	Superpower	Ind. violent	Influence	USA	Violence	Serious clashes	Victory
9400	Afghanistan	15/07/79–25/12/79	Small	Pol. (verbal)	Pol. regime	USSR	Violence	Serious clashes	Defeat
9402	Pakistan	24/12/79–02/02/80	Middle	Ext. change	Pol. regime	USSR	Negotiation	No violence	Stalemate
9403	USA	24/12/79–28/02/80	Superpower	Ext. change	Influence	USSR	Mult. no viol.	No violence	Stalemate
274									
(2731)	Chad/Libya IV	12/04/79–10/11/79	(Subsystem)						
9373	Libya	12/04/79–10/11/79	Great	Political	Influence	Chad	Mult. inc. viol.	Full-scale war	Victory
9375	Chad	25/06/79–10/11/79	Small	Violent	Pol. regime	Libya	Mult. inc. viol.	Full-scale war	Compromise
9376	France	25/06/79–10/11/79	Great	Ind. violent	Influence	Libya	Violence	Full-scale war	Compromise
275									
(2725)	Goulimime-Tarfaya Road	01/06/79–25/06/79	(Subsystem)						
9371	Morocco	01/06/79–25/06/79	Middle	Violent	Territory	Algeria	Mult. inc. viol.	Serious clashes	Victory
9372	Algeria	06/06/79–25/06/79	Middle	Pol. (verbal)	Territory	Morocco	Non-viol. mil.	No violence	Victory
276									
(2726)	Soviet Threat to Pakistan	01/06/79–03/07/79	(Subsystem)						
9374		01/06/79–03/07/79	Middle	Pol. (verbal)	Limited	USSR	Negotiation	No violence	Stalemate
277									
(2780)	Rhodesian Settlement	15/07/79–04/03/80	(Subsystem)						
9436	Rhodesia	15/07/79–04/03/80	Middle	Internal chal.	Pol. regime	Mozambique	Mult. inc. viol.	Serious clashes	Defeat
9437	Botswana	08/08/79–21/12/79	Small	Violent	Limited	Rhodesia	Violence	Minor clashes	Victory
9438	Mozambique	05/09/79–21/12/79	Small	Violent	Economic	Rhodesia	Violence	Serious clashes	Victory
9435	Zambia	17/11/79–31/01/80	Small	Violent	Economic	Rhodesia	Non-viol. mil.	No violence	Victory
278									
(2735)	Raid on Angola	28/10/79–02/11/79	(Subsystem)						
9380	Angola	28/10/79–02/11/79	Middle	Violent	Limited	S. Africa	Negotiation	No violence	Stalemate
279									
(2860)	US Hostages in Iran	04/11/79–20/01/81	(Subsystem)						
9335	USA	04/11/79–20/01/81	Superpower	Political	Limited	Iran	Mult. no viol.	No violence	Compromise
9340	Iran	24/04/80–20/01/81	Middle	Violent	Pol. regime	USA	Mult. no viol.	Minor clashes	Compromise
280									
(2910)	Nicaragua/Colombia	12/12/79–08/07/81	(Subsystem)						
9410	Colombia	12/12/79–08/07/81	Middle	Pol. (verbal)	Territory	Nicaragua	Mult. no viol.	No violence	Victory
281									
(2920)	Raid on Gafsa	27/01/80–00/04/80	(Subsystem)						
9460	Tunisia	27/01/80–00/04/80	Small	Internal chal.	Pol. regime	Libya	Mult. inc. viol.	Serious clashes	Victory
9461	Libya	28/01/80–27/02/80	Middle	Non-viol. mil.	Influence	France	Non-viol. mil.	No violence	Defeat
282									
(2925)	Operation Iman	01/03/80–09/05/80	(Subsystem)						
9465	Morocco	01/03/80–09/05/80	Great	Violent	Territory	Algeria	Violence	Serious clashes	Victory

Case and crisis actors	Duration	Power status (system level)	Trigger	Gravity of threat	Source of threat	Crisis management technique	Intensity of violence as CMT	Substance of outcome
283								
(2930) Operation Smokeshell	07/06/80–02/07/80	(Subsystem)						
9470 Angola	07/06/80–02/07/80	Middle	Violent	Territory	S. Africa	Mult. inc. viol.	Serious clashes	Stalemate
284								
(2940) Libyan Threat-Sadat	11/06/80–	(Subsystem)						
9475 Egypt	11/06/80–	Great	Pol. (verbal)	Pol. regime	Libya	Non-viol. mil.	No violence	Victory
9476 Libya	16/06/80–	Middle	Non-viol. mil	Grave damage	Egypt	Mult. no viol.	No violence	Stalemate
285								
(2950) Malta/Libya Oil Dispute	20/08/80–15/09/80	(Subsystem)						
9480 Malta	20/08/80–15/09/80	Small	Non-viol. mil.	Economic	Libya	Negotiation	No violence	Compromise
286								
(2960) Onset Iran/Iraq War	17/09/80–00/11/80	(Subsystem)						
9486 Iran	17/09/80–00/11/80	Great	Pol. (verbal)	Territory	Iraq	Violence	Full-scale war	Stalemate
287								
(2970) Libyan Intervention/Gambia	27/10/80–07/11/80	(Subsystem)						
9490 Gambia	27/10/80–07/11/80	Small	Internal chal.	Pol. Regime	Libya	Mult. no viol.	No violence	Victory
288								
(2990) Jordan/Syria Confrontation	25/11/80–14/12/80	(Subsystem)						
9497 Jordan	25/11/80–14/12/80	Middle	Non-viol. mil.	Territory	Syria	Non-viol. mil.	No violence	Victory
289								
(2995) East Africa Confrontation	05/12/80–29/06/81	(Subsystem)						
9498 Somalia	05/12/80–29/06/81	Small	Political	Territory	Ethiopia	Non-viol. mil.	No violence	Compromise
290								
(3000) Chad/Libya V: Merger	06/01/81–16/11/81	(Subsystem)						
9500 France	06/01/81–16/11/81	Superpower	Political	Influence	Libya	Negotiation	No violence	Victory
291								
(3010) Peru/Ecuador	22/01/81–02/02/81	(Subsystem)						
9504 Peru	22/01/81–02/02/81	Middle	Violent	Territory	Ecuador	Mult. inc. viol.	Minor clashes	Defeat
9505 Ecuador	22/01/81–02/02/81	Small	Violent	Territory	Peru	Mult. inc. viol.	Minor clashes	Stalemate
292								
(3020) Mozambique Raid	30/01/81–00/03/81	(Subsystem)						
9510 Mozambique	30/01/81–00/03/81	Small	Violent	Territory	S. Africa	Negotiation	No violence	Stalemate
293								
(3035) Essequibo II	04/04/81–00/03/83	(Subsystem)						
9513 Guyana	04/04/81–00/03/83	Small	Pol. (verbal)	Territory	Venezuela	Mult. no. viol.	No violence	Stalemate
294								
(3040) Biqa Missiles	28/04/81–24/07/81	(Subsystem)						
9516 Syria	28/04/81–24/07/81	Great	Violent	Influence	Israel	Non-viol. mil.	No violence	Victory
9517 Israel	29/04/81–24/07/81	Great	Non-viol. mil.	Influence	Syria	Negotiation	No violence	Stalemate
295								
(3050) Nigeria/Cameroon Border	16/05/81–24/07/81	(Subsystem)						
9520 Nigeria	16/05/81–24/07/81	Superpower	Violent	Influence	Cameroon	Non-viol. mil.	No violence	Victory
9521 Cameroon	17/05/81–24/07/81	Small	Pol. (verbal)	Economic	Nigeria	Negotiation	No violence	Defeat
296								
(3060) Iraqi Nuclear Reactor	08/06/81–19/06/81	(Subsystem)						
9524 Iraq	08/06/81–19/06/81	Middle	Violent	Influence	Israel	Negotiation	No violence	Defeat
297								
(3070) Coup Attempt-Gambia	30/07/81–31/01/82	(Subsystem)						
9527 Senegal	30/07/81–31/01/82	Small	Ind. violence	Influence	Gambia	Violence	Serious clashes	Victory
298								
(3080) Gulf of Syrte	12/08/81–01/09/81	(Subsystem)						
9529 Libya	12/08/81–01/09/81	Middle	Pol. (verbal)	Territory	USA	Non-viol. mil.	No violence	Defeat
299								
(3090) Operation Protea-Angola	23/08/81–30/09/81	(Subsystem)						
9532 Angola	23/08/81–30/09/81	Small	Violent	Territory	S. Africa	Mult. inc. viol.	Serious clashes	Stalemate
300								
(3095) Polisario Attack	13/10/81–09/11/81	(Subsystem)						
9535 Morocco	13/10/81–09/11/81	Great	Violent	Territory	Algeria	Mult. inc. viol.	Serious clashes	Defeat

APPENDIX B. – *continued*

Case and crisis actors	Duration	Power status (system level)	Trigger	Gravity of threat	Source of threat	Crisis management technique	Intensity of violence as CMT	Substance of outcome
301								
(3120) Coup Attempt-Bahrain	13/12/81–08/01/82	(Subsystem)						
9546 Bahrain	13/12/81–08/01/82	Small	Internal chal.	Pol. regime	Iran	Negotiaton	No violence	Victory
9547 Saudi Arabia	13/12/81–19/12/81	Middle	Other	Influence	Iran	Negotiation	No violence	Victory
302								
(3130) Khoramshar	22/03/82–30/07/82	(Subsystem)						
9549 Iraq	22/03/82–30/07/82	Great	Violent	Grave damage	Iran	Mult. inc. viol.	Full-scale war	Defeat
303								
(3135) Falklands/Malvinas	31/03/82–14/06/82	(Subsystem)						
9551 UK	31/03/82–14/06/82	Great	Non-viol. mil.	Territory	Argentina	Mult. inc. viol.	Full-scale war	Victory
9552 Argentina	05/04/82–14/06/82	Great	Non-viol. mil.	Territory	UK	Mult. inc. viol.	Full-scale war	Defeat
304								
(3150) Lebanon War	05/06/82–17/05/83	(Subsystem)						
9554 Lebanon	05/06/82–17/05/83	Small	Violent	Territory	Israel	Negotiation	No violence	Stalemate
9555 Syria	07/06/82–01/09/82	Great	Violent	Influence	Israel	Mult. inc. viol.	Full-scale war	Compromise
9556 Israel	09/06/82–01/09/82	Great	Violent	Influence	Syria	Mult. inc. viol.	Full-scale war	Compromise
305								
(3155) Ogaden III	30/06/82–00/08/82	(Subsystem)						
9557 Somalia	30/06/82–00/08/82	Small	Violent	Territory	Ethiopia	Mult. inc. viol.	Serious clashes	Stalemate
306								
(3170) Lesotho Raid	09/12/82–15/12/82	(Subsystem)						
9564 Lesotho	09/12/82–15/12/82	Small	Violent	Territory	S. Africa	Negotiation	No violence	Stalemate
307								
(3180) Libya Threat-Sudan	11/02/83–22/02/83	(Subsystem)						
9567 Sudan	11/02/83–22/02/83	Middle	Non-viol. mil.	Pol. regime	Libya	Non-viol. mil.	No violence	Victory
9568 Egypt	11/02/83–22/02/83	Great	Non-viol. mil.	Influence	Libya	Non-viol. mil.	No violence	Victory
9569 Libya	17/02/83–22/02/83	Middle	Non-viol. mil.	Influence	USA	Mult. no viol.	No violence	Compromise
308								
(3190) Chad/Nigeria Clashes	18/04/83–02/07/83	(Subsystem)						
9573 Chad	18/04/83–02/07/83	Small	Violent	Territory	Nigeria	Mult. inc. viol.	Serious clashes	Victory
9574 Nigeria	18/04/83–02/07/83	Great	Violent	Territory	Chad	Mult. inc. viol.	Serious clashes	Victory
309								
(3210) Chad/Libya VI	24/06/83–11/12/84	(Subsystem)						
9580 Chad	24/06/83–10/10/84	Small	Violent	Existence	Libya	Mult. no viol.	Minor clashes	Defeat
9581 France	31/07/83–11/12/84	Superpower	Ind. violent	Influence	Libya	Mult. inc. viol.	Minor clashes	Compromise
9582 Libya	09/08/83–10/11/84	Great	Non-viol. mil.	Influence	France	Negotiation	Minor clashes	Victory
310								
(3230) Invasion of Grenada	19/10/83–28/10/83	(Subsystem)						
9585 USA	19/10/83–28/10/83	Superpower	Ind. violent	Influence	Grenada	Violence	Serious clashes	Victory
9586 Grenada	22/10/83–28/10/83	Small	Non-viol. mil.	Pol. regime	USA	Negotiation	Serious clashes	Defeat
311								
(3250) Botswana/Zimbabwe Border	08/11/83–21/12/83	(Subsystem)						
9597 Botswana	08/11/83–21/12/83	Small	Violent	Limited	Zimbabwe	Negotiation	Minor clashes	Victory
312								
(3260) Sudan/Ethiopia Border	20/11/83–20/02/84	(Subsystem)						
9599 Sudan	20/11/83–20/02/84	Middle	Non-viol. mil.	Pol. regime	Ethiopia	Non-viol. mil.	No violence	Victory
313								
(3270) Operation Askari	06/12/83–16/02/84	(Subsystem)						
9600 Angola	06/12/83–16/02/84	Middle	Violent	Territory	S. Africa	Mult. inc. viol.	Serious clashes	Compromise
314								
(3275) Basra/Kharg Island	21/02/84–11/07/84	(Subsystem)						
9601 Iraq	21/02/84–00/03/84	Great	Violent	Grave damage	Iran	Violence	Full-scale war	Stalemate
9602 Iran	01/03/84–10/06/84	Great	Violent	Economic	Iraq	Violence	Serious clashes	Stalemate
9603 Kuwait	13/05/84–11/07/84	Small	Violent	Economic	Iran	Negotiation	No violence	Stalemate
9604 Saudi Arabia	16/05/84–20/06/84	Middle	Violent	Territory	Iran	Mult. inc. viol.	Minor clashes	Victory
315								
(3280) Aegean Naval Crisis	08/03/84–09/03/84	(Subsystem)						
9605 Greece	08/03/84–09/03/84	Small	Violent	Limited	Turkey	Negotiation	No violence	Victory

Case and crisis actors		Duration	Power status (system level)	Trigger	Gravity of threat	Source of threat	Crisis management technique	Intensity of violence as CMT	Substance of outcome
316									
(3290)	Omdurman Bombing	16/03/84–	(Subsystem)						
9608	Sudan	16/03/84–	Middle	Violent	Pol. regime	Libya	Negotiation	No violence	Victory
9609	Egypt	16/03/84–	Great	Ind. violent	Influence	Libya	Non-viol. mil.	No violence	Victory
9610	Libya	18/03/84–	Middle	Ext. change	Influence	USA	Negotiation	No violence	Compromise
317									
(3292)	Thai Border Incident	25/03/84–17/04/84	(Subsystem)						
9611	Thailand	25/03/84–17/04/84	Middle	Violent	Limited	Vietnam	Negotiation	Minor clashes	Stalemate
318									
(3295)	Sino/Vietnam Clashes	02/04/84–00-06/84	(Subsystem)						
9612	Vietnam	02/04/84–00/06/84	Great	Violent	Influence	PRC	Mult. inc. viol.	Serious clashes	Stalemate
319									
(3310)	Village Border Clashes	05/06/84–00/10/84	(Subsystem)						
9620	Thailand	05/06/84–17/07/84	Middle	Non-viol. mil.	Limited	Laos	Mult. inc. viol.	Minor clashes	Compromise
9621	Laos	06/06/84–00/10/84	Small	Violent	Territory	Thailand	Negotiation	Minor clashes	Compromise
320									
(3320)	Nicaragua MIG-21s	06/11/84–12/11/84	(Dominant)						
9625	USA	06/11/84–09/11/84	Superpower	Ext. change	Influence	USSR	Non-viol. mil.	No violence	Stalemate
9626	Nicaragua	07/11/84–12/11/84	Small	Non-viol. mil.	Pol. regime	USA	Negotiation	No violence	Stalemate
321									
(3440)	Botswana Raid	14/06/85–21/06/85	(Subsystem)						
9660	Botswana	14/06/85–21/06/85	Small	Violent	Territory	S. Africa	Negotiation	No violence	Stalemate
322									
(3480)	Expulsion/Tunisians	21/08/85–26/09/85	(Subsystem)						
9680	Tunisia	21/08/85–26/09/85	Small	Non-viol. mil.	Pol. regime	Libya	Non-viol. mil.	No violence	Victory
323									
(3510)	Burkina Faso/Mali Border	20/12/85–18/01/86	(Subsystem)						
9686	Mali	20/12/85–18/01/86	Small	Non-viol. mil.	Territory	Burkina Faso	Violence	Serious clashes	Stalemate
9687	Burkina Faso	25/12/85–18/01/66	Small	Violent	Pol. regime	Mali	Violence	Serious clashes	Stalemate

References

ABEL, Elie. *The Missile Crisis*. Philadelphia, PA: Lippincott, 1966.

ABOLFATHI, Farid, John J. HAYES and Richard E. HAYES. "Trends in United States Response to International Crises: Policy Implications for the 1980s," in Charles W. KEGLEY, Jr. and Patrick J. McGOWAN. *Challenges to America*. Beverly Hills, CA: Sage, 1979, 57–85.

ACHESON, Dean. *Present at the Creation: My Years in the State Department*. New York: New American Library, 1969.

ADOMEIT, Hannes. *Soviet Risk-Taking and Crisis Behavior: A Theoretical and Empirical Analysis*. London: Allen and Unwin, 1982.

ALKER, Hayward R. and Thomas J. BIERSTEKER. "The Dialectics of World Order: Notes for a Future Archaeologist of International Savoir Faire," *International Studies Quarterly*, **28**, 2 (1984), 121–142.

ALLISON, Graham T. *Essence of Decision: Explaining the Cuban Missile Crisis*. Boston, MA: Little, Brown, 1971.

——. "Conceptual Models and the Cuban Missile Crisis," *American Political Science Review*, **63**, 3 (1969), 689–718.

ALPEROVITZ, Gar. *Atomic Diplomacy: Hiroshima and Potsdam*, 2nd ed. New York: Penguin Books, 1985.

ANDRIOLE, Stephen J. "The Levels of Analysis Problems and the Study of Foreign, International, and Global Affairs: A Review, Critique, and Another Final Solution," *International Interactions*, **5** (1978), 113–133.

ANGELL, R. C. "Social Values of Soviet and American Élites: Content Analysis of Élite Media," *Journal of Conflict Resolution*, **8**, 4 (1964), 330–385.

ANGLIN, Douglas G. *Zambian Crisis Behavior: UDI in Rhodesia, 1965–66* (forthcoming).

ARON, Raymond. *Peace and War*. Garden City, NY: Doubleday, 1966.

——. *On War*, Garden City, NY: Doubleday, 1959.

——. "Conflict and War from the Viewpoint of Historical Sociology," in *The Nature of Conflict*. Paris: UNESCO, 1957.

ARROW, Kenneth J. "Economic Equilibrium," in David L. SILLS (ed.), *International Encyclopedia of the Social Sciences*, Vol. 4. New York: Macmillan, 1968, 376–389.

ARURI, Naseer H. (ed.). *Middle East Crucible: Studies on the Arab-Israeli War of October 1973*. Wilmette, IL: Medina University Press International, 1975.

ASHBY, William R. *Design for a Brain: The Origin of Adaptive Behavior*. London: Chapman and Hall, 1952.

ASHLEY, Richard K. "The Poverty of Neorealism," *International Organization*, **38** (1984), 225–286.

AVAIZIAN, Varouj A. and Jeffrey L. CALLEN. "The Coase Theorem and the Empty Core," *Journal of Law and Economics*, **24** (1981), 175–181.

AZAR, Edward E. "Protracted International Conflicts: Ten Propositions," *International Interactions*, **12**, 1 (1985), 59–70.

——. "The Conflict and Peace Data Bank (COPDAB) Project," *Journal of Conflict Resolution*, **16** (1980), 143–152.

——. "Peace Amidst Development: A Conceptual Agenda for Conflict and Peace Research," *International Interactions*, **6**, 2 (1979), 123–143.

——. "Conflict Escalation and Conflict Reduction in an International Crisis: Suez, 1956," *Journal of Conflict Resolution*, **16** (1972), 183–201.

——, Richard BRODY and Charles A. McCLELLAND. "International Events Interaction Analysis: Some Research Considerations," *Sage Professional Papers in International Studies*, 02-001. Beverly Hills, CA: Sage, 1972.

——, *et al*. "A System for Forecasting Strategic Crises: Findings and Speculations about Conflict in the Middle East," *International Interactions*, **3** (1977), 193–222.

——, and N. FARAH. "The Structure of Inequalities and Protracted Social Conflict: A Theoretical Framework," *International Interactions*, **7**, 4 (1981), 317–335.

——, Paul JUREIDINI and Robert McLAURIN. "Protracted Social Conflict: Theory and

Practice in the Middle East," *Journal of Palestine Studies*, VIII, 29 (1978), 41–60.

——, and Thomas J. SLOAN. *Dimensions of Interaction*. Pittsburgh, PA: International Studies Association, 1975.

BACKMAN, Carl W. "Role Theory and International Relations: A Commentary and Extension," *International Studies Quarterly*, **14**, 3 (1970), 310–319.

BANDMANN, Yona and Yishai CORDOVA. "The Soviet Nuclear Threat Towards the Close of the Yom Kippur War," *Jerusalem Journal of International Relations*, **5**, 1 (1980), 94–110.

BARNDS, William J. *India, Pakistan and the Great Powers*. New York: Praeger, 1972.

BARNET, Richard J. *Intervention and Revolution: The United States in the Third World*. New York: World, 1968.

BARRINGER, Richard E. *Patterns of Conflict*. Cambridge, MA: MIT Press, 1972.

BARTOV, Hanoch. *Dado: Forty-Eight Years and Another Twenty Days*, 2 vols. (Hebrew). Tel Aviv: Ma'ariv Library, 1978.

BEER, Francis. *Peace Against War*. San Francisco, CA: Freeman, 1981.

BELL, Cora. *The Conventions of Crisis*. New York: Oxford University Press, 1971.

BENDER, Gerald, James COLEMAN and Richard L. SKLAR. *African Crisis Areas and United States Foreign Policy*. Berkeley, CA: University of California Press, 1986.

BERGESEN, Albert (ed.). *Crises in the World-System*. Beverly Hills, CA: Sage, 1983.

BERNARD, Jessie. "The Sociological Study of Conflict," in *The Nature of Conflict*. Paris: UNESCO, 1957.

——. "Where is the Modern Sociology of Conflict?" *American Journal of Sociology*, **56** (1950), 11–16.

BETTS, Richard K. *Nuclear Blackmail and Nuclear Balance*. Washington DC: Brookings, 1987.

BINDER, Leonard. "The Middle East as a Subordinate International System," *World Politics*, **X** (1958), 408–429.

BLAINEY, Geoffrey. *The Causes of War*. New York: Free Press, 1973.

BLECHMAN, Barry M. and Stephen S. KAPLAN. *Force without War: U.S. Armed Forces as a Political Instrument*. Washington, D.C.: Brookings, 1978.

BLOOMFIELD, Lincoln P. *The United Nations and U.S. Foreign Policy*, rev. ed. Boston, MA: Little, Brown, 1967.

BOBROW, Davis B. "The Perspective of Great Power Foreign Policy: Steps in Context," in J. RUBIN (ed.), *Dynamics of Third Party Intervention: Kissinger and the Middle East*. New York: Praeger, 1981.

——, Steve CHAN and John A. KRINGEN. *Understanding Foreign Policy Decisions: The Chinese Case*. New York: Free Press, 1979.

——. "Understanding How Others Treat Crises," *International Studies Quarterly*, **21** (1977), 199–223.

BOHLEN, Charles E. *Witness to History, 1929–1969*. New York: Norton, 1973.

BORISOV, Oleg B. and B.T. KOLOSKOV. *Soviet-Chinese Relations, 1945–1970*. Bloomington, IN: Indiana University Press, 1975.

BOULDING, Kenneth E. *Ecodynamics: A New Theory of Societal Evolution*. Beverly Hills, CA: Sage, 1978.

——. *Conflict and Defense*. New York: Harper, 1962.

——. "General Systems Theory – The Skeleton of Science," *Management Science*, **2** (1956), 197–208.

BOWMAN, Larry W. "The Subordinate State System of Southern Africa," *International Studies Quarterly*, **12** (1968), 231–261.

BRACKEN, Paul. *The Command and Control of Nuclear Forces*. New Haven, CT: Yale University Press, 1983.

BRECHER, Michael. "International Crises and Protracted Conflicts," *International Interactions*, **11**, 3–4 (1984), 237–297.

——. "State Behavior in International Crises: A Model," *Journal of Conflict Resolution*, **23**, 3 (1979), 446–480.

——. (ed.). *Studies in Crisis Behavior*, New Brunswick, NJ: Transaction Books, 1979.

——. "Toward a Theory of International Crisis Behavior," *International Studies Quarterly*, **21** (1977), 39–74.

——. *The Foreign Policy System of Israel*. London: Oxford University Press, 1972.

——. "International Relations and Asian Studies: The Subordinate State System of Southern Asia," *World Politics*, **XV** (1963), 213–235.

——, and Hemda BEN YEHUDA. "System and Crisis in International Politics," *Review of International Studies*, **11** (1985), 17–36.

——, with Benjamin GEIST. *Decisions in Crisis: Israel 1967 and 1973*. Berkeley and Los Angeles: University of California Press, 1980.

——, and Patrick JAMES. *Crisis and Change in World Politics*. Boulder, CO: Westview Press, 1986.

——, Blema S. STEINBERG and Janice STEIN. "A Framework for Research on Foreign Policy Behavior," *Journal of Conflict Resolution*, **XIII** (1969), 75–101.

——, and Jonathan WILKENFELD. "Crises in World Politics," *World Politics*, **34** (1982), 380–417.

——, *et al. Crises in the Twentieth Century: Vol. I, Handbook of International Crises*. Oxford: Pergamon Press, 1988.

——, and Stephen R. HILL. "Threat and Violence in International Crisis," in K. MUSHAKOJI and H. USUI (eds.), *Theoretical Frameworks of the Contemporary World in Transition: Vol. I. Interstate Relations and Decision-Making*. Tokyo: Yushindo Kobunsha, 1987, 57–102.

BREMER, Stuart A. "The Contagiousness of Coercion: The Spread of Serious International Disputes, 1900–1976," *International Interactions*, **9**, 1 (1982), 29–55.

BRIERLY, James L. *The Law of Nations*. Oxford: Clarendon Press, 1928.

BRINES, Russell. *The Indo-Pakistani Conflict*. London: Pall Mall Press, 1968.

BRODIE, Bernard. *War and Politics*. New York: Macmillan, 1973.

BROWN, Seyom *The Causes and Prevention of War*. New York: St. Martin's Press, 1987.

BRZEZINSKI, Zbigniew and Samuel P. HUNTINGTON. *Political Power: USA/USSR*. New York: Viking Press, 1964.

BUENO de MESQUITA, Bruce. "Toward a Scientific Understanding of International Conflict: A Personal View," *International Studies Quarterly*, **29**, 2 (1985), 121–136.

——. *The War Trap*. New Haven, CT: Yale University Press, 1981.

——. "Theories of International Conflict: An Analysis and Appraisal," in Ted R. GURR (ed.), *Handbook of Political Conflict*. New York: Free Press, 1980, 361–398.

——. "Systemic Polarization and the Occurrence and Duration of War." *Journal of Conflict Resolution*, **22** (1978), 241–268.

——. "Measuring Systemic Polarity," *Journal of Conflict Resolution*, **19** (1975), 187–216.

BULL, Hedley. *The Anarchical Society*. New York: Columbia University Press, 1977.

——. "International Theory: The Case for a Classical Approach," *World Politics*, **XVIII** (1966), 361–377.

BURGESS, Phillip M. and Raymond W. LAWTON. *Indicators of International Behavior: An Assessment of Events Data Research, Sage Professional Papers, International Studies*, Vol. 1. Beverly Hills, CA: Sage, 1972.

BUTTERWORTH, Robert L. "Do Conflict Managers Matter: An Empirical Assessment of Interstate Security Disputes and Resolution Efforts, 1945–1974," *International Studies Quarterly*, **22**, 2 (1978), 195–214.

——. *Managing Interstate Conflict: Data with Synopses*. Pittsburgh, PA: University Center of International Studies, 1976.

CACI. *Analysis of Superpower Crisis Management Behavior: Final Report*. Arlington, VA: CACI, Inc. – Federal, 1980.

——. *Analysis of the Soviet Crisis Management Experience: Technical Report*. Arlington, VA: CACI, Inc. – Federal, 1978.

——. *Planning for Problems in Crisis Management*. Arlington, VA: CACI, Inc. – Federal, 1976.

CALLAHAN, Patrick, Linda P. BRADY and Margaret G. HERMANN (eds.). *Describing Foreign Policy Behavior*. Beverly Hills, CA: Sage, 1982.

CANTORI, Louis J. and Steven L. SPIEGEL. *International Politics of Regions*. Englewood Cliffs, NJ: Prentice-Hall, 1970.

CARR, Edward H. *The Twenty Years' Crisis, 1919–1939*. London and New York: Macmillan, 1939.

CHAN, Steve. "Chinese Conflict Calculus and Behavior: Assessment from a Perspective of Crisis Management," *World Politics*, **30**, 3 (1978), 391–410.

CHAYES, Abram. *The Cuban Missile Crisis: International Crises and the Role of Law*. London: Oxford University Press, 1974.

CHOUCRI, Nazli and Robert C. NORTH. *Nations in Conflict: National Growth and International Violence*. San Francisco: W. H. Freeman, 1975.

CHOUDHURY, Golam W. *Pakistan's Relations with India, 1947–1966*. New York: Praeger, 1968.

CLAUDE, Inis L., Jr. *Swords into Plowshares*, New York: Random House, 1964.

COASE, R.H. "The Coase Theorem and the Empty Core: A Comment," *Journal of Law and Economics*, **24** (1981), 183–187.

——. "The Problem of Social Cost," *Journal of Law and Economics*, **3** (1960), 1–44.

COLLINS, John N. "Foreign Conflict Behavior and Domestic Disorder in Africa," in Jonathan WILKENFELD (ed.). *Conflict Behavior and Linkage Politics*. New York: David McKay, 1973.

CONFINO, Michael and Shimon SHAMIR (eds.). *The U.S.S.R. and the Middle East*. New York: John Wiley, 1973.

COOLEY, Charles H. *Social Process*. New York: Scribner, 1918.

CORSON, Walter H. *Conflict and Cooperation in East-West Crises*. Ph.D dissertation, Harvard University, 1970.

COSER, Lewis A. "Conflict: Social Aspects," in David A. SILLS (ed.). *International Encyclopedia of the Social Sciences*, **3**, 232–236. London: Collier-Macmillan, 1968.

——. *The Functions of Social Conflict*. Glencoe, IL: Free Press, 1956.

CRAIG, Gordon A. and Alexander L. GEORGE. *Force and Statecraft: Diplomatic Problems of Our Time*. New York: Oxford University Press, 1983.

CRANKSHAW, Edward. *Khrushchev: A Career*. New York: Viking Press, 1966.

DAHRENDORF, Ralf. *Class and Class Conflict in Industrial Society*. Stanford, CA: Stanford University Press, 1959.

DALLIN, Alexander. *The Soviet Union at the United Nations*. New York: Praeger, 1962.

DAVID DAVIES MEMORIAL INSTITUTE OF INTERNATIONAL STUDIES. *International Disputes: The Legal Aspects*. London: Europa Publications, 1972.

DAVIS, W.W., G.T. DUNCAN and R.M. SIVERSON. "The Dynamics of Warfare, 1816–1965," *American Journal of Political Science*, **22**, 4 (1978), 772–792.

DAVISON, Walter P. *The Berlin Blockade: A Study in Cold War Politics*. Princeton, NJ: Princeton University Press, 1962.

DAWISHA, Adeed I. *Syria and the Lebanese Crisis*. London: Macmillan, 1980.

DAWISHA, Karen. *The Kremlin and the Prague Spring*. Berkeley and Los Angeles: University of California Press, 1984.

——. "Limits of the Bureaucratic Politics Model: Observations on the Soviet Case," *Studies in Comparative Communism*, **13** (1980), 300–346.

DAYAN, Moshe. *Story of My Life*. Jerusalem and Tel Aviv: Steimatzky's, 1976.

DDIR (Data Development in International Relations). "Rethinking Interstate Conflict Data," ISA Annual Convention, 1987.

DEAN, P.D. and John A. VASQUEZ. "From Power Politics to Issue Politics," *Western Political Quarterly*, **29** (1976), 7–28.

DEUTSCH, Karl W. *Politics and Government*, 2nd ed. Boston, MA: Houghton Mifflin, 1974.

——, and J. David SINGER. "Multipolar Power Systems and International Stability," *World Politics*, **XVI** (1964), 390–406.

DINERSTEIN, Herbert S. *The Making of a Missile Crisis: October 1962*. Baltimore, MD: Johns Hopkins University Press, 1976.

DOMINGUEZ, Juan E. "Mice That Do Not Roar," *International Organization*, **25** (1971), 175–208.

DOUGHERTY, James E. and Robert L. PFALTZGRAFF, Jr. *American Foreign Policy: FDR to Reagan*. New York: Harper and Row, 1986.

DOWTY, Alan. *Middle East Crisis: US Decision-Making in 1958, 1970, and 1973*. Berkeley and Los Angeles: University of California Press, 1984.

EAGLETON, Clyde. *International Government*. New York: Ronald Press Co., 1932.

EAST, Maurice, Stephen A. SALMORE and Charles F. HERMANN (eds.). *Why Nations Act*. Beverly Hills, CA: Sage, 1978.

EBAN, Abba. *An Autobiography*. Jerusalem and Tel Aviv: Steimatzky's, 1977.

ECKHARDT, William and Edward E. AZAR. "Major World Conflicts and Interventions, 1945–1975," *International Interactions*, **5** (1978), 75–110.

FALK, Richard A. and Saul H. MENDLOVITZ (eds.). *The Strategy of World Order, 3, The United Nations*. New York: World Law Fund, 1966.

FELD, Werner J. and Gavin BOYD. *Comparative Regional Systems*. New York: Pergamon Press, 1980.

FINK, Clinton F. "Some Conceptual Difficulties in the Theory of Social Conflict," *Journal of Conflict Resolution*, XII, 4 (1968), 412–459.

FINLAYSON, J.A. and Mark W. ZACHER. *The United Nations and Collective Security: Retrospect and Prospect*. United Nations Association of America, 1980.

FREEDMAN, Robert O. *Soviet Policy Towards the Middle East Since 1970*. New York: Praeger, 1975.

GADDIS, John L. *The Long Peace*. New York: Oxford University Press, 1987.

——. "The Long Peace: Elements of Stability in the Postwar International System," *International Security*, 10 (1986), 99–142.

——. *Strategies of Containment: A Critical Appraisal of Postwar American National Security Policy*. New York: Oxford University Press, 1982.

GARNHAM, David. "The Causes of War: Systemic Findings," in Alan Ned SABROSKY (ed.), *Polarity and War: The Changing Structure of International Conflict*. Boulder, CO: Westview Press, 1985, 7–23.

GARTHOFF, Raymond L. *Reflections on the Cuban Missile Crisis*. Washington, D.C.: Brookings, 1987.

GEIST, Benjamin. *Hungary 1956: Crisis Decision-Making in a Socialist State* (forthcoming).

GEORGE, Alexander L. "US–Soviet Global Rivalry: Norms of Competition," *Journal of Peace Research*, 23, 3 (1986), 247–262.

——. "Political Crises," in Joseph S. NYE, Jr. (ed.), *The Making of America's Soviet Policy*. New Haven, CT: Yale University Press, 1984, 129–157.

——. *Managing US–Soviet Rivalry: Problems of Crisis Prevention*. Boulder, CO: Westview Press, 1983.

——, and Richard SMOKE. *Deterrence in American Foreign Policy*. New York: Columbia University Press, 1974.

——, D.K. HALL and W.E. SIMONS. *The Limits of Coercive Diplomacy*. Boston, MA: Little, Brown, 1971.

GHOSHAL, U.N. "The System of Inter-State Relations and Foreign Policy in the Early Arthasastra State," in *India Antiqua*. Leiden: E.J. Brill, Ltd., 1947.

GILPIN, Robert. *War and Change in World Politics*. New York: Cambridge University Press, 1981.

GOCHMAN, Charles S. and Zeev MAOZ. "Militarized Interstate Disputes, 1816–1976: Procedures, Patterns, Insights," *Journal of Conflict Resolution*, 28, 4 (1984), 585–615.

GOLAN, Galia. *Yom Kippur and After: The Soviet Union and the Middle East Crisis*. Cambridge: Cambridge University Press 1977.

——. *The Soviet Union and the Arab–Israel War of October 1973*. Jerusalem Papers on Peace Problems, No. 7. Jerusalem: Leonard Davis Institute for International Relations, 1974.

GOLAN, Matti. *The Secret Conversations of Henry Kissinger: Step-by-Step Diplomacy in the Middle East*. New York: Bantam Books, 1976.

GOLDSTEIN, Joshua S. *Long Cycles: Prosperity and War in the Modern Age*. New Haven, CT: Yale University Press, 1988.

GOODSPEED, Stephen S. *The Nature and Function of International Organization*. New York: Oxford University Press, 1967.

GOTTLIEB, M. *The German Peace Settlement and the Berlin Crisis*. New York: Paine-Whitman, 1960.

GRIFFITHS, Franklyn. "The Sources of American Conduct: Soviet Perspectives and Their Policy Implications," *International Security*, 9, 2 (1984), 3–50.

GULICK, Edward V. *Europe's Classical Balance of Power*. Ithaca, NY: Cornell University Press, 1955.

GURR, Ted R. (ed.). *Handbook of Political Conflict*. New York: Free Press, 1980.

HAAS, Ernst B. *Why We Still Need the United Nations*. University of California Policy Papers in International Affairs, No. 26. Berkeley, CA: Institute of International Studies, 1986.

——. "Regime Decay: Conflict Management and International Organizations, 1945–1981," *International Organization*, 37 (1983), 189–256.

——. "On Systems and International Regimes," *World Politics*, XXVII (1975), 147–174.

——. *Collective Security and the Future International System*. Monograph Series in World Affairs, Vol. 5. Denver, CO: University of Denver Press, 1967–68.

——. *Beyond the Nation State*. Stanford, CA: Stanford University Press, 1964.

——, Robert L. BUTTERWORTH and Joseph S. NYE, Jr. *Conflict Management by International Organizations*. Morristown, NJ: General Learning Press, 1972.

HAAS, Michael. "Research on International Crisis: Obsolescence of an Approach?" *International Interactions*, **13**, 1 (1986), 23–58.

——. *International Conflict*. Indianapolis: Bobbs-Merrill, 1974.

——. "International Subsystems: Stability and Polarity," *American Political Science Review*, **64** (1970), 98–123.

HAGGARD, Stephan and Beth A. SIMMONS. "Theories of International Regimes," *International Organization*, **41** (1987), 491–517.

HALPERIN, Morton H. and Arnold KANTER (eds.). *Readings in American Foreign Policy: A Bureaucratic Perspective*. Boston, MA: Little, Brown, 1973.

HANRIEDER, Wolfram F. "The International System: Bipolar or Multibloc?" *Journal of Conflict Resolution*, **9** (1965), 299–307.

HART, Jeffrey A. "Power and Polarity," in Alan Ned SABROSKY (ed.), *Polarity and War*. Boulder, CO: Westview Press, 1985, 25–40.

HAZLEWOOD, Leo *et al*. "Planning for Problems in Crisis Management: An Analysis of Post-1945 Behavior in the U.S. Department of Defense," *International Studies Quarterly*, **21** (1977), 75–106.

HEIKAL, Mohamed. *The Road to Ramadan*. London: Collins, 1975.

HENKIN, Louis. *How Nations Behave*. New York: Praeger, 1965.

——. *The Berlin Crisis and the United Nations*. New York: Carnegie Endowment for International Peace, 1959.

HERMANN, Charles F. "Enhancing Crisis Stability: Correcting the Trend Toward Increasing Instability," in Gilbert R. WINHAM (ed.), *New Issues in International Crisis Management*. Boulder, CO: Westview Press, 1988, 121–149.

——. "Superpower Involvement with Others: Alternative Role Relationships," in Stephen G. WALKER (ed.), *Role Theory and Foreign Policy Analysis*. Durham, NC: Duke University Press, 1987, 219–240.

—— (ed.). *International Crises: Insights from Behavioral Research*. New York: Free Press, 1972.

——. "International Crisis as a Situational Variable," in James N. ROSENAU (ed.), *International Politics and Foreign Policy*, rev. ed. New York: Free Press, 1969, 409–421.

HERZ, John. *International Politics in the Atomic Age*. New York: Columbia University Press, 1959.

HERZOG, Chaim. *The War of Atonement*. London: Weidenfeld & Nicholson, 1975.

HILSMAN, Roger. *To Move a Nation*. New York: Doubleday, 1967.

HOFFMANN, E.P. and F.J. FLERON, Jr. *The Conduct of Soviet Foreign Policy*. New York: Aldine, 1980.

HOFFMANN, Stanley. "Muscle and Brains," *Foreign Policy*, **37** (1979–80), 3–27.

——. *Gulliver's Troubles, or the Setting of American Foreign Policy*. New York: McGraw-Hill, 1968.

——. "Discord in Community," *International Organization*, **17** (1963), 521–549.

——. "International Systems and International Law," *World Politics*, **XIV** (1961), 205–237.

HOFFMANN, Steven. *India and the China Crisis* (forthcoming).

HOLLIST, W. Ladd and James N. ROSENAU (eds.). *World System Structure, Continuity and Change*. Beverly Hills, CA: Sage, 1981.

——. "World System Debates," special issue of *International Studies Quarterly*, **25**, 1 (1981).

HOLSTI, Kalevi J. *The Dividing Discipline: Hegemony and Diversity in International Theory*. London: Allen & Unwin, 1985.

——. *International Politics*, 2nd ed., 4th ed. Englewood Cliffs, NJ: Prentice-Hall, 1972, 1983.

——. "National Role Conceptions in the Study of Foreign Policy," *International Studies Quarterly*, **14**, 3 (1970), 233–309.

——. "Resolving International Conflicts," *Journal of Conflict Resolution*, **X**, 3 (1966), 272–296.

HOLSTI, Ole R. "Historians, Social Scientists and Crisis Management: An Alternative View," *Journal of Conflict Resolution*, **24** (1980), 665–682.

——. *Crisis Escalation War*. Montreal: McGill-Queen's University Press, 1972.

——. "The 1914 Case," *American Political Science Review*, **59** (1965), 365–378.

——, and Alexander L. GEORGE. "The Effects of Stress on the Performance of

Foreign Policy Makers," *Political Science Annual*, **6** (1975), 255–319.

——, Richard H. Brody and Robert C. North. "The Management of International Crises: Affect and Action in American-Soviet Relations," *Journal of Peace Research*, **3–4**, (1964), 170–190.

Hopkins, Raymond F. and Richard W. Mansbach. *Structure and Process in International Interactions*. New York: Harper and Row, 1973.

Hopmann, Terrence, Dina A. Zinnes and J. David Singer (eds.). *Cumulation in International Relations Research*, Monograph Series in World Affairs, Vol. 18, Book 3. Denver, CO: University of Denver Press, 1981, 65–97.

Hopple, Gerald W. and Paul J. Rossa. "International Crisis Analysis: Recent Developments and Future Directions," in P. Terence Hopmann, Dina A. Zinnes, and J. David Singer (eds.). *Cumulation in International Relations Research*. Denver, CO: University of Denver Press: Monograph Series in World Affairs, 1981.

——, Jonathan Wilkenfeld, Paul J. Rossa and R. N. McCauley. "Societal and Interstate Determinants of Interstate Conflict," *Jerusalem Journal of International Relations*, **2**, 4 (1977), 30–66.

Horelick, Arnold L. "The Cuban Missile Crisis: An Analysis of Soviet Calculations and Behavior," *World Politics*, **16**, 3 (1964), 363–389.

——, and Myron Rush. *Strategic Power and Soviet Foreign Policy*. Chicago, IL: University of Chicago Press, 1964.

Howard, Michael E. *The Causes of War and Other Essays*. Cambridge, MA: Harvard University Press, 1984.

Howe, J. T. *Multicrises: Sea Power and Global Politics in the Missile Age*. Cambridge, MA: M.I.T. Press, 1971.

Huth, Paul. *Deterrence and War*. New Haven, CT: Yale University Press, 1988.

——, and Bruce Russett, "Deterrence Failure and Crisis Escalation," *International Studies Quarterly*, **32**, 1 (1988), 29–45.

——, "What Makes Deterrence Work? Cases from 1900 to 1980," *World Politics*, **XXXVI**, 4 (1984), 496–526.

Ikle, Fred C. *How Nations Negotiate*. New York: Harper and Row, 1964.

Jackson, William D. "Polarity in International Systems: A Conceptual Note," *International Interactions*, **4** (1977), 87–96.

James, Alan. *The Politics of Peacekeeping*. New York: Praeger, 1969.

James, Patrick. *Crisis and War*. Montreal: McGill-Queen's University Press, 1988.

——, and Michael Brecher. "Stability and Polarity: New Paths for Inquiry," *Journal of Peace Research*, **25**, 1 (1988), 31–42.

——, Michael Brecher and Tod Hoffman. "International Crises in Africa, 1929–1979: Immediate Severity and Long-Term Importance," *International Interactions*, **14** (1988), 51–84.

——, and Jonathan Wilkenfeld, "Structural Factors and International Crisis Behavior," *Conflict Management and Peace Science* (1984), 33–53.

Janis, Irving L. and Leon Mann. *Decision-Making*. New York: Free Press, 1977.

Jervis, Robert. "Pluralistic Rigor: A Comment on Bueno de Mesquita," *International Studies Quarterly*, **29** (1985), 145–149.

——. "Security Regimes," in Stephen D. Krasner (ed.), *International Regimes*. Ithaca, NY: Cornell University Press, 1983, 173–194.

——, R. Ned Lebow and Janice G. Stein. *Psychology and Deterrence*. Baltimore, MD: Johns Hopkins University Press, 1985.

Jonsson, Christer. *Superpower: Comparing American and Soviet Foreign Policy*. New York: St. Martin's Press, 1984.

Jukes, Geoffrey. *Hitler's Stalingrad Decisions*. Berkeley and Los Angeles: University of California Press, 1985.

Kahn, Herman. *On Thermonuclear War*. Princeton, NJ: Princeton University Press, 1960.

Kaiser, Karl. "The Interaction of Regional Subsystems," *World Politics*, **XXI** (1968), 84–107.

Kalb, Marvin and Bernard Kalb. *Kissinger*. Boston, MA: Little, Brown, 1974.

Kaplan, Morton A., "The Great Debate: Traditionalism vs. Science in International Relations," *World Politics*, **XIX** (1966), 1–20.

——. *System and Process in International Politics*. New York: John Wiley, 1957.

——, and Nicholas deB. Katzenbach. *The Political Foundations of International Law*. New York: John Wiley, 1961.

KAPLAN, Stephen S. *Diplomacy of Power: Soviet Armed Forces as a Political Instrument.* Washington, D.C.: Brookings, 1981.

KAUFMANN, William W. *The McNamara Strategy.* New York: Harper & Row, 1964.

KEGLEY, Charles W. Jr. and Pat McGOWAN (eds.). *Foreign Policy: USA/USSR,* Volume 7, Sage International Yearbook of Foreign Policy Studies. Beverly Hills, CA: Sage, 1982.

——, and Eugene WITTKOPF. *World Politics: Trend and Transformation.* New York: St. Martin's Press, 1985.

——. *American Foreign Policy: Pattern and Process,* 2nd ed. New York: St. Martin's Press, 1982.

KENNAN, George. "Two Views of the Soviet Problem," in Charles W. KEGLEY and Eugene WITTKOPF (eds.), *Perspectives on American Foreign Policy.* New York: St. Martin's Press, 1983, 40–46.

——. "The Sources of Soviet Conduct," *Foreign Affairs,* vol. 25 (1947), 566–582.

KENNEDY, John F. *The Burden and the Glory.* New York: Harper & Row, 1964.

——. "The Cuban Crisis," *US Information Service,* 1962.

KENNEDY, Robert F. *Thirteen Days – A Memoir of the Cuban Missile Crisis.* New York: Norton, 1969.

KEOHANE, Robert O. *After Hegemony: Cooperation and Discord in the World Political Economy.* Princeton, NJ: Princeton University Press, 1984.

——. Letter to the authors (1981).

——, and Joseph S. NYE, Jr. *"Power and Interdependence* Revisited," *International Organization,* **41**, 4 (1987), 725–753.

——. *Power and Interdependence.* Boston, MA: Little, Brown, 1977.

——. (eds.). *Transnational Relations and World Politics.* Cambridge, MA: Harvard University Press, 1972.

KEYLOR, William R. *The Twentieth-Century World: An International History.* New York: Oxford University Press, 1984.

KHRUSHCHEV, Nikita. *Khrushchev Remembers.* Boston, MA: Little, Brown, 1970.

KISSINGER, Henry A. *Years of Upheaval.* London: Weidenfeld & Nicholson, 1982.

KNORR, Klaus. "Failures in National Intelligence Estimates: The Case of the Cuban Missiles," *World Politics,* **XVI** (1964), 455–467.

KOLKO, Joyce, and Gabriel M. KOLKO. *The Limits of Power.* New York: Harper & Row, 1972.

KOLKOWICZ, R. *The Soviet Military and the Communist Party.* Princeton, NJ: Princeton University Press, 1967.

KRASNER, Stephen D. "Toward Understanding in International Relations," *International Studies Quarterly,* **29** (1985), 137–144.

——. (ed.). *International Regimes.* Ithaca, NY: Cornell University Press, 1983.

KRATOCHWIL, F. "Of Systems, Boundaries, and Territoriality: An Inquiry into the Formation of the State System," *World Politics,* **XXXIX** (1986), 27–52.

LAMB, Alistair. *Crisis in Kashmir, 1947-1966.* London: Routledge and Kegan Paul, 1966.

LAMPERT, D.E. "Patterns of Transregional Relations," in Werner J. FELD and Gavin BOYD (eds.), *Comparative Regional Systems.* New York: Pergamon Press, 1980, 429–81.

LASSWELL, Harold D. "Conflict: Social," in SELIGMAN, Edwin R. and Alvin JOHNSON (eds.). *Encyclopedia of the Social Sciences,* IV. New York: Macmillan, 1931, 194–196.

——, and Abraham KAPLAN. *Power and Society.* New Haven, CT: Yale University Press, 1950.

LAZARUS, Richard S. "Stress," in David L. SILLS (ed.), *International Encyclopedia of the Social Sciences,* Vol. 15. New York: Collier Macmillan, 1968, 337–348.

——, and Susan FOLKMAN. *Stress, Appraisal, and Coping.* New York: Springer, 1984.

LEBOW, R. Ned. *Nuclear Crisis Management: A Dangerous Illusion.* Ithaca, NY: Cornell University Press, 1987.

——. *Between Peace and War.* Baltimore, MD: Johns Hopkins University Press, 1981.

——, and Janice G. STEIN. "Beyond Deterrence" and "Beyond Deterrence: Building a Better Theory," *Journal of Social Issues,* **43**, 2 (1987), 5–72, 155–170.

LENG, Russell J. "Crisis Learning Games," *American Political Science Review,* **82**, 1 (1988), 1179–1194.

——. "When Will They Ever Learn? Coercive Bargaining in Recurrent Crises," *Journal of Conflict Resolution,* **27**, 3 (1983), 379–419.

——, and Charles S. GOCHMAN. "Dangerous Disputes: A Study of Conflict Behavior and War," *American Journal of Political Science*, **26**, 4 (1982), 664–687.

——, and J. David SINGER. "Militarized International Crises: The BCOW Typology and its Applications," *International Studies Quarterly*, **32**, 2 (1988), 155–173.

——, and H.G. WHEELER, "Influence Strategies, Success and War," *Journal of Conflict Resolution*, **23**, 4 (1979), 655–684.

LEVY, Jack S. "The Polarity of the System and International Stability: An Empirical Analysis," in Alan Ned SABROSKY (ed.), *Polarity and War*. Boulder, CO: Westview Press, 1985, 41–66.

——. *War in the Modern Great Power System, 1495–1975*. Lexington, KY: University Press of Kentucky, 1983

——, and T.C. MORGAN. "The War Weariness Hypothesis: An Empirical Test," *American Journal of Political Science*, **30**, 1 (1986), 26–49.

LEWIN, Kurt. *Resolving Social Conflicts*. New York: Harper, 1948.

LISKA, George. *International Equilibrium*. Cambridge, MA: Harvard University Press, 1957.

LUARD, Evan. *War in International Society*. New Haven, CT: Yale University Press, 1987.

MACK, R. W. and Richard C. SNYDER. "The Analysis of Social Conflict – Toward an Overview and Synthesis," *Journal of Conflict Resolution*, I, **2** (1957), 212–248.

MACKINTOSH, J.M. *Strategy and Tactics of Soviet Foreign Policy*. New York: Oxford University Press, 1963.

MAILLARD, Pierre. "The Effect of China on Soviet–American Relations," in *Soviet–American Relations and World Order: The Two and the Many*. London: International Institute for Strategic Studies, Adelphi Papers, **66** (1970), 42–50.

MANSBACH, Richard W. and John A. VASQUEZ. *In Search of Theory*. New York: Columbia University Press, 1981.

MAOZ, Zeev. "Joining the Club of Nations: Political Development and International Conflict, 1816–1976" (paper presented at the American Political Science Association Annual Meeting, Chicago, 1987).

——, and N. ABDOLALI. "Regime Types and International Conflict, 1816–1976," *Journal of Conflict Resolution*, **33**, 1 (1989), 3–35.

MASTERS, Roger D. "A Multi-Bloc Model of the International System," *American Political Science Review*, **LV** (1961), 780–798.

MATTINGLY, Garrett. *Renaissance Diplomacy*. London: Jonathan Cape, 1955.

McCLEARY, Richard and Richard A. HAY, Jr. *Applied Time Series Analysis for the Social Sciences*. Beverly Hills and London: Sage, 1980.

McCLELLAND, Charles A. "Access to Berlin: The Quantity and Variety of Events, 1948–1963," in J. David SINGER (ed.), *Quantitative International Politics: Insight and Evidence*. New York: Free Press, 1968, 159-186.

——. *Theory and the International System*. New York: Macmillan, 1966.

——. "Systems and History in International Relations: Some Perspectives for Empirical Research and Theory," in *General Systems*, Yearbook of the Society for General Systems Research, Vol. III (1958), 221–47.

——. "Applications of General Systems Theory in International Relations," *Main Currents in Modern Thought*, **12** (1955), 27–34.

McCORMICK, James M. "International Crises: A Note on Definition," *Western Political Quarterly* (September 1978), 352–358.

McGOWAN, Patrick J. and Helen E. PURKITT. *Demystifying 'National Character' in Black Africa: A Comparative Study of Culture and Foreign Policy Behavior*. Denver, CO: Graduate School of International Studies, University of Denver, 1979.

McNEILL, E. (ed.). *The Nature of Human Conflict*. Englewood Cliffs, NJ: Prenctice-Hall, 1965.

MEIR, Golda. *My Life*. Jerusalem and Tel Aviv: Steimatsky's, 1975.

MERRITT, Richard L. (ed). *Communication in International Politics*. Urbana, IL: University of Illinois Press, 1972.

MIDLARSKY, Manus. *The Onset of World War*. Boston: Unwin, Hyman, 1988.

——. "A Hierarchical Equilibrium Theory of Systemic War," *International Studies Quarterly*, **30**, 1 (1986), 77–105.

MILBURN, Thomas W. "The Management of Crisis," in Charles F. HERMANN (ed.). *International Crises: Insights from Behavioral Research*. New York: Free Press, 1972, 259–280.

MITCHELL, C. R. *The Structure of International Conflict*. New York: St Martin's Press, 1981.

MODELSKI, George. *Long Cycles in World Politics*. Seattle, WA: University of Washington Press, 1987.

——. "The Long Cycle of Global Politics and the Nation-State," *Comparative Studies in Society and History*, **20** (1978), 143–235.

——. "Kautilya: Foreign Policy and International System in the Ancient Hindu World," *American Political Science Review*, **LVIII** (1964), 549–560.

——. "International Relations and Area Studies: The Case of Southeast Asia," *International Relations*, **II** (1961), 143–55.

——, and Patrick M. MORGAN. "Understanding Global War," *Journal of Conflict Resolution*, **29**, 3 (1985), 391–417.

MONROE, Elizabeth and A. H. FARRAR-HOCKLEY. *The Arab-Israel War, October 1973 – Background and Events*. London: International Institute for Strategic Studies, Adelphi Papers, **3**, (1975).

MORGAN, Patrick M. *Theories and Approaches to International Politics*. New Brunswick, NJ: Transaction, 4th ed., 1987.

MORGENTHAU, Hans J. *Politics Among Nations*, New York: Alfred A. Knopf, 1st ed., 5th ed., 1948, 1973.

——. *Scientific Man Vs. Power Politics*. Chicago: University of Chicago Press, 1946.

MORRISON, Donald G. and H. Michael STEVENSON. "Cultural Pluralism, Modernization, and Conflict: An Empirical Analysis of Sources of Political Instability in African Nations," *Canadian Journal of Political Science*, **5**, 1 (1972), 82–103.

MOST, Benjamin A. and Harvey STARR. "Polarity, Preponderance and Power Parity in the Generation of International Conflict," *International Interactions*, **13** (1987), 255–262.

——. "Diffusion, Reinforcement, Geopolitics, and the Spread of War," *American Political Science Review*, **74**, 4 (1980), 932–946.

MUELLER, John. *Retreat from Doomsday: The Obsolescence of Major War*. New York: Basic Books, 1989.

MURPHY, Robert. *Diplomat Among Warriors*. London: Collins, 1964.

NACHT, Michael. *The Age of Vulnerability: Threats to the Nuclear Stalemate*, Washington, D.C.: Brookings, 1985.

NASH, Henry T. *American Foreign Policy: A Search for Security*, 3rd ed. Homewood, IL: Dorsey Press, 1985.

NELSON, Keith L. and Spencer C. OLIN, Jr. *Why War? Ideology, Theory, and History*. Berkeley and Los Angeles: University of California Press, 1979.

NICHOLAS, Herbert G. *The United Nations*. New York: Oxford University Press, 1971.

NICHOLSON, Michael. *Conflict Analysis*. London: English Universities Press, 1970.

NIXON, Richard M. *RN: The Memoirs of Richard Nixon*. New York: Grosset & Dunlop, 1978.

NOGEE, Joseph L. "Polarity: An Ambiguous Concept," *Orbis*, **XVIII** (1975), 1193–1224.

——, and John SPANIER. *Peace Impossible—War Unlikely*. Glenview, IL: Scott, Foresman/Little, Brown, 1988.

NORTH, Robert C. "Conflict: Political Aspects," in David A. SILLS (ed.). *International Encyclopedia of the Social Sciences*, **3**, 226–232. London: Collier-Macmillan, 1968.

——. "Research Pluralism and the International Elephant," *International Studies Quarterly*, **11** (1967), 394–416.

——, Richard A. BRODY and Ole R. HOLSTI. "Some Empirical Data on the Conflict Spiral," *Peace Research Society (International) Papers*, **1** (1964), 1–14.

——. Howard E. KOCH and Dina A. ZINNES. "The Integrative Functions of Conflict," *Journal of Conflict Resolution*, **IV**, 3 (1960), 355–374.

NYE, Joseph S. Jr. "Nuclear Learning and U.S.–Soviet Security Regimes," *International Organization*, **41**, 3 (1987), 371–402.

OPPENHEIM, Franz L. *International Law*, 1st ed., 8th ed. (H. LAUTERPACHT, ed.). New York: Longmans, Green, 1905, 1906, 1955.

ORGANSKI, A. F. Kenneth and Jacek KUGLER. *The War Ledger*. Chicago: University of Chicago Press, 1980.

OSGOOD, ROBERT E. *Alliances and American Foreign Policy*. Baltimore, MD: Johns Hopkins University Press, 1968.

OYE, Kenneth, Donald ROTHCHILD and Robert J. LIEBER (eds.). *Eagle Defiant: US Foreign Policy in the 1980s*. Boston, MA: Little, Brown, 1983.

PAIGE, Glenn D. "Comparative Case Analysis of Crisis Decisions: Korea and

Cuba," in Charles F. Hermann (ed.). *International Crises: Insights from Behavioral Research*. New York: Free Press, 1972, 41–55.

——, *The Korean Decision*. New York: Free Press, 1968.

Park, Robert E. and Ernest W. Burgess. *Introduction to the Science of Sociology*. Chicago: University of Chicago Press, 1924.

Patchen, Martin. *Resolving Disputes between Nations: Coercion or Conciliation?* Durham, NC: Duke University Press, 1988.

Pearson, Frederic S. and J. Martin Rochester. *International Relations: The Global Condition in the Late Twentieth Century*. Reading, MA: Addison-Wesley, 1984.

Pelcovits, Nathan A. and Kevin L. Kramer. "Local Conflict and UN Peace-keeping," *International Studies Quarterly*, **20** (1976), 533–552.

Peterson, Sophia. "Research on Research: Events Data Studies, 1961–1972," in Patrick J. McGowan (ed.), *Sage International Yearbook of Foreign Policy Studies*, Vol. 3. Beverly Hills, CA: Sage, 263–309.

Phillips, Warren R. "Prior Behavior as an Explanation of Foreign Policy," in Maurice East, Stephen Salmore and Charles F. Hermann (eds.), *Why Nations Act*. Beverly Hills, CA: Sage, 1978.

——. "The Conflict Environment of Nations," in Jonathan Wilkenfeld (ed.), *Conflict Behavior and Linkage Politics*. New York: McKay, 1973.

Pipes, Richard. *U.S.-Soviet Relations in the Era of Détente*. Boulder, CO: Westview Press, 1981.

Potter, William C. "Issue Area and Foreign Policy Analysis," *International Organization*, **34** (1980), 405–27.

Pruitt, Dean G. "Stability and Sudden Change in Interpersonal and International Affairs," *Journal of Conflict Resolution*, **XIII** (1969), 18–38.

——, and Richard C. Snyder. *Theory and Research on the Causes of War*. Englewood Cliffs, NJ: Prentice-Hall, 1969.

Quandt, William B. *Decade of Decisions: American Policy Toward the Arab–Israeli Conflict 1967–1976*. Berkeley and Los Angeles: University of California Press, 1977.

Rapkin, David, William Thompson with Jon Christopherson. "Bipolarity and Bipolarization in the Cold War Era," *Journal of Conflict Resolution*, **23** (1979), 261–295.

Rapoport, Anatol. *Conflict in Man-Made Environment*. Middlesex: Penguin, 1974.

——. *Fights, Games and Debates*. Ann Arbor, MI: University of Michigan Press, 1960.

Richardson, Lewis F. *Arms and Insecurity*. Pittsburgh, PA: Boxwood Press, 1960a.

——. *Statistics of Deadly Quarrels*. Pittsburgh, PA: Boxwood Press, 1960b.

Riker, William H. *The Theory of Political Coalitions*. New Haven. CT: Yale University Press, 1962.

Robinson, James A. *The Concept of Crisis in Decision-Making*, Washington D.C.: National Institute of Social and Behavioral Science, Symposia Study Series, No. 11, 1962.

Ro'i, Yaacov (ed.). *The Limits of Power: Soviet Policy in the Middle East*. New York: St. Martin's Press, 1979.

Rosecrance, Richard N. "Long Cycle Theory and International Relations," *International Organization*, **41** (1987), 283–301.

——. "Bipolarity, Multipolarity, and the Future," *Journal of Conflict Resolution*, **X** (1966), 314–27.

——. *Action and Reaction in World Politics*. Boston, MA: Little, Brown, 1963.

Rosenau, James N. "Patterned Chaos in Global Life: Structure and Process in the Two Worlds of World Politics," *International Political Science Review*, **9**, 4 (1988), 327–364.

——. "Before Cooperation: Hegemons, Regimes and Habit-driven Actors in World Politics," *International Organization*, **40**, 4 (1986), 849–894.

——. "The External Environment as a Variable in Foreign Policy Analysis," in James N. Rosenau, Vincent Davis and Maurice East (eds.), *The Analysis of International Politics*. New York: Free Press, 1972, 145–165.

——. "Pre-Theories and Theories of Foreign Policy," in R. Barry Farrell (ed.), *Approaches to Comparative and International Politics*. Evanston, IL: Northwestern University Press, 1966, 27–92.

Ross, Edward A. *Principles of Sociology*. New York: Century, 1930.

Rubinstein, Alvin Z. *Red Star Over the Nile: The Soviet-Egyptian Influence Relationship Since the June War*. Princeton, NJ. Princeton University Press, 1977.

RUMMEL, Rudolph J. "Libertarian Propositions on Violence Between and Within Nations: A Test Against Published Research Results," *Journal of Conflict Resolution*, **29**, 3 (1985), 419–455.

——. "Libertarianism and International Violence," *Journal of Conflict Resolution*, **27**, 1 (1983), 27–71.

——. *Understanding Conflict and War (5 Vols.)*. Beverly Hills, CA: Sage, 1975–81.

RUSSETT, Bruce M. "The Young Science of International Politics," *World Politics*, **XXII** (1969), 87–94.

——. *International Regions and the International System*. Chicago, IL: Rand McNally, 1967.

——. *Trends in World Politics*. New York: Macmillan, 1965.

——, and Harvey STARR. *World Politics: The Menu For Choice*, New York: W.H. Freeman, 2nd ed., 1985.

SADAT, Anwar. *In Search of Identity: An Autobiography*. New York: Harper & Row, 1978.

SCHELLING, Thomas C. *Arms and Influence*. New Haven, CT: Yale University Press, 1966.

——. *The Strategy of Conflict*. Cambridge, MA: Harvard University Press, 1960.

SCHICK, Jack M. "American Diplomacy and the Berlin Negotiations," *Western Political Quarterly*, **18** (1965), 803–820.

SCHIFF, Zeev. "The Full Story of the Encirclement That Ended the Yom Kippur War," *Ha'aretz*, (14 September 1975) (Hebrew).

SCHLESINGER, Jr., Arthur. *A Thousand Days*. Boston, MA: Houghton Mifflin, 1965.

SCHUMAN, Frederick L. *International Politics*. New York: McGraw-Hill, 1933.

SHAKED, Haim and Itamar RABINOVICH (eds.). *The Middle East and the United States: Perceptions and Politics*. New Brunswick, NJ: Transaction, 1980.

SHEEHAN, Edward R.F. "Step by Step in the Middle East," *Foreign Policy*, **22** (1976), 3–70.

SHIMONI, Yaacov. *The Arab States*. Tel Aviv: Am Oved, 1977 (Hebrew).

SHLAIM, Avi. *The United States and the Berlin Blockade, 1948–1949: A Study of Crisis Decision-Making*. Berkeley and Los Angeles: University of California Press, 1983.

SHULMAN, Marshall D. "The Future of Soviet–American Competition," in *Soviet–American Relations and World Order: The Two and The Many*. London: International Institute for Strategic Studies, Adelphi Papers, **66**, 1970, 1–10.

SIMMEL, George. *Conflict: The Web of Group Affiliations*. Glencoe, IL: Free Press, 1908.

SINGER, J. David. "Accounting for International War: The State of the Discipline," *Journal of Peace Research*, **XVII**, 1 (1981), 1–18.

——. "Theorists and Empiricists: The Two-Culture Problem in International Politics," in James N. ROSENAU, Vincent DAVIS and Maurice A. EAST (eds.), *The Analysis of International Politics*. New York: Free Press, 1972, 80–95.

——. *A General Systems Taxonomy for Political Science*. New York: General Learning Process, 1971.

——. "Soviet and American Foreign Policy Attitudes: Content Analysis of Elite Articulations," *Journal of Conflict Resolution*, **8**, 4 (1964), 424–485.

——. "The Level-of-Analysis Problem in International Relations," *World Politics*, **XIV**, 1 (1961), 77–92.

——, et al. *Explaining War: Selected Papers from the Correlates of War Project*. Beverly Hills, CA: Sage, 1979.

——, and Melvin SMALL. *The Wages of War 1816–1965: A Statistical Handbook*. New York: John Wiley, 1972.

——. "Alliance Aggregation and the Onset of War," in J. David SINGER (ed.) *Quantitative International Politics*. New York: Free Press, 1968, 247–286.

——, and Michael D. WALLACE. *To Augur Well: Early Warning Indicators in World Politics*. Beverly Hills, CA: Sage, 1979.

——, Stuart BREMER and John STUCKEY. "Capability Distribution, Uncertainty and Major Power War, 1820–1965," in Bruce M. RUSSETT (ed.), *Peace, War and Numbers*. Beverly Hills, CA: Sage, 1972, 19–48.

SINGER, Marshall R. *Weak States in a World of Powers: The Dynamics of International Relationships*. New York: Free Press, 1972.

SIVERSON, Randolph M. and Michael R. TENNEFOSS. "Power, Alliance, and the Escalation of International Conflict, 1815–1965," *American Political Science Review*, **78**, 4 (1984), 1057–1069.

SLAWITSKY, Bruce. "UN Activity and the Pace of Crisis Abatement," MA Thesis, The Hebrew University of Jerusalem, 1982.

SMALL, Melvin and J. David SINGER. *Resort to Arms: International and Civil Wars, 1816–1980*. Beverly Hills, CA: Sage, 1982.

SNYDER, Glenn H. "Crisis Bargaining," in Charles F. HERMANN (ed.). *International Crises: Insights from Behavioral Research*. New York: Free Press, 1972, 217–256.

——, and Paul DIESING. *Conflict Among Nations: Bargaining, Decision Making and System Structure in International Crises*. Princeton, NJ: Princeton University Press, 1977.

SNYDER, Richard C., H.W. BRUCK and Burton SAPIN. *Foreign Policy Decision-Making*. New York: Free Press, 1962.

SORENSEN, Theodore. *Kennedy*. New York: Harper & Row, 1965.

SOROKIN, Pitirim A. "Sociological Interpretation of the 'Struggle for Existence' and the Sociology of War," in Sorokin, *Contemporary Sociological Theories*. New York: Harper, 1928.

SPANIER, John W. *Games Nations Play: Analyzing International Politics*. New York: Praeger, 1972.

SPIEGEL, Steven L. *Dominance and Diversity*. Boston, MA: Little, Brown, 1972.

——. "Bimodality and the International Order: Paradox of Parity," *Public Policy*, **18** (1970), 383–412.

STEIN, Janice G. "The Managed and the Managers: Crisis Prevention in the Middle East," in Gilbert R. WINHAM (ed.), *New Issues in International Crisis Management*. Boulder, CO: Westview Press, 1988, 171–198.

——, and Raymond TANTER. *Rational Decision Making: Israel's Security Choices, 1967*. Columbus, OH: Ohio State University Press, 1980.

STEINBERG, Blema S. "Goals in Conflict: Escalation, Cuba, 1962," *Canadian Journal of Political Science*, **14**, 1 (1981), 83–105.

STEPHENS, Jerome, "An Appraisal of Some Systems Approaches in the Study of International Systems," *International Studies Quarterly*, **16**, 3 (1972), 321–349.

STOESSINGER, John G. *Why Nations go to War*. New York: St Martin's Press, 4th ed., 1985.

STONE, Julius. *Legal Controls of International Conflict*. New York: Rinehart, 1975.

STRAUSZ-HUPÉ, Robert, *et al. Protracted Conflict*. New York: Harper, 1959.

STREMLAU, John J. *The International Politics of the Nigerian Civil War, 1967–1970*. Princeton, NJ: Princeton University Press, 1977.

TANTER, Raymond. "International Crisis Behavior: An Appraisal of the Literature," *Jerusalem Journal of International Relations*, **2–3** (1978), 340–74.

——. *Modelling and Managing International Conflicts: The Berlin Crises*. Beverly Hills, CA: Sage, 1974.

——. "Dimensions of Conflict Behavior Within and Between Nations, 1958–1960," *Journal of Conflict Resolution*, X (1966), 41–64.

TATU, Michel. *Power in the Kremlin*. New York: Viking, 1969.

THOMPSON, William R. *On Global War*. Columbia SC: University of South Carolina Press, 1988.

——. "Polarity, the Long Cycle, and Global Power Warfare." *Journal of Conflict Resolution*, **30** (1986), 587–615.

——. "The Regional Subsystem," *International Studies Quarterly*, **17** (1973), 89–117.

THUCYDIDES. *A History of the Peloponnesian War*. Trans. by Benjamin JOWETT. Oxford: Shendene Press, 1930.

TOUVAL, Saadia. "Biased Intermediaries: Theoretical and Historical Considerations," *Jerusalem Journal of International Relations*, **1**, 1 (1975), 51–70.

TRISKA, Jan F. and David D. FINLEY. *Soviet Foreign Policy*. New York: Macmillan, 1968.

TRUMAN, Harry S. *Years of Trial and Hope*. New York: Doubleday, 1956.

ULAM, Adam. *Expansion and Coexistence*. New York: Praeger, 1974.

——. *The Rivals – America and Russia since World War II*. New York: Viking, 1971.

VALENTA, Jiri. *Soviet Intervention in Czechoslovakia 1968: Anatomy of a Decision*. Baltimore, MD: Johns Hopkins University Press, 1979.

——, and William C. POTTER (eds.). *Soviet Decision-Making for National Security*. Boston, MA: Allen & Unwin, 1984.

VASQUEZ, John A. "The Steps to War: Toward a Scientific Explanation of Correlates of War Findings," *World Politics*, **XL**, 1 (1987), 108–145.

——. *The Power of Power Politics*. New Brunswick, NJ: Rutgers University Press, 1983.

——, and Richard W. Mansbach. "The Issue Cycle: Conceptualizing Long-Term Global Political Change," *International Organization*, **37** (1983), 257–279.

Vertzberger, Yaacov Y. I. *Misperceptions in Foreign Policymaking: The Sino-Indian Conflict, 1959–1962*. Boulder, CO: Westview Press, 1984.

Walker, Richard L. *The Multi-State System of Ancient China*. Hamden, CT: Shoe String Press, 1953.

Walker, Stephen G. (ed.). *Role Theory and Foreign Policy Analysis*. Durham, NC: Duke University Press, 1987.

——. "The Correspondence Between Foreign Policy Rhetoric and Behavior: Insights From Theory and Exchange Theory," *Behavioral Science*, **26** (1981), 272–280.

——. "National Role Conceptions and Systematic Outcomes," in L. Falkowski (ed.), *Psychological Models of International Politics*. Boulder, CO: Westview Press, 1979, 169–210.

Wallace, Michael D. "Polarization: Towards a Scientific Conception," in Alan Ned Sabrosky (ed.), *Polarity and War*. Boulder, CO: Westview Press, 1985, 95–113.

——. "Alliance Polarization, Cross-Cutting, and International War, 1815–1964: A Measurement Procedure and Some Preliminary Evidence," *Journal of Conflict Resolution*, **17** (1973), 575–604.

Wallerstein, Immanuel. *The Modern World System II*. New York: Academic Press, 1980.

——. *The Modern World System*. New York: Academic Press, 1974.

Waltz, Kenneth N. *Theory of International Politics*. Reading, MA: Addison-Wesley, 1979.

——. "Theory of International Relations," in Fred I. Greenstein and Nelson W. Polsby (eds.), *Handbook of Political Science, Vol. 8, International Politics*. Reading, MA: Addison-Wesley, 1975, 1–85.

——. "International Structure, National Force, and the Balance of World Power," *Journal of International Affairs*, **XXI**, 2 (1967), 215–231.

——. "The Stability of a Bipolar World," *Daedalus*, **XCIII**, 3 (1964), 881–909.

——. *Man, the State, and War*. New York: Columbia University Press, 1959.

Ward, Michael D. "Cooperation and Conflict in Foreign Policy Behavior," *International Studies Quarterly*, **26** (1982), 87–126.

Wayman, Frank W. "Bipolarity and War: The Role of Capability Concentration and Alliance Patterns Among Major Powers, 1816–1965," *Journal of Peace Research*, **21** (1984), 61–78.

Weber, Max. *The Methodology of the Social Sciences*. Glencoe, IL: Free Press, 1917, 1949.

Weiner, A.J. and Herman Kahn (eds.). *Crisis and Arms Control*. Harmon-on-Hudson, NY: Hudson Institute, 1962.

Welch, William. *American Images of Soviet Foreign Policy*. New Haven, CT: Yale University Press, 1970.

Whiting, Allen S. *The Chinese Calculus of Deterrence: India and Indochina*. Ann Arbor, MI: University of Michigan Press, 1975.

——. *China Crosses the Yalu: The Decision to Enter the Korean War*. Stanford, CA: Stanford University Press, 1960.

Wilkenfeld, Jonathan. "A Time Series Perspective on Conflict in the Middle East," in Patrick J. McGowan (ed.), *Sage International Yearbook of Foreign Policy Studies*, Vol. 3. Beverly Hills, CA: Sage, 1975.

——. "Domestic and Foreign Conflict Behavior of Nations," *Journal of Peace Research*, **5** (1969), 56–69.

——, and Michael Brecher. "Crisis Management, 1945–1975: The UN Dimension," *International Studies Quarterly*, **28** (1984), 45–67.

——. "Superpower Crisis Management Behavior," in Charles W. Kegley and Patrick J. McGowan (eds.), *Foreign Policy: US/USSR*. Sage International Yearbook of Foreign Policy Studies, VIII. Beverly Hills, CA: Sage, 1982, 185–212.

——, *et al. Crises in the Twentieth Century, Vol. 2: Handbook of Foreign Policy Crises*. Oxford: Pergamon Press, 1988.

——, Virginia Lussier and Dale Tahtinen. "Conflict Interactions in the Middle East, 1949–1967," *Journal of Conflict Resolution*, **16** (1972), 135–154.

——, Gerald W. Hopple, Stephen J. Andriole and Robert N. McCauley. "Profiling States for Foreign Policy Analysis," *Comparative Political Studies*, **11** (1980).

——, Gerald W. Hopple, Paul J. Rossa and Stephen J. Andriole. *Foreign Policy Behavior: The Interstate Behavior Analysis Model*. Beverly Hills, CA: Sage 1980.

Williams, Phil. *Crises Management: Confrontation and Diplomacy in the Nuclear Age*. New York: John Wiley, 1976.

Windsor, Philip. *City on Leave: A History of Berlin, 1945–1962*. New York: Praeger, 1963.

Winham, Gilbert R. (ed.). *New Issues in International Crisis Management*. Boulder, CO: Westview Press, 1988.

Wish, Naomi B. "Foreign Policy Makers and Their National Role Conceptions," *International Studies Quarterly*, **24**, 3 (1980), 532–544.

——. "Relationships Between National Role Conceptions, National Attributes, and Foreign Policy Behavior," unpublished PhD dissertation, Rutgers University, 1977.

Wohlstetter, Albert and Roberta Wohlstetter. *Controlling the Risks in Cuba*. London: International Institute of Strategic Studies, Adelphi Paper, **17**, 1965.

Wolf, Charles. *United States Policy and the Third World*. Boston, MA: Little, Brown, 1967.

Wolfers, Arnold. *Discord and Collaboration*. Baltimore, MD: Johns Hopkins University Press, 1962.

Wright, Quincy. *A Study of War*, (2 Vols.). Chicago, IL: University of Chicago Press, 1942.

Yalem, Ronald J. "Tripolarity and the International System," *Orbis*, **XV** (1972), 1051–1063.

Young, Oran R. "International Regimes: Toward a New Theory of Institutions," *World Politics*, **XXXIX** (1986), 104–122.

——. *Compliance and Public Authority*. Baltimore, MD: Johns Hopkins University Press, 1980.

——. "Anarchy and Social Choice: Reflections on the International Polity," *World Politics*, **30** (1978), 241–263.

——. "The Perils of Odysseus: On Constructing Theories of International Relations," in Raymond Tanter and Richard H. Ullmann (eds.), *Theory and Policy in International Relations*. Princeton, NJ: Princeton University Press, 1973, 179–203.

——. "Professor Russett: Industrious Tailor to a Naked Emperor," *World Politics*, **XXI** (1969), 486–511.

——. *A Systemic Approach to International Politics*. Princeton, NJ: Princeton University Press, 1968a.

——. *The Politics of Force*. Princeton, NJ: Princeton University Press, 1968b.

——. "Political Discontinuities in the International System," *World Politics*, **XX** (1968c), 369–392.

——. *The Intermediaries: Third Parties in International Crisis*. Princeton, NJ: Princeton University Press, 1967.

Zacher, Mark W. *International Conflicts and Collective Security*. New York: Praeger, 1979.

Zagoria, Donald S. *The Sino-Soviet Conflict, 1956–1961*. Princeton, NJ: Princeton University Press, 1962.

Zartman, I. William. "Africa as a Subordinate State System in International Relations," *World Politics*, **XX** (1967), 545–64.

Ziegler, David W. *War, Peace, and International Politics*, 3rd ed. Boston, MA: Little, Brown, 1984.

Zimmerman, William. "Hierarchical Regional Subsystems and the Politics of System Boundaries," *International Organization*, **26** (1972), 18–26.

——. "Elite Perspectives and the Explanation of Soviet Foreign Policy," *Journal of International Affairs*, **24**, 1 (1970), 84–98.

Zimmern, Alfred. *The League of Nations and The Rule of Law 1918–1935*. London: Macmillan, 1936.

Zinnes, Dina A. "Prerequisites for the Study of System Transformation," in Ole R. Holsti, Alexander L. George and Randolph M. Siverson (eds.) *Change in the International System*. Boulder, CO.: Westview Press, 1980, Chap. 1.

——. "An Analytic Study of Balance of Power Theories," *Journal of Peace Research*, **3** (1967), 270–288.

——. "The Expression and Perception of Hostility in Prewar Crisis: 1914," in J. David Singer (ed.), *Quantitative International Politics*. New York: Free Press, 1968, 85–119.

——, and Jonathan Wilkenfeld. "An Analysis of Foreign Conflict Behavior of Nations," in Wolfram F. Hanrieder (ed.), *Comparative Foreign Policy*. New York: McKay, 1971, 167–213.

——, Joseph L. Zinnes and Robert D. McClure. "Hostility in Diplomatic Communications: A Study of the 1914 Crisis," in Charles F. Hermann (ed.), *International Crises*. New York: Free Press, 1972, 139–162.

Zolberg, Aristide R. "The Structure of Political Conflict in the New States of Tropical Africa," *American Political Science Review*, **62**, 1 (1968), 70–87.

Zoppo, Ciro E. "Nuclear Technology, Multipolarity and International Stability," *World Politics*, **XVIII** (1966), 579–606.

Name Index

Subject Index

Note: Crisis case numbers for 1979–85 cases appear in parentheses after each crisis title when it appears as a main entry. In addition to the Subject Index, readers are advised to make full use of the List of Figures and Tables in the preliminary pages and the Appendices of this volume.